Between Compliance and Conflict

RENEWALS 458-4574

WITHDRAWN
UTSA LIBRARIES

Between Compliance and Conflict

East Asia, Latin America, and the "New" Pax Americana

Edited by

Jorge I. Domínguez
and
Byung-Kook Kim

NEW YORK AND LONDON

Published in 2005 by
Routledge
Taylor & Francis Group
270 Madison Avenue
New York, NY 10016

Published in Great Britain by
Routledge
Taylor & Francis Group
2 Park Square
Milton Park, Abingdon
Oxon OX14 4RN

© 2005 by Taylor & Francis Group, LLC
Routledge is an imprint of Taylor & Francis Group

Printed in the United States of America on acid-free paper
10 9 8 7 6 5 4 3 2 1

International Standard Book Number-10: 0-415-95124-0 (Hardcover) 0-415-95125-9 (Softcover)
International Standard Book Number-13: 978-0-415-95124-1 (Hardcover) 978-0-415-95125-8 (Softcover)
Library of Congress Card Number 2004019528

No part of this book may be reprinted, reproduced, transmitted, or utilized in any form by any electronic, mechanical, or other means, now known or hereafter invented, including photocopying, microfilming, and recording, or in any information storage or retrieval system, without written permission from the publishers.

Trademark Notice: Product or corporate names may be trademarks or registered trademarks, and are used only for identification and explanation without intent to infringe.

Library of Congress Cataloging-in-Publication Data

Between compliance and conflict : East Asia, Latin America, and the "new" Pax Americana / edited by Jorge I. Domínguez, Byung-Kook Kim.
   p. cm.
   Includes bibliographical references and index.
   ISBN 0-415-95124-0 (hc: alk. paper) -- ISBN 0-415-95125-9 (pbk. : alk. paper)
   1. United States--Foreign relations--1989- 2. United States--Foreign relations--East Asia. 3. Balance of power. 4. East Asia--Foreign relations--United States. 5. United States--Foreign relations--Latin America. 6. Latin America--Foreign relations--United States. I. Domínguez, Jorge I., 1945- II. Kim, Byung-Kook.

E840.B48 2005
327.7305'09'0511--dc22   2004019528

Taylor & Francis Group
is the Academic Division of T&F Informa plc.

Visit the Taylor & Francis Web site at
http://www.taylorandfrancis.com

and the Routledge Web site at
http://www.routledge-ny.com

Library
University of Texas
at San Antonio

Contents

List of Figures and Tables		vii
Acknowledgments		ix
Contributors		xi

1. Between Compliance and Conflict: Comparing U.S.–East Asian and U.S.–Latin American Relations ... 1
   JORGE I. DOMÍNGUEZ AND BYUNG-KOOK KIM

2. A New Pax Americana? The U.S. Exercise of Hard Power in East Asia and Latin America ... 33
   ROBERT PAARLBERG

3. A Rise of Regionalist Ideas in East Asia: New East Asian Regionalism and Pax Americana ... 55
   YOUNG JONG CHOI

4. Pax Americana in Latin America: The Hegemony behind Free Trade ... 77
   PAMELA K. STARR

5	The U.S.–China Peace: Great Power Politics, Spheres of Influence, and the Peace of East Asia ROBERT S. ROSS	111
6	Japan's Ambition for Normal Statehood TAKASHI INOGUCHI	135
7	Brazilian Foreign Policy since 1990 and the Pax Americana MÔNICA HERZ	165
8	Cuba and the Pax Americana: U.S.–Cuban Relations Post-1990 JORGE I. DOMÍNGUEZ	193
9	To Have a Cake and Eat It Too: The Crisis of Pax Americana in Korea BYUNG-KOOK KIM	219
	Index	251

List of Figures and Tables

Figures

1.1	Bilateral free trade talks and "regionalism" in East Asia	19
2.1	Alternative regional security systems	52
9.1	Public sentiments toward U.S. foreign policy goal and style	236

Tables

1.1	Interplay between Economic and Security Dynamics	20
1.2	Free Trade Area and Collective Security Understandings	20
2.1	Selected U.S. Military Deployments/Engagements, 1975–2001	36
2.2	U.S. Military Deployments/Engagements in Latin America and East Asia, 1975–2001	37
8.1	Cuba's Main International Economic Partners at the End of the Twentieth Century	204

Acknowledgments

This book is the result of collaboration and good will among many participants. The editors, Domínguez and Kim, have worked with each other on and off for a quarter century. For this project, they are grateful to have obtained help from many colleagues and various institutions. The East Asia Institute (Seoul, Korea) and Harvard University's Weatherhead Center for International Affairs (Cambridge, MA) cosponsored a conference at the Center held in February 2003. Papers presented at that meeting were subsequently substantially revised. We also thank Joongang Ilbo for its generous financial backing. Specifically, we express our gratitude to Chairman Hong Seok-Hyun and Vice President Kwon Young-Bin at Joongang Ilbo. We also very much appreciate the assistance from Kim Hajeong and Jeon Eun-Kyung from the East Asia Institute and Jeana Flahive, Nadine Gerstler-Lopes, and Kathleen Hoover from the Weatherhead Center to enable us to prepare the conference and the book.

Contributors

Young Jong Choi is a research professor at the Asiatic Research Center at Korea University. He earned his Ph.D. from the University of Washington in 1998. He is interested in regional integration, international institutions, and U.S.–Japan economic relations. His research has focused on the institutionalization of regional economic relations in East Asia and the Pacific. His recent works include "Comparative Regional Integration" (with James A. Caporaso), published in the *Handbook of International Relations* (Sage Publications, 2002) and "A Comparative Study of Regionalism in East Asia and the Americas," *Asian Perspective*, vol. 26, no. 3 (2002). His current research project concerns bilateral free trade agreements (FTAs) in East Asia.

Jorge I. Domínguez is the director of the Weatherhead Center for International Affairs and the Clarence Dillon Professor of International Affairs at Harvard University. His current research focuses on public opinion and voting in Mexico's 2000 presidential election. He is the author (with Rafael Fernández de Castro) of *The United States and Mexico: Between Partnership and Conflict* (Routledge, 2001). He edited and contributed the synthetic chapter to *The Future of Inter-American Relations* (Routledge, 2000). He is a past president of the Latin American Studies Association.

Mônica Herz has a Ph.D. in international relations from the London School of Economics. She is a professor at the Institute of International Relations at the Catholic University of Rio de Janeiro. She has written publications on Latin America security and Brazilian foreign policy. She recently published *Ecuador vs. Peru: Peacemaking Amid Rivalry,* (Lynne Rienner, 2002) with coauthor João Pontes Nogueira.

Takashi Inoguchi has been a professor of political science at the Institute of Oriental Culture, University of Tokyo, since 1988. After he earned his Ph.D. in political science at the Massachusetts Institute of Technology in 1974, he taught as an associate professor at Sophia University (until 1977) and the University of Tokyo (until 1988). He has held various visiting positions at such universities as Geneva, Harvard, Australian National, Johns Hopkins, California (Berkeley), Aarhus (Denmark), Gadjah Mada (Indonesia), Delhi (India), Peking (China), and National Singapore. Also he was Assistant Secretary General of the United Nations Senior Vice Rector of the United Nations University Headquarters (1995–1997). He has published 41 books and numerous articles in English and in Japanese. His latest books include *Japan's Asian Policy* (editor, Palgrave, 2002), *Global Change* (Palgrave, 2001), *American Democracy Promotion* (coeditor, Oxford University Press, 2000), *Japanese Foreign Policy Today* (coeditor, Palgrave, 2000), *Encyclopedia of Political Science* (principal editor, Kobundo, 2000), and *Democracy, Governance and Economic Performance* (coeditor, United Nations University Press, 1999). He is also the editor of two journals: *International Relations of the Asia-Pacific* (Oxford University Press) and *Japanese Journal of Political Science* (Cambridge University Press). He is a member of the Legal Council of the Japanese Government. He frequently offers comments on Japan and international affairs on BBC, CNN, Reuters-TV, and CNBC and in the *International Herald Tribune, Asahi, Mainichi, Chosun Ilbo,* and *Straits Times.*

Byung-Kook Kim is currently at the Department of Political Science, Korea University, where he teaches party politics, methodology, Latin American politics, and comparative political theory. Dr. Kim graduated Phi Beta Kappa from Harvard University with a B.A. in economics in 1982 and received a Ph.D. from the Department of Government, Harvard University, six years later. He served on the Editorial Board of *Hankukilbo* as well as the Presidential Commission on Policy Planning. His published works include: *Hopes and Disillusions of Latin American Politics and Society* (1991), *Dynamics of National Division and Revolution: The Political Economy of Korea and Mexico* (1994), *State, Region and International System: Change and Continuity* (1995), *Korean Politics* (1998), and *Consolidating*

Democracy in South Korea (2000). Dr. Kim received the Award for Distinguished Publication on Liberal Democracy and Market Economy from the Federation of Korean Industries in 1995. He currently directs the East Asia Institute, a private nonprofit organization, founded in May 2002 under the initiative of former Prime Minister Lee Hong Koo with the goal of transforming East Asia into a society of nations based on democracy, market economy, open society, and peace. To this end, the East Asia Institute works to propagate liberal values and ideas including diversity, tolerance, accountability, and transparency through research, education, international exchange, and civic activism. The institute edits the *Journal of East Asian Studies*, for which Dr. Kim chairs the Executive Editorial Committee.

Robert Paarlberg is a professor of political science at Wellesley College and an associate at the Weatherhead Center for International Affairs at Harvard University. He has published books on the use of food as a weapon (*Food Trade and Foreign Policy*, Cornell University Press), on international agricultural trade negotiations (*Fixing Farm Trade*, Council on Foreign Relations), on environmentally sustainable farming in developing countries (*Countrysides at Risk*, Overseas Development Council), on U.S. foreign economic policy (*Leadership Abroad Begins at Home*, Brookings Institution), and on the reform of U.S. agricultural policy (*Policy Reform in American Agriculture*, Chicago University Press, with David Orden and Terry Roe). He has also been a member of the Board of Directors of Winrock International, a member of the Emerging Markets Advisory Committee at the U.S. Department of Agriculture, a scientific liaison officer to the International Food Policy Research Institute, and a consultant to the National Intelligence Council (NIC), United States Agency for International Development (USAID), International Food Policy Research Institute (IFPRI), and the World Bank. His research has recently concentrated on policies toward genetically modified agricultural crops in developing countries, particularly Kenya, Brazil, Cameroon, Senegal, India, China, and Argentina. His latest book, *The Politics of Precaution: Policies toward GM Crops in the Developing World*, was published by the Johns Hopkins University Press in November 2001. He received his undergraduate degree in political science from Carleton College and his Ph.D. in government from Harvard University. He has also served as an officer in the United States Navy and as a legislative aide in the U.S. Senate.

Robert S. Ross is a professor of political science, Boston College, and associate of the John King Fairbank Center for East Asian Research, Harvard University. His research focuses on Chinese security policy, including Chinese use of force and deterrence strategies, U.S.–China relations, and East Asian security. His most recent publications include *Re-examining the Cold War: U.S.–China Diplomacy, 1954–1973* (coeditor) and *Engaging China: Management of an Emerging Power* (coeditor). He is the author of articles on Chinese security policy and U.S.–China relations in various scholarly and policy journals.

Pamela K. Starr is a professor of international studies at the Instituto Tecnológico Autónomo de México (ITAM), where she teaches courses on the political economy of development, globalization, and developing countries, and the politics of economic reform in Latin America. She is the coeditor of *Markets and Democracy in Latin America* (Lynne Rienner, 2000). Her recent articles focus on dollarization in Latin America, the origins of the Argentine crisis, and the broader political economy of economic reform and exchange rate regimes in Latin America. She is currently working on two book manuscripts, one on the viability of dollarization in Latin America and another analyzing the Fox Administration in Mexico. Dr. Starr has worked extensively in seminars designed to help secondary school teachers integrate economic concepts into their course cirricula, and as a consultant to private corporations, investment banks, and governmental agencies.

CHAPTER 1

Between Compliance and Conflict: Comparing U.S.–East Asian and U.S.–Latin American Relations

JORGE I. DOMÍNGUEZ AND BYUNG-KOOK KIM

Introduction

The triple transformation of the international system at the end of the 1980s and start of the 1990s had specific effects on U.S. relations with East Asia and Latin America. These effects highlighted shared traits in the relations between the United States and these two regions that distinguished them from U.S. relations with other parts of the world. The United States played an important role in each of these three major international transformations. These three transformations were as follows:

- The collapse of the Soviet Union and all European communist regimes with the consequent end of the Cold War in Europe, the worldwide weakening or outright disappearance of communist parties, and the collapse of most, though not all, communist revolutionary movements in Third World countries.
- The opening of political systems, often leading to democratic regimes.

- The spread of market-oriented economic practices including substantial trade liberalization.

Since the end of the Cold War in Europe, U.S. relations with East Asia and Latin America bear four distinctive and uniquely shared characteristics. First, only in these two regions did communist regimes survive following the collapse of the Soviet Union. Second, the United States became least likely to go to war where communist legacies endured in East Asia and Latin America, deterred as it had been during the Cold War, and more likely to go to war in Europe and the Middle East, where it felt undeterred after the end of the Cold War. In East Asia and Latin America, but not elsewhere, after 1990 the United States also found two new strategic partners — the People's Republic of China and Mexico — notwithstanding persisting conflicts with each of these new partners. The rediscovery of China and Mexico as strategic partners consolidated the peace-building efforts inherited from the Cold War years in these two regions.

Third, in East Asia and Latin America, but not elsewhere, the United States, belatedly and reluctantly, became a major force to help overturn the authoritarian political regimes to which it was long allied. This change in the U.S. role from dictator hugger to dictator slayer in the same country (often with regard to the same dictator, once an ally, then an adversary) began late in the twentieth century, uninterruptedly so from the mid-1980s onwards. This change in the U.S. role was possible thanks to the diffusion of democratic norms worldwide to which the United States had contributed and the substantial international and domestic political stability that came to characterize both East Asia and Latin America.

Fourth, East Asia and Latin America witnessed far more dramatic economic change — both economic growth and financial crises — than any other region in the noncommunist world during the closing quarter of the twentieth century. Along with India, no other noncommunist countries liberalized their economies as much as those in these two regions. The United States brokered the accession of Mexico and later China into the General Agreement of Tariffs and Trade (GATT) and the World Trade Organization (WTO). It backed the International Monetary Fund's (IMF's) discovery in Brazil and the Republic of Korea (South Korea) of the utility — albeit still officially unacknowledged by the IMF — of democratic practices for the implementation of IMF stabilization programs.

East Asia and Latin America share some traits with other regions of the world. They have adjusted to the new U.S. military supremacy and complied with U.S. demands for economic openness and, except for the communist countries, political openness. In these ways, they accepted the new Pax Americana — the bundle of unprecedented and unrivaled U.S. military, political, and economic power evident in the last decade of the twentieth century and the first of the twenty-first. Even North Korea, the bluntest dissenter from U.S. power in these regions, has had to negotiate concerning its nuclear weapons programs and has begun to modify its policies toward Japan and South Korea. Cuba, the next most important dissenter, actively cooperates with the United States over migration and security around the U.S. naval base at Guantanamo and in the Straits of Florida and, under President George W. Bush's administration, since 2001 has been importing large quantities of agricultural products from the United States.

However, adjusting to the new U.S. military supremacy and U.S. demands for economic openness is an ongoing process that engenders domestic and international conflicts. In a myriad of ways, East Asian and Latin American countries have resisted many implications of the new U.S. supremacy. In each East Asian and Latin American country, there is a heated debate about how much compliance and conflict there should be vis-à-vis the United States. Even beyond North Korea and Cuba, Malaysia's then Prime Minister Mohammed Mahathir rhetorically, if not actually, opposed U.S. leadership as neocolonialism, whereas President Roh Moo-hyun's South Korea and President Luiz Inácio Lula da Silva's Brazil uneasily waver between compliance and resistance. Domestic political struggles and values, as well as international considerations, shape the responses to the new role of the United States and the concurrent reshaping of national identities, politics, economic policies, and military policies.

The Worldwide Effects of the Collapse of the Soviet Union

The end of the Cold War in Europe removed the fear of thermonuclear or major conventional war in that continent, dissolving the Warsaw Pact alliance of formerly communist countries and challenging the need for the continued existence of the North Atlantic Treaty Organization (NATO), which, since the late 1940s, had bound together the security policies of North America and most of Western Europe. On the military front, however, brutal war accompanied the breakup of Yugoslavia, engaging NATO in war over Kosovo's status — NATO's first war ever. War also marked the experiences of former-Soviet, newly independent states in the Caucasus region.

Freed from the constraints of the Cold War, the United States displayed its military power to bring about regime change in Panama in 1989, Haiti in 1994 and 2004, the former Yugoslavia in Bosnia and Kosovo in the late 1990s, Afghanistan in 2001, and Iraq in 2003. In all but Panama and Iraq,

U.S. interventions in these countries received substantial backing from allies and others — in Haiti in 1994 and in Bosnia, from the United Nations Security Council. But the United States also demonstrated a willingness to intervene militarily despite the opposition of some of its key international allies. It intervened in Panama in 1989 over the opposition of most Latin American governments and in Iraq in 2003 over the opposition of France, Germany, Canada, and other allies. This display of U.S. military power worldwide with or without the support of allies and multilateral organizations is a key building block of a Pax Americana. The United States seemed prepared to fight any foe anywhere, preemptively at times, to impose its will.

The concern with international terrorism after the terrorist attacks on New York and Washington on September 11, 2001, involved the United States more deeply in internal wars in Colombia and the Philippines, supplying higher levels of military aid (including military specialists) to fight insurgents suspected of ties to international terrorist organizations but stopping well short of major U.S. military deployments.

This widespread military activity was no longer related to the Cold War, however. The United States was ready to fight adversaries except the few extant communist regimes. The communist regimes of East Asia and Cuba had not collapsed. The Democratic People's Republic of Korea (North Korea) underwent a dynastic leadership transition in the 1990s just as Cuba formalized the rules for its own possible dynastic transition at the time of President Fidel Castro's passing. The United States chose nonmilitary means to deal with these two communist states that are still unwilling or unable to follow the Chinese and Vietnamese path of substantial economic reform and fuller-scale military accommodation to U.S. leadership. The United States increased the severity and comprehensiveness of some of the sanctions it applied on Cuba to bring about regime change. The United States also challenged North Korea's development of nuclear and chemical weapons and efforts to build missile delivery systems for such weapons. It retained economic sanctions on North Korea and brought China into the framework of six-party talks to pressure North Korea to end its programs of weapons of mass destruction.

U.S. policies toward Cuba and North Korea since 1990 differed sharply from those that the United States pursued toward these countries during the Cold War. The United States went to war in the Korean peninsula in 1950. With regard to Cuba, in 1961 the United States sponsored the Bay of Pigs invasion to seek unsuccessfully to overthrow the Castro government and, in 1962, it confronted the Soviet Union over Cuba, as both the United States and the USSR brought the world to the brink of nuclear war. These military episodes were key building blocks for the North Korean and Cuban communist regimes, but they were also the last instances of war or near-war between the United States and either North Korea or Cuba. U.S. relations with the governments of both countries remained extremely tense, but also peaceful. North Korea and Cuba deterred U.S. military action — the only sites in the international system featuring those outcomes after the Cold War had ended in Europe.

The end of the Cold War in Europe had other important, albeit less dramatic, effects in both East Asia and Latin America. The United States reestablished diplomatic and economic relations with Vietnam and Cambodia and it welcomed their wider engagement in the international affairs of Southeast Asia. With the Soviet collapse and Cuba's decision to stop supporting insurgencies in Central America, the United States became a willing participant in peace negotiations to end the long domestic and international wars that had swirled in and about Nicaragua, El Salvador, and Guatemala. These indirect effects of the end of the Cold War in Europe contributed to peace in Central America and Southeast Asia.

Freed from worries about the Cold War and thus able to overcome suspicions and disagreements related to it, the United States built new relationships with Mexico and the People's Republic of China. These new relationships resembled the long-term U.S. relationship with France because new partnership combined with persisting friction. It differed from Cold War hostile U.S. relations with China or the Soviet Union and long-time neglectful relations with Mexico and cordial relations with the Federal Republic of Germany. It differed also from continuing relations of close collaboration with the United Kingdom and continuing neglectful relations with Brazil and early twenty-first century frostiness with Germany.

The United States looked creatively and freshly at Mexico, its neighbor of over one hundred million people, conscious of its growing potential and existing importance for the U.S. economy and the very demography of the United States, but unconcerned about Mexican military clout. In 1994 Mexico, Canada, and the United States signed the North American Free Trade Agreement (NAFTA) as a new compact for North America — an agreement with no formal military significance.[1] U.S.–Mexican disputes persisted over migration and drug traffic control, however.

The United States came to see the People's Republic of China as a major power, perhaps an emerging superpower, but one whose military capacity in the late twentieth and early twenty-first centuries was limited to the exertion of pressure on its immediate neighbors. Alas, even at the peak of the Cold War, little Cuba deployed hundreds of thousands of troops across the oceans and continents while giant China did not. Disputes were salient over China's relations with Taiwan, but U.S.–Chinese collaboration developed not only through economic relations but also in the U.S.–Chinese endeavor, joined by Japan and South Korea, to prevent North Korea's full acquisition of nuclear weapons and the means to deliver them.

Thus, as a direct or indirect consequence of the end of the Cold War in Europe, East Asia and Latin America shared distinctive traits in their relations with the United States that rendered them alike in important respects and also different from other regions of the world:

- East Asia and Latin America were the only regions of the world where communist regimes continued to exist.
- The United States remained least likely to go to war where Cold War legacies remained most acute (North Korea, Cuba) and more likely to go to war in regions other than East Asia and Latin America.
- The end of the U.S.–Soviet struggle had indirect benefits for peace making in Southeast Asia and Central America.
- After 1990, U.S. relations with European countries on both sides of the Cold War divide, and with the Arab Middle East after the first U.S.–Iraqi war in 1991, changed much more dramatically than did U.S. relations with most countries of East Asia or Latin America.
- Under the new era of Pax Americana, the United States constructed a more cooperative relationship with a key large country in both East Asia and Latin America — China and Mexico, respectively — albeit with persistent instances of conflict.

The Worldwide Processes of Democratization

The opening of political systems, often leading to democratic regimes, proceeded principally for domestic reasons within each country, imparting distinctive characteristics to each instance of regime change. Nevertheless, international processes contributed to democratization as well. The tolerance for authoritarian regimes declined markedly in Western Europe and North America in the 1960s and 1970s. The European Economic Community (EEC) required the prior existence of a democratic regime for accession to membership through the Treaty of Rome, thereby creating both sanctions and an eventual inducement that facilitated regime change and democratic consolidation in Southern and Eastern Europe. European Christian Democratic and Social Democratic parties, through their respective international party federations, provided guidance and financial and other support to kin parties in other parts of the world, including Latin

America. Like the European Union, the Southern Common Market (MERCOSUR), which includes Argentina, Brazil, Uruguay, and Paraguay, also has a "democracy clause."

The United States lagged in some respects behind its European allies, Canada, and MERCOSUR in the promotion of democracy. The United States was an early contributor to the spread of democracy and human rights norms at the end of World War II, but its government responded fitfully and erratically to the spread of such norms — supportive during the Kennedy and Carter presidencies but not at other times — until the mid-1980s when it joined the consensus of consolidated democracies in Europe and Canada opposed to authoritarian regimes. That shift in U.S. policies contributed (a) decisively to the end of the dictatorships of hitherto allies Ferdinand Marcos in the Philippines and Manuel Antonio Noriega in Panama; (b) significantly to political openings in Chile and Paraguay at the expense of yet other former allies Augusto Pinochet and Alfredo Stroessner; and (c) indirectly to other openings in Mexico, South Korea, and Taiwan, also weakening former allies in those authoritarian regimes. Working through the United Nations, the United States helped the political opening in Cambodia as well.

NAFTA still does not have a democracy clause to make democratization a prerequisite for membership. Nonetheless, the deeper intertwining of U.S.–Mexican relations in the 1990s contributed to Mexico's democratization and the election in 2000 of its first president from an opposition political party. At the Quebec Summit of Heads of State and Government in 2001, moreover, the United States agreed to a first-ever democracy clause for the negotiations of the Free Trade Agreement of the Americas (FTAA) that the governments still hoped to sign.

Domestic political openings did not occur in a vacuum, therefore. There was a systematic worldwide normative change adverse to authoritarian regimes. This change affected both East Asia and Latin America. The collapse of European communist regimes also contributed to this shift, delegitimizing an authoritarian option on the political left and depriving the political right of a pretext to establish authoritarian rule in order to repress political radicalization. In the second half of the 1970s, nearly all Central and South American countries were under authoritarian regimes. After 1990, only Cuba qualifies as an authoritarian regime in the Americas (on its own, Haiti has also been unable to sustain a democratic regime), even though important limitations on democracy and abuses of human rights still mark political experience in some Latin American countries. In the 1990s in East Asia, democratization advanced gradually but inexorably in Taiwan, South Korea, and Thailand; by the end of the decade, Taiwan and South Korea had elected the candidate of a main opposition party for president. Democratization came precipitously to Indonesia after the 1997 Asian financial crisis. Malaysia's "soft" authoritarian regime, anchored on the United Malays National Organization (UMNO), also showed signs of pluralization in the aftermath of the 1997 financial crisis and Deputy Prime Minister Anwar Ibrahim's split with Mahathir.

The remaining communist regimes in East Asia and Latin America did not democratize, but China and Vietnam adopted major market-oriented economic changes that transformed their economies, especially China's, and contributed to elements of societal opening consistent with those changes. Cuba adopted a much more limited version of such economic reforms, with consequently much more modest results. North Korea's economic reforms were the least significant.

Thus, as a direct or indirect consequence of these worldwide forces pushing for political opening and democratization, East Asia and Latin America shared yet again some distinctive traits that rendered them alike in important respects and also different from other regions of the world:

- East Asia and Latin America were the only regions of the world where many long-time authoritarian-regime U.S. allies experienced political regime changes. They were also the only regions marked by extensive and numerous regime changes in countries that never had communist regimes.
- The United States was long an unlikely partner of democratizers in East Asia and Latin America, just as it was in the rest of the world, but it became a significant force for democratization in both of these regions and not in other regions from the mid-1980s onward.
- The United States played no role in the democratization of most South American countries, which occurred before the mid-1980s, and had only modest impact on political change in the remaining communist countries in East Asia and Latin America.
- The modal pattern for East Asian and Latin American communist regimes features some at times dramatic market-oriented reforms and societal changes but few, if any, changes in the political regime.
- The United States has been opposed or reluctant to accept democracy clauses in international economic agreements such as NAFTA or the Asia Pacific Economic Community (APEC).
- After 1990, the domestic characteristics of political regimes, specifically democracy, became a more important element in

shaping the content and quality of U.S. bilateral relations with East Asian and Latin American countries. In that way, these regions differ from U.S. relations with the independent countries that emerged from the former Soviet Union, Africa, the Middle East, and Central and South Asia, where the United States retained cordial relations with governments under authoritarian regimes.

The Worldwide Processes of Market-Oriented Reforms

Market-oriented practices were long part of the policy repertoire of noncommunist East Asian and Latin American economic regimes. After World War II, however, most Latin American states intruded systematically and deeply in their country's economies through state enterprises and extensive microeconomic regulation, seeking economic independence. Noncommunist East Asian economic regimes were more market friendly, in the 1950s to 1960s modeling their development strategies after the Japanese path to growth, even though the state often played a very important role — especially in Japan and South Korea — in directing economic strategy and providing strong positive and negative incentives for the behavior of business firms. By the 1960s, East Asian economies became strong exporters. Latin America's economic depression of the 1980s and the East Asian financial crisis of 1997 each propelled market-oriented economic liberalization. The extent of the change was greater in Latin America because the economic distortions had been greater. East Asian macroeconomic policies had been sounder; the post-1997 East Asian economic reforms focused on such microeconomic issues as transparent corporate governance structures, bank and corporate restructuring, prudential regulations in the financial sector, and rules regarding competition and oligopolistic market structures.

Of course, the most impressive changes in economic policy and results anywhere occurred in China since the start of its economic reforms in 1979. Once economically prostrate, China became one of the world's leading exporters over the course of a single generation and dramatically lifted the standard of living of its people. Reforms in Vietnam have also been important, though less spectacular in their results than in China.

The pattern of economic reforms had mixed international and domestic origins. The accelerated period of reforms started with international financial crises whose roots and tentacles reached beyond each region. Rising worldwide interest rates triggered Latin America's crash in 1982–1983 through the mechanism of an international debt crisis. The 1997 financial crisis had major international repercussions, but its origin and worst effects were in East Asia, where finance companies and banks collapsed because they had borrowed foreign loans short-term and re-lent the money to domestic borrowers long-term without hedging their foreign exchange exposure. In both regions, the principal antecedents of the crisis were rooted in the domestic economies and the policies of governments and firms in each country, and so too would be the principal remedies.

The Latin American experience with tariff rates illustrates the salience of domestic factors in enacting change with international repercussions. In 1985, the average tariff rates (unweighted) of Argentina, Brazil, Colombia, Peru, Mexico, and Venezuela all exceeded 30 percent, with Mexico at 34 percent and Brazil at 55 percent. Peak tariff rates in both Mexico and Brazil exceeded 100 percent. By the end of the 1990s, none of these countries had average tariff rates above 15 percent, and no single tariff rate exceeded 60 percent.[2] For the most part, Latin American governments enacted these changes unilaterally, that is, not as part of international trade negotiations. On the other hand, international factors mattered. The Uruguay Round of the GATT, which would culminate in 1994 with the establishment of the WTO, supplied context, norms, and incentives for such unilateral steps.

With regard to China and Mexico, however, the United States played a key role in their trade liberalization. Mexico joined the GATT in 1986 and China joined the WTO in 2001. Under the rules of each organization, much of the active negotiation for accession is conducted between the candidate country and its principal trading partner within the GATT or WTO. In each case, this was the United States. The timing, rhythm, and pattern of China's and Mexico's trade liberalization and associated economic reforms depend directly, therefore, on U.S. bilateral relations with each of them.

In both regions, capital markets liberalization was also propelled by the joint forces of U.S. pressures and domestic political–economic dynamics. Latin America dramatically opened up its capital markets in the 1990s to attract scarce foreign capital and suffered adverse effects when some of this capital flowed out, as in Mexico in late 1994 and Brazil and Argentina in the late 1990s. The East Asian newly industrializing countries (NICs), too, joined the worldwide trend of capital market liberalization in the early 1990s from a much stronger position but with equally destabilizing results. The East Asian NICs accommodated the U.S. demands, but on their own terms. Taiwan liberalized its capital markets gradually, while Thailand established unregulated offshore capital market facilities both to meet U.S. demands for liberalization and to satisfy the local business firms' insatiable appetite for relatively inexpensive foreign loans. South Korea, too, liberalized short-term but not long-term financial markets in order to meet the demands of the United States and the *chaebol* business conglomerates and to clear the way for its membership in the Organisation for Economic Co-operation and Development (OECD) as a political showcase of its economic modernization. Both Thailand and South Korea got into financial distress as a result.

The international role at the remedy stage was more marked in financial crises. The United States operated directly and through the international financial institutions in the Latin American crisis of the 1980s, but it relied relatively more on the IMF to address the financial crises of the late 1990s. The U.S. response in the 1980s was slow and uncreative, though beginning with the so-called Brady Plan in 1989, it became more effective. The international response to the 1997 East Asian financial crisis and to the Brazilian financial crises of 1999 and 2002 varied widely. The international response may have aggravated the Indonesian crisis.

In Brazil and South Korea (after some initial fumbling), the international response proved both successful and favorable to democratic consolidation. In South Korea in 1997 and in Brazil in 2002, all key presidential candidates from the incumbent and the opposition parties signed on to their respective government's agreement with the IMF. In each case, international support helped to prevent the breakdown of the financial system and hence the democratic political system. In turn, the procedures of democracy provided long-term credible guarantees for the implementation of an effective economic reform program. The election of leftist or progressive candidates in South Korea and Brazil — Kim Dae-jung and Lula da Silva — facilitated reform. It deprived the political left of the option of opposing liberalization. Moreover, the two presidents felt free to break with their countries' established model of economic growth, given their long exclusion from policy-making processes, and aggressively pushed for major changes in macro- and microeconomic policy.

Thus, with regard to market-oriented reforms, East Asia and Latin America shared yet again some distinctive traits that rendered them alike in important respects and also different from other regions of the world:

- The East Asian and Latin American economies had long been hybrids of market practices with varieties of statist economics. Each had sufficient economic prosperity to participate actively in the international economy. Their economies were vulnerable to financial crises, with high potential for adverse repercussions on the international economy. They thus differed from economically successful Western Europe but also from more statist and less economically successful Africa, the Middle East, and South Asia.

- East Asia and Latin America were at the heart of the worldwide economic liberalization that marked the last decade of the twentieth century.
- The two most severe international financial crises in developing countries that threatened the stability of the international financial system took place in Latin America in 1982–1983 and East Asia in 1997. The potential worldwide repercussions of these crises compelled the IMF and the United States to intervene actively to mitigate the resulting market panics and foster economic reforms. By comparison, economic crises in Africa, and even in Russia in 1998, occurred in economies too small to have sufficient impact on the world system.
- South Korea and Brazil have been trailblazers in combining the adoption of IMF austerity packages with democratic procedures, where IMF policies supported democracy and democracy made the IMF package more credible for implementation.
- The United States played a direct and salient role in promoting trade liberalization in China and Mexico. Partly because of this trade liberalization, China and Mexico became — along with Canada — the top U.S. trade partners. U.S. trade with European countries became proportionately much less significant.

In this book, we are conscious of the enormous differences between countries within and between regions. On some dimensions, these are among the most different countries in the world. But comparison between them is possible because they share important similarities in elements of their relations with the United States.

This book's aim is to provide a better understanding of the several dimensions of such U.S. relations with both regions. In the recent past, each region at some point has had an active dissenter (Cuba and North Korea) from Pax Americana that supported revolutionary movements in other countries and retained relations with groups that the U.S. government classified as terrorist. Both regions have had strong U.S. allies that once served as Cold War outposts (Japan, South Korea, and, until the late 1970s, Brazil). More recently, each region has witnessed substantial ideological change in terms of their relations with the United States (oscillation in anti-American sentiments in Latin America and increase in East Asia). The two regions now resemble each other more in how they think about the United States. And, especially, the similar pattern of change in bilateral relations between the United States and each of these two regions makes them more similar to each other and more different from the rest of the world in terms of their relations with the United States. They share sufficient similarities in such relations to enable us to explore both divergences and key joint outcomes.

The New Pax Americana

When, therefore, did the "new" Pax Americana emerge and how does it differ from predecessor arrangements? In the world history after Word War II, the concept *Pax* did not literally mean the absence of war. There have been many wars before as well as after the Soviet Union collapsed in December 1991, the year demarcating the "old" and "new" age of the international system. Whatever peace may have existed before 1991 was certainly not for Afghans, Koreans, Nicaraguans, Salvadorans, and Vietnamese, who saw their land torn apart by civil wars that Moscow and Washington prolonged, escalated, and at times instigated. The two superpower rivals were on virtually permanent military alert, clamping down with military force on ideological "heretics" in their respective spheres of dominance in Eastern Europe and Latin America, and fighting and intervening in civil wars worldwide.

The new Pax was ushered in with a war over Saddam Hussein's takeover of Kuwait in 1991, just as the old Pax had gestated in Harry Truman's dispatch of U.S. troops to the Korean peninsula more than four decades earlier. The second Iraq War (2003) promises future bellicosity. War making was and remains an integral part of each Pax.

Yet there was one kind of peace. Unlike the world before 1945, after World War II there was peace between the major global military powers. The two superpowers of the Cold War era waged "proxy wars" with client states as their vehicle to further ideological interests but avoided directly confronting each other in battlefields. When a client state threatened to drag its patron into a superpower military confrontation, both Moscow and Washington stopped their client from dictating their fate and thus sustained the peace with each other, though success varied. In 1950, Joseph Stalin successfully persuaded China to take on the United Nations allied forces on the Korean peninsula. Nikita Khrushchev was forced to back down from his Cuban adventure in 1961 before John F. Kennedy's naval quarantine and was punished three years later with loss of power.

Since 1991, there has also been a peaceful coexistence between major powers under the new Pax. The global military structure is unipolar, thus by definition diminishing the threat of war with global systemic consequences. Even where military power is regionally distributed in a bipolar but highly asymmetrical way, as in East Asia with Washington showing preponderance in air and naval powers and Beijing commanding a colossal land army, regional powers opt for accommodation rather than confrontation.

The Pax between major powers before as well as after 1991 was a product of U.S. leadership, but U.S. leadership also accounted for many "limited wars" fought during the Cold War and the military campaigns waged against "rogue states" thereafter. The United States has been a container of challengers, a patron of client states, a discipliner of ideological heretics, and a cop against rogues — all at the same time. The active military role, however, comprised only one aspect of its leadership. Reacting against World War II, the United States also became a builder of international organizations in economic as well as military realms at global and regional levels. Many of its institutional inventions from the 1940s have survived. The IMF is as strong as ever, running rescue operations in East Asia and Latin America, both shaken by financial crises in the late 1990s and opening years of the current decade, with the U.S. Federal Reserve Board playing a key supporting role. The forces of free trade show equal resilience, with the WTO tightening loopholes in trade regulation. The idea of free trade agreements (FTAs) has spread in North and South America and also in hitherto mercantilist East Asia. Even NATO survives, though its original raison d'être of ensuring collective security against the Soviet threat no longer exists. In short, three key features marked the Pax Americana before and after 1991:

- Peace between the global powers
- United States leadership
- Institutionalized forms of collective action

Nevertheless, there is something new about the post-1991 Pax Americana. The intensity of relations between and among states deepened significantly. The volume and speed of transnational flows of money, goods, humans, and ideas grew geometrically. As a result, the frequency, level, and scope of political conflict between countries whose experiences became profoundly affected by each other's actions intensified as well. Because of this sharing of a common fate, which Joseph Nye and Robert Keohane termed "sensitivity" under complex interdependence,[3] conflicts proliferated but without a rupture of ties. Severing relations would incur prohibitively high costs. Costs would be higher for some than others, resulting in different levels of "vulnerability." The United States is sensitive but less vulnerable toward others, given its economic size, military prowess, technological lead, and "soft power."[4] This enabled it to assemble more effectively than other states a diverse mix of multilateral, bilateral, and unilateral foreign policy styles in pursuit of its national interests.

Before 1991, the U.S. sought to forge unity with allies and clients facing the Soviet Union, thereby restraining its bias for unilateralism. The collapse of bipolarity freed it from this constraint, enabling it to confront allies and clients with demands for greater burden sharing in collective security and economic globalization. The combination of more intense transnational relational processes and a rapidly emerging unipolar structure of global power made conflict with allies a distinctive trait of the new Pax Americana, given also a new United States less willing to accommodate others as part of being a hegemony.

The world's appraisal of globalization and the role of the United States within it, however, is neither stable nor uniform. In the aftermath of the disastrous "Asian Crisis" of 1997,[5] significant numbers of people in East Asia's NICs moved toward the "globalophobe" end of the international spectrum of preferences from their previous "globalophile" stance. In contrast, Latin America slowly emerged from its "lost decade" of debt crisis with a newly discovered commitment toward more open markets, only to see it profoundly shaken up by financial crises in the late 1990s and early 2000s. The U.S. image rose and fell in both regions in tandem with booms and busts, swinging between friend and foe, helping or sabotaging development. Ironically, the United States also had had its days of globalophobia in the 1980s, as its manufacturers looked helpless against competition from imports. Then, it thought itself as a victim of globalization, too.

Perceiving the industrial policies of East Asia and Latin America's NICs as threatening global liberal trade norms and U.S. jobs, in 1994 the United States launched the WTO to close loopholes in international regulations over subsidy, trade barriers, and intellectual property rights. From the U.S. perspective, moreover, regionalism was acceptable only if the United States led the regionalist effort. Joint with Canada and Mexico, in 1994 the United States formed NAFTA while opposing APEC's formation of a trade bloc from its simple status of "open regionalism." It battled against Malaysian Prime Minister Mohammed Mahathir's East Asian Economic Grouping (EAEG) proposal and its Association of Southeast Asian Nations (ASEAN) Plus Three (APT) successor while advocating the integration of North and South America into one free trade area. In the late 1990s, Japan proposed but was quickly compelled to withdraw its idea regarding an Asian Monetary Fund (AMF) in the aftermath of the Asian Crisis, once the United States warned against weakening the IMF role and power. The United States has become dexterous in creating new multilateral options for itself while preempting those of its allies and friends in East Asia through flexibly choosing and dropping partners from various continents.

The surge of a nationalistic strand in U.S. security policy owes much to the September 11 terrorist attacks. Even so, signs of change were visible as early as 1990 when Defense Secretary Richard Cheney unilaterally drew up an East Asia Strategic Initiative, planning for a staged reduction of U.S. troops in South Korea to adjust military capability to the end of the Cold War.[6] The policy was abruptly suspended in 1992 amidst reports of Pyongyang's nuclear development program[7] and then reversed with the release of the "Nye Report" in 1995, which endorsed a continuous forward deployment of U.S. troops in East Asia.[8]

The triumphant Desert Storm war campaign of 1991 and the spread of international terrorism in the 1990s led gradually to a reformulation of U.S. strategy. Predicting future wars to be "asymmetric" in character, with enemies focusing on the development of "niche capabilities" including weapons of mass destruction and striking at U.S. vulnerabilities in unconventional ways such as terrorist attacks, the U.S. Joint Chiefs of Staffs envisioned making the army, navy, air force, and marines more "interoperable," supporting each other as members of a joint force through a systematic application of information technology in weapons as well as command systems.[9] The new policy, announced in May 2000 as Joint Vision 2020, was a culmination of strategic rethinking unleashed by the end of the Cold War.

In 1997, the National Defense Panel warned against "nuclear, chemical, or biological attacks by a rogue state." Judging traditional deterrence policy as inadequate in thwarting this new threat, it called for fully exploiting information technology to build up U.S. military capabilities to "detect, identify, and track far greater numbers of targets over a larger area for a longer time than ever before." The U.S. armed forces would need "greater mobility, precision, speed, stealth, and strike ranges while it sharply reduces its logistics footprint."[10] That required a comprehensive overhaul of military organization, away from the Cold War forward deployment of large land forces in a few fixed bases ready for simultaneous engagement in two regional theaters of conventional war, toward an extensive network of much smaller ground units operating like "expeditionary" forces with "lighter and more agile automated systems" and projecting power "within hours or days rather than months" against unconventional provocations.[11] The U.S. military readied for change in its force organization well before Osama bin Laden's attack on New York, though it did not yet know how to do it or at what pace.

Any transformation of force structure on the scale in accord with the National Defense Panel's vision was bound to cause resistance from allies and clients. The September 11 attacks and the second Iraqi War prompted

Defense Secretary Donald Rumsfeld to accelerate force restructuring and redeployment, making alliance conflict a distinctive trait of the new Pax Americana in both economic and military areas.

The newness of the new Pax Americana has, therefore, these distinctive traits:

- A unipolar structure of worldwide military power
- Increased likelihood that the United States would act unilaterally
- Accelerated speed and intensity of global transnational relations
- Manifold sources of conflict between the United States and its allies in the context of U.S. alliances
- U.S.-led bilateral and regionalist endeavors and U.S. resistance toward similar endeavors that it does not lead.

Three Kinds of Regionalism

The construction of a unipolar global power structure made Washington less tolerant of "free riders" and more willing to act unilaterally. The response of U.S. allies and client states toward this new form of U.S. leadership varied over space and time, however, sometimes driven by domestically based political dynamics but more frequently influenced by Washington's behavior. Unilateralism constitutes a key trait of U.S. leadership in the new Pax; regionalism has been the focal point of foreign policy innovation for most of its allies during the new Pax. We note three types of regionalism.

The European Union (EU) is the most ambitious example, seeking to create a regional economic union with free flows of capital and labor backed by a single currency, with elements of political coordination to share sovereignty between supranational, national, provincial, and local authorities. It has the potential of growing into a rival of the United States outside the area of military security, where U.S. preponderance is overwhelming. The EU is propelled by more than its member states' fear of outside challengers driving their firms out of markets. Its success lies fundamentally in its teleology, namely, its goal to create unity among the states of Europe, itself a constantly reconstructed and expanding regional identity.

A second kind of regionalism is reflected in trade blocs proliferating or under gestation at subregional, regional, or hemispheric levels, such as NAFTA, MERCOSUR, and FTAA in North and South America and ASEAN in Southeast Asia. They are not conceived as an integral part of a larger program of community building, laying the groundwork for the next phases of regional cooperation or supplementing national life with supranational identity. Instead, they are intended as free trade areas.[12] These trade blocs are justified narrowly in terms of how to advance member state interests, not by a teleological vision of a regional community valued in and of itself.

A third type of regionalism has become popular in East Asia in recent years. Bilateral regionalism engages a country simultaneously in multiple bilateral free trade talks.[13] This happens in part because these countries lack political parties capable of organizing the public into a domestic coalition supportive of wider regional free trade areas and because they are deprived of easily identifiable natural free trade zones with trade partners eager for multilateral cooperation. Such experiments with bilateral free trade have not been conceived as parts of a larger regionalist initiative. Given huge obstacles at home and abroad, each country makes the best of what it has, engaging in free trade talks with a more eager trade partner with the hope of triggering similar talks on other fronts, or simply gaining access to already existing trade blocs. Figure 1.1 reports East Asia's bilateral free trade talks.

Two countries in particular are innovative networkers: Singapore and Chile. Singapore features a thoroughly open economy free of agricultural lobbies demanding protection. It has capitalized on its membership in the ASEAN Free Trade Area to lure a wide range of states into free trade talks. It has reached bilateral agreements with Australia, New Zealand, Japan, and even the European Free Trade Association (EFTA) member states. To acquire a gateway to the MERCOSUR and NAFTA, it started negotiations with Chile and Mexico. Chile projects itself as a doorway to a regional trade bloc, too, as it seeks to penetrate deep into Japan and South Korea's huge markets for agricultural goods. Chile has also signed bilateral free trade agreements with many countries of the Americas, including Canada, Mexico, and the United States, strengthening its attractiveness as an FTA partner for East Asian countries.

Trailing not far behind in reaching out for free trade partners are Japan and South Korea, which are pulled by contradictory forces. Each competes with China in signing a free trade agreement with ASEAN. Yet each also knows that the real battle is fought over Northeast Asia. Whereas Japan focuses on second tier states such as South Korea and Mexico for free trade talks, South Korea has engaged Japan and the United States in negotiations and envisaged a free trade area with China to balance Japanese and U.S. power. China has thus far taken a third route, focusing only on ASEAN.

A country's choice between the three kinds of regionalism as a means to cope with the challenges of globalization, unipolarity, and U.S. unilateralism is shaped by several variables. The presence of a politically powerful but

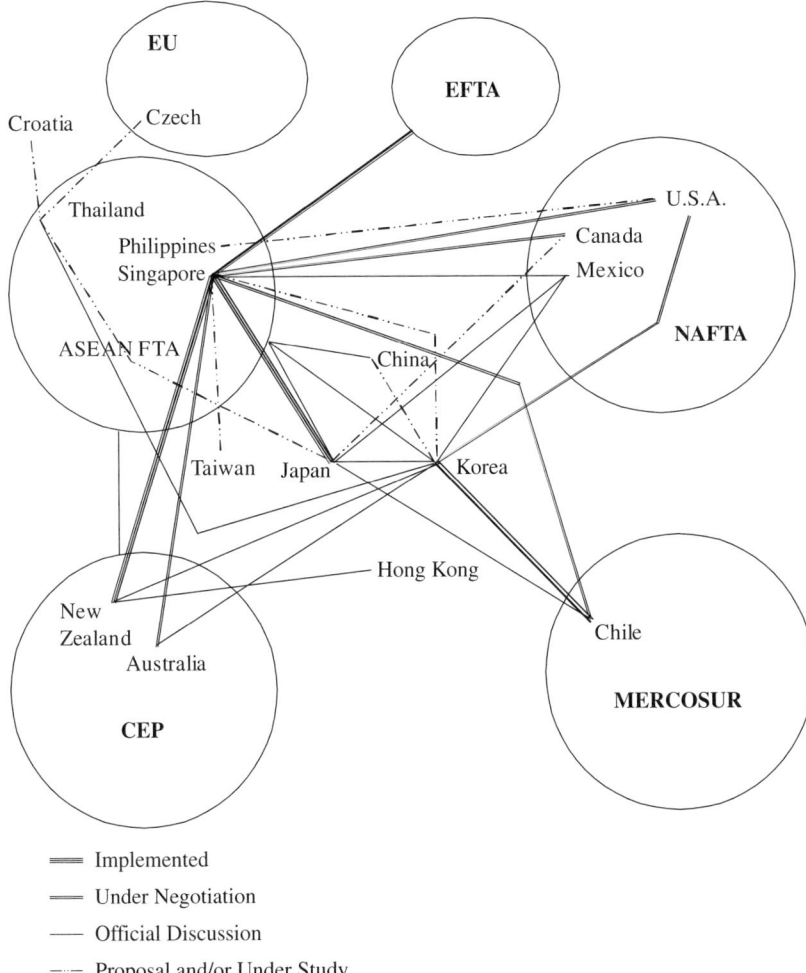

- ═══ Implemented
- ─── Under Negotiation
- ─── Official Discussion
- ─·─ Proposal and/or Under Study

Figure 1.1 Bilateral free trade talks and "regionalism" in East Asia. Adapted from Table 1, Samuel S. Kim, "Regionalization and Regionalism in East Asia," *Journal of East Asian Studies* 4, No. 1 (January–April 2004), based on Kathie Krumm and Homi Kharas, eds., *East Asia Integrates: A Trade Policy Agenda for Shared Growth* (Washington, DC: The World Bank, 2003), 83. ASEAN FTA, Association of Southeast Asian Nations Free Trade Area; CEP, Australia–New Zealand Closer Economic Partnership; EFTA, European Free Trade Association; EU, European Union; NAFTA, North American Free Trade Agreement; MERCOSUR, Southern Common Market.

economically stagnant primary, secondary, or tertiary sector frequently deters policymakers from engaging in more ambitious types of free trade talks. The capability of political parties for interest intermediation is also critical because, without their advocacy of new policy ideas, organization of supporters, and engineering of political bargains, proposals for a free trade area become mere intellectual exercises even if there exists public support for regionalism. Then, there is the problem of finding the right partners with complementary economic structures and ideological affinities.

Each region's military security dynamics matter greatly for regionalism (see Tables 1.1 and 1.2). The most successful experiment of integration after World War II started as an effort to build a better security environment. To stop their rivalry from escalating into World War III, France and West Germany joined forces with four others in collectively managing coal and steel resources — two strategic goods thought then to be essential for war making. The resulting European Coal and Steel Community (ECSC) drew U.S. support in spite of its contribution to trade diversion because Washington, too, placed military security before economics. The ECSC contributed to a long process of Franco–German reconciliation, enabling Washington and Western Europe to confront Soviet expansionism. This experiment sowed the seeds for a trade bloc founded through the Treaty of Rome in 1957 — what today we know as the European Union.

Table 1.1 Interplay between Economic and Security Dynamics

U.S. Role in Regional Security Dynamics	Primary Economic Partners[a]	
	Within Region Trade Arrangements	**Outside Region Trade Arrangements**
Integrative	EC, 1967	ECSC, 1952
	EU, 1994	EEC, 1958
	NAFTA, 1994	
	MERCOSUR, 1995	
Divisive	APEC, 1994	ASEAN FTA, 1993

[a] See Figure 1.1 for ASEAN FTA, EU, NAFTA, and MERCOSUR. APEC, Asia Pacific Economic Community; EC, European Community; ECSC, European Coal and Steel Community; and EEC, European Economic Community.

Table 1.2 Free Trade Area and Collective Security Understandings[a]

	Free Trade Area Embedded in Collective Security Understandings	Free Trade Area without Collective Security Understandings
Interregional	FTAA negotiation	APEC talks
Regional	EU, NAFTA	ASEAN
Subregional	MERCOSUR	
National	Japan–Korea talks	Korea–Chile negotiation

[a] See Figure 1.1 for ASEAN, EU, MERCOSUR, and NAFTA. APEC, Asia Pacific Economic Community; FTAA, Free Trade Area of the Americas.

The importance of regional military security is borne out in the history of MERCOSUR. The MERCOSUR experiment was possible only after South America's two giants, Argentina and Brazil, gave up their aspiration for regional hegemony and renounced the use of military force against one another. Their process of reconciliation began with a 1979 agreement regarding the use of the Paraná River system's waters. The change accelerated as a product of a paradigmatic change of domestic politics and economics. The lost decade ushered in by a debt crisis in 1982 made the rhetoric of military buildup implausible and illegitimate; the free fall of their two economies helped to drive the military out of power and unleash the forces of democratization. Empowered with newly acquired ideas and organizations, democratic governments channeled resources away from defense into welfare and growth programs. In 1985, the two countries pledged to use nuclear energy exclusively for peaceful purposes, and in 1986, they began to lift trade barriers selectively, eventually joining Uruguay and Paraguay to launch MERCOSUR through the 1991 Treaty of Asunción.

Moreover, as with the birth of ECSC, the United States supported the long journey toward reconciliation between Argentina and Brazil in the context of their acceptance of U.S. hegemony and the U.S.-led international institutions, after years of mistrust and vacillation, if not outright resistance. In 1990, Argentina and Brazil confirmed their adherence to the U.S.-led regime for nuclear nonproliferation, pledging cooperation with the International Atomic Energy Agency's program of safeguard measures over national nuclear programs and endorsing the Treaty of Tlatelolco's vision of a nuclear-free Latin America. The U.S. government concluded that MERCOSUR posed little threat to U.S. interests, seeing it as an instrument to strengthen the shift in their domestic politics and economics toward U.S.-propagated ideas of neoliberal reform. The Argentine and Brazilian governments created MERCOSUR as an integral part of a larger systemic liberalization and deregulation whose goal was to dismantle the enduring legacies of Juan Perón's "populism" and Getúlio Vargas' "corporatism," respectively.

The launching of NAFTA in 1994 was also a triumph of U.S. values and norms. The debt crisis of the 1980s destroyed Mexico's faith in its import substitution industrialization strategy based on populist or corporatist ideas and institutions. In 1986, President Miguel de la Madrid Hurtado led Mexico's entry into the GATT to consolidate U.S. support for debt rescheduling and strengthen his domestic political and economic reforms by opening to the pressures of international competition. Mexico's joining of NAFTA eight years later constituted a similar act of ideological convergence toward U.S. values and norms, albeit on a much larger scale.

By contrast, Northeast Asia has opened up only toward regionalist ideas of the third kind. This ideational shift is at its preliminary stage, with FTA talks proceeding at a bilateral rather than multilateral level, engaging a very limited pool of elite segments of the state bureaucracy and think tanks to learn each other's thoughts on opportunities for partnership. The region's lag in organizing multilateral organizations either in defense against trade blocs or in hopes of preventing a spread of financial instability owes much to its singularly unique asymmetric bipolarity in military security matters. The United States and Japan keep order in maritime East Asia through naval supremacy, while China predominates over continental East Asia with its land power, to quote Robert S. Ross. The three collaborate over regional peace but also deter each other from becoming a hegemon on both land and sea.

This rivalry occurs as a dynamic power game because everyone extrapolates China's future power capability from its two decades of high growth and sees its transformation into a global power as an irreversible international trend. Interested in taming China's ambition before it grows too strong and too big, Washington and Tokyo encourage its entry into multilateral economic institutions to inculcate the values and norms of the Pax Americana in China's ruling elite. To let China emerge as a center of FTA initiatives among East Asian NICs would undermine this effort of acculturation. China, too, looks cautiously at FTAs, but for the opposite reason. Believing that time is on its side, it delays, perhaps indefinitely, FTA talks with Japan and continues to strengthen its developmental state's unilateralist strategy of economic growth, with a spice of bilateral FTA initiatives newly added.

The recent Chinese and Japanese overtures toward an ASEAN FTA are a product of this intraregional split. To make Southeast Asia not only a de facto but also a de jure Japanese sphere of influence before China makes a further inroad, Tokyo seeks a trade bloc with ASEAN. China woos ASEAN, too. South Korea, as a midsized power, fears any hegemony, whether Chinese or Japanese, and searches for a balance by inviting both China and Japan to FTA talks.

This fear of neighbors does not by itself prevent Northeast Asia from forming FTAs. As noted in the discussion of regional integration initiatives in Western Europe and North and South America, security conflicts or rivalries have been critical and often more important than economic interests in launching regional FTAs. Regionalism is a distinctive method of problem solving. States pool parts of their sovereignties selectively and even transfer segments of political authority to a supranational entity because they face a problem they cannot effectively address alone. Had a unilateralist way of problem solving yielded fruit, they would have not given up parts of sovereignty and subjected themselves to supranational or intergovernmental policymaking. Regionalism is their second-best method of problem solving. FTAs ameliorate security conflicts through building a structure of mutual hostages between member states. States agree simultaneously to tie their hands by entering a regional FTA. By deepening and widening the depth and scope of interdependence, FTAs raise the costs of war prohibitively between its members.

Northeast Asia is, nevertheless, a less fertile ground for regional integration because of its power structure, not because of extant security conflicts. The strategy of mutual hostages works only when key rival states are roughly on par with each other in terms of power both dynamically and statically, as were France and West Germany in 1951 and Argentina and Brazil in 1979. Western Europe had an additional advantage of having other "floating" powers such as Italy and later Great Britain preventing any member state from ruling regional policy-making bodies. That helped France and West Germany to collaborate without fearing each other as a potential regional hegemon. The power structure of Northeast Asia, by contrast, is bipolar and asymmetric, locking China and Japan in a dynamic power game that renders mutual accommodation more difficult.

Confident of its status tomorrow as Northeast Asia's regional hegemon but fearful of its vulnerabilities today as a newly industrializing country facing economically and technologically powerful Japan, China prefers to dither. Japan opposes integration, too, but for the opposite fear of inadvertently aiding China's rise to the rank of a regional hegemon. Whereas FTAs were looked on as mechanisms to formalize and strengthen fragile balances of power in Western Europe and South America, in Northeast Asia they are judged as part of hegemonic struggles. Northeast Asia's second tier state, South Korea, is also too small to ameliorate the fear of a hegemon through a floater role.

The United States and East Asian Regionalism

The security role of the United States exacerbates the Sino–Japanese rivalry. In Western Europe and South America, the United States took a benign posture toward, if not actively prodded, integration experiments because they were embedded in a collective security framework that the United States dominated. With NATO's integration of West Germany into a collective military command structure, the United States feared neither the reconstruction of West Germany nor the integration of Western Europe into a trade bloc. Both were assets in its containment policy in global and regional arenas. The same was true for MERCOSUR, nested in the myriad of U.S.-centric regional and global organizations under the shadow of U.S. power. By contrast, China lies outside any global or regional collective security apparatus and shows ambition for independence; the United States has played the role of a spoiler in FTA talks involving Northeast Asia.

APEC is a case in point. The United States backed it as an instrument to integrate the Asia Pacific region when regionalism became a new global fad with the launching of ASEAN FTA, EU, NAFTA, and MERCOSUR between 1991 and 1994. APEC could strengthen global but not regional integration because of its extremely heterogeneous membership. With 21 member states widely dispersed from Canada to Australia and from China to Chile, in 1994 APEC predictably came out in favor of building a liberal global trade regime through "open regionalism" with nondiscrimination toward outside regions.

In 1994, APEC was launched to brake the global proliferation of regionalism, not as an effort to construct a new trade bloc or regional identity. Those with ASEAN FTA, NAFTA, and MERCOSUR membership welcomed APEC because it enabled them to encourage Northeast Asia's economic liberalization without compromising their exclusive trade blocs. By contrast, Japan and South Korea joined the bandwagon to slow down the regionalist experiments of other APEC members and to pressure China to enter global markets on their free trade terms. This explains why much of regionalist talk in East Asia after the 1997 Asian crisis occurred outside the APEC framework. Fearing another region-wide epidemic of bank failures, and also intertwined by security rivalries, China, Japan, and South Korea linked up with some of the ASEAN FTA states to search for new ways to collaborate. Given APEC's extreme internal heterogeneity, they created new channels of political dialogue. To borrow EU jargon, APEC "widened" its membership too much before it "deepened" its level of cooperation to make it a promising ground for regional institution building. Unable to find a common denominator in economic or security realms, APEC members split into smaller groups to engage in "combinations and permutations of two-power, three-power, four-power, and even two-plus-four power or three-plus-three power FTA talks."[14]

U.S. hostility toward the idea of Northeast Asian or East Asian regionalism remains strong, whether it is anchored on China or Japan. The ASEAN plus Three, linking Southeast Asia with Northeast Asia's three trade powers, formed in 1990, found itself undermined by the United States, which also killed Japan's idea of establishing an Asian Monetary Fund (AMF) in the aftermath of the 1997 Asian Crisis, as already noted, lest it weaken the U.S.-led IMF and transform East Asia into a yen bloc.

This U.S. hostility arises from East Asia's power structure. Unlike Latin America and Europe, East Asia lacks collective security mechanisms to tone down and control the military ambition of a rising regional power. That rising power, China, has such size and growth record to make it look like a contender for regional hegemony even more than post-war Germany and Brazil ever were in their respective regions. And because of the absence of second tier powers capable of balancing Japan unilaterally or as a group in East Asia, any FTA or AMF that Japan establishes with South Korea and ASEAN countries would be unlike the EEC or the later European Monetary System (EMS). Western Europe's regionalist experiments were driven by three or four states with more or less equal power, but any FTA or AMF anchored around Japan would be internally vertical. The power disparity between Japan and its second tier neighbors is too great to make regionalism a union of equals. The U.S. government opposes its Japanese ally's regionalist ambition because U.S. power in East Asia critically depends on its ability to maintain Japan's dependence on the United States for security and on its preempting Japan from coming too close to China.

Despite the formidable obstacles, it is still too early to give the final verdict on East Asian regionalism. As Singapore's Lee Kuan Yew diagnosed, merging East Asia's southern and northern parts into some collaborative endeavor is an "idea that would not go away."[15] The Asian Crisis of 1997 created a profound sense of vulnerability before global market forces and a deep resentment of what many saw as U.S. exploitation of that vulnerability to further its economic interests. These perceptions helped to spread what were condemned as heretical ideas only a few years before. Mahathir's idea of ASEAN plus Three suddenly acquired legitimacy, bringing the heads of state of Northeast and Southeast Asia to a summit meeting for the first time in December 1997 in the middle of the Asian Crisis. Some ASEAN member states and South Korea, moreover, called on Japan's leadership to forge regional FTAs despite their collective memory of prewar Japanese colonial aggression.

U.S. Defense Secretary Donald Rumsfeld's program of U.S. troop reallocation imposed on South Korea unilaterally, without much consultation, heightened the search for alternatives. The way that the U.S. government reshaped its military posture and presence in South Korea at the start of the twenty-first century alienated even South Korea's pro-U.S. conservative camp. The reallocation policy would make South Korea push even more aggressively for a free trade agreement with Japan for the sake of closer security ties with Japan and as leverage to lure China into a free trade agreement with South Korea.

The new Pax Americana is too strong to be undermined by these efforts, however. South Korea is too small to affect Northeast Asia's asymmetric bipolarity, upon which new Pax Americana rests in East Asia, and it has no intention of weakening the U.S. regional military security role. South Korea requires a very strong U.S. presence in Northeast Asia for a peaceful resolution of the North Korean nuclear crisis and to hold both China and Japan in check. Rather, South Korea's FTA overtures toward its giant neighbors are likely to strengthen Northeast Asia's asymmetric bipolarity unless China and Japan join hands. That possibility is extremely low because Japan has sought to strengthen its military alliance with the United States for the past decade. The new Pax Americana is likely to continue with a proliferation of bilateral and even regional FTAs in East Asia.

The chapters that follow explore several of these topics in detail. The chapters by Young Jong Choi and Pamela K. Starr analyze the variations in regionalist experimentation and trends. Those by Robert Paarlberg, Robert S. Ross, Takashi Inoguchi, Mônica Herz, and the two of us consider principally political and military issues in the two regions with regard to each region's principal powers, namely, China, Japan, Brazil, South Korea, and Cuba.

How Do East Asia and Latin America Compare in Detail?

Robert Paarlberg's chapter argues that the new Pax Americana after the end of the Cold War in Europe did not bring about increased use of U.S. military power in either region. In neither region did the collapse of the Soviet Union create a significant vacuum of power waiting for the United States to fill. The Soviet Union never had much impact in Latin America outside Cuba, and by the mid-1980s China overshadowed its influence in East Asia. In contrast, there was much more U.S. attention to Europe and, after the terrorist attacks of September 11, 2001, to the Middle East. The exercise of U.S. "hard power" peaked and began to decline in East Asia and Latin America well before the end of the Cold War in Europe. In each region, substantial stability in the pattern of regional international relations carried through from the 1980s to the 2000s.

Changes did occur, however, in each of the two regional systems. Regional integration schemes advanced and, to some extent, deepened in both. The reasons differed. East Asian regionalism had both defensive security and economic logics: how to prevent the repeat of the 1997 Asian financial crisis through regional cooperation and how to tame and incorporate China into the existing world economy. Latin American regionalism had a predominantly economic logic: how to emerge from the collapsed economic models of the past. Despite these differences, the result was comparable in both: deepened regionalism, for the most part not at odds with U.S. interests.

East Asia had long been the least institutionalized of the world's regions in terms of regional international economic cooperation. The East Asian financial crisis of 1997 propelled governments to find better ways to cooperate, as Young Jong Choi shows in his chapter. The long-time members of ASEAN began to consult more closely with China, South Korea, and Japan over economic and some security issues. The actual processes of regional integration have been modest, however, and for the most part have not clashed with U.S. interests.

Since the late nineteenth century, Latin Americans had spurned U.S. proposals for free trade agreements. In the 1990s, as Pamela K. Starr demonstrates, they reversed those views and sought to promote new economic partnerships with the United States. Mexico, the Central American and Caribbean countries, Chile, and Colombia sought the closest forms of trade integration. Brazil and, less consistently, Argentina sought forms of trade integration with the United States that nonetheless retained a substantially independent trade policy as well as a separate trading bloc in southern South America (MERCOSUR). Despite these intraregional divergences, by the 2000s the thrust of Latin American trade policy had changed from emphasizing distance from, to engaging, the United States.

Changes occurred as well in some of the key actors within each of the two regional international systems: China, Japan, and Brazil. From the last two decades of the twentieth century to the start of the twenty-first, changes within China and in China's role in the world were extraordinary. Changes within Japan and Brazil and their respective roles in the world have been subtler. All three patterns of change affect their future relations with the United States, but at the start of the twenty-first century none had provoked a crisis in such relations, nor did such a crisis seem likely. In its own way, each was eager to find ways to cooperate with the United States.

Since the collapse of the Soviet Union, only China emerged as a significant potential worldwide challenger of Pax Americana and a possible U.S. rival, as Robert S. Ross shows in his chapter. China's emergence as a major power and possible superpower depends, of course, on its spectacular economic growth, including growth in international trade as well as its Leninist party-state's ability to deal with myriad political, economic, and social problems that accompany its growth. Yet China has also been a conservative power in several ways. It defended the territorial status quo relative to the Soviet Union (later, Russia) and North Korea. It conserved its military resources, emphasizing the capacity of its land armies to uphold China's interests at its borders, but it has not challenged U.S. maritime superiority in the Pacific Ocean. It asserted military power to advance its territorial interests vis-à-vis India and Vietnam but all well before its spectacular economic growth. It continued to limit Taiwan's international freedom of action, but it has not broken the understandings of decades consistent with a two-China policy. East Asia has been peaceful since the end of the Cold War in Europe in part because the United States and China, and China and its neighbors, developed an effective, albeit asymmetric, balance of power. The United States has been deterred from deploying its forces, but China has also been careful not to provoke U.S. security alarms.

Japan has long been a close partner of the United States within the context of Pax Americana, but its international role, as Takashi Inoguchi demonstrates in his chapter, has been constrained by the persistent legacies of its defeat in World War II: a permanent U.S. military presence in Japan, the abrogation of the use of military force in the Japanese Constitution, a strong sense in Japanese society and polity in support of those constitutional clauses, and the legacy of war that generated suspicion and resentment toward Japan in several East Asian countries. Yet, since the collapse of the Soviet Union, Japan has changed its international role and its relations with the United States. It built up its self-defense forces and deployed them short of combat outside Japan, pursued a more dynamic diplomatic initiative toward North Korea with both carrots and sticks, and engaged in free trade agreement negotiations, successfully with Singapore and inconclusively in the wider context of East and Southeast Asia. In the long term, Japan has been successful in its international relations: it has achieved peace and prosperity. Since 1990, the questions that some in its society, as well as in the United States, have posed is whether Japan ought to contribute more to international stability in alliance with, or as a counterweight to, the United States, and whether Japan could afford a more activist policy in either direction, given its relatively stagnant economy since the start of the 1990s. On balance, Japan incrementally transformed itself into a "normal state" within the framework of the U.S.–Japanese security alliance.

Brazil has long accepted the core values and norms of Pax Americana, as Mônica Herz makes clear, but it sought, more than Japan but less than China, to carve and sustain a posture in the international system independent of the United States. It also became an international regime-abiding cooperative democratic state. Brazil's assets include its size as one of the largest countries and economies of the world as well as an experienced and sophisticated diplomatic corps. As with Japan, Brazilian foreign policy eschewed the use of force toward its neighbors. Since 1990, Brazil moved to accept the international regimes in trade, human rights, and nuclear weapons nonproliferation and harness them to increase its clout in international forums, deepen its relations with its immediate neighbors, especially Argentina, and broaden the reach of its foreign policy toward Lusophone countries worldwide. Brazil has cooperated with the United States on many issues but it has also differed on such topics as regional security in the Amazon basin and Colombia's civil wars as well as on regional economic integration. Brazilian policy navigates between its desires to cooperate with the United States and to sustain its distinctive interests in the face of U.S. inattention to Brazilian concerns.

Pax Americana, in contrast, had long been unacceptable to Cuba. The U.S. and Cuban governments, adversaries since 1959, fought each other at the Bay of Pigs in 1961 and again in Grenada in 1983 and sought to thwart each other's security objectives worldwide until Cuba's loss of its Soviet ally impaired its ability to behave as if it were a global power. Cuba adjusted well to the post-1990 international system, Jorge I. Domínguez argues in his chapter. It designed a foreign policy expecting that others would in due course balance U.S. power, enlisted international support in its confrontation with the United States through active participation in multilateral institutions, changed its international economic relations to diversify political risk, broadcast the attractive qualities of its society to build a constituency abroad, and even cooperated with the U.S. government where interests coincided, as over drug traffic, migration, and the Guantanamo base. Of all U.S. adversaries worldwide, none was as effective as Cuba in frustrating the exercise of U.S. power and retaining freedom for international maneuvering.

Pax Americana was becoming unacceptable to South Korea, which is in the midst of a transition whose endpoint is uncertain, as Byung-Kook Kim points out in his chapter. On the one hand, its people aspire to an "equal security alliance" with the United States, which they believe their country deserves because it is a major trading power. On the other hand, the power disparity with China and Japan, coupled with the nuclear threat from North Korea, makes South Korea still a small country unable to live without U.S. support. Caught between its ideal of equal alliance and the reality of security vulnerability, South Korea sometimes acquiesces to, sometimes resists U.S. hegemony. Its population is divided between these two camps along generational lines. The younger generations do not share the older generations' pro-alliance sentiments born during the Korean War. Unilateral Bush administration policies to confront North Korea with a de facto diplomatic blockade over its nuclear development program, and to reassign and restructure the U.S. troops in South Korea as part of a larger effort to adjust to the security requirements of the post-9/11 war on terror, rendered U.S.–South Korean relations more complex, alienating even the older generations from the United States. Many South Koreans came to believe that the United States put its global strategic goals ahead of the security requirements of the Korean peninsula without consulting its South Korean ally, refusing to exclude the option of surgical air strikes against North Korea's nuclear facilities (thus provoking a war scare in South Korea), and restructuring its military presence in South Korea to release some of its troops for U.S. wars elsewhere, notwithstanding the nuclear crisis in the Korean peninsula.

Conclusion

The fundamental features of U.S. relations with East Asia and Latin America, set in the early to middle decades of the twentieth century, changed less than U.S. relations with other regions in the post-1990 period. International peace, domestic political openings including democratic transitions, and substantial market-oriented economic reforms framed U.S. relations with both regions. Pillars of continuity existed: U.S.–Cuban and U.S.–North Korean relations remained little changed and rather adversarial. Subtle changes unfolded as well, in the widening and deepening of economic regionalism in both regions — most in NAFTA and MERCOSUR, less so in East Asia — and the evolution of the international roles of Brazil and Japan.

The main future scenarios, therefore, were posed by China and South Korea in their relations with the United States. China demonstrated a capacity for self-transformation, the deployment of power simultaneous with self-restraint, and a continuing ability for its government, rather than its society, to set the terms for China's international relations. South Korea, too, showed enormous self-transformation and even a willingness to deploy its military power beyond the seas in alliance with the United States, but, in South Korea as in much of Western Europe, domestic society had increasingly begun to say "no" to Pax Americana. Will the future foreign policies of these East Asian and Latin American countries remain driven by the state's interests, as in China, or by the society's interests, as in South Korea?

Notes

1. For the impact of the end of the Cold War on U.S.–Mexican relations leading to NAFTA, see Jorge I. Domínguez and Rafael Fernández de Castro, *The United States and Mexico: Between Partnership and Conflict* (New York: Routledge, 2001), 19–23.
2. Robert Devlin, Antoni Estevadeordal, and Luis Jorge Garay, "Some Economic and Strategic Issues in the Face of the Emerging FTAA," in *The Future of Inter-American Relations*, ed. Jorge I. Domínguez (New York: Routledge, 2000), 157.

3. Joseph S. Nye and Robert O. Keohane, *Power and Interdependence* (Boston: Pearson Addison Wesley, 2000).
4. Joseph S. Nye, *Bound to Lead: The Changing Nature of American Power* (Boston: Basic Books, 1991).
5. Samuel S. Kim, "East Asia and Globalization: Challenges and Responses," in *East Asia and Globalization*, ed. Samuel S. Kim (Lanham, MD: Rowman & Littlefield, 2000), 2–5.
6. U.S. Department of Defense, *A Strategic Framework for the Asia Pacific Rim: Looking toward the 21st Century* (Washington, DC: U.S. Government Printing Office, 1990).
7. U.S. Department of Defense, *A Strategic Framework for the Asia Pacific Rim: Report to Congress 1992* (Washington, DC: U.S. Department of Defense, May 1992).
8. U.S. Department of Defense, Office of International Security Affairs, *United States Security Strategy for the East Asia-Pacific Region* (Washington, DC: U.S. Government Printing Office, February 1995).
9. See U.S. Joint Chiefs of Staff, "Joint Vision 2020," May 30, 2000. http://www.dtic.mil/jointvision/jvpub2.htm.
10. See National Defense Panel, "Transforming Defense: National Security in the 21st Century," December 1997, iii. http://www.dtic.mil/ndp/FullDoc2.pdf.
11. National Defense Panel, "Transforming Defense: National Security in the 21st Century," 33–34, 47.
12. MERCOSUR members greatly improved their interstate security relations parallel to, but outside of, the formal MERCOSUR framework.
13. Mireya Solís, "Japan's New Regionalism: The Politics of Free Trade Talks with Mexico," *Journal of East Asian Studies* 3, no. 2 (September–December 2003), 377–404. See also Samuel S. Kim, "Regionalization and Regionalism in East Asia," *Journal of East Asian Studies* 4, no.1 (January–April 2004), 39–67.
14. Samuel S. Kim, "Regionalization and Regionalism in East Asia," 59.
15. Paul Evans, "Between Regionalization and Regionalism: Policy Networks and the Nascent East Asian Institutional Identity," in *Remaking Asia*, ed. T. J. Pempel (Ithaca: Cornell University Press, forthcoming).

CHAPTER 2

A New Pax Americana?
The U.S. Exercise of Hard Power in East Asia and Latin America

ROBERT PAARLBERG

Introduction

American primacy since the end of the Cold War means different things in different regions. In some regions where the power of the Soviet Union had previously blocked or deterred outsiders, U.S. foreign policy has become more assertive. This has been seen most clearly in the Persian Gulf, the Horn of Africa, the Balkans, and Southwest Asia. The United States began deploying significant military forces for the first time to the Arabian Peninsula to fight a war against Iraq in 1990–1991, to Somalia in 1992–1992 to engage in humanitarian relief and nation-building, to Bosnia and Kosovo in 1995–1999 to check Serb ambitions, to Afghanistan in 2001–2002 to force a regime change in Kabul and to deny sanctuaries to al-Qaeda, and in 2003 to change the regime of Iraq.

This unmistakable expansion in U.S. foreign policy ambition was officially acknowledged and explained in a new National Security Strategy (NSS) promulgated by the Bush administration in September 2002. According to this document, a "moment of opportunity" had been created by America's "unparalleled military strength and political influence." The United States, in keeping with its heritage and principles, would not use its new strength to press for unilateral advantages. Instead, it would "use this moment of opportunity to extend the benefits of freedom across the globe" (White House 2002).

This official declaration of a new Pax Americana was big news for the Middle East, Africa, South Asia, the Former Soviet Union, and even Western Europe. But was it anything new for Latin America and East Asia? Even compared to Europe, these two regions had long histories of direct exposure to U.S. military and economic power. Both, at different times, had been badly bruised by the old Pax Americana.

In Latin America and East Asia, the new Pax Americana can indeed be considered something new, but not in the sense we might expect. The post–Cold War period has not brought an increased use of U.S. power in these regions; so far it has brought instead a diminished use of U.S. military and economic power. In these two regions, the collapse of the Soviet Union after 1990 produced fewer power vacuums waiting to be filled by U.S. ambition. In Latin America, Soviet influence had never been a strong barrier to U.S. activity, except in Cuba, and in East Asia even if the Soviet barrier was now gone, a significant and increasingly strong Chinese barrier remained. Also, in both Latin America and East Asia the explicit objective of the new U.S. National Security Strategy (to "extend the benefits of freedom") was already on its way to being attained without further U.S. power exertions. Latin America in the 1980s and 1990s had transformed itself into a region governed almost entirely by democratic states, and these states were pursuing increasingly open and market-oriented economic policies. With the exception once again of Cuba, there were few freedom-denying nondemocracies left in the region for the United States to struggle against. In East Asia as well, political and economic freedoms had advanced dramatically. By the 1990s, with the sad exception of North Korea, all the states of East Asia were either democratic, open to market capitalism, or both.

As a result, neither Latin America nor East Asia emerged as a central target for U.S. power efforts under the so-called new Pax Americana, and U.S. power efforts in both regions actually decreased in intensity during the decade following the end of the Cold War, and even following the September 11, 2001, al-Qaeda attacks. This pattern of diminished U.S. power use in Latin America and East Asia could be interrupted at any time, particularly on the Korean peninsula, yet it is a pattern that has been sufficiently visible up through 2003 to merit closer examination.

The international power of the United States originally came of age in Latin America and East Asia. It was in precisely these two regions that big stick diplomacy and Coca-Colonization first became prominent, more than a century ago, and in Latin America the Monroe Doctrine — the original old Pax Americana — dates back to 1823. The U.S. established itself as a formal colonial power in both of these regions (and nowhere else) following the military conquests of Spanish–American War of 1898. The Second World War and the subsequent Cold War eventually extended U.S. power efforts far beyond these two core regions, yet throughout the Cold War, Latin America and East Asia remained subject to intense efforts at U.S. foreign policy influence. Using the terminology that has been popularized by Joseph S. Nye, Jr., the U.S. repeatedly exercised "hard power" in both of these regions through direct military interventions, alliance formation and forward basing, military and economic aid, continuous diplomatic and political exertions, and also through covert politico–military actions. American society also exercised unofficial "soft power" in both regions, through bank finance, corporate investments, commercial and labor markets, cultural exports, tourism, and the media (Nye 2002).

Compared to this historical baseline, we discover that the exercise of U.S. hard power in these two regions has actually been in decline over the past several decades. In part because fundamental U.S. interests and values are now so much better protected in these two regions compared to the Cold War era, U.S. hard power efforts have become less vigorous. In both regions the U.S. government is now intervening less often with military force, is imposing fewer significant manipulations on flows of economic resources, and is making fewer unwelcome political demands on local regimes. The Pax has generally been increasing in both regions since the end of the Cold War, but the Americana has not.

The Diminished Exercise of U.s. Military Hard Power

The U.S. has a long history of using military hard power beyond its own borders. The U.S. Congressional Research Service (CRS) has calculated that over the period 1798–1993, the United States used its military forces abroad, in situations of conflict or potential conflict, 234 different times. This CRS inventory confirms that during the early history of the Republic, most of these military actions took place either in Latin America and the Caribbean, or in East Asia and the Pacific. Prior to 1914, 80 percent of these U.S. military hard power exercises took place in these two traditional "backyard" regions. After 1914 the focus of U.S. military actions abroad became more diffuse, but more than two thirds of all U.S. military actions between 1914 and 1974 still took place in just these two regions (CRS 1993).

Following the final withdrawal of U.S. forces from Vietnam in 1975, the frequency of U.S. military action abroad was for a time reduced everywhere, and permanent overseas basing in all regions was temporarily scaled down. But with the end of the Cold War in 1989, fears of stumbling into a deadly clash with Moscow declined, so in areas where Soviet power had previously been a constraint, U.S. military deployments and actions began to rise. Permanent basing did not always grow, but operational military deployments increased dramatically. The Center for Defense Information (CDI) in Washington, DC, counts U.S. military deployments and engagements and found that the frequency these U.S. military actions nearly tripled after 1989. More important, the regional focus of these actions shifted. The most frequent post–Cold War deployments and engagements were now focused primarily in the Persian Gulf, the Balkans, and Africa, rather than in Latin America or East Asia. Following the end of the Cold War, the frequency of U.S. military actions in both Latin America and East Asia actually declined. Table 2.1 shows that in the post–Cold War new Pax Americana era, only 16 percent of all U.S. military engagements and deployments have taken place in Latin America or East Asia.

A review of the specific individual deployments or engagements summarized in Table 2.1 provides further evidence of the diminished use of U.S. military hard power in these two regions. Table 2.2 summarizes these specific deployments.

Table 2.1 Selected U.S. Military Deployments/Engagements, 1975–2001

	Cold War: 1975–1989 (15 years)	Post–Cold War: 1990–2001 (12 years)
Latin America and Caribbean	8	6
East Asia and Pacific	4	4
Sub-Saharan Africa	2	18
North Africa, Middle East, Persian Gulf	13	17
Balkans	0	15
Other	0	2
Total	27	62

Source: Calculated from *Military Almanac 2001–02*, Center for Defense Information, pp. 50–53.

Table 2.2 shows that in post–Cold War Latin America, four of the six U.S. military events counted by CDI were either refugee assistance or humanitarian relief, while the fifth event was logistical support for an observation mission. Only in one of these Latin American cases since 1990 — the nation-building troop deployment to Haiti in 1994 — was a significant

Table 2.2 U.S. Military Deployments/Engagements in Latin America and East Asia, 1975–2001

	Cold War: 1975–1989 (15 years)	Post–Cold War: 1990–2001 (12 years)
Latin America and Caribbean	1981–1990: Advisors to government forces in El Salvador 1983–1989: Helos and pilots for Honduran force deployment versus Nicaragua 1983–1985: 8,800 troops to Grenada 1986: Army helos and personnel to assist Bolivia 1988: 1,000 added troops to Panama 1989: 1,900 added troops to Panama 1989: 100 troops for transport and antinarcotics training in Bolivia, Peru, and Colombia 1989–1990: 14,000 troops to Panama	1991–1994: Coast Guard and Navy assistance to Haitian refugees 1993–1995: 21,000 troops for nation building in Haiti 1994–1996: Coast Guard and Navy assistance to Cuban refugees 1995–1998: Logistics assistance for military observation mission at Ecuador–Peru border 1998–1999: Hurricane disaster relief in Central America 2000: Humanitarian aid to Venezuela
East Asia and Pacific	1975: Evacuation of Saigon 1975: Mayaguez Rescue 1976: Korea "tree cutting incident" 1989: Aircraft from Clarke and 100 Marines to U.S. Embassy Manila	1994: Deployment of Patriot Batteries and aircraft with support to Korea 1999–2000: Rotational force to East Timor 2000: Military observers to East Timor 2000: Rotational force to East Timor

Source: Calculated from *Military Almanac 2001-02*, Center for Defense Information, pp. 50–53.

U.S. force deployed for a coercive hard power political purpose. It is not clear why this count of Latin American military deployments failed to include the July 2000 dispatch to the region of 500 permanent and temporary duty U.S. military personnel to support the government of Colombia's drug control efforts (under Plan Colombia), but even if this intervention were included, the pattern of less frequent post–Cold War intervention in the region would remain. In the case of post–Cold War East Asia, the Table 2.2 CDI list of deployments and engagements may understate the activity of U.S. forces in the region somewhat more, since it does not include President Clinton's important decision in 1996 to send an aircraft carrier to the Western Pacific in response to the People's Republic of China's (PRC) intimidation of Taiwan. On the other hand, this tally counts three times what was essentially one action in East Timor. Fundamentally, these CDI counts fail to show any increase in the assertive use of U.S. military hard power in either Latin America or East Asia since the end of the Cold War.

Latin America

Explaining these trends in Latin America, the diminished use of U.S. military power reflects in part a dramatic political change within the region itself: a shift away from violent political struggles over socialist revolutionary change. The 30-year period between the Cuban revolution of 1959 and the collapse of socialist regimes in Eastern Europe in 1989 has been described by Jorge Castaneda as nothing less than a "thirty years war" between a Latin American political left inspired to seek revolutionary change and a (usually more powerful) political right firmly opposed to such change. This left–right struggle in the region invited frequent interventions and counter-interventions by both the United States and the Soviet Union, at times bringing the region to the brink of nuclear war (in Cuba in 1962) and finally culminating during the Reagan administration with a protracted battle over the future of a Marxist insurgency in El Salvador and the survival of a Marxist (Sandinista) regime in Nicaragua.

This intense left–right political struggle within Latin America finally weakened in the 1980s, replaced by an unexpected wave of centrist democratizations (often redemocratizations). As late as 1975, there were only three fully democratic regimes in the region: Costa Rica, Venezuela, and Colombia. But then a democratic opening in Spain following the death of General Francisco Franco helped inspire similar events in Latin America (Colburn 2002). Ecuador restored democratic procedures in 1979, followed by Peru in 1980, Argentina in 1983, Uruguay in 1984, El Salvador in 1984,

Bolivia and Honduras in 1985, Guatemala in 1986, Brazil in 1989, Chile and Nicaragua in 1990, and Paraguay in 1993.

The United States at times used hard power to support and promote this Latin American democratic wave. In 1978 U.S. military forces were deployed to ensure a fair election count in the Dominican Republic; the United States intervened to prevent planned military coups in El Salvador in 1980, Honduras in 1983, and Bolivia in 1984; in 1989 U.S. diplomacy helped prevent a military coup in Peru, and that same year the United States staged a military invasion of Panama to reverse a coup there against free electoral processes (Huntington 1991; Smith 1994). Finally, in 1994, U.S. military forces were deployed to Haiti to create political space for democratic elections on that troubled island.

U.S. economic values also triumphed in Latin America in the 1980s and 1990s, as most of the new democratic regimes that came to power embraced market-oriented rather than state-socialist economic policies. The debt crisis and economic depression of the 1980s, alongside the failures of state socialism in Eastern Europe and the apparent success of market capitalism in East Asia, had diminished political support for statist and protectionist policy approaches. Monetary prudence was embraced, which cut inflation to single digits almost everywhere in the region. Fiscal discipline reduced average budget deficits from 5 percent of GDP to about 2 percent and lowered average public external debt from about 50 percent of GDP to less than 20 percent. Trade liberalization brought average tariffs down from more than 40 percent to nearly 10 percent. More than 800 public enterprises were officially privatized, and private capital was welcomed back into the region. These private capital inflows increased from a level of just $14 billion in 1990 up to $86 billion by 1997 (Birdsall and de La Torre 2001).

By the late 1990s, then, Latin America no longer presented any strong direct challenges to the major goals of U.S. foreign policy. Most events in the region seemed to support the U.S. foreign policy preference for open markets and functioning democracies. In 1992, President George Bush even proclaimed the region, apart from Cuba, to be the "first completely democratic hemisphere in human history," and two years later President Bill Clinton officially celebrated this foreign policy victory by hosting a regional "summit" in Miami with all the democratically elected heads of government from the region (Lowenthal and Dominguez 1996). Cuba remained an anti-American and undemocratic thorn, but with Castro's Soviet patron now gone, most U.S. hard power decision makers lost interest in the island. The regime in Havana remained of intense concern to the Cuban exile community in Miami, and to some in Congress, but it fell off the radar screen at the Pentagon.

This U.S. foreign policy triumph in Latin America was accompanied by a substantial withdrawal of U.S. military assets from the region. Except for the Joint Task Force-Bravo facility in Honduras, with 190 U.S. military personnel assigned, and two forward operating locations (FOLs) in Manta, Ecuador, and in Comalapa, El Salvador, for support of the host country drug interdiction efforts, there are no longer any U.S. military installations located anywhere in Central or South America. The U.S. Southern Command, long headquartered in Panama, was relocated to Miami on September 26, 1997. This command still has 3,000 permanently assigned military personnel, but most are now in Puerto Rico or in Florida. The only significant U.S. military base on foreign soil in the region today is, ironically, in Cuba. This venerable outpost at Guantánamo Bay is now serving mostly as a penal colony for hundreds of captives taken in the U.S. war against terrorism, rather than an active instrument of U.S. military hegemony in the region.

Stubborn believers in the importance of U.S. military hard power in Latin America have tried to identify a new kind of "stealth imperialism" in the region, managed through military training and weapons sales programs (Johnson 2001). But sales of advanced U.S. weapons to militaries in the region had actually ceased for human rights reasons prior to the end of the Cold War and were not reauthorized by the Clinton administration until 1997, after the regimes in the region had all become democratic. The left seeks to depict U.S. military sales and training assistance to Plan Colombia as a project to shape political developments throughout the Andes region according to Washington's preferences (Monthly Review 2002). The U.S. role in Plan Colombia is scarcely that ambitious; when Congress approved funding in support of Plan Colombia in July 2000, it placed strict limits on the numbers of U.S. military and civilian personnel that could be involved (500 military, 300 civilian contractors).

Nor was there any evidence, up through early 2003, of a hard power exercise by the United States government against any of the new populist regimes in the region — particularly in Venezuela, Ecuador, and Brazil — that had begun challenging (at least rhetorically) the wisdom of Washington Consensus neoliberal economic policies. A few conservative members of Congress pointed with alarm to this new "Axis of Populism" in the region, but executive branch foreign policy makers remained calm. In Venezuela in April 2002, when confused and violent street demonstrations in Caracas led to the temporary ouster of the country's erratic but elected president Hugo Chavez, suspicions arose of an official U.S. hand behind the coup attempt. But in July 2002, the Office of the Inspector General of the State Department released a 92-page report, based on an internal review of 2000 memos, e-mails, cables, and interviews, which found "nothing to indicate that the Department or Embassy Caracas planned, participated in, aided or encouraged the brief ouster" of Mr. Chavez (OIG 2002).

In the current era, has the exercise of U.S. hard power in Latin America only shifted into new areas, such as the war against terrorism or against drugs? The post-9/11 U.S. war against terrorism does create a new political situation in some parts of East Asia, but in Latin America the impact has so far been minimal, since Muslim communities in the region are small and links to al-Qaeda are hard to find. In October 2001, the Bush administration officially dismissed the notion that the new war on international terror would imply any change in its policies in the region. The only Latin country from which any officially listed international terrorist organizations were known to operate was Colombia, and in that country the Bush administration's existing support for Plan Colombia was considered a sufficient response. In 2002 the U.S. Justice Department did announce the indictment of members of the Revolutionary Armed Forces of Colombia (FARC) as terrorists, for having caused the deaths of three U.S. citizens in 1999, but this was mostly a public relations effort to put some non-Muslim balance into the new war on international terror. The absence of an al-Qaeda link (the FARC's suspected international ties were instead to the Irish Republican Army) ensured that little new attention would be paid. Latin Americans seeking to enter or remain in the United States illegally did face tighter scrutiny at the border and closer supervision by the INS, and in some cases national authorities (e.g., in Brazil) were pressed to work more closely with U.S. intelligence services, but in most respects the new preoccupation with terrorism only gave Washington a new reason to ignore Latin America. Late in 2002, Mexican Foreign Minister Jorge Castaneda resigned from President Vicente Fox's cabinet partly over his inability to command attention in post-9/11 Washington for a bilateral immigration treaty he had been seeking.

The U.S. war against narcotics production and trafficking has been another matter for the region. Most of the drugs consumed illegally in the United States are produced in Latin America, and in 1986, Congress amended the foreign assistance act to include a provision that bars countries from receiving several forms of assistance if they are not annually certified by the president as cooperating in the war on drugs. U.S. representatives to multilateral banks (such as the World Bank and the Inter-American Development Bank) were required to vote against all loans or grants to decertified countries, and the president was given permission to impose additional economic sanctions on such countries as he saw fit. In order to avoid decertification, some governments in Latin America had to enact tougher laws against drug traffickers; in 1989 the Bolivian Congress passed a tougher law to regulate coca and controlled substances, and Ecuador enacted a similar law, also under U.S. pressure. But in most cases the certification process has been a hollow exercise, an embarrassing (to both sides) charade designed to satisfy only the letter of the law. Governments in Latin America are routinely certified (e.g., Mexico) even when their efforts against narcotics trafficking have been minimal, and when governments are occasionally decertified (e.g., Colombia several times in the late 1990s), the option to impose more than minimal sanctions has not been exercised.

The United States does exercise enormous power over the Latin American region in the area of illicit drugs, but mostly in the form of unofficial soft market power rather than direct foreign policy hard power. U.S. citizens consume $50 billion worth of illegal drugs every year, and the price they are willing to pay on the street to get these illegal drugs is high, currently more than ten times the cost of production in Latin America (Thompson 2002). These huge premiums inevitably inspire illegal production and trafficking, often with devastating consequences for the governments as well as the societies in question. The criminal organizations that make the largest profits from drugs bribe ill-paid law enforcement and security forces, assassinate judges, intimidate or corrupt elected politicians, and arm themselves to take over land or fight wars with the state — and with each other — in search of larger market shares. Entire countries in Latin America have come to resemble the city of Chicago during prohibition, thanks to the domestic drug habits and drug criminalization policies of the United States. This profound penalty has been imposed on the region by the United States, but not through an official hard power foreign policy exercise, least of all one based on military power.

East Asia

Tables 2.1 and 2.2 also reveal a minimal post–Cold War use of U.S. hard power in East Asia. This is more surprising, given that the Cold War has never fully ended in East Asia (Communist Party regimes persist in Beijing, Pyongyang, and Hanoi) and given that Eastern Asia is a region of many more potential international military flash-points than Latin America. One 1990 study of disputed international borders found the highest ratio of unresolved disputes (as a fraction of total contested borders) to be in East and Southeast Asia (Friedberg 1993/1994). Some of these unresolved disputes even pit nuclear-armed communist states directly against U.S. military clients. The China–Taiwan conflict across the straits and the conflict between North and South Korea on the Korean peninsula stand out as particularly dangerous conflicts, with the full potential to involve the United States in nothing less than nuclear war.

In response to such East Asian threats, the United States has remained willing to deploy and exercise hard military power in East Asia. In 1994 the United States went to the brink of war in hopes of preventing North Korea from producing the plutonium it would need to build a larger stock of nuclear weapons. A U.S. military strike was threatened but then averted at the last minute through negotiation of an "agreed framework" committing North Korea first to freeze and then later to dismantle its most controversial nuclear facilities and to permit the eventual verification of its nuclear activities. In return, the United States agreed to lead an international effort to build modern, more proliferation-resistant nuclear reactors in North Korea. Then in March 1996, prior to Taiwan's first-ever democratic election for president, China sought to intimidate Taiwan by conducting elaborate military maneuvers in the straits, including live-fire war games plus a launching of missiles with dummy warheads close to Taiwan's commercial seaports. The U.S. response was to brand China's actions "both provocative and reckless" and dispatch two naval carrier battle groups to the region. At one point the USS Independence, with 70 aircraft on board, approached to within an hour's flying time of the Chinese military exercises.

Continued hard power actions such as these confirm that U.S. military influence efforts in the region remain strong. But the trend in the region, since the end of the Cold War, has not been toward an increased use of U.S. hard power. Instead the United States has withdrawn forces from numerous forward bases in East Asia while tolerating a growth in the local military capabilities of increasingly independent allied regimes.

In 1975, at the close of the Vietnam War, the U.S. still maintained a massive forward military presence in East Asia. In addition to U.S. naval and air bases in Japan (Yokosuka and Okinawa) and U.S. army troops stationed in South Korea, the U.S. also had major air and naval facilities in the Philippines (Clark and Subic) and a complex of air bases in Thailand (Udorn, Takli, Korat, and Ubon). Some key elements of this forward presence are still maintained today. Yokosuka, a 568-acre complex on the coast south of Tokyo, remains the largest overseas U.S. naval installation in the world, supporting the U.S. Seventh Fleet including a permanently forward-deployed attack aircraft carrier. The island of Okinawa was nominally returned to Japan in 1973, but it continues to play host to an elaborate complex of U.S. air, marine, and intelligence gathering facilities. U.S. aircraft take off and land 142 times a day from Futenma Marine Corps Air Station alone (Johnson 2001). The United States also maintains an Asian mainland presence on the Korean peninsula, with approximately 37,000 U.S. military personnel assigned in South Korea at any one time, most stationed as a tripwire to help deter a North Korean attack across the demilitarized zone.

Beyond these core areas in and around Japan, the forward U.S. military presence in the region has significantly receded over the past several decades. Following defeat in Vietnam in 1975, the U.S. forces expelled from that country left the rest of Southeast Asia as well. In 1976, at the insistence of the Thai government, the U.S. agreed to withdraw all 23,000 U.S. personnel remaining in that country. The Southeast Asian Treaty Organization (SEATO) was quietly dissolved in 1977, and Southeast Asia has retained this arms-length posture toward U.S. military forces in the decades since.[1] A century-long U.S. military basing presence in the Philippines finally ended in 1991–1992, when the U.S. Air Force formally transferred Clark Airbase in its entirety over to the Philippine government and when the U.S. Navy withdrew the last of its forces from Subic Bay. U.S. military forces remain present in Southeast Asia, but mostly through U.S. naval port visits or occasional regional exercises with cooperating states (for example, the annual Cobra Gold military exercises conducted with Thailand and Singapore).

This U.S. withdrawal from forward basing in East Asia to some extent reflects the evolution of weapons systems in the post–Cold War era. The so-called Revolution in Military Affairs (RMA) has given the U.S. military more options to project power around the globe from a safe distance, without relying as much on "boots on the ground." Satellite based information systems, geographic positioning systems (GPS), and precision-guided smart bombs and missiles delivered from long-range bombers or long-cruising (nuclear powered) aircraft carriers and submarines provide options to conduct military strikes with far greater precision even while pulling back on the forward basing of some military personnel. But the U.S. pullback reflects other factors as well.

First is a greater willingness to encourage the growth of military strength among allied or client states in the region. In 1996–1997 the United States and Japan agreed on a Joint Declaration of Security and on Revised Guidelines for Defense Cooperation. The new guidelines called for a significantly enlarged role for Japan's Self-Defense Forces (SDF) in the event of a crisis in the region. SDF operations would no longer focus only on the defense of Japan's home islands, but would now include actions to enhance regional stability more broadly (Katzenstein and Okawara 2001/2002). Rather than seeking to exercise greater military hard power over Japan, the United States was inviting Japan to exercise greater military hard power of its own over the region.

Likewise for Taiwan and South Korea. The 1979 Taiwan Relations Act passed by Congress calls on the United States to "enable Taiwan to maintain a sufficient self-defense capability," and during the 1990s, the U.S. Defense Department concluded more than $10 billion worth of direct arms sales to Taiwan, usually over the opposition of the PRC. In 2001 the Bush administration stopped short of selling advanced Aegis naval air defense systems to Taiwan, but otherwise it continued and strengthened the policy of providing generous military supplies. In contrast U.S. arms sales to South Korea declined during the 1990s, but one reason was the growth of South Korea's own indigenous arms industry. U.S. arms sales to Korea over the years had included offset agreements that gave aid to Korean weapons industries, so Korea was able to build its own weapons and also to export arms. During 1994–1998, South Korea exported more than $100 million worth of arms, according to the Stockholm Peace Research Institute.

A second reason for the U.S. military hard power pullback in Eastern Asia was the enlargement of democracy in the region. Eastern Asia is not yet a zone of democratic peace, but since the 1980s a number of previously authoritarian states in this region have become democratic. The 1986 the People Power Revolution ended authoritarian rule in the Philippines and helped inspire a subsequent victory for democratization in South Korea. The East Asian financial crisis of 1997–1998 then helped bring democracy to Thailand and eventually brought an end to the nondemocratic Suharto regime in Indonesia. In May 2000, Taiwan held a direct presidential election in which the candidate of the former ruling party, the Kuomintang, was defeated. This regional democratization trend had not yet reached Malaysia or Singapore — let alone China, Vietnam, Cambodia, or North Korea — but it was a significant trend just the same, one that allowed the United States to lighten its military hand on the region.

This trend toward decreased U.S. military involvement in Eastern Asia was to some extent interrupted following the al-Qaeda attacks in New York and Washington on September 11, 2001. The United States began more intense efforts to destroy al-Qaeda terror networks active in Southeast Asia, and in Northeast Asia the United States found itself again in a confrontation with North Korea, following that regime's provocative decision, after being branded as "evil" by President Bush, to reject the constraints of the 1994 nuclear weapons freeze agreement. The U.S. responded with military hard power to both of these new post-9/11 challenges, but the response was limited in both cases.

In Southeast Asia, the greater U.S. effort after 2001 to break up Islamist terror networks was welcomed by most regimes in the region as a means to reengage with the United States and perhaps regain access to U.S. economic and military assistance. The Philippine government welcomed U.S. military assistance in the fight against Abu Sayyaf, a violent terrorist group active in the southern islands that was seeking an Islamic state and had embarrassed Manila with a series of kidnappings and beheadings. By the summer of 2002, the Philippines had welcomed back 1,200 U.S. American troops, including 160 Green Beret advisors, to build rural roads and train Philippine soldiers to fight Abu Sayyaf.

This might look like a U.S. military hard power exercise over the Philippines, but it could just as easily be viewed as a bilateral exchange of favors between Washington and Manila. In return for accepting this more intrusive form of militarized U.S. counterterror activity, the Philippines received $100 million in bilateral security assistance, a pledge of over $1 billion in Generalized System of Preferences (GSP) trade access benefits, $150 million in U.S. agricultural sales credit guarantees, up to $40 million in U.S. food aid, $29 million from Congress to support poverty alleviation, economic growth, and anticorruption efforts throughout the Philippines, a special $200 million credit line from the Overseas Private Investment Corporation (OPIC), and eligibility to participate in a U.S. tropical forest conservation act program that would swap a portion of Philippine concessional debts owed to the United States (totaling $430 million) for pledges to support domestic forest conservation (U.S. Department of State 2001). The U.S. military departure from Clark and Subic in the early 1990s had left the Philippines, for a decade, without any excuse to ask for side payments of this kind. As a U.S. partner in the new war against Islamist terror, the opportunity to ask for side payments was back.

The limited nature of this new U.S. military involvement in the Philippines was underscored in March 2003, when the United States backed away from a plan to send an additional 1,750 marines and Special Operations troops to operate jointly with Philippine soldiers against Abu Sayyaf. The U.S. Department of Defense dropped this idea following broad popular protests in the Philippines, and upon being reminded that the Constitution of the Philippines prohibited foreign troops from fighting on national soil.

Beyond the Philippines the United States has not sought to reinsert military forces in the region, but nonetheless it has pledged increased assistance to any regime that will assist in the war against terror. In return for such pledges, the United States was able to secure, from a summit of the ten ASEAN nations in August 2002, a unified promise to "prevent, disrupt and combat" global terrorism. In some cases, states in the region voluntarily sought closer military cooperation with the United States. In 2002, Malaysia and the Philippines sought an opportunity to join Singapore,

Thailand, and the United States as participants in Cobra Gold regional military exercises. Malaysia was a prominent launching pad for al-Qaeda activity and was struggling with its own internal Kumpulan Mujahideen Malaysia (KMM) movement, which wanted to overthrow the government and create a single Islamic state in the region, joining Malaysia with Indonesia and the southern Philippines. In support of the United States after 9/11 the government of Malaysia arrested dozens of members of the Islamist network Jemaah Islamiyah (JI) and agreed to share intelligence with the United States. In September 2002, Singapore showed its support by announcing the arrest of 21 suspected JI members.

In Indonesia, the one state in the region where a more coercive approach might have been needed to wage an effective war on international Islamist terror, the United States government has so far stopped short of reverting to coercion. President Megawati's initial response to the September 11 attacks was ineffectual, and leaders of Islamist groups with links to al-Qaeda were effectively permitted to roam free. The United States at first tolerated this response from the political leadership and began rebuilding bridges to the Indonesian military, which the United States had shunned ever since the bloody events in East Timor in 1999. In August 2002, the United States in effect set aside these human rights concerns and announced it would resume direct military training to Indonesia for the first time in a decade, $50 million worth in counterterrorism programs over the next two years, most to train Indonesia's fledgling national police force. Then in September 2002, U.S. officials leaked news of an alleged JI attempt to assassinate President Megawati, hoping to secure greater political leadership cooperation. This step, plus the Bali bombing in October 2002, eventually produced a visible strengthening of Indonesian pressure on JI leaders.

In Korea as well, the U.S. policy response to 9/11 stopped short of a convincing exercise of hard power. Having defined North Korea early in 2002 as part of an Axis of Evil, alongside Iraq and Iran, and having defined its case for military action against Iraq in terms of denying weapons of mass destruction to such regimes, the Bush administration might have been expected to mobilize its military might against North Korea as well, once it learned in October 2002 that North Korea was moving ahead with a nuclear weapons program in violation of a number of bilateral and international agreements. The United States responded instead with mild economic sanctions suspending fuel shipments. North Korea responded by escalating the dispute: expelling nuclear monitors, withdrawing from the Nuclear Nonproliferation Treaty, and moving spent nuclear fuel rods at the Yongbyon reactor complex into position for possible reprocessing, to be able to divert weapons-grade plutonium. At this point, the Bush administration put 24 long-range bombers on alert for possible deployment to Guam, but rather than shifting to a path of militarized confrontation the U.S. remained committed to intense multilateral diplomacy and went out of its way to say it had no plans to invade North Korea.

The evolution of this 2002–2003 crisis underscored some of the new limitations on U.S. hard power in Korea. U.S. military action against North Korea was now deterred partly by knowledge that Pyongyang already had one or two nuclear weapons at its disposal, along with the means to use them in retaliation against either South Korea or Japan. Preemptive air strikes against North Korea's nuclear facilities would be resisted by Seoul, because of the risk of a wider war plus the danger of radioactive pollution in the region.

U.S. economic and diplomatic influence over South Korea had diminished as well, relative to the enlarged influence of China. Korea's economic ties to China have grown rapidly. More Chinese than Americans now visit South Korea, and South Koreans now invest more money in China than in the United States. In 2002, China's two-way trade with South Korea increased by roughly 20 percent to exceed $100 billion, and China replaced the United States as the largest trading partner for the Korean peninsula as a whole (Brooke 2003). These expanding economic ties, plus China's unique diplomatic influence over North Korea, have increasingly turned South Korea's political attention away from Washington and toward Beijing, a significant change from a decade ago when South Korea did not even have diplomatic relations with China. In 2002 China and South Korea exchanged naval port calls for the first time, and in deference to China South Korea began to discourage visa applications by former leaders of Taiwan.

This political reorientation in Seoul is one reason U.S. military hard power has not been more vigorously exercised against the North since 9/11, and the decision to brand North Korea as an Axis of Evil state appears so far to have weakened rather than strengthened U.S. military and diplomatic influence over the peninsula. Rather than finding itself trapped in a new Pax Americana, Seoul appears to be breaking out of its Cold War isolation and building stronger bridges both to Pyongyang and Beijing. Early in 2003, newly elected President Roh Moo Hyun (elected in part on a wave of anti-American sentiment) defied U.S. preferences and initiated cabinet-level meetings with the regime in the North. President Roh began speaking of establishing an economic community with North Korea and even of personally guaranteeing its security.

Economic Hard Power

Perhaps the strength of the new Pax Americana is to be found in the exercise of economic hard power rather than military hard power. The remarkable growth of the U.S. economy during the eight years of the Clinton presidency left an impression that U.S. influence in the world derived now as much from its mastery of the "new economy" (knowledge-based, networked, and computer driven) as from the Pentagon's command of new RMA military technologies. Economic as well as military triumphalism certainly marked the official rhetoric of U.S. diplomacy during the early post–Cold War period. Yet in Latin America and East Asia, the exercise of economic hard power by agencies of the U.S. government (as opposed to simple market power) once again did not increase following the end of the Cold War; if anything, it declined.

In Latin America, the U.S. exercise of state-to-state economic hard power had been in decline for decades. It remained strong during the Cold War, particularly following the Cuban revolution when the U.S. government dedicated significant treasury resources to the support of client regimes in the region through the Alliance for Progress. Meanwhile, regimes that defied U.S. Cold War policies were subject to economic sanctions (originally Cuba, and then Chile under Allende and Nicaragua under the Sandinistas). During the Latin American debt crisis of the 1980s, the United States government again exercised considerable direct economic hard power, through its dominating position within key international financial institutions such as the World Bank and the International Monetary Fund (IMF). In return for Bank and Fund assistance in rolling over or reducing debts, governments in the region were compelled to accept Washington Consensus macroeconomic policies.

By the 1990s, however, the Cold War had ended, democracy had spread, most regimes in the region were embracing some form of Washington Consensus policies, and private investment flows to the region were moving sharply upward. Between 1990 and 1998, foreign direct investments in Latin America and the Caribbean increased more than eightfold, from $8.1 billion up to $69.3 billion, and net private capital flows into the region increased tenfold, from $12.4 billion up to $126.8 billion (World Bank 2000). Under these circumstances the United States had fewer reasons to attempt to exercise economic hard power in the region, and Latin American governments seeking economic resources had new alternatives to official aid from Washington. The episodic financial crises that hit Mexico (1994–1995), Brazil (1998–1999), and Argentina (2001–2002) during this period did not trigger the same degree of hard power effort from the United States, or from the IMF, partly because ending the panic was seen by all as more important than coercing a specific policy change, and also because — once again — the policy changes that the United States might demand had for the most part already been made.

By the 1990s, the U.S. foreign economic policy agenda in Latin America was dominated not by contentious investment protection issues (as in the 1970s), or debt service issues (as in the 1980s), but instead by the challenge of reciprocal trade liberalization, first within the North American Free Trade Agreement (NAFTA) and then within the Free Trade Area of the Americas (FTAA). Since most Latin regimes were eager as ever for lower barriers to the U.S. market, and now ideologically more comfortable with import liberalization at their end as well, this U.S. pursuit of reciprocal trade liberalization did not require much of a hard sell. Hemispheric free trade ran into trouble after 1994 because it was resisted within the U.S. Congress, not in Latin America.

In Eastern Asia, where U.S. economic hard power was never wielded as strongly as in Latin America, economic power efforts diminished even more. U.S. leverage in this region has been even more undercut by rapid economic growth locally. In the 1950s, and even into the 1960s, some client states such as South Korea and Taiwan were significantly dependent on direct U.S. economic as well as military assistance. This dependence evaporated in the 1970s and 1980s when these and other states in the region performed their "East Asian miracle" of sustained rapid growth. By the 1990s, this region (with the possible exception of the Philippines) had transformed itself from a Third World region into an independent economic power center in its own right. During the financial crisis of 1997–1998, some nations, including Thailand, Indonesia, and even South Korea, were briefly susceptible once again to a measure of U.S. economic hard power (exercised through the U.S. Treasury and the IMF), but the need to end the panic quickly restrained the inclination of the United States to exploit this power, and the crisis proved temporary in any case.

The new center of economic influence in Eastern Asia was not the United States or Japan, but China. Strengthened by its absorption of Hong Kong in 1997 and its entry into the World Trade Organization (WTO) in 2001, China emerged as a newly prominent trading state in the region. The PRC's share of exports and imports for developing East Asia grew throughout the 1990s, at the expense of both U.S. and Japanese trade shares. In 2001, the ASEAN 10 sensed where their future trade interests would lie and agreed to trade zone talks with China. Early in 2002, when China surpassed the United States as Taiwan's largest export market, the Taiwanese government lifted what had been a 50-year ban on direct trade and investment links with the mainland. Also in 2002, China passed the

United States as the leading trade partner for the Korean peninsula. China also became a growing foreign direct investor in the region, a rapidly growing source of tourist money, and increasingly a financial power, with the Bank of China operating branches in Thailand, Malaysia, Singapore, and Indonesia. It was China, not just the United States, that worked to block Japan's 1997 proposal to create an Asian Monetary Fund independent of the IMF (Bergsten 1998). This dramatic strengthening of economies throughout developing East Asia, plus the economic emergence of China, left the United States much less well positioned to exercise state-to-state economic hard power in the region, compared to the earlier Cold War era.

What New Pax Americana?

We have seen that in both Latin America and East Asia, the exercise of U.S. hard power has been declining rather than rising since the end of the Cold War, and the U.S. response to 9/11 did not alter this reality. This need not imply any foreign policy frustration for the United States. The exercise of hard power is costly, and the United States can count itself as fortunate if its interests and values in these two regions can be secured with a less rather than a more vigorous power effort. In different ways and to differing degrees this has been the story of U.S. foreign policy in both Latin America and East Asia since the end of the Cold War and the onset of the war on terrorism.

The altered circumstances of U.S. policy in these two regions can be understood through a larger framework of comparative regional security theory, which recognizes the exercise of hard power by a hegemon as only one path to regional peace and prosperity in the modern age. As distributions of power and values change, other regional security strategies can become available to powers such as the United States. By drawing on several strains of international relations theory, we can imagine at least four regional security systems capable of satisfying the needs of U.S. foreign policy, and only one of these is a hegemonic Pax Americana system based U.S. preponderance and a frequent exercise of hard power. Regional security can also be attained within a stable bipolar balancing system, such as the one that kept the peace in divided Europe during the Cold War. Alternatively, as democratic institutions spread within a region, it might be possible to rely for security on what has been identified as the "democratic peace," the fact that no democratic state has yet fought a war against another democratic state (Russett 1993). United Europe may be at peace for this reason today despite a relative absence of hard power use in the region by the United States (either balancing or hegemonic) or by any one else. Even better might be the emergence of a genuine "security community," where democratic states halt even their contingency planning for militarized conflict within a region. North America, at present, comes closest to approximating this ideal.

These alternative regional security systems can be mapped spatially along two dimensions, as shown in Figure 2.1. On a horizontal axis we can measure how concentrated hard power has become in a region (especially military hard power) in the hands of one state, several states, or many states, and on a vertical axis we can measure movement toward joint democracy (implying how frequently hard power must be exercised to preserve regional peace). The regional system described by concentrated power in the hands of one state and limited joint democracy, just slightly up the left-hand margin of this space, was the regional security system favored by the United States in Latin America during the Cold War — the old Pax Americana. Multipolarity in power concentration and even less joint democracy was East Asia's condition during the Cold War; this was not a regional security system so much as a regional war-fighting system. As democracy spread in Latin America, this region moved in the direction of becoming a zone of democratic peace. As East Asia saw democracy spread, and as the decline of Soviet power left this region less multipolar more nearly bipolar (U.S. versus PRC) in terms of hard power, this region has moved toward bipolar stability.

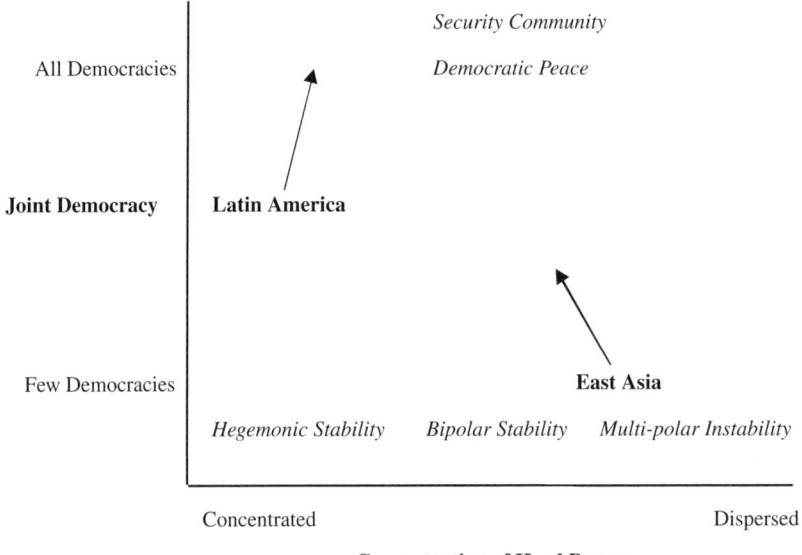

Figure 2.1 Alternative regional security systems (arrows show changes since end of Cold War).

The United States was content to pursue different regional security strategies in different regions throughout the Cold War. The United States provided peace and security to Europe during the Cold War through bipolar stability, while in North America it worked to achieve something close to a full security community. A century ago in Latin America the United States imposed hegemonic stability under Pax Americana, and variants of this strategy continued during the Cold War era. In East Asia none of these strategies was traditionally available, since power was not sufficiently concentrated (the region was neither unipolar nor bipolar — it was multipolar and unstable) and democracy was hardly pervasive.

Since the end of the Cold War, we have seen significant changes in U.S. policy because we have seen significant changes in the systemic options available to the United States. Post–Cold War Europe has moved from bipolar stability to a democratic peace. In the Persian Gulf and the Balkans following the demise of Soviet power, the United States increasingly used international police power and war hoping to impose hegemonic stability. And in Latin America and East Asia we have also seen change.

In Latin America the United States has been able to move away from the old Pax Americana based on frequent exercises of hard power, in part because the region is now so close to becoming a zone of market-oriented democratic peace. In the past decade and a half this region has managed to pacify itself, into what might now be called a Pax Latin Americana. In East Asia, where the United States never had unipolar dominance, an old Pax Americana never really existed. Nor was there much bipolarity in this region, so during most of the Cold War East Asia was more prone to military conflict than Europe. In East Asia today, the regional security system now emerging is made possible by the demise of Soviet power and the rise of a more powerful China. The region may now be stabilized through some form of Sino–American bipolarity. Such an outcome could be less stable than the Soviet–American bipolarity system in Cold War Europe, because China has unsatisfied ambitions in Taiwan and because of nuclear ambitions and unpredictabilities in North Korea. Yet this emergent Pax Sino–Americana in East Asia could in other ways be more stable than the Cold War system in Europe, because of the more open, less ideological, and less imperial nature of politics in post-Mao Beijing, compared to politics in post-Stalin Moscow.

Note

1. In 1994, President Clinton asked Thailand to allow the United States to anchor six civilian ships containing "prepositioned" U.S. military equipment in the Gulf of Thailand, but the Thais turned down the request, and Malaysia and Indonesia immediately expressed support for Thailand's decision.

References

Albright, David, and Kevin O'Neill, eds. 2000. *Solving the North Korean Nuclear Puzzle.* Washington, DC: ISIS Press.
Bergsten, Fred. 1998. "Reviving the Asian Monetary Fund." *International Economy,* 98, no. 8 (November/December), available at http://www.iie.com/newsletr/news98-8.htm
Birdsall, Nancy, and Augusto de la Torre. 2001. *Washington Contentious.* Findings of the Commission on Economic Reform in Unequal Latin American Societies. Washington, DC: Carnegie Endowment for International Peace and Inter-American Dialogue.
Brooke, James. 2003. "China 'Looming Large' in South Korea as Biggest Player, Replacing the U.S." *New York Times,* January 3, 2003: A10.
Colburn, Forrest D. 2002. *Latin America at the End of Politics.* Princeton, NJ: Princeton University Press.
Congressional Research Service (CRS). 1993. "Instances of Use of United States Forces Abroad, 1798–1993," http://www.history.navy.mil/wars/foabroad.htm
Domínguez, Jorge I., and Abraham F. Lowenthal. 1996. *Constructing Democratic Governance: Latin America and the Caribbean in the 1990s.* Baltimore: Johns Hopkins University Press.
Friedberg, Aaron L. 1993/1994. "Ripe for Rivalry: Prospects for Peace in Multipolar Asia." *International Security,* 18, no. 3 (Winter): 5–33.
Huntington, Samuel P. 1991. *The Third Wave: Democratization in the Late Twentieth Century.* Norman, OK: University of Oklahoma Press.
Johnson, Chalmers. 2001. *Blowback: The Costs and Consequences of American Empire.* New York: Owl Books.
Katzenstein, Peter J., and Nobuo Okawara. 2001/2002. "Japan, Asian-Pacific Security, and the Case for Analytical Eclecticism," *International Security,* 26, no. 3 (Winter): 153–185.
Monthly Review. 2002. "U.S. Military Bases and Empire." *Monthly Review,* 53, no. 10, http://www.monthlyreview.org/0302editr.htm
Nye, Joseph S., Jr. 2002. *The Paradox of American Power: Why the World's Only Superpower Can't Go It Alone.* New York: Oxford University Press.
Office of Inspector General (OIG), U.S. Department of State. 2002. "Review of U.S. Policy Toward Venezuela: November 2001–April 2002. Redacted for Public Release." Washington, DC, July 29, 2002.
Russett, Bruce. 1993. *Grasping the Democratic Peace.* Princeton, NJ: Princeton University Press.
Smith, Tony. 1994. *America's Mission: The United States and the Worldwide Struggle for Democracy in the Twentieth Century.* Princeton, NJ: Princeton University Press.
Thompson, Tom. 2002. "Drug War Strategy Fatally Flawed." *Seattle Post-Intelligencer,* June 21, 2002.
United States Department of State. 2001. "Joint Statement between the U.S. and the Philippines." Office of the Press Secretary, U.S. Department of State, November 20, 2001.
White House. 2002. "The National Security Strategy of the United States of America." www.whitehouse.gov/nsc/nss.html
World Bank. 2000. *World Development Report 2000/2001: Attacking Poverty.* New York: Oxford University Press.

CHAPTER 3

A Rise of Regionalist Ideas in East Asia: New East Asian Regionalism and Pax Americana

YOUNG JONG CHOI

Introduction

Regionalism is a widespread phenomenon that occurs in almost every part of the world. About 140 regional preferential trading arrangements are presently in force. Almost every member of the World Trade Organization (WTO) is a member of at least one such arrangement. East Asia, however, long existed outside this global trend at least until the mid-1990s. It was commonly argued that the most striking feature of East Asia was the underdevelopment of regional institutions in the midst of rapidly deepening economic interdependence (Grieco 1997; Katzenstein 1997; Choi and Caporaso 2002).

In the past decade, however, regionalism has engulfed East Asia like any other regions in the world. Proposals for regional cooperation in East Asia have proliferated, particularly after the financial crisis of 1997, at regional, subregional, and bilateral levels. East Asia is now more identified as a region, whose members include ten Association of Southeast Asian Nations (ASEAN) members plus three Northeast Asian countries, China,

Japan, and South Korea. This ASEAN plus Three (APT) process, which was dormant after its birth in 1990 by Malaysian Prime Minister Mahathir due to the absence of regional support as well as U.S. opposition, finally came to life in 1997. At present, numerous free trade agreements (FTAs) have been proposed, and many of them are either under study or being negotiated in East Asia. More concrete progress has been made in the monetary field in the form of several bilateral currency swap arrangements. Regionalism is no longer a stranger to East Asia.

This chapter explores this drastic turn in the fate of East Asian regionalism with a focus on the causes, future prospects, and global ramifications of the recent development of East Asian regionalism. This chapter specifically answers the following questions: Why was there a sudden rise in talks on regional economic integration or regionalism in East Asia? What is the future prospect of these talks to materialize into working regional entities that may push forward regional economic and political integration? And how will East Asian regionalism be linked to the U.S.-led regional and global order?

The recent rise of regionalist ideas in East Asia may not be so puzzling since regionalism is a global phenomenon. East Asia has been mysteriously "under-identified" and "under-institutionalized" as a region in spite of a high level of economic interactions. Therefore, the recent development may indicate that East Asia is on its way to becoming a normal region. Still, we need to figure out the underlying factors behind the recent proliferation of regionalist ideas to see its future prospects as well as its global ramifications.

This chapter argues that the rise of regionalism in recent years is largely driven by external factors. More specifically, the economic crisis that began in July 1997 not only created some functional demands to manage monetary matters jointly but also drove East Asian countries to pool their political power against international financial institutions like the international monetary fund (IMF) and the United States. In addition, a sense of common identity was fostered among the countries experiencing the same crisis. The prospect of these regionalist ideas materializing into working regional institutions will depend on how lasting these impacts of economic crisis will be on the supply and demand sides of regional integration. Judging from the fact that the enthusiasm for building an East Asian community has subsided substantially in the past couple of years when the region largely overcame the crisis, their staying power seems to be waning. Therefore, we can expect that the future prospect of East Asian regionalism is not bright and that there will be no imminent danger of East Asian regionalism running into U.S. hegemony in the near future.

The rest of the chapter is organized in the following way. The first section explores the causes of the rise of regionalism in East Asia. The second section examines the future prospect of East Asian regionalism. The third section evaluates the relationship between the rise of East Asian regionalism and the U.S. regional and global order. The conclusion includes a brief summary and the implications of this chapter.

Explaining the Rise of Regionalism in East Asia

Theoretical Overview

East Asian regionalism raises interesting puzzles surrounding its long stagnation in the middle of rapid growth in regional economic interdependence and a sudden surge of regionalist interests in recent years. These puzzles lead us to examine key conditions necessary for the success of regional integration.

Regional integration has both demand and supply sides. Functionalist approaches (e.g., functionalism, neofunctionalism, and transaction cost theories) represent sophisticated theorizing about the demand side. They start from groups and individuals who are involved in trans-border economic exchanges and therefore have intense interests in breaking down barriers to economic exchange. Reduction of transaction costs, elimination of red tape, and removal of tariff and nontariff barriers will increase the geographic scope of production and exchanges and enhance overall economic efficiency. The process of economic integration involves not just economic exchange but also rules and institutions. Even the simplest economic exchanges require regulations and standard setting as well as specification of property rights. Separate national legal regimes constitute the crucial source of transaction costs for those who wish to engage in exchanges across borders (Stone Sweet and Sandholtz 1998, 11).

Although a well-developed demand side is necessary for integration, it is not sufficient. Without political mechanisms to provide leadership, aggregate interests, and convert them into policy, even the most intense interests may not lead to policy consequences. In this sense, regionalism has a supply side. Institutional arrangements, however, do not automatically come into being just because they are efficient. There are many potential regional arrangements that would be beneficial but have not come into effect. Efficiency at the regional level may be sidestepped by national or subnational actors that would benefit from the status quo.

Specifying the supply-side conditions of regional integration has been one of the major subjects of international relations theories and regional integration theories. One plausible answer coming out of this theoretical journey is the presence of a core area or a small group of committed members among the potential integrating countries. Successful regional arrangements have a hegemonic core, for example, Germany or Germany–France in the case of the European Union (EU) and the United States in the case of North America. Hegemonic stability theory argues that the presence of a hegemonic power increases the prospects for cooperation of all kinds. The ensuing theoretical development shows that, short of a single large power whose interests lie in integration, a small number of committed countries favorable to integration can help. Since regional integration contains aspects of public goods, the presence of a committed core of countries (the so-called privileged k) that benefit from integration even in the face of free riding will facilitate integration.

In recent years, researchers have been paying increased attention to domestic politics, which is at the center of liberalism and liberal intergovernmentalism. Their basic idea is that economic and social interests provide only the raw material of politics but that these interests have to be recognized and mobilized before they become active in politics. Therefore, researchers focus their efforts on explaining the formation of groups pursuing interests and the political process through which interests are converted into actual policies. Pluralist interest group theory, the logic of collective action, and institutional theory are instrumental in understanding how economic demands are translated into political results. Liberalism and liberal intergovernmentalism provide a sophisticated theory of preference formation regarding regional integration (Moravcsik 1998).

Strategic concerns (e.g., relative power concerns and opportunistic behaviors) are at the center of realism. They were commonly used to show the difficulties of regional integration among sovereign states. The agenda of realist researches has, however, gradually shifted to explaining regional integration as an indisputable political reality. A stable bipolar system (Gowa 1989) and the incentive of secondary states to bind the powerful countries (Grieco 1995) are exemplary realist explanations for the successful regional integration in Western Europe. According to the realist logic, the existence of a security community will contribute to the success of regional integration. History shows, however, that regional integration can proceed without a security community. History also shows that many regional integration initiatives are driven by the incentive to counter integration in other regions or to increase collective power against external powers. Therefore, being in a similar strategic situation (e.g., facing common threats or crises) will make it easier for a group of geographically contiguous countries to form a regional entity.

In addition, ideational factors like mutual trust or common identity deserve attention as facilitators of region integration. Mutual trust among member countries provides an important aspect of social capital to economic and political actors, and therefore many potential economic exchanges will not take place without it. Common identity will also facilitate integration, particularly the deepening of already existing regional entities. This concern belongs to early functionalists like Deutsch (1957), who focused on community and the development of "we-feelings," and in recent years to constructivists like Checkel (1999). It is also not unusual for a group of countries that experience common threats or crises to develop a strong sense of community or common identity.

In view of these underlying forces of regional integration, the long stagnation of regionalism in East Asia can be attributed to the deficiency of these forces. For instance, according to neofunctionalism, integration is most likely to emerge among countries with a certain type of domestic environment, that is, liberal democratic countries with advanced capitalist economies, differentiated social structures, and highly pluralistic interest group structures (Haas and Schmitter 1964). A transnational society has a better chance to emerge among such countries. East Asia, however, does not meet these basic conditions. Even the multinational capitalists of the East Asian origin working in East Asia are so nationalistic or ethnically based that a powerful transnational capitalist class has yet to develop (Katzenstein 1997, 38–40). Moreover, formal regional institutions are either underdeveloped or intentionally avoided in East Asia. In short, both transnational societies and transnational institutions, the prime movers of regional integration in neofunctionalism, are very weak in East Asia.

Realists generally list the continuation of the Cold War, an unstable power distribution, the absence of a security community, the deficiency of a working regional leadership, and, most important, the opposition from the United States as the factors that have prevented integration in East Asia (Choi and Caporaso 2002, 493). Intergovernmentalism would take note of the divergence of national preferences concerning regional integration, particularly between Japan and the rest of the regional countries, particularly China (Choi 1998). If we follow the logic of constructivism, East Asia lacks coherence as a geopolitical entity, let alone as a communal consciousness or common identity.

Until the financial crisis in 1997, East Asian countries, with their impressive economic track records, had not experienced common exigencies that might justify joint actions. East Asian economies had been "ruthlessly successful domestic adjusters but slower than the United States and European states to recognize the international dimensions of adjustment via collective regional action" (Higgott 1998b, 45). Most of the East Asian states maintained a high degree of domestic economic control, and therefore domestic adjustments were both available and feasible. The nationalistic nature of their economic policies was reinforced by the close government–business ties in most of the East Asian countries. All these factors had long deterred any serious debate about regional integration that would go beyond intergovernmental cooperation.

Factors Contributing to the Rise of Regionalism

In recent years, the long-dormant East Asian Economic Group/East Asian Economic Caucus proposal has sprung back to life, and numerous trade and monetary cooperation initiatives are on the table in East Asia. The enthusiasm for free trade agreements, which was unknown only to East Asian countries, has finally taken over the East Asian region in less than a decade. This new development leads us to suspect that significant changes might have occurred to the factors behind the underdevelopment of East Asian regionalism. As we will see, two changes stand prominent in relation to the rise of regionalist ideas in East Asia: U.S. policy shift and the economic crisis of 1997.

U.S. Policy Shift and Systemic Changes. Realism explains international phenomena with the changes in power distribution in the international system. The recent proliferation of regional blocs, according to the leading neo-realist Kenneth Waltz, is an indication that the international system is moving from a bipolar into a multipolar world (Waltz 1995, 59). As is commonly known, U.S. opposition has been the major obstacle to the development of East Asian regionalism. The recent surge of regionalist talks leads us to suspect that U.S. power to suppress the East Asian desire for regionalism might have declined substantially.

There is, however, not sufficient evidence in support of this proposition. To the contrary, the United States became the sole military superpower with the end of the Cold War. Its unprecedented economic prosperity in the 1990s revived its economic hegemony. The significance of U.S. markets for East Asian exports remained largely unchanged throughout the 1990s, indicating that the United States is still the single largest market for most of East Asian economies.

What has changed for the United States is not its global power position but the way it exercises its power and its perception of regionalism. The character of the leading state and the manner in which it wields its power, according to Kupchan, determine how other states react to its power preponderance. More specifically, states that exercise unfettered power and that engage in predatory and exploitative behaviors are likely to trigger balancing coalitions and strategic rivalry (Kupchan 1998, 46). There is a well-developed argument that East Asian regionalism was an attempt to counterweigh U.S. influence (Higgott 1998a; Stubbs 2002; Ravenhill 2002). Ravenhill argues that it was not the decline of U.S. power but the arrogance of the United States that drove East Asian countries to come together to form regional institutions that excluded the United States. This attitude was expressed vividly in the aftermath of the financial crisis of 1997 when the U.S. Treasury Department, in cooperation with the IMF, used the conditionality attached to financial assistance packages to mold East Asian economies in its own design (Ravenhill 2002, 171).

There is no denying that such a motivation is more or less behind the recent drive for East Asian regionalism. In particular, China's recent assertiveness regarding East Asian regionalism is largely attributable to the absence of the United States. The ensuing development of East Asian regionalism shows, however, that the claims of anti-U.S. motivation are largely overblown. East Asian countries, including highly intransigent Malaysia and China, have been very cautious not to instigate the United States in pursuing their versions of regionalism.

Consequently, none of the regional initiatives seems to pose a particular threat to U.S. interests these days. For that reason, they have not attracted much attention from the United States. The silence of the U.S. government about the rise of East Asian regionalism is quite different from its clear and strong objection to Mahathir's EAEG and Japan's Asian Monetary Fund (AMF) proposals. We may assume that the United States is not worried about the current direction of new East Asian regionalism, particularly the FTA drive that appears to reinforce the commitment to free trade and economic liberalization.

Moreover, the United States has become more receptive toward regionalist options. Since the conclusion of an FTA with Canada in 1988 and its expansion into North American Free Trade Agreement (NAFTA) in the early 1990s, the United States has proposed the Free Trade Area of the Americas (FTAA) in the Western Hemisphere, the Trans Atlantic Free Trade Area (TAFTA) with Europe, and many other FTA talks. These efforts suggest that the attention of U.S. trade policy has increasingly shifted from multilateral arrangements to regional arrangements. Therefore, the proliferation of FTA talks in East Asia is nothing to worry about for the United States. Still, the U.S. government is casting a watchful eye on the APT process, which is more likely to turn into a political force against the U.S.-led global and regional order. It is certain that the United States will act resolutely to abort any regional initiative that may seriously undermine its strategic and economic interests.

Economic Crisis. There is no denying that underneath the recent launching of a regionalist drive in East Asia, some meaningful changes occurred in the levels of "functional demands," "regional leadership," "the incentive to increase collective power," and "common identity." These changes were, however, largely driven by the economic crisis of 1997. The future development of East Asian regionalism will depend on the staying power of these changes.

The financial crisis of 1997 was a watershed in the history of East Asian regionalism. Since that crisis, there have been heated debates about the limitations of an East Asian development model. A number of East Asian countries have rejected nationalistic economic policies and are experimenting with an Anglo-Saxon model of economic management. In addition, there have been serious discussions about the necessity of regional-level institutions designed to prevent the recurrence of financial crises. The dormant EAEC proposal had finally come back to life in the aftermath of the financial crisis. The first annual APT heads of state summit was held in Manila in November 1999.

The economic crisis created a functional demand for collective action to manage monetary matters jointly. Consequently, regional cooperation was most notable in the financial sector. The crisis also drove East Asian countries to pool their political power against international financial institutions like the IMF and the United States. In fact, conspiracy theories that blame the international financial establishment and the United States for the crisis had a large audience in East Asia (Gilpin 2000, 153–54). The IMF and the United States dictated much of the East Asian response to the crisis, and the "Washington consensus" was imposed upon the crisis-stricken countries as a condition for help. The widespread view that the IMF programs deteriorated the situation made the East Asians even more resentful, driving them further in the direction of regionalism.

In addition, the crisis fostered a sense of common identity, particularly "the image of a region in adversity besieged by outsiders 'ganging up' in their attempts to exploit the difficulties that East Asian governments faced" (Ravenhill 2002, 175). This sense of common destiny must have pushed them to act together and facilitated the process of institutionalization in East Asia. The leadership problem, which had long hampered the progress of East Asian regionalism, could also be attenuated by the crisis as well as by the formation of a common identity. For the first time in history, Japan and China worked together to come up with a financial arrangement to prevent the recurrence of financial crises, and both of them became active participants in the talks to build regional institutions.

In spite of these positive effects of the crisis on the recent surge of interests in regionalism, East Asia is still not a fertile ground for regional integration. The foundation of contemporary East Asian regionalism is the deepening of economic interactions (e.g., intra-regional trade, investment flows, and production networks) after the Plaza Accord of 1985. The level of economic interdependence in East Asia has not changed much throughout the 1990s, and "the vectors of trade flows, investment flows, electronic bank transfers, telephone calls and travel still center on the United States" (Evans 2002, 134). Domestic political changes conducive to regional integration such as democratization, liberalization, and power shift from protectionist to pro-liberalization forces fall short of bringing about the convergence of national preferences among major countries in favor of regional economic integration. Transnational societies and institutions are still largely underdeveloped in East Asia.

The seed of expanding ASEAN to include Northeast Asia was laid in 1993 and 1994, prior to the economic crisis in 1997, when the ASEAN countries (at that time only six) invited South Korea, Japan, and China to join them in broader discussions. Since then, the APT formula has become the foundation for the current discussions of East Asian regionalism. There is no denying that a degree of convergence of national interests between Japan and China contributed to the launching of this East Asian initiative.

Both Japan and China have been, however, not only widely apart in their national preferences toward specific details about East Asian regionalism but also engaged in an intense rivalry over the control of the region. China was an early supporter of the EAEC, seeing it as a means of countering pressures from the United States and other Western countries on various fronts, particularly human rights. China strongly prefers an East Asia independent from U.S. influence. Japan cannot be overly enthusiastic about a well-developed East Asian identity or a regional bloc since that has the potential to damage its relationship with the United States.

In addition, Japan and China are reluctant to take the leadership role to provide various public goods for the region. Secondary powers like South Korea and the ASEAN have taken the initiative in region-wide cooperation initiatives like the East Asian Free Trade Area (EAFTA) and an East Asian community proposal. Japan and China have instead struggled to prevent each other from taking the dominant position in the region. At present, both countries are competing intensely to pull the ASEAN into their own sphere of influence by proposing FTAs with ASEAN. Both of them are extremely sensitive to any attempts by the other to expand political clout in the region. This leadership problem persists even after the financial crisis of 1997.

We cannot deny that East Asia is more of a region at present than in the early 1990s when Mahathir proposed EAEG. If identity determines the boundaries of a region, as constructivists argue, East Asia has a stronger common identity now than a decade ago. The question still remains regarding the extent of newly forged collective identity as well as the magnitude of its impact on government policies (Ravenhill 2002, 175). Furthermore, it is unclear what constitutes the East Asian-ness or East Asian identity and what is left after the crisis swept through the region. The divergence of historical experiences, cultural and linguistic diversity, and differing political ideologies still pose formidable barriers to regional economic cooperation. A neoliberal consensus, which has propelled regional integration in other regions, is still weak in East Asia.

Another burden to the constructive argument is to refute the powerful claim that ideas are only tenuously linked as an independent variable to regional integration (Moravcsik 1998, 73–77). The stagnation of various East Asian community initiatives (e.g., EAFTA and East Asian Summit), combined with the surge of interest in functional arrangements like bilateral FTAs, indicates that it is interest, rather than common identity, that drives East Asian regionalism today.

Domestic politics has the weakest causal link to the rise of interest in East Asian regionalism. According to functionalist approaches, the pressure for regional integration becomes stronger along with democratization and economic liberalization. In most of East Asian countries, however, state is still stronger than society, protectionist forces are influential in domestic policy making, and economic policies are largely mercantilist in nature. However, the growing interests in bilateral FTAs indicate that the pro-liberalization forces are gaining strength in domestic politics of some East Asian countries, particularly in Japan and South Korea. The pro-liberalization forces strive to take advantage of bilateral FTAs as a means of facilitating economic reforms. Once these pro-liberalization forces take the upper hand in domestic politics, regionalism will take root in East Asia.

In short, the future of East Asian regionalism depends on the staying power of the impacts of the economic crisis exerted on the demand and supply conditions of regional integration. So far the picture seems not so promising. The crisis-driven regionalism in East Asia somewhat lost its momentum once the crisis was over. There are few concrete outcomes from a flood of FTA talks in East Asia, either.

Future Prospect of East Asian Regionalism

The APT Process and an East Asian Community

The APT process is at the center of East Asian regionalism. As a direct descendant of Mahathir's EAEG proposal, it is the most elaborate form of regional integration initiative in terms of regional boundary, identity, and institutions (Evans 2002, 137). Informal APT summit meetings began in 1997 in the aftermath of the East Asian economic crisis, and they became an official gathering in 1999. At the first annual APT summit held in Manila in November 1999, the participating leaders agreed to strengthen cooperation with a view to advancing East Asian cooperation in priority areas of shared interest and concern even as they look to future challenges. Its ultimate goal was to form an East Asian Free Trade Area by 2020.

The level of institutionalization is low in the APT process without an independent secretariat. It remains basically a consultative forum of thirteen member governments, and bureaucrats have frequent meetings at various levels to discuss issues of concern. Its future blueprint is well elaborated in the works of the two commissioned groups: the East Asian Vision Group (EAVG) and, its successor, the East Asian Study Group (EASG).[1]

In its annual summit meeting in November 2001, the APT member countries agreed to launch an East Asian Summit (EAS) in the foreseeable future, as well as to scrutinize a plan for EAFTA on the basis of the EAVG report. An East Asian community, though poorly defined, appeared in sight considering the great enthusiasm and strong rhetoric exuded by participating leaders. When the EAVG handed in its final report to the 2002 APT summit, most of the key proposals contained in it were either watered down or relegated to long-term goals (Evans 2002, 139). The EASG final report did not receive much media attention due to the high publicity of the China–ASEAN framework agreement on the bilateral FTA. Major actors of the APT, particularly Japan, were more interested in assessing the repercussions of the possible China–ASEAN economic alliance and figuring out countermeasures against it.

These two reports are very optimistic about the possibility of an East Asian community. East Asian cooperation, according to the EASG report, is "both inevitable and desirable, and that such integration in East Asia will evolve over time" (p. 5). The reality, however, does not justify this optimism. There is a serious leadership problem in East Asia. Right now, neither China nor Japan intends to play a leadership role. A kind of dual power structure has emerged in East Asia. Specifically, secondary powers like ASEAN and South Korea are taking the initiative in the APT process;

major powers like China and Japan are in the backseat. This dual power structure is definitely not conducive to the success of the APT. China prefers ASEAN to continue to play a leading role while aggressively seeking close economic alliance with ASEAN at the same time. Japan is nervous about the possibility of an East Asian bloc led by the China–ASEAN alliance.

Monetary Cooperation in East Asia

While East Asian community initiatives (e.g., EAFTA and EAS) are stagnating, regional monetary cooperation is proceeding rapidly. Since financial problems lay at the heart of the economic crisis of 1997, it is not surprising that regional cooperation has proceeded more rapidly on monetary issues than on trade. Moreover, monetary cooperation, unlike most trade deals, does not create powerful domestic losers. This is why Japan, a hegemonic defector from regional cooperation, could play a leadership role in monetary cooperation.

In the aftermath of the regional financial crisis, Japan proposed an AMF in September 1997. Although the proposal was rejected immediately by the United States on the grounds that it might undermine the IMF, it was just the beginning. The Japanese government not only provided liquidity to the crisis-hit economies through the Mayazawa Plan, but also proposed the "Chiang Mai Initiative" in May 2000, which was basically an effort to set up a region-wide currency swap arrangement to prevent currency crises and the escalation of such crises in the case of recurrence in the future. Japan has not yet provided a clear framework for genuine monetary integration in East Asia, and its exact shape will have to be determined through arduous consultations with the IMF, the United States, and other regional countries.

The likely result of current talks of regional currency swap arrangements will be "a series of bilateral swap arrangements" rather than a genuine regional institution (Ravenhill 2002, 187). As the European experience shows, monetary integration poses more threats to national sovereignty. It is therefore more difficult than market integration, but with much less spillover effect on societal integration. Monetary and financial cooperation achieved so far in East Asia, in spite of its symbolic value, will have only a limited impact on the actual progress of regional integration.

Bilateral FTAs and East Asian Regionalism

Generally speaking, regional groupings with a small membership are more likely to succeed than those with a large membership. Accordingly, bilateral FTAs will be the easiest to establish, followed by subregional groupings and finally by region-wide or trans-regional arrangements. The evolution of the EU from a five-member group and the development of NAFTA and FTAA support this logic. In the Americas, a bilateral FTA between the United States and Canada set off a new wave of regionalism. It was soon expanded into NAFTA, and at about the same time MERCOSUR was formed. Now, a region-wide FTAA negotiation is under way. This developmental sequence indicates that regional integration has a better chance to succeed if it starts from bilateral FTAs.

Regionalism in East Asia, however, started from an opposite direction, that is, trans-regional cooperation. This foreboded great troubles for East Asian regionalism. Trans-Pacific cooperation, despite a long history dating back to the pre–World War period, could not bear fruit until 1989 when the Asia Pacific Economic Cooperation (APEC), the first-ever intergovernmental institution in the Asia-Pacific region, was formed. APEC has yet to make a quantum leap to accomplish its professed goal of regional free trade. Interestingly, the region had not known bilateral FTAs until recently. It is expected that bilateral FTAs, particularly between core countries in the region, will increase the chance of successful regional integration in East Asia.

Currently a strong wind of regionalism, represented by the proliferation of FTAs, is blowing throughout East Asia. The Japan–Singapore Economic Partnership Agreement (JSEPA) signed in January 2002 was the first ever between East Asian countries. For the two concerned parties, the JSEPA represented a significant break from the past in terms of trade policy and policy toward regional integration. Japan had held strong reservations against regionalism for a long time. Although Singapore is one of the most liberalized economies in East Asia, its trade policy has been constrained by the preferences of other more protectionist members of the ASEAN.

As is well-known, the most critical factor for the successful launching of NAFTA was the reversal of traditional U.S. opposition to regionalism. In addition, Mexico's defection from the cause of Latin American integration by proposing an FTA with the United States drastically changed the dynamics of regional politics, sending shock waves throughout Central and South America. This move not only weakened the Latin American resistance to U.S. hegemony but also stirred worries about the potential economic costs arising from the favorable treatment of Mexico by the United States. In the aftermath, Latin American countries were forced to search for FTAs of their own (Mattli 1999, 153–54).

Similar to Mexico's defection, Singapore's plan to strike a free trade accord with Japan and several other countries outside ASEAN drew strong criticism from other ASEAN members, notably Malaysia and Indonesia.

Nevertheless, Singapore accelerated its FTA drive by launching negotiations with the United States, Mexico, Canada, and Australia. Its first bilateral FTA, with New Zealand, came into effect in 2001. In response, other ASEAN members became serious about FTAs. For example, Thailand is scrutinizing the possibility of an FTA with several countries outside of ASEAN.

Similar to U.S. policy change, Japan's policy shift in favor of FTAs has the potential to ignite a regionalist drive in East Asia. The Japanese government acknowledged officially the value of regional integration for the first time in the 1999 issue of its annual "White Paper on Trade" (*Tsusan Hakusho*), and the same report published in 2000 made this policy more vivid. The report pointed out that regional integration in East Asia was the way to go for Japan in light of the steady deepening of economic interdependence between East Asia and Japan. The Japanese government was worried that the proliferation of FTAs on a global scale might put Japanese businesses at a disadvantage due to the discriminatory nature of FTAs. If Japan were left out, Japanese businesses would be adversely affected when entering markets with FTAs. Japan's receptiveness of FTAs also reflected political interests of pro-liberalization forces, whose political power was growing but not sufficient to bring about liberalizing reforms. FTAs were expected to expedite and lock in domestic reforms.

The Japanese government has sought FTA deals with several countries in recent years.[2] The first accomplishment was JSEPA. The biggest stumbling block to Japan has been its protectionist agriculture sector. Singapore is an exception in this regard since it has no meaningful agricultural sector. Moreover, the Singaporean economy is highly advanced, and its income level is higher than that of Japan. Even with these favorable conditions for economic integration, the Japan–Singapore FTA deal did not sail through due to the opposition from the farm lobby against the inclusion of Singaporean products like ornamental fish and cut flowers. These items were dropped out in the final agreement. Japan's leadership capability as well as the future of East Asian regional integration will hinge on Japan's ability to overcome its agricultural protectionism.

It will be interesting to see whether the Japan–Singapore FTA has an explosive power comparable to that of the drastic policy shifts made by the United States and Mexico in the late 1980s by setting off the domino of FTAs in East Asia. For now, JSEPA has created some momentum for emulation throughout East Asia. China, casting a wary eye on the possibility of Japan's enhanced position in Southeast Asia, proposed a China–ASEAN free trade area. China's Premier Zhu Rongji suggested in November 2000 on the occasion of the APEC Summit Meeting in Brunei that ASEAN and China work toward a bilateral FTA. In November 2001, both sides officially agreed on a timetable, that is, a free-trade area within 10 years. Japan answered by unveiling a new initiative to deepen economic ties with ASEAN in January 2002, including pacts on investment, services, education, tourism, and science and technology, when Prime Minister Koizumi made a tour of five major ASEAN countries (Kajita 2002). In November 2002, the Japanese government, witnessing the possibility of a China–ASEAN FTA in the near future, grudgingly proposed an FTA with ASEAN. Even this proposal was overshadowed by a more ambitious call by China for a Northeast Asian FTA (NEAFTA) encompassing China, South Korea, and Japan. The Japanese government had to dismiss China's proposal in consideration of the strong domestic opposition against such trade liberalization.

The China–ASEAN FTA talks came in the midst of Japan's growing fear of the rapidly rising China — particularly its rapid economic growth and enhanced regional political clout. Japan was shocked by the joint announcement of China and ASEAN at the APT summit in November 2002 to go ahead with a bilateral FTA. There is a strong worry, both within and outside Japan, that such a grouping may turn into an anti-Western pressure group rather than a catalyst for trade liberalization.

Japan's best chance to effectively balance China (or a China–ASEAN FTA) may lie in a bilateral FTA with South Korea. A Japan–South Korea FTA would bring together the two biggest democratic, capitalist economies in East Asia. A better scenario is to form a zone of peace among developed capitalist countries in East Asia by adding Singapore. Currently, South Korea–Singapore and South Korea–Japan FTA deals are already on the table. What is at issue is the scope and degree of liberalization of the agricultural sector of Japan and South Korea. This grouping, if properly managed and open to outsiders, can gradually expand to include those who meet the membership requirements, similar to the expansion of Canada–U.S. FTA (CUSFTA) into NAFTA and a series of EU widening. The United States will have no reason to fear this version of East Asian regionalism.

A more serious problem resides with South Korea, where protectionist agriculture makes it almost impossible for its government to cut an FTA deal. In spite of its domestic rigidity, the South Korean government has been a strong advocate of larger regional groupings like EAFTA or NEAFTA rather than bilateral FTAs. South Korea's enthusiasm for EAFTA and NEAFTA makes sense economically. A region-wide FTA is more profitable than subregional or bilateral level FTAs in light of the increasing returns to scale. In terms of feasibility, however, bilateral pacts are likely to be far easier than plurilateral deals. In short, South Korea's strong attachment to

EAFTA and NEAFTA does make sense economically, but it has a serious feasibility problem. The South Korean government, with a high degree of domestic rigidity, seems to advocate EAFTA just because it is beyond reach in the near future.

At present, the South Korean government has three options concerning East Asian regionalism. The first is to continue to hold on to its grand design, that is, an East Asian community built upon East Asian Summit and EAFTA. This option is not mutually exclusive to the other two options and is therefore very likely to be taken in view of its domestic rigidity. The idea of an East Asian community is, however, a long shot. The opportunity costs of the lost bilateral FTAs in the process will be substantial as well.

The second option is to strike bilateral FTAs with Japan and Singapore. This option has a fair chance to succeed since all the concerned parties share some common interests. If Japan and South Korea can agree on an FTA, it will create a strong momentum for region-wide trade liberalization. Just like the expansion of CUSFTA into NAFTA, a Japan–South Korea FTA may easily develop into a trilateral FTA including Singapore. The result will be as good as a rich-men's club in East Asia. One reservation is that this grouping may enter into conflict with the less-developed "ASEAN-China bloc."

Another option left for South Korea is to be immersed in inter-Korean relations. The Roh administration is putting more weight on this option than the second one. An open, liberalized North Korea can be an ideal outlet for South Korean manufacturers troubled by rising production costs. Furthermore, economic integration with North Korea and possibly with China may offer an alternative to the FTAs with Japan and Singapore.

Considering North Korea's strong reluctance to open up its economy, this option has a serious feasibility problem. Worse still, Korea's domestic politics is deeply divided concerning its policy toward North Korea. Its domestic rigidity will add more difficulty for the South Korean government to pursue a clearly defined policy toward East Asian regionalism. As before, South Korea will stick to the idea of an East Asian community for a long while, avoiding the tough choice that may involve high domestic adjustment costs. President Roh Moo-hyun did not betray this prediction when he announced in his inauguration speech delivered in February 2003 that his administration's top policy agenda was to elevate South Korea into the leadership position in an emerging Northeast Asian community, which is also a long shot.

East Asian Regionalism and Pax Americana

The recent rise of regionalism (particularly the APT process) has laid the foundation for an East Asia more independent of U.S. influence or the U.S.-led global order. East Asian regionalism is, however, still at the adolescent stage. Its deep internal divide (e.g., between China and Japan and between the developing and advanced countries) poses formidable barriers to East Asia's becoming a third pillar in global politics along with the EU and the United States. Furthermore, the present assertiveness of Washington in regional and global affairs may provide little room for an independent East Asia.

The enthusiasm expressed by the APT members in the 2000 and 2001 summits to build an East Asian community has subsided since then. The momentum has been taken over by a race for FTAs, which is at this stage propelled more by parochial, strategic interests than by a genuine commitment to economic liberalization and free trade. Only a few FTA talks, particularly those between the advanced economies, are seriously committed to trade liberalization and economic integration. In this sense, the new interest in regionalism is not a result of the triumph of pro-liberalization ideas and forces (Ravenhill 2002, 176).

A case in point is the China–ASEAN FTA proposal. ASEAN has experienced more than enough difficulties in carrying out its AFTA scheme. Although AFTA is in force among its original members from January 1, 2003, regional free trade is still far away since the list of free trade is not comprehensive and its four new members (Vietnam, Laos, Cambodia, and Myanmar) are allowed to delay their tariff reductions. A bilateral FTA with China will pose more challenges and difficulties to the domestic politics of ASEAN members. Furthermore, it makes little sense to liberalize trade between underdeveloped countries with similar product compositions.

It is also well-known that China is not ready for another dose of liberalization on top of the requirements imposed by the WTO. The ASEAN–China FTA is a token proposal driven by political motivations. East Asian regionalism or a close cooperation with ASEAN can serve several political purposes for the Chinese government. That is to say, it may tame the fear of the "China threat" among East Asian countries, particularly ASEAN members; serve its foreign policy goal of "anti-hegemonism"; and undermine Japan's dominant position in Southeast Asia.

Japan is extremely worried that an East Asian community, envisioned by the leaders of the APT, may turn into a collectivity against Japan, led by China and other less developed countries in the group. Therefore, whenever the issue of regional development and income redistribution issues came up in East Asia, Japan resorted to broader frameworks that encompass the

United States, Australia, and other advanced countries in the Asia–Pacific region. Japan's intention was to diffuse the influence of less developed countries within a larger grouping, as well as to reduce its share of burden (Choi 1998, 301–4).

"The Initiative for Development in East Asia," suggested by Koizumi in the early 2002, was the latest example of Japan's clear preference for Asia–Pacific regionalism to East Asian regionalism. The Japanese Prime Minister wanted to include Australia and New Zealand in an East Asian community due to the fear of rapidly rising China. Malaysia, China, and Indonesia were, however, reluctant to accept outside members, stressing that the APT should be the center of regional cooperation. In the face of opposition, Japan changed its position and decided to focus on the APT, as well as to continue its support for the development of Southeast Asia (*The Economist*, Jan. 19, 2002, 34). It is expected that Japan will continue to strike a balance between its East Asian and trans-Pacific interests (Maswood 2001, 15).

Given all these considerations, there will be no imminent danger that U.S. hegemony and East Asian regionalism might enter into an open conflict with each other. The long-term relationship between East Asia and the United States will, however, depend on which version of East Asian regionalism wins the day, one centered around China or one led by Japan. If China emerges as the champion of East Asian regionalism, we may expect more confrontation between East Asia and the U.S. hegemony. If Japan's current FTA drive bears fruit and spreads across East Asia, a more amicable relationship is likely to develop between the two. The rapid rise of China and the long stagnation of Japan, however, seem to foretell more trouble for the United States.

A China-centered regional bloc is taking on a more concrete shape as the Chinese economy makes strides. The very foundation of Chinese regionalism is the presence of Overseas Chinese networks in Southeast Asia. Recently, the Chinese government has seen strategic as well as economic value in strengthening economic ties with the Overseas Chinese through investment, trade, and tourism. Beijing is fully supportive of the idea of closely connecting Hong Kong, Taiwan, and Overseas Chinese in Southeast Asia with the Chinese mainland (Katzenstein 2000, 12). An FTA between China and ASEAN will have the effect of setting already vibrant Overseas Chinese networks free from the arbitrary, interventionist hands of ASEAN governments. To the contrary, Japanese networks, built upon intimate relationships with ASEAN governments (frequently through bribes), will be adversely affected by economic liberalization in Southeast Asia (Hatch and Yamamura 1996, 131–32). Although Overseas Chinese networks in Southeast Asia may not develop into a China-dominated regional bloc in the near future, China is likely to exercise increasingly more influence in regional politics.

The most serious problem with Japan is that it has no clear vision for East Asia and in particular for East Asian regionalism. Japan is also disadvantaged, as compared with China, in approaching East Asia since its options are tightly constrained by the need to maintain an amicable relationship with the United States. Japan is a commercial giant without much military power or soft power. Consequently, Japan has difficulty keeping ASEAN under its umbrella. Its most promising partner to counter a rising China, South Korea, is still a suspicious neighbor. Historical animosity runs deep in China and the two Koreas. Singapore is a political dwarf. Taiwan is probably the only country to accept Japanese leadership.

Another factor that may determine the nature of future relationship between East Asian regionalism and U.S. hegemony is U.S. policy itself. The recent rise of regionalism in East Asia offers both challenges and opportunities to the United States. On the one hand, an integrating East Asia may pose increasing challenges to U.S. economic ideas (free trade, market economy, and liberalization), concept of human rights, efforts to execute anti-terrorist wars, and, the most serious of all, its hegemonic position itself. On the other hand, the recent interests in liberalization and free trade, as manifested in the proliferation of FTAs, may transform East Asia into a more liberal, open, and peaceful area. If the United States cannot take advantage of this opportunity while taking up challenges wisely at the same time, East Asian regionalism is more likely to run a collision course vis-à-vis U.S.-led regional and global order.

The best alternative for the United States is to strengthen its economic diplomacy leveled at fostering a zone of peace in East Asia, an EU-like community of advanced, democratic, capitalist countries. This job has to start from FTAs with advanced economies like Japan, South Korea, and Singapore. The United States has already made a significant move in relation to Singapore. While in Brunei for the 12th APEC Ministerial Meeting in November 2000, President Clinton met with Prime Minister Goh Chok Tong of Singapore and launched negotiations for a U.S.–Singapore Free Trade Agreement (USSFTA). The deal finally came through in May 2003.

The United States is well aware of the significance of the USSFTA. In addition to the economic benefits arising from trade liberalization, Washington also expects some positive externalities from the deal, for example, to send a clear signal that the United States will keep its presence in the region and that it is really serious about trade liberalization in East Asia and the Pacific (U.S.–Singapore FTA Business Coalition 2003).

The U.S. government, however, remains silent about FTAs with its two most important alliance partners in East Asia: Japan and South Korea. The United States has consistently argued that bilateral FTAs with them are not effective in liberalizing these economies due to the existence of structural barriers (USTR 1997; USITC 1989).

U.S. reluctance will turn positive if Japan and South Korea agree to form a free trade area. In addition to the strategic value, an FTA between Japan and South Korea will create a huge potential market for U.S. trade and investment. The United States cannot afford to forgo this market in light of the discriminatory nature of FTAs. The U.S. hegemony will also have the best chance to continue in East Asia if the advanced, capitalist economies in the region (e.g., Japan, Singapore, and South Korea) are linked together through FTAs, preferably with the United States as well.

Conclusion

Regionalism has finally come to life in East Asia. Proposals for regional cooperation in East Asia have proliferated at regional, subregional, and bilateral levels, particularly after the financial crisis of 1997. This paper has examined the causes, future prospects, and global ramifications of the recent development of East Asian regionalism.

This paper argues that the economic crisis of 1997 was the catalyst for the recent development of East Asian regionalism by creating a strong demand for regional integration. The economic crisis not only created functional demands to manage monetary matters jointly but also drove East Asian countries to pool their political power against international financial institutions like the IMF and the United States. The crisis also fostered a sense of common identity, which in turn facilitated the process of institutionalization in East Asia. The active participation by the regional leaders like Japan and China into regional cooperation initiatives, along with the benign neglect of the United States, added momentum to East Asian regionalism.

The future prospect of East Asian regionalism is not so rosy since the underlying forces are largely propelled by the economic crisis. The enthusiasm for an East Asian community subsided recently when the region largely overcame the crisis. I conclude that there will be no imminent danger of East Asian regionalism colliding with U.S. hegemony.

We cannot evaluate the prospect of East Asian regionalism without taking into account U.S. interests. The United States has played the role of a spoiler to many East Asian initiatives from EAEG to AMF. Strangely, the United States has remained silent regarding the new regionalism in East

Asia that transpired after the economic crisis of 1997. Given the near disappearance of the distance between China and ASEAN in recent years, East Asian regionalism led by ASEAN and China has a good chance to materialize in the future. They will try to use it to stand up against the United States and to a degree to constrain Japan's exercise of economic power. In that case, the United States will intervene and try to abort any Asian-only regional scheme. Japan will have no choice but to side with the United States.

Notes

1. The EAVG was created in 1998 by the leaders of the ATP in response to the suggestion of South Korean President Kim Dae-jung. Its task was to study ultimate objectives and the ways to effectively achieve them. The vision group was made up of two academics from thirteen member countries. After a three-year study, they submitted an ambitious plan for a regional bloc in November 2001. The EASG, composed of senior officials from the member states, was set up in 2001 to assess the recommendations of the EAVG.
2. The list includes Canada, Chile, South Korea, Mexico, Singapore, and Thailand.

References

Bergsten, Fred C. 2000. "Towards a Tripartite World." *The Economist*, July 15.
Checkel, Jeffrey T. 1999. "Norms, Institutions, and National Identity in Contemporary Europe." *International Studies Quarterly*, 43(1): 83–114.
Choi, Young Jong. 1998. "Institutionalizing Asia and the Pacific: Interdependence, States, and Institutional Preferences – Japan's Policy in Comparative Perspective," PhD dissertation, University of Washington, Seattle, WA.
Choi, Young Jong, and James A. Caporaso. 2002. "Comparative Regional Integration." In *Handbook of International Relations*, ed. W. Carlsnaes, T. Risse, and B. Simmons, pp. 480–499. Thousand Oaks, CA: Sage Publications.
Deutsch, Karl W. et al. 1957. *Political Community and the North Atlantic Area: International Organization in the Light of Historical Experience*. Princeton, NJ: Princeton University Press.
Evans, Paul. 2002. "East Asian Regionalism: Supplement or Alternative to an American-Centered Pacific Order?" In *Proceeding for Annual International Conference (Building an East Asian Community: Visions and Strategies)*, pp. 130–51. Seoul: Asiatic Research Center.
Gilpin, Robert. 2000. *The Challenge of Global Capitalism: The World Economy in the 21st Century*. Princeton, NJ: Princeton University Press.
Gowa, Joanne. 1989. "Bipolarity, Multipolarity and Free Trade." *American Political Science Review*, 83(4): 1245–56.
Grieco, Joseph M. 1995. "The Maastricht Treaty, Economic and Monetary Union, and the Neo-realist Research Programme." *Review of International Studies*, 21(1): 21–40.
Grieco, Joseph M. 1997. "Systemic sources of variation in regional institutionalization in Western Europe, East Asia, and the Americas." In *The Political Economy of Regionalism*, ed. E. D. Mansfield and H. V. Milner, pp. 164–87. New York: Columbia University Press.
Haas Ernst B., and Philippe C. Schmitter. 1964. "Economics and Differential Patterns of Political Integration: Projections about Unity in Latin America." *International Organization* 18(3): 705–37.
Hatch, Walter, and Kozo Yamamura. 1996. *Asia in Japan's Embrace*. London: Cambridge University Press.
Higgott, Richard. 1998a. "The Asian Economic Crisis: A Study in the Politics of Resentment." *New Political Economy* 3(3): 333–56.

Higgott, Richard. 1998b. "The Political Economy of Regionalism: The Asia-Pacific and Europe Compared." In *Regionalism and Global Economic Integration: Europe, Asia and Americas,* ed. C. D. William and G. R. D. Underhill, pp. 42–67. London: Routledge.

Kajita, Takehiko. "Japan's New ASEAN Policy Comes as China Rises." *The Japan Times,* January 15, 2002.

Katzenstein, Peter J. 1997. "Introduction: Asian Regionalism in Comparative Perspective." In *Network Power: Japan and Asia,* ed. Peter J. Katzenstein and Takashi Shiraishi, pp. 1–46. Ithaca, NY: Cornell University Press.

Katzenstein, Peter J. 2000. "Varieties of East Asian Regionalisms." In *Asian Regionalism,* ed. P. J. Katzenstein et al. pp. 1–34. Ithaca: Cornell University East Asia Program.

Kupchan, Charles A. 1998. "After Pax Americana: Benign Power, Regional Integration, and the Sources of a Stable Multipolarity." *International Security, 23*: 2 (Fall): 42–79.

Mansfield, Edward D., and Helen V. Milner. 1999. "The New Wave of Regionalism." *International Organization,* 53(3): 589–628.

Maswood, Javed S. 2001. "Japanese Foreign Policy and Regionalism." In *Japan and East Asian Regionalism,* ed. Javed S. Maswood, pp. 6–25. London/New York: Routledge.

Mattli, Walter. 1999. *The Logic of Regional Integration: Europe and Beyond.* London: Cambridge University Press.

Moravcsik, Andrew. 1998. *The Choice for Europe.* Ithaca, NY: Cornell University Press.

Ravenhill, John. 2002. "A Three Bloc World? The New East Asian Regionalism." *International Relations of the Asia–Pacific,* 2: 167–195.

Stone Sweet, Alec, and Wayne Sandholtz. 1998. "Integration, Supranational Governance, and the Institutionalization of the European Polity." In *European Integration and Supranational Governance,* ed. W. Sandholtz and A. Stone Sweet, pp. 1–26. Oxford: Oxford University Press.

Stubbs, Richard. 2002. "ASEAN Plus Three: Emerging East Asian Regionalism?" *Asian Survey,* XLII, no. 3 (May/June): 440–455.

U.S.–Singapore FTA Business Coalition. 2003. "Reasons to Support the US–Singapore Free Trade Agreement." http://www.us-asean.org/ussfta/index.asp (January 12, 2003).

U.S. International Trade Commission. 1989. *Pros and Cons of Entering Free Trade Agreements with Taiwan, the Republic of Korea, or the Pacific Rim in General.* Washington, DC.

USTR. 1997. *Recommendations on Future Trade Area Negotiations.* Washington, DC: Office of the U.S. Trade Representative.

Waltz, Kenneth N. 1995. "The Emerging Structure of International Politics." In *The Peril of Anarchy: Contemporary Realism and International Security,* ed. M. E. Brown et al., pp. 42–77. Cambridge, MA: The MIT Press.

CHAPTER 4

Pax Americana in Latin America: The Hegemony behind Free Trade

PAMELA K. STARR

Introduction

For more than a century, Latin America struggled to escape U.S. pressures to institutionalize its commercial relationship with its southern neighbors. The first inter-American conference, held in Washington in 1989–1990, was called by the U.S. government for the explicit purpose of promoting U.S. trade with Latin America. Latin Americans complained that the United States seemed to want "to make Latin America a market, and sovereign states tributaries" and opposed the formation of a "New World chancellery without the authorization of the rest of the states [of Latin America]." Owing to Latin American opposition, the outcome of the conference was limited to the establishment of an inter-American bureaucracy to promote trade through the dissemination of information about regional trade opportunities, far less than the United States had envisioned.[1]

Throughout most of the twentieth century, the U.S. pursuit of deeper and freer trading relations with Latin America was a common theme in U.S.–Latin American relations: from dollar diplomacy's emphasis on opening the Latin market to U.S. trade and investment and linking Latin currencies to the U.S. dollar, to pockets of World War II era support for encouraging dollarization in Latin America to reinforce regional trade and hence U.S. influence over Latin America,[2] to Eisenhower and Kennedy administration use of economic assistance through the World Bank and the Alliance for Progress to encourage freer markets and more open trade, to George H.W. Bush's 1990 proposal for an Enterprise of the Americas Initiative, the promotion of freer trade has been a constant in U.S. policy toward Latin America. Yet equally consistent were Latin American efforts to keep U.S. economic might at arm's length. It is not that Latin America did not want to trade with the United States or was opposed to economic regionalism more generally. To the contrary, the U.S. market has always presented an important opportunity for the Latin economies. What Latin America opposed was the institutionalization of this relationship because, given the power disparities involved, it seemed inevitable that such a relationship would favor U.S. interests. This was particularly true in the post–World War II era when Latin America actively pursued an economic development model based on protection of their domestic markets from international competition (Import Substitution Industrialization). Further, during the 1960s Latin American countries attempted to build a regional trading arrangement, but one that explicitly excluded the United States.[3] Latin American states preferred to keep the terms of their economic relationship with the United States vague, both to increase their economic policy freedom and to prevent the deepening of their economic dependence on the "Colossus of the North."

Given this historic background, Latin American efforts during the 1990s to deepen and institutionalize its trading relationship with the United States are puzzling. It seems that Latin America has done a complete about-face. After a hundred years of struggling to keep U.S. economic hegemony at bay, the region suddenly reversed course. Instead of the United States pushing a reticent Latin America to negotiate free regional trade, Latin American countries did lead the charge for freer trade in the 1990s. Why has Latin America suddenly decided to embrace its economic dependence on the United States and to formalize this relationship through the creation of a Free Trade Area of the Americas?

The answer lies in the forces that have long driven Latin American foreign policy. First and most obvious, the disparity of political and economic power within the hemisphere imposes sharp constraints on Latin America's freedom of action. Second is the ideology of regional policy makers and the nature and extent of U.S. pressure that combine to shape Latin America's response to the reality of regional hegemony (Hey 1997). The question thus becomes: How did these three variables change prior to the 1990s and how does this explain Latin America's policy shift. The answer is disturbingly simple and bears little resemblance to the security-driven model of regionalization described in the Choi chapter in this volume. The manner in which the United States implemented its international and regional hegemony during the 40 years following World War II gradually modified conditions in the international economy and in Latin America. This combined with the failure of the import substitution model of development in the early 1980s to shift Latin American attitudes toward a free trade agreement with the United States. These two factors led to a gradual change in the global and regional environment within which Latin America operated, a significant alteration in the economic ideology of Latin American policy makers and a moderation in popular attitudes toward the United States, and a different means of applying U.S. pressure in the region. This combination of factors motivated Latin America's change of heart about institutionalizing the economic core of Pax Americana in the Western Hemisphere.

Within this broad argument about Latin America, there is significant intra-regional variance that reflects differing degrees of dependence on the U.S. economy and hence different responses to U.S. hegemony. Where economic dependence is deepest — in the Caribbean, Central America, and Mexico — the acceptance of a formalization of U.S. economic hegemony has been greatest. Where economic dependence is weakest — in the Southern Cone and particularly Brazil — doubts about formalization are evident, with the obvious exception of Chile. The Andean countries occupy an intermediate position, while Cuba has been excluded from the process owing to its history of hostility with the United States.

This chapter will elaborate on the preceding argument as follows: The first section illuminates how the application of U.S. hegemony in the post–World War II period led to the institutionalization of market-based rules of international economic interaction. By separating these rules from direct association with U.S. economic power, post–World War II economic institutions such as the General Agreement on Tariffs and Trade (GATT) legitimated market-based rules of economic interaction and encouraged states to adopt gradually freer trade and freer global interactions. Without the resulting political will to open markets, globalization of the world economy would have been impossible. And without economic globalization, there would have been little incentive for Latin America to open its economies to world markets.

The second section explains the shift in ideas and ideology in Latin America toward market economics. Essential to the change in economic ideas was the failure of the import substitution (statist and protectionist) model of development and the examples of market-based success stories such as South Korea, Chile, Spain, and even the United Kingdom. But this shift in ideas toward acceptance of the market would have been impossible without two additional factors: the globalization of U.S. economic thinking driven by the education of rising Latin American technocrats in U.S. universities and the so-called nonbiased advise offered by U.S. economics professors to regional economies in crisis. The third section of the paper discusses the emergence in Latin America of a less adversarial view of the United States. The evident softening of popular attitudes toward the United States was driven by an explosion of new sources of information about the United States offered by the Internet, television, movies, and so on. At the elite level, this attitudinal shift is also a direct consequence of democratization in the region and the revised view of external intervention in the domestic affairs of Latin American states this produced. In conjunction with the nature of U.S. policy in the region, these developments help to explain a reduced suspicion of the United States and its objectives in Latin America.

The fourth section explains how U.S. policy toward Latin America at the end of the Cold War further motivated interest in a more formalized economic relationship with the United States and a reduced fear of closer ties to the United States. First, and as is well-known, the United States directly pressured Latin America to adopt a market-oriented economic model more reliant on interaction with the international community. Second, owing to a clear reduction in extra-hemispheric economic influences in the region, the United States became the absolutely undisputed economic (and political) hegemon in the Western Hemisphere, leaving Latin America few options other than dealing with the United States. Equally important, however, were two changes in U.S. policy toward Latin America. In the wake of the Cold War, the U.S. policy in the region was ambiguous at best, raising concern about the U.S. commitment to freer regional trade and a possible U.S. abandonment of Latin America. (Smith 2000; Lowenthal 2000) At the same time, a clear shift emerged in U.S. policy preferences away from its historical preference for unilateral intervention (often to the detriment of regional democracy) and toward negotiation and multilateral action designed to preserve democracy and human rights. This not only lessened Latin America's fear of the behemoth to the north; it also created a perception of a growing body of shared interests between Latin American democracies and the United States and the potential for regional cooperation to achieve them.

The fifth section of the chapter breaks Latin America down into subregions to understand better how the broader argument explains differing attitudes about the formalization of economic relations with the United

States — from enthusiastic support in the Caribbean Basin and Mexico, to less enthusiastic support in the Andean Region, and to hesitant participation in Brazil.

By way of conclusion, the final section addresses the probability that a Free Trade Area of the Americas (FTAA) will come into being. It argues that the new calculus in Latin American foreign policy that has placed free trade on the regional policy agenda could change in the near future. But any such change would most likely be the result of recent shifts in U.S. policy toward the region — toward increased unilateralism, neglect, and hard-handedness — rather than changes in the international structural or domestic variables also driving Latin America's newfound interest in free trade. When combined with the nature of U.S. trade politics, this suggests that the prospects for an FTAA are much less bright than the rhetoric of the U.S. government would suggest, and less bright than much of Latin America would hope.

U.S. Power and Economic Globalization

The globalization of the world economy, whether in the late nineteenth or in the late twentieth century, is the consequence of technological advances and political will. During the last four decades of the twentieth century, advances in communications, transport, and business operations made the exchange of goods and services across large distances less costly and hence more common. Yet the ability of firms to trade and produce across national borders would be impossible without the decision of sovereign states to authorize the movement of goods and services into and out of their territory. Without the political determination to open national economies to international competition, economic globalization would be severely truncated, if not rendered impossible. The question is then why would national governments be willing to make such a decision?

Analysts of the last two globalization episodes have demonstrated that many variables — domestic and international, political, economic, and ideological — are involved in such decisions. In the post–World War II era, however, the hegemonic power of the United States and the manner in which it was exercised was the dominant factor.

As World War II moved toward its climax, the governments of the United States and the United Kingdom met to consider the character of the postwar economic order. Both countries brought to the table three key lessons drawn from the events of the previous 15 years. First, free trade was essential to global prosperity and peace. It was the collapse of free trade in the early 1930s, the delegates believed, that led to the Great Depression. Economic crisis then reinforced the interstate tensions that culminated in world war. Second, any free trade regime must be as inclusive as possible. The decision of Germany and Japan to remain outside of the free trade system after 1880 ensured that these two countries would have little interest in helping to maintain free trade and eliminated the possibility that economic interdependence could have mitigated their bellicose intents.[4] Third, the management of free trade and its monetary support system must be institutionalized. The economic decline of England made it increasingly difficult for this nation to pay the costs of sustaining the free trade order in the early twentieth century, rendering free trade vulnerable to economic downturns and political machinations. It was necessary, therefore, to design a system that was not dependent on the hegemonic power of a single nation.

Although the hegemonic power of the United States will ultimately be the means by which a liberal international economic order will be established in the aftermath of World War II, the manner in which the United States employed this power explains how the core objectives of the system's designers — inclusive and institutionalized free trade — were gradually met, and economic globalization thereby advanced. To encourage free trade in the world economy, the United States did not follow the English model of unilaterally opening its economy to the world's exports. Instead, it used its political and economic power to leverage trade openings throughout the West.

Although the Soviet Bloc countries were invited to join the Bretton Woods economic order at the end of World War II, their decision against joining meant that free trade would develop within an anticommunist alliance of nations. In this context, the security of the West became entwined with freer trade. The United States was able to encourage its allies to liberalize their economies as a friendly repayment for the security from Soviet aggression the U.S. provided. To the extent that freer trade strengthened allied economies, this met U.S. security needs and thereby reinforced the U.S. preference for free trade (Lake 1991).

Equally important was (and is) the structural foundation of U.S. economic hegemony, the size of the U.S. domestic economy, and its lack of dependence on international trade. The dominant size of the U.S. economy (3 times the size of its nearest rival during the 1950s; 2.5 times in 2001) enabled the United States to leverage concessions from its trading partners in exchange for expanded access to the U.S. market. In this manner, the United States was able to encourage countries to find the political will to open their national economies to international trade (Lake 1991).

Most important, however, was the U.S. decision to formalize the rules of international trade in multilateral institutions — GATT and the International Monetary Fund (IMF). By distancing itself from management of the liberal international economic order and by empowering allied countries to share in this responsibility, these institutions made liberalization politically more feasible. Countries would be liberalizing not under direct pressure from the United States, it now seemed, but as a consequence of their commitment to cooperate in the construction of global prosperity and peace.

Finally, the success of free trade in creating economic prosperity in the North generated ideological and political support for the process and a powerful example for the countries of the South. The correlation between the rapid expansion of trade and economic prosperity during the 1960s and again during the late 1980s and 1990s created the impression that free trade was, on balance, a good thing. Further, as trade expanded, it generated domestic interests whose economic well-being were directly tied to trade. This was especially true given the close relationship between trade and foreign direct investment in the late twentieth century globalization episode. These trade and investment interests translated into political pressures in support of a continued process of international economic opening (Milner 1987; Gourevitch 1989).

The consequence was a marked reduction in protectionist measures limiting international trade in goods and services and the flow of investment capital (direct and portfolio) across national borders. This process of economic globalization created new development opportunities for the South. For the first time since the 1920s, active participation in the global economy could become a viable foundation for economic development, a lesson reinforced by the success of the East Asian tigers by the late 1970s. The closure of the global economy in the 1930s had forced Latin America to adopt a development model based on self-reliance, and the perpetuation of high international barriers to trade and investment for 30 years reinforced this logic. In a world of mercantilism, a development strategy based on trade would have made little sense. By the late 1960s, and with renewed force by the mid-1980s, however, the rebirth of a globalizing international economy presented Latin America with a series of international opportunities for development not seen for nearly half a century. When the import substitution model entered into crisis, therefore, economic globalization provided a strong incentive to move toward a more liberal, export-based development model.

Changing Economic Ideas

"The ideas of economists and political philosophers, both when they are right and when they are wrong, are more powerful than is commonly understood."[5]

"The triumph of the West, of the Western idea, is evident."[6]

By the early 1990s, a shift in thinking about development and about the United States was evident in Latin America. A region that had favored a statist model of development for over a half century initiated a dramatic move toward a market-based development strategy. Further, a region that had long mistrusted the United States and feared political, economic, and cultural intervention from the north now exhibited a much more positive image of the United States and even embraced broad swaths of its political, economic, and popular culture. These changes were driven by seven factors, four of which clearly derived from U.S. power.

There can be no doubt that the most important force reshaping economic ideas in Latin America during the 1980s was the spectacular failure of the import substitution development model.[7] This failure was almost exclusively a Latin American affair, with international forces playing a supporting role at best. Even as import substitution pushed the economies of Taiwan and Korea toward rapid development, poor implementation of the same development model produced less auspicious results in the West. Protectionism and state direction of the Latin American economies did lead to growth and development in much of the region into the 1950s, but by the 1960s the shortcomings of the model became increasingly evident. A strong bias against export production, inefficient industries, and recurrent macroeconomic instability restricted Latin America's ability to import essential production inputs, undermined demand, and hindered investment. Latin America was able to evade most of the economic implications of these implementation failures and thereby extend the life of this development model through the 1970s by borrowing heavily on international capital markets. When the markets closed to Latin America in 1982–1983, the latent, unresolved problems of import substitution — most particularly, its inability to generate sufficient investment capital — exploded into public view.[8] The recognition that Latin America's statist model of development was the principle cause of economic crisis came at different points in time in different Latin American countries owing to distinct domestic environments. By the end of the decade, however, accepted wisdom in the region was that import substitution had failed.[9]

Simply admitting that Latin America needed a new strategy to guide its economic development, however, did not automatically lead to the adoption of a market-based model of development. At least theoretically, there were other options. Four factors ensured that Latin America would turn to the market. First, clear examples of market-based success stories — the economic turnaround in the United Kingdom beginning in the late 1970s under the Thatcher government, the spectacular development successes of South Korea and Taiwan beginning in the 1960s, and most importantly, the rapid return to growth following the debt crisis in Latin America's only market-based economy, Chile — suggested that reliance on the market promoted growth and development rather than obstructed it (as structuralist economists had argued for decades). Further, the success of economic liberalization in Spain under a social–democratic government during the 1980s demonstrated that the market model could complement both democratic development and a center–left political agenda, very much unlike Latin America's recent history in which market economics was correlated exclusively with repressive authoritarian governments. Second, the victory of the West in the Cold War further discredited statist economic strategies. There could be little doubt that the failings of the communist economic model — a model even more statist and protectionist than import substitution in Latin America — played a determining role in the Soviet loss and the ensuing collapse of communism throughout Europe. Global events thereby suggested a marked-based approach to development might make sense in Latin America.

This perception was reinforced by the power of U.S. economic ideas. Ideas are among the most subtle and yet most efficient means by which a state can exert influence internationally. If a state can export its way of thinking, this will increase the likelihood that other states will operate in a manner that does not threaten, and that even advances, the interests of the first state. Further, this benefit can be obtained without paying the costs of exerting coercive force. The United States exported its economic ideas to Latin America in two ways. First, via educational exchanges — American professors teaching at Latin American universities and Latin American students studying at U.S. universities. The Fulbright program was designed to achieve precisely this objective. Latin American students and universities gradually turned away from their traditional academic ties to Europe and toward the United States beginning in the late 1960s and 1970s. This initial current turned into a torrent by the 1990s, especially in the field of economics. When Latin America initiated economic reform, it was led by technocrats educated at universities such as Chicago, MIT, Yale,

Stanford, and Harvard, where the curriculum was heavily biased toward liberal market economics.[10]

The second means by which the United States has exported its economic thinking to Latin America is the parade of U.S. economists who have visited Latin America during the past 15 years to advise regional governments on the implementation of economic reform.[11] As academic economists, their ideas are presented as independent of the U.S. government and free of any political bias. Yet the mere fact that these economists were among the most decorated in North American academia meant that they were mainstream economists. In a country with the most competitive market in the world — competition being an essential prerequisite to the efficient operation of a market economy — it is not surprising that nonbiased, mainstream economic analysis should demonstrate the efficiency of the market.

Examples of market successes and statist failures at the end of the 1980s combined with the export of U.S. economic ideas, and the opportunities offered by a globalizing international economy, to convince Latin American leaders that the market was the best development option available. Now came the task of implementation. Latin American countries did not implement economic reform at the same moment or with the same fortitude. These variations were closely tied to the nature of the national political debate about economic policy, the degree of insulation of economic policy makers, and the ability of political leaders to form governing coalitions around the new economic model.[12] Initially, most Latin American countries blamed volatility in the international financial system and/or previous authoritarian regimes for the onset of economic crisis. As long as import substitution was not seen as the culprit, liberal economic ideas made little headway in the hemisphere. The persistence of crisis for the better part of a decade, however, gradually redirected blame toward the statist model of development. This new atmosphere was much more receptive to neoliberal ideas. Once convinced of the wisdom of neoliberalism, however, political leaders needed to find the means to implement the requisite reforms. This process was eased by the insulation of economic policy makers, the so-called technocrats, from political pressures. Where this existed, such as Argentina, Mexico, and Peru, reform proceeded rapidly. Where policy makers were exposed to political pressures, as in Costa Rica and Uruguay, reform proceeded much more slowly and was much less extensive. Finally, reforms would have been impossible if political leaders had not been able to construct a new policy coalition to support them. The process of constructing such a coalition also influenced the timing of the initiation of reform in the region.

Regardless of the precise moment and degree of reform, virtually every Latin American country had adopted market-based economic policies by the mid-1990s. This implied a dramatic reduction in the role of the state in the economy and an equally dramatic reduction in protectionism.[13] The consequence was a shift in the dynamic poll of development from production for the domestic economy to production for export. For such a model to be effective, however, Latin America required two things: access to export markets and foreign sources of investment capital. The most desirable export market in the hemisphere, indeed in the world, and the most important source of investment capital (whether foreign direct investment or portfolio investment) was and is found in the United States. Latin America's decision to adopt a market-based, export-oriented model of development thereby inevitably implied a large increase in its economic dependence on the United States.

Changing Ideas about the United States

The large potential economic benefits from a deepened dependency on the United States were thus determined by Latin America's decision to adopt a market-based model of development. But what of the costs of increased dependency? If domestic public opinion were to react poorly or if the United States were poised to exploit Latin America's increased dependence to coerce the region into acting against its interests, the political costs of economic reform could have outweighed the benefits (a particularly relevant consideration since variation in the domestic political calculus among Latin countries is one of the factors explaining the implementation of economic reform at different times in different countries). Three factors combined to produce the perception among Latin American leaders that the costs of increased dependence on the United States would be far less than the potential benefits — a shift in popular attitudes about the United States, democratization in Latin America at the close of the Cold War, and the nature of post–Cold War U.S. policy toward Latin America. The first two will be discussed in this section, while U.S. policy is the subject of the following section.

Historically, public attitudes toward the United States were not extremely positive in Latin America. This can be explained in part by the inevitable suspicion the weak have about the actions of the strong. This inclination toward mistrust born of regional power disparities was reinforced by two additional factors. First, the U.S. penchant for intervention in the internal affairs of Latin American states — to exclude extra-hemispheric powers from the region, to promote market economies, to promote democracy (or not), to prevent excessive migration, and to police the drug trade.

For Latin Americans, it seemed that the United States would find any excuse to justify its preference for interventionism in "its backyard." Latin American popular suspicions about the United States were further reinforced by a nearly monolithic intellectual elite that monopolized the dissemination of information about the United States. In Latin American universities, in the media, and in the arts, the anti-American attitudes of intellectuals monopolized debate well into the 1980s. Latin American citizens also had few sources of information about the United States independent of their local intellectual class.

This situation has changed markedly, however, as a result of technological advances associated with globalization and increased competition in local media and entertainment outlets. The advent of satellite and cable television provided easy access to U.S. news and entertainment shows offering a very different view of the "colossus of the north" (the importance of CNN en Español is hard to overestimate). The Internet provided access to U.S. newspapers, archives, and shopping. Most importantly, it made direct communication with average Americans through e-mail and chat groups easier than ever before. New privately owned theater chains dramatically increased the number of first-run American movies available to Latin audiences. And reduced transportation costs made travel to the United States (both legal and illegal) a much more common phenomenon, particularly from South America. The democratization of access to information about the United States enabled Latin Americans to access less biased sources of information and thereby helped to temper views about this country.

Poll numbers demonstrate the impact of this attitudinal shift in most of Latin America. The 1995 Latin American Barometer survey showed that in seven of the eight countries included in this initial poll, at least 47 percent of the public held a positive opinion about the United States.[14] More importantly, the same survey registered significant popular support for closer economic relations with the United States in the four largest economies included in the survey: Mexico, Argentina, Brazil, and Venezuela.[15] By 2002, the positive image of the United States had grown even further, to 65 percent of South Americans, 85 percent of Central Americans, and 63 percent of Mexicans. Of the 17 countries in the 2002 survey, only Argentina registered a net negative view of the United States (reflecting the country's sense of abandonment by the U.S. in its time of economic need).

One should not read into these statistics a disappearance of negative images and suspicions about the United States in Latin America. Quite to the contrary, the flip side of these numbers reflects a very large number of Latin Americans who still hold a negative view of the United States, a fact reinforced by the ballooning of anti-American sentiment in the region during early 2003 fueled by Latin American opposition to the U.S. invasion of Iraq. Further, research in Mexico indicates that positive views of the United States are concentrated in the middle and upper classes, those sectors that enjoy access to the new sources of information about the United States. Poor Latin Americans, the majority of the regional population, hold a much more negative view of the United States than their more affluent countrymen (Moreno 2002). Nevertheless, the numbers do demonstrate that a large and growing percentage of the Latin American populace saw the United States in a relatively positive light during the 1990s. As a consequence, the domestic political costs of closer economic ties with the United States were more manageable at the end of the twentieth century than at any other point in recent memory.

Democratization in Latin America during the waning years of the Cold War reinforced the perception among regional leaders that the costs of increased economic dependence on the United States would be manageable. The emergence of democracy in Latin America and its historic timing had two tangible consequences for Latin America's thinking about the interventionist impulse of the United States: that it would be both less likely and more tolerable when it occurred. It would be less likely because of a shift in the nature of the U.S.–Latin American relationship at the end of the Cold War. Lacking a global adversary, the United States would be less likely to see Latin America as a potential conduit for threats to U.S. national security (although certainly not immune to this, as the war on drugs demonstrates). The emergence of market democracies in Latin America, meanwhile, fulfilled a long-time goal of U.S. hemispheric policy. This not only denied the United States a justification for intervention, but it also established a foundation for cooperation based on shared interests. Intra-hemispheric relations could now focus on building economic cooperation and protecting democracy, issue areas where military intervention was a less effective foreign policy tool (Smith 2000, 249; Hakim and Shifter 1995).

The interventionist impulse of the United States would also be more tolerable in democratic Latin America. The new democratic regimes of Latin America feared they might need to protect democracy from surviving authoritarian interests, most particularly the armed forces. They saw international intervention to preserve democracy, most often with the cooperation of the United States under the auspices of the Organization of American States, as an essential deterrent to opponents and opportunists in Latin America's less than fully democratic political cultures (Domínguez 1998). In the eyes of many Latin American governments, intervention in the internal affairs of regional states ceased to be a tool solely of unilateral U.S. meddling in Latin America and became a useful multilateral mechanism to support regional democracies.

U.S. Policy toward Latin America

Latin America's decision to adopt a market-based economic model and thereby increase its economic dependence on the United States thus reflected the indirect consequences of U.S. power (globalization, the end of the Cold War, and the spread of U.S. ideas) combined with domestic developments (economic crisis, domestic politics, and democratization). But it also reflected the direct impact of U.S. policy in the region.

Developments during the 1980s deepened U.S. hegemony in Latin America. The onset of the debt crisis dramatically undermined the economic and political clout of Latin America. During the 1970s, flush with capital from high prices for their raw material exports and huge inflows of capital from the international financial system, Latin American countries possessed sufficient economic freedom to question openly and even challenge U.S. actions affecting the region. Latin American countries supported developing country efforts to build a "New International Economic Order," purchased military equipment denied them by the United States from France and the Soviet Union, and actively opposed U.S. policies in Central America. Following the onset of the debt crisis, however, Latin American leaders found their power resources slashed and their capacity to stand up to the United States dramatically diminished.

The end of the Cold War further revised the distribution of regional power in favor of the United States by virtually eliminating the economic presence of extra-hemispheric powers in Latin America. The Soviet Union first retrenched and then dissolved, Europe turned its attention eastward, and Japan hesitated to fill the void for fear of ruffling U.S. feathers by encroaching on its traditional sphere of influence.[16] The Latin American strategy (or dream in many cases) of balancing the regional economic might of the United States by expanding economic ties with Europe and Japan was thereby undercut in the immediate aftermath of the Cold War. The fruitless efforts of Mexican President Carlos Salinas to open trade negotiations with the European Union and Japan in early 1989 has become a legendary example of this reality. By the end of the 1980s, a weakened Latin America thus faced the hegemonic power of the United States alone.

In these circumstances direct U.S. pressure for market reforms in Latin America, most tangibly expressed through the Brady Plan (an offer of debt relief in exchange for market reforms), was difficult to resist. When added to the international economic opportunities, domestic economic and ideological incentives, and domestic political space for adopting reform, direct U.S. pressure helped turn the economic policy tide in Latin America.

During the 1990s, two changes in U.S. policy toward Latin America also helped to reinforce the initial perception in Latin America (discussed above) that the United States would not exploit the increased capacity for economic coercion inherent in regional economic liberalization. First, U.S. foreign policy during the 1990s, both internationally and regionally, exhibited an increased reliance on multilateral means to resolve problems. This does not mean that the United States eschewed unilateral solutions in Latin America (the invasions of Panama in 1989 and of Haiti in 1994 demonstrate this fact). Rather, U.S. policy exhibited a relative move away from near exclusive reliance on unilateral action toward increased use of multilateral options, most notably in its willingness to work through the Organization of American States to promote regional democratic governance (Domínguez 1998; Millett 1994). For Latin America, this shift was very important. In a region where Latin opinions about solutions to regional problems were regularly overlooked or ignored by the United States, a move toward multilateralism implied that the United States would listen to the concerns of Latin American nations and potentially incorporate some of them into regional policy. Multilateralism could thereby help both to cushion Latin America from any U.S. effort to exploit the economic vulnerability of regional states and to restrain U.S. unilateralism, something the Latin America nations had strived to achieve for over a hundred years.

Second, U.S. policy toward Latin America in the first decade of the post–Cold War era was ambiguous (Lowenthal 2001). Throughout the1990s, U.S. leaders referred to Latin America as a foreign policy priority (a Clinton aide even declared 1994 to be the "year of Latin America" in U.S. foreign policy[17]), professed their interest in a new relationship with the region, and actively participated in two inter-American summit meetings (the first since 1967) designed to promote increased hemispheric cooperation on a variety of issues, trade being the most important. At the same time, however, the United States unilaterally ousted governments in Panama and Haiti and it dealt with issues from drug-trafficking to immigration in a heavy handed and often unilateral fashion. More troubling still was the inability of the Clinton Administration to win approval for Trade Promotion Authority in the U.S. Congress, effectively blocking all U.S. trade negotiations and raising fears about increased U.S. protectionism, and following this failure the disappearance of Latin America from the administration's policy agenda. For Latin America these events created confusion, and more importantly they raised the possibility of a renewal of benign neglect on the part of the United States just as Latin America was committing itself to an economic model that demanded increased U.S. economic cooperation in the region. Latin America, therefore, did not fear increased economic coercion on the part of the United States in the early 1990s so much as it feared an abandonment of Latin America by the United States.

Region-Wide Conclusions

Latin America's decision not only to accept the formation of an FTAA but to promote it actively is thus the direct result of U.S. hegemony and the manner in which the United States employed its power in the years and decades following the World War II. Quite unlike the Asian experience with regionalism (Choi in this volume), Latin America's interest in regionalism was not driven by security concerns or a perceived need to join forces against liberalizing pressures of the United States and the IMF. To the contrary, the FTAA was on the Latin American policy agenda in large part because of the region-wide decision to abandon import substitution in favor of market economies. And although the U.S. role in Latin America's decision to change is model of development was pivotal, it was somewhat more subtle than in the aftermath of the 1997 Asian financial crisis. The U.S. determination to reestablish open international markets in the wake of World War II, to encourage broad participation in world trade and finance, and to institutionalize this system in a series of international organizations designed to define and oversee its rules laid the political foundation for economic globalization in the late twentieth century. Freer trade in goods and services thereby provided significant economic opportunities for any country willing to open its economy to global markets. The ideological victory of the United States in the Cold War and the dissemination of American economic ideas made the idea of economic opening seem increasingly logical and viable to Latin American leaders struggling to find a means to reestablish economic growth, while increased access to positive information about the United States helped mitigate the negative view of the United States long held by the majority of the Latin American populace. The reemergence of full U.S. economic hegemony in the Western Hemisphere, meanwhile, enabled the United States to apply an effective coup de grâce in favor of policy change by pressuring Latin countries to undertake market-based economic reforms.

Any explanation of Latin America's decision to adopt a market model of economic development, however, would be incomplete and misleading if it did not include an analysis of the domestic factors also driving this decision, including a deep and enduring economic crisis and the particulars of domestic politics. Yet even in the presence of these factors, it is hard to imagine the region shifting its development strategy in the absence of the opportunities offered by economic globalization (the reflection of U.S. structural power), an ideology identifying the wisdom and efficiency of markets, and the financial carrot offered by the Brady Plan. U.S. power was determining.

Once Latin America determined to adopt a liberal, market model of development, increased economic dependence on the United States was all but inevitable. With only a few exceptions, the United States has long been the most important trading partner and the dominant source of foreign investment throughout the region. With Europe withdrawing from Latin America and Japan hesitant to increase its economic contacts in the region at the end of the Cold War, the U.S. market dominated Latin America's future opportunities. Opening to increased international flows of goods and finance would thus inevitably deepen Latin America's economic reliance on the United States.

Latin American access to U.S. consumers and foreign direct investment, however, was limited and unpredictable. Access to the U.S. market was limited by trade restrictions directed at precisely the sorts of products Latin America countries tended to export — agricultural goods, textiles, and steel — and the U.S. tendency to suddenly reduce market access in response to the demands of U.S. domestic politics. In recent years the United States had blocked a very long list of Latin American imports including steel, beef, avocados, orange juice, tomatoes, tuna, and even honey, most often to protect U.S. producers from lower cost Latin American producers. Access to U.S. foreign direct investment was also constrained by one of two factors, depending on the type of investment involved. Investment in the fabrication of production inputs and the assembly of final goods for export was constrained by a lack of guarantees for the rules under which these goods would enter the U.S. market. Should these products suddenly face higher import duties, the lower production costs of the foreign investment could be erased. Assured market access, therefore, should increase investment to these sectors. Investment in production for the Latin American domestic market, most particularly in the service sector, depended on the degree of investor confidence in the potential for growth in the Latin economy. If economies structured to export were to gain assured access to their main foreign market, however, investor confidence should receive a significant boost.

In the second half of the 1990s, the theoretic benefits of a free trade agreement with the United States to improve market access, increase flows of foreign direct investment, and thereby promote growth were transformed into empiric reality by the North American Free Trade Agreement (NAFTA). The post-NAFTA boom in Mexican exports to the United States, the explosion of foreign direct investment in the Mexican economy (not only from U.S. companies, but also from European and Asian firms interested in duty-free access to the U.S. market for their products), and the speed with which the Mexican economy recovered from the 1994 peso crisis (a recovery led by exports to the United States) offered a glimpse at the sort of economic benefits an FTAA could generate for the rest of Latin America.[18] Further, the trade diversion suffered by Caribbean, Central American, and some Andean countries as a consequence of NAFTA made clear the costs of not entering into a preferential trading arrangement with the United States.

A free trade agreement with the United States would not only provide improved access to the U.S. market and encourage foreign investment; it would regularize the rules of trade and investment. An international trade treaty would help to limit the capacity of the United States to exploit regional power differentials to manipulate trade and investment flows at will (although the inability of NAFTA to control fully U.S. protectionist impulses — the exclusion of Mexican tuna and Mexican trucks from the U.S. market offer two outstanding examples — suggests that no trade treaty will ever be able to eliminate completely this U.S. tendency). Such a strategy was also nothing new in Latin American foreign policy. Latin American countries have struggled for more than a century to limit U.S. freedom of action in hemispheric affairs by relying on international law and regional treaties, a traditional tactic of the weak to tie the hands of the strong. Throughout the late nineteenth and early twentieth centuries Latin America worked to convince the United States to sign a resolution renouncing its perceived right to intervene in the internal affairs of Latin American states. Although these efforts failed for over 40 years, they finally met with success in 1933 when the United States formally agreed that "no state has the right to intervene in the internal or external affairs of another" and again in 1948 when this nonintervention resolution was included in the treaty of the Organization of American States (OAS) (Smith 2000, 104).[19]

A region-wide free trade treaty had four additional advantages from the Latin American perspective. First, it would prevent the inefficiencies and trade diversion inherent in a complex web of autonomous free trade treaties throughout the region. Second, negotiating as a group would enhance the leverage of the Latin American states. Third, a region-wide negotiation promised to be sufficiently interesting to the United States to mitigate the likelihood that the United States would abandon much of the region. Fourth, the FTAA was initially a U.S. proposal (George Bush's Enterprise of the Americas Initiative), suggesting that its probability for success was significant.

As noted previously, the costs associated with the decision to negotiate the FTAA seemed manageable during the 1990s. Shared interests in promoting markets, democracy, and human rights; the reduced effectiveness of military intervention to resolve disputes in these issue areas; and an increased U.S. tendency to operate multilaterally in the hemisphere suggested that the United States was not likely to exploit Latin America's increased economic dependence often. Latin America also hoped that an FTAA would deepen U.S. economic reliance on Latin American markets, creating a mutual dependency that would assure long-term U.S. attention to regional economic matters and hopefully produce a degree of Latin American leverage over the United States (Feinberg 2002). Despite the potential benefits of an FTAA and the seemingly limited costs associated with the increased dependency on the United States, the decision to negotiate a free trade agreement with the United States was nevertheless a calculated risk, and one that was calculated differently throughout the hemisphere due to variations in geographic proximity to the United States.

Regional Variations

Mexico and the Caribbean Basin

The region with the greatest zeal for free trade agreements with the United States is without doubt Mexico and the Caribbean Basin. Mexico was the first to negotiate such a pact with the United States in the post–Cold War era, but the Caribbean countries and Central America have enjoyed privileged access to the U.S. market since the first Caribbean Basin Initiative of 1983, and a U.S.–Central America free trade agreement was moving toward approval in early 2003. This interest in formalizing their trading relationship with the United States is a direct reflection of the region's geographic location. Sitting on the southern border of the United States, the U.S. market has always been the locus of Caribbean Basin trade. Mexico historically sent 75 percent of its exports to the United States and as a consequence of NAFTA now relies on the U.S. market to absorb nearly 90 percent of its exports, accounting for nearly a quarter of the country's total production (GDP).[20] Caribbean and Central American countries on average send about 40 percent of their exports to the United States, but there is enormous variation among the countries of these subregions.[21]

The United States is the overwhelming source of regional foreign direct investment, and capital remittances from nationals living and working in the United States is one of the most important sources of foreign capital inflows throughout the region.[22] Meanwhile, the U.S. dollar operates as an unofficial currency throughout much of the region, and does so officially in El Salvador, Panama, and Guatemala. Deep economic dependence on the United States is a fact of life for Mexico and the Caribbean Basin with or without a free trade treaty. Formalizing this relationship would thereby produce significant economic benefits and few economic costs.

Beyond economics, geography has also determined that Mexico and the Caribbean Basin have been the focus of U.S. policy in Latin America. As the southern border of the United States, political stability in the Caribbean Basin and Mexico has long been a preoccupation of the United States, leading to repeated interventions in the internal affairs of these states. Although this geographic reality has been costly at times, it also assures this region that whatever U.S. policy toward South America might be in the years to come, the United States cannot afford to ignore its closest neighbors. U.S. hegemony in all its forms is an inevitability for this subregion, but geographic proximity also provides these countries with an important measure of leverage over the United States, making U.S. regional hegemony more a story of interdependence than pure dependency.

Although Mexico and the Caribbean Basin are highly dependent on their trade relationship with the United States, the United States is increasingly dependent on this same trade relationship. Mexico is the second largest trading partner of the United States, and virtually no U.S. car maker could turn out any of their North American models without the participation of their Mexican affiliates. The countries of the Caribbean Basin absorb 30 percent more U.S. exports than does China, and this trade flow has grown exponentially over the past decade. Central America takes more U.S. exports than Eastern Europe and the Soviet Union combined. Mexico and the Caribbean also possess sources of "soft power," providing increased leverage over U.S. policy. The most important such source of power is migration. Cuba, the Dominican Republic, Haiti, and Jamaica have 10, 12, 14, and 15 percent, respectively, of their total population living in the United States, and generations of Mexican migration have transformed Latinos into the largest minority in the United States at the opening of the twenty-first century (Lowenthal 2000). For the United States, there are two consequences of this reality. First, political or economic instability in this region is a clear threat to the U.S. ability to police its national borders and hence is an issue to be dealt with before a crisis develops. Second, its foreign policy toward these countries is increasingly a domestic policy matter as well (Mexican-Americans now account for over a third of the population of Los Angeles County, and the power of Cuban-American voters in Florida is legendary). Under these circumstances, deepening their economic ties with the United States promises to increase the interdependence between Mexico, Central America, and the Caribbean and the United States instead of merely augmenting dependence on their northern neighbor.

Chile

Chile also forms part of the group of countries highly receptive to negotiating the FTAA with the United States. This is surprising because Chile possesses a very different cost/benefit calculus than Mexico and the Caribbean Basin. Its geographic distance from the United States has limited both trade with, and foreign direct investment from, the regional economic power house.[23] It has been historically distant in U.S. thinking about Latin America (with the important exception of the mid-1970s) and it possesses few sources of soft power that might translate into leverage over the United States. Nevertheless, Chile is one of the most enthusiastic regional proponents of free trade with the United States. Chile seems to believe that promoting freer trade with the United States will once again confer on it the stamp of the Latin American leader in the economic liberalization process (a status Chile lost during the 1990s as other Latin American countries followed Chile's lead and implemented far-reaching economic reforms). Investors will thereby see Chile in a more favorable light than its South American neighbors, leading to an increased flow of direct investment toward this pacific country. The fact that this strategy is unlikely to produce the expected benefits does not negate the power this perception holds over Chilean trade policy (Edwards 2003).

Brazil and Mercosur

At the other extreme of the policy spectrum is Brazil, which along with Venezuela is one of the least receptive Latin American countries to the idea of an FTAA (excluding Cuba, which is excluded from the FTAA negotiations). The Brazilian position reflects its diversified profile of international economic relations, the industrial structure of its economy and the physical distance of Brazil's manufacturing center from the United States, and the Brazilian self-image as a middle power that should naturally play an important role in international affairs and a dominant role in South American affairs (Herz in this volume). Although the United States and Brazil have enjoyed basically good relations throughout the twentieth century, underlying this friendship are clear differences in economic and political interests that limit Brazil's enthusiasm for any FTAA that deepens U.S. hegemony in South America or increases Brazilian economic dependence on the United States.

Brazil is neither heavily dependent on trade in general nor on its trade with the United States. Brazil trades only a quarter of its GDP (compared with nearly 50 percent for Mexico) and is considered one of the most insular economies in the Americas. Nor does Brazil have any great interest in becoming a trading nation. Despite significant trade liberalization throughout the 1990s, the Brazilian industrial sector remains well protected (the 1994 adoption of Mercosur's common external tariff required Argentina to raise many of its trade duties to match Brazil's higher rates rather than requiring Brazil to lower its tariff rates).[24] Of what Brazil does trade, by far the largest portion is directed toward Argentina. The United States absorbs less than a quarter of Brazilian exports, accounting for less than 5 percent of Brazilian production. And although Brazil imports huge quantities of foreign direct investment, its origin is balanced between Europe and the United States.

Brazil has never fully adopted the logic of comparative advantage, in which it is considered unimportant what products a country produces, as long as it is the product in which national production is least inefficient. For Brazil, there is a huge difference between producing computer chips or potato chips. Advanced industrial production creates high value-added products and technological advances that are the foundation for the development of a strong, modern economy. Economic strength in turn is an essential prerequisite to the effective projection of national power, and hence to Brazil's capacity to play its natural role as a middle power in the international system and as a leader in South America (Hirst 2001). Brazil is thus unwilling to risk the health of its national industries to a blind faith in the efficiency of free trade, and much less so if free trade is with an industrial powerhouse such as the United States.

Brazil's physical size and its distance from the United States have also given it the geographic potential (it borders every other South American country except one) and the freedom of action (owing to the absence of a direct application of U.S. hegemony, quite unlike the Mexican experience) that have made its self-image as the leader of South America seem natural. Brazil's wariness of free trade with the United States and its interest in solidifying its leadership role in South America have been key forces driving the deepening of Mercosur during the past decade, efforts to expand Mercosur's trade ties throughout South America, and Brazilian pretensions to form a South American free trade area dominated by the Brazilian economy. Not unlike Chinese ambitions in East Asia (Choi in this volume), Brazil would prefer to trade freely within South America, free of U.S. influence, rather than within a hemispheric trading arrangement. Brazil prefers to trade with a region where Brazil's industrial prowess will dominate trade, where trade will stimulate Brazilian industrial development, and where deeper economic integration will enhance Brazilian regional influence.

Brazil nevertheless determined to take an active part in the FTAA negotiations, albeit much later than most of its hemispheric neighbors. This decision was a direct reflection of a political–economic calculus inspired by Brazilian interests outlined above. Brazil would have preferred to avoid the FTAA altogether, but when Mercosur members Argentina and Uruguay along with other South American countries expressed their interest in a free trade agreement with the United States, Brazil was forced to join the negotiations as a defensive maneuver to prevent the collapse of Mercosur and the end of any hope for Brazil's preferred outcome — a South American Free Trade Area (SAFTA). Brazil's negotiating strategy within the FTAA has been characterized by efforts to form a common negotiating position within Mercosur and among as many other South American countries as possible (Hirst 2001; da Motta Veiga 2001). This will increase Brazil's negotiating strength, place it in the position of leading South America in the negotiations, and should the FTAA negotiations fail, enable Brazil to exploit its leadership role and South America's shared negotiating position to construct a SAFTA.

In the negotiations, Brazil has insisted on deep concessions by the United States in exchange for U.S. access to the Brazilian market (most notably, sharp restrictions on the U.S. use of antidumping duties and compensatory tariffs, huge reductions in U.S. agricultural subsidies, and an only gradual reduction of industrial tariffs to provide Brazilian industries the time they will need to adjust to increased competition) and has made it clear that it is in no rush to complete the negotiation process. This bargaining strategy has two aims. First, it is an attempt to ensure that any FTAA will increase U.S.–Brazilian economic interdependence rather than imposing increased economic dependence on Brazil. In the words of Brazilian Vice President José Alencar, "We needn't be afraid of an FTAA, because we can compete. But if we're starting from the idea that the United States is going to impose conditions, then that to me is no longer an FTAA but something else that we are not going to enter" (*New York Times*, April 13, 2003). Failing this and given strong opposition in the U.S. Congress to the concessions demanded by Brazil, the Brazilian strategy also seems designed to make sure that any regional trading arrangement that does not meet Brazil's minimum demands will collapse under the weight of U.S. domestic politics (Otteman 2002).

Andean Community

In between these two extremes lie the Andean countries. The countries in this region are less dependent on their economic ties with the United States than Mexico and the Caribbean Basin, but more so than Brazil and Mercosur. The Andean countries export 20 percent of their GDP, and 40 percent of their exports are destined for the United States (totaling 12 percent of regional production of GDP). Yet the rate of growth in Andean trade with the United States currently lags behind every other Latin American region. They have also been less susceptible historically to U.S. interventionism than their northern neighbors, but more so than the Southern Cone. As a group, therefore, the Andean countries are somewhat more ambiguous about FTAA than other subregional groupings of states.

Generalizing about the Andean countries, however, is as perilous as generalizing about Latin America with regard to FTAA. The importance of oil exports to the Venezuelan economy contrasts with the economy's relative closure to imported goods (Venezuela trades 40 percent of its GDP yet imports just 14 percent of its GDP; by comparison Brazil imports 12 percent and Mexico 24 percent). And although Venezuela sits tightly within the U.S. sphere of influence in the Caribbean, it has not been a historic target of U.S. intervention. One would thus expect an ambiguous position relative to FTAA, but under the nationalist and populist leadership of Hugo Chavez, Venezuela has tightly aligned itself with Brazil in the FTAA negotiations.

Like the Southern Cone countries, Colombia historically has had limited direct interaction with the United States politically or economically (with the glaring exception of the 1904 Panama episode). Over the past decade, however, its interactions with the Untied States deepened dramatically owing to the war on drugs. Colombia receives more U.S. security assistance than any other country outside of the Middle East, and as a consequence of the war on drugs, the United States extended to Colombia (along with Ecuador, Bolivia, and Peru) modest preferential access to the U.S. market under the Andean Trade Preferences Act.[25] Colombia now exports 12 percent of its GDP to the United States. This mixed political and economic profile has produced a mixed stance on FTAA. Colombia was an early promoter of free trade with the United States. Yet this support for an FTAA is colored by tangible reservations and efforts to ensure that the negotiation process is not rushed.

Ecuador is a regional laggard in the area of economic reform, yet it trades 55 percent of its economic production and sends nearly half of these goods to the United States. Ecuador has adopted the U.S. dollar as its national currency and receives remittances from the United States totaling

10 percent of the Ecuadorian GDP. These economic figures imply that Ecuador should be following the lead of Mexico and the Caribbean Basin countries in active pursuit of a formalization of its inevitably dependent trading relationship with the United States. Strong nationalist and antimarket forces within Ecuadorian domestic politics, however, have generated significant obstacles to an FTAA. In particular, the determined opposition to FTAA from the country's large and politically mobilized indigenous movement has tangibly constrained government enthusiasm for FTAA.

Future Prospects

But how likely is it that a Free Trade Agreement of the Americas will come to fruition? What is the likelihood that the United States will be able to reach an accommodation with the most important Latin American economy, Brazil, and what is the likelihood that Latin America's attitude toward FTAA could change in the future? To what extent might the factors that have brought Latin American foreign economic policy to the point of accepting (more or less grudgingly) a formalization of their economic reliance on the U.S. market change in the coming years? Since the key factor shaping Latin America's interest in a free trade agreement with the United States is the market-based, export-oriented development model the region has adopted during the past decade, were Latin America to abandon this economic model, interest in an FTAA would fall off markedly. Yet it is hard to imagine that this model, albeit with some significant revisions, will not guide Latin American economic interactions for the foreseeable future.

The opportunities offered by economic globalization are unlikely to disappear. Despite concerns that the Doha round of trade negotiations (under the auspices of the World Trade Organization) might fail due to increased global protectionist pressures, the same fears have plagued every set of global trade negotiations over the past 30 years, yet each time agreement has been reached (Bergesten 2002). Associated fears that weaknesses in international financial markets will eventually undermine the process are well considered but somewhat overstated. And the ability of the anti-globalization forces to undermine the political will needed to sustain globalization will be constrained by the ever-expanding set of economic interests that benefit from the process. Although one should never be sanguine about the future of economic globalization, especially since the previous episode collapsed so spectacularly in a few short years, it seems that the current globalization experience is not destined to disappear any time soon.

The export of U.S. ideas about markets and economics also appears to be a well-established process. More and more Latin American students travel to the United States to study economics, as well as other fields. Although the extreme neoliberal view of the market that characterized a U.S. economics education in past years seems to be yielding somewhat to a more nuanced view of the market (considering its failings as well as its benefits), there is no alternate theory of economic development to challenge market economics for predominance. Despite loud complaints in Latin America about the implementation of this model, moreover, the dominant opinion among leaders and the public is that the market is the best (even if far from perfect) option for organizing economic interaction in the early twenty-first century (Weyland 2002; Latinobarómetro 2002). Meanwhile, the democratization of the access to information about the United States, its people, and its culture should continue and even increase in the future as the costs of technology fall further and as incomes in the hemisphere (hopefully) rise.

A decade after the end of the Cold War, both the European Union and Japan have begun to expand their economic presence in the hemisphere. Through increased foreign direct investment in Latin America and free trade treaties of their own, these powers have ended the United States' unipolar moment in the Western Hemisphere. Nevertheless, with the exception of a few South American countries, this extra-hemispheric economic influence remains miniscule when compared with the economic presence of the United States. Further, the differential between the power of the United States and that of its global rivals remains enormous (the U.S. economy is 2.5 times the size of its nearest rival). U.S. hegemony in the Western Hemisphere will remain a fact of regional life well into the future.

The impact of Latin American domestic politics on the sustainability of the market-model of development is a bit more of a wild card, but it is ultimately unlikely to significantly alter Latin American support of an FTAA. It seems logical to assume that where popular support for the market wanes because of economic crisis or unfulfilled expectations, politicians will offer populist solutions in the hopes of riding the wave of popular discontent into office. What is striking about current Latin American politics, however, is the extent to which this has not occurred despite the disappointing results of the new market model in generating sustained growth and reduced poverty during the late 1990s. Although voices have risen to protest the perceived shortcomings of Latin America's new development model (most strikingly in Bolivia, Ecuador, and southern Mexico), these voices have been sporadic, and politicians have been either unable or unwilling to exploit this opposition to promote policy change. To the contrary, leftist presidential candidates in Brazil and Ecuador dropped their antimarket rhetoric after their 2003 inaugurations in favor of a more moderate discourse calling for improvements in the operation of the market and better relations with Washington. In Argentina, the country that arguably suffered the most at the hands of the neoliberal economic model, populist and leftist candidates faded in the polls in advance of the 2003 presidential elections. Even in Venezuela, despite President Hugo Chávez's populist and nationalist rhetoric, little was done to reverse the broad economic course set by Chávez's predecessors until serious economic problems in early 2002 produced some significant tinkering at the margins (devaluation and capital controls). And when Mexicans voted to replace the long-ruling PRI in July 2000, they chose a market populist over the antimarket alternative.

It thus seems unlikely that Latin America will soon turn away from the market model of development. This means that for those countries with a deep economic dependence on the United States, the institutionalization of this inevitably close relationship will remain an important policy objective. For those with a more limited economic association with the United States, and most particularly for Brazil, preferences for an FTAA will be driven more by the behavior of the United States. The likelihood of achieving a hemisphere-wide FTAA, therefore, depends on the United States, on the broad foreign policy path it pursues in the Americas during the early twenty-first century, and on its domestic politics.

The historic ambivalence in Washington about Latin America threatened to reemerge following the terrorist attacks of September 11, 2001. President George W. Bush's stark statement following the attacks, insisting that the nations of the world were either "with us or with the terrorists" sent shudders up the collective Latin American spine. Was the United States returning to a Cold War–style view of the region as either allies or enemies and to a preference for unilateralism in its foreign policy? These concerns were reinforced by three other events. First, the limited but nevertheless symbolic U.S. support for the April 2001 failed coup against a democratically elected government in Venezuela did little to reassure Latin Americans about U.S. willingness to rely on multilateralism in Latin America. Second, the Bush administration's decision to abandon Argentina to its fate as the country faced a devastating economic crisis in 2002 reinforced fears throughout the region that Washington would once again turn its back on Latin America (with the obvious exceptions of Colombia and Mexico). Third, U.S. behavior as it prepared to go to war with Iraq in late 2002 and early 2003 further deepened Latin American concerns. In part this reflected the Bush administration's public expressions of disappointment with Latin American states that did not support the war. This created the impression that reprisals could ensue and reinforced concerns that Washington once again saw Latin Americans as allies or enemies. But it also reflected the ease with which the United States shunted aside the very sort of institutionalized multilateralism that Latin America hoped to use in the guise of an FTAA to constrain U.S. actions.

It remains unclear if these tendencies toward renewed unilateralism, neglect, and heavy-handedness are excesses driven by global circumstances or if they reflect a more permanent shift in U.S.–Latin American policy. Should the United States succumb to the temptation of either "bullying or retreat" in the hemisphere, however, the positive attitude evident in much of Latin America during the 1990s about deepening regional dependence on the United States could fade (Shifter 2002).

Within this context, Congressional approval of Trade Promotion Authority in late 2002 (an essential first step for any serious negotiations on trade liberalization), the push for FTAA coming from the Office of the U.S. Trade Representative, and President Bush's repeated expressions of strong support for FTAA have carried great weight in Latin America. Yet even if the White House were to remain devoted to negotiating the FTAA, the willingness of the U.S. Congress to approve a completed treaty remains unclear. Any hemispheric trade treaty that includes Brazil will require the United States to make significant concessions. In a country where public opinion is hesitant at best about free trade (less than 10 percent of Americans defined themselves as "free traders" in a 2000 poll, while nearly 40 percent defined themselves as "protectionist" and another 50 percent saw themselves as "fair traders"[26]) and where important, organized segments of the U.S. polity oppose free trade treaties (most prominently labor unions, environmental groups, and a politically important segment of agricultural and textile producers), however, Congressional support for an FTAA is far from assured.

This reality was demonstrated by the very close vote approving Trade Promotion Authority in 2002. After eight years of unsuccessful executive efforts to win its renewal and despite heavy lobbying from the Bush administration, including its decision to entice key congressmen to vote favorably by raising steel tariffs and increasing farm subsidies, the House of Representatives approved the bill by just three votes. The fact that the final treaty must be approved only in the U.S. Senate, where the Trade Promotion Authority legislation fared much better (mustering nearly a two-thirds majority), will help matters greatly. Nevertheless, the U.S. Congress will be reluctant to cede its capacity to protect constituents harmed by trade, most particularly by accepting limitations to the use of anti-dumping duties and safeguard clauses (two of Brazil's key demands), while individual congressmen will be wary of opposing powerful constituents.

Despite its historic misgivings about the political costs of free trade, however, the U.S. Congress has not voted down a single global trade agreement in the past 30 years. But a regional trade agreement is a very different animal from its global counterpart. Global trade negotiations have a historic momentum and take place under the auspices of an international institution (initially the GATT and since 1995 the World Trade Organization). As such, Congress is afraid that casting the vote of the world's largest trading economy against freer trade could permanently damage the negotiation process and potentially undermine the commercial globalization from which the United States economy has benefited enormously. The same calculus does not apply to a new, regional trade agreement, however. Further, the relative unimportance of an FTAA to the U.S. economy (U.S. regional trade is very heavily dominated by the two countries with which it already has a free trade agreement: Canada and Mexico[27]) combined with the perception in the United States that free trade agreements with developing countries tend to eliminate U.S. jobs and damage the environment, will make the FTAA extremely vulnerable to a congressional vote directed toward satisfying constituent demands against free trade. Responsible congressmen could easily vote for global free trade where the economic costs of a "no" vote would be great while voting against regional free trade where the economic costs of a "no" vote are low and the political gain high.

These final paragraphs are not intended to suggest that the FTAA is a political impossibility. Rather they demonstrate that the greatest obstacles to an FTAA will emanate not from Latin America but from the United States. Latin America has opted for market economies in which exports and foreign direct investment are key drivers of growth. Such economies need to gain market access and investor confidence, and in the Western Hemisphere a useful tool to that end is a free trade accord with the United States. Given that the variables behind this economic policy decision are unlikely to change in the near future, Latin support for an FTAA is unlikely to wane. Some argue that Canada, the other non-Latin participant in the FTAA talks, might help to bridge the gap between Brazil and the United States. Canada is a developed country like the United States, but it is also an economy highly dependent on the United States, like Latin America, and one that successfully institutionalized its trading relationship with the United States, first in the U.S.–Canada Free Trade Agreement and later as a member of NAFTA. At the same time, however, as a developed economy, Canada favors a tight, rule-based agreement along the lines of NAFTA, which protects its exports and investments from policy discrimination — precisely the sort of position that makes Brazil hesitant to join. In short, Canadian economic interests in an FTAA parallel those of the United States, making Canada a less than perfect interlocutor between the United States and Brazil (Roy 1999). Although Canada may help on the margin, in the final analysis the success of the FTAA depends on the United States. When it comes to free trade in the Western Hemisphere, the power behind the Pax Americana continues to be determining.

Notes

1. Argentine delegate and future president, Roque Sáenz Peña. Cited in Schoultz, 1998, p. 283).
2. "Since we are engaged in the most difficult task of creating and perpetuating a complex as well as peaceful area of influence, we must be clear about our long range approaches to the attainment of the material and intangible bonds upon which this empire depends. Since trade is a permanent foundation of such influence, the whole series of inter-American economic institutions should be molded toward the simplification of the currencies and customs regulations now in force in the twenty-one republics; they should be attached inseparably to the dollar." Internal State Department Memo, September 1939, cited in Schoultz, 1998, p. 374. On U.S. support for dollarization in the Americas, see Eric Helleiner, 2002, "Dollarization Diplomacy: US Policy Toward Latin America Coming Full Circle?" TIPEC Working Paper 02/8. www.trent.ca/tipec/working/html.
3. The Latin American Free Trade Association was formed in 1960 and ultimately met with little success. In the words of Mexican President Gustavo Díaz Ordaz, this process of "Latin American integration is, and we should make every effort so that it continues to be, an exclusively Latin American process." The President of Chile, Eduardo Frei, went even further. He argued that any attempt by the United States to force its way into the regional trading arrangement based on its role as a provider of economic aid to the region would be unacceptable. "This would constitute an intolerable infringement of national sovereignty" (Mattli 1999, 150–51).
4. The role of non–free trade powers in undermining the nineteenth century free trade system is discussed in Lake 1983. Although the delegates to the meetings leading up to the 1944 Bretton Woods conference believed in the power of economic interdependence to mitigate against war, the academic literature has long questioned this simplistic relationship. See for example Albert Hirschman, *National Power and the Structure of Foreign Trade*, Berkeley/Los Angeles: University of California Press, 1945; and Dale C. Copeland, "Economic Interdependence and War: A Theory of Trace Expectations," *International Security*, 20, no. 4 (Spring 1996): 5–41.
5. John Maynard Keynes, *The General Theory of Employment, Interest and Money* (London: Macmillian, 1936), p. 383.
6. Francis Fukuyama, "The End of History?" *The National Interest* (Summer 1989), p. 3.
7. The conceptualization of how economic ideas spread presented in this and the following sections is influenced by previous research on the spread of Keynesian economic ideas from the late 1930s until the 1960s. See Hall 1989.
8. On the central importance of foreign capital to economic growth in Latin America, see Hausmann 2003.
9. On Latin America's experience with import substitution, see Cardoso and Helwege 1992; Thorp 1998; and Iglesias 1992.
10. For a discussion of the process by which ideas are formed, translated into the Latin American context, and become policy, see Camp 2002; Valdés 1995; and Domínguez 1997.
11. On the impact of neutral economic advisers as a tool of U.S. Latin American policy throughout the twentieth century, see Drake 1994.

12. The literature on the domestic politics of economic reform in Latin America is substantial. A few representative works include Joan Nelson, ed., *Economic Crisis and Policy Choice: The Politics of Adjustment in the Third World* (Princeton, NJ: Princeton University Press, 1990); Adam Przeworski, *Democracy and the Market: Political and Economic Reforms in Eastern Europe and Latin America* (New York/London: Cambridge University Press, 1991); Stephan Haggard and Robert Kaufman, eds., *The Politics of Economic Adjustment*, Princeton, NJ: Princeton University Press, 1992); and Joan Nelson, ed., *A Precarious Balance: Democracy and Economic Reforms in Latin America* (San Francisco, CA: Institute for Contemporary Studies, 1994).
13. Regional average tariff rates fell from 40 percent in the mid-1980s to 10 percent in 2000, while average maximum tariffs fell from 80 percent to 40 percent (IDB 2002, p. 62).
14. The exceptions were Uruguay at 35 percent, Argentina at 47 percent, and Mexico at 49 percent. The other countries were Peru at 69 percent, Paraguay at 68 percent, Brazil at 55 percent, and Venezuela at 50 percent (Moreno 2002).
15. Mexico 64 percent, Argentina 57 percent, Brazil, 43 percent, and Venezuela 41 percent (Moreno 2002).
16. Japan was reluctant to take a leadership role in Latin America during the 1990s because of Latin America's geographic distance from Japan, a Japanese perception of the region as being unstable and risky, Latin America's economic crisis as Asian economies boomed, and Japan's own economic slump. This reluctance also prominently reflected the importance of the United States to Japanese security and international economic policy. Given the U.S. perception of Latin America as being within its sphere of influence, the importance of good relations with the U.S. to Japan, and Japan's only limited economic interest in Latin America, the costs of playing a more prominent role in Latin America far outweighed its benefits to Japan during the 1990s. Japanese Latin American policy would thus be "contingent on its own relations with the United States" (Berríos 2001, 152). In Latin America Japan would follow, not lead (Berríos 2001; Yopo 1991).
17. Cited in Hakim and Shifter 1995, p. 49.
18. Mexican exports nearly doubled during the first three years of NAFTA and continued to increase at a double digit rate until the U.S. economy entered into recession in 2001. Foreign direct investment tripled during the first year of the NAFTA agreement, after increasing 35 percent in 1993 in anticipation of the NAFTA agreement. Although FDI fell back somewhat in subsequent years, it remained three to four times the pre-NAFTA (1992) rate.
19. The fact that the OAS treaty has not prevented the United States from intervening in internal affairs of various Latin American states does not negate the Latin American attempt to use international law and regional treaties to constrain the regional behavior of the United States. It merely demonstrates the limitations of this strategy.
20. All trade data is derived from IMF, Direction Trade Statistics.
21. The Dominican Republic sends 87 percent of its exports to the United States accounting for 22 percent of its GDP; Honduras sends 70 percent of its exports to the United States accounting for a whopping 51 percent of its GDP; yet El Salvador sends just 19 percent of its exports to the United States, accounting for just 1.6 percent of GDP.
22. Remittances in Mexico are greater than tourism receipts and in 2002 totaled three quarters of total inflows from foreign direct investment despite Mexico being the world's third largest developing country recipient of FDI. In El Salvador remittances total over 10 percent of the national product.
23. In a preliminary but illuminating study, UCLA economist Edward Leamer has estimated that every 1000 miles of distance a good must travel is the equivalent of a tariff of between 7 and 17 percent.
24. Although Brazil's average tariff rate is just over 15 percent (compared with 9 percent for Chile), this reflects low tariff rates within Mercosur and high for countries outside of this preferential trading arrangement. In its trade with the United States, a significant industrial competitor, Brazilian tariffs on light manufactured goods average 18 percent, 21 percent on capital goods and food processing and 33 percent on consumer durables (Hinojosa-Ojeda 2000; IDB 2002, Chapter 3).

25. The Andean Trade Preferences Act was initially approved by the U.S. Congress in December 1991, benefiting exports from Bolivia, Colombia, Ecuador, and Peru to support the drug control effort. The act expired in 2001, but it was finally renewed in mid-2002 until the end of 2006.
26. Louis Harris & Associates, April 2000, published by The Odum Institute, www2.irss.unc.edu/irss/home.asp
27. In 2001 Canada accounted for 20 percent of total U.S. trade and Mexico for another 12.3 percent, while the rest of Latin America combined accounted for just 6.8 percent of U.S. trade.

References

Bergesten, C. Fred. 2002. "A Renaissance for U.S. Trade Policy?" *Foreign Affairs* 81, no. 6 (November/December): 86–98.
Berríos, Rubén. 2001. "Japan's Economic Presence in Latin America." *Latin American Politics and Society* 43, no. 2 (Summer): 147–61.
Camp, Roderic Ai. 2002. *Mexico's Mandarins: Crafting a Power Elite for the Twenty-First Century*. Berkeley/Los Angeles: University of California Press.
Cardoso, Eliana, and Ann Helwege. 1992. *Latin America's Economy: Diversity, Trends, and Conflicts*. Cambridge, MA: MIT Press.
da Motta Veiga, Pedro. 2001. "Brasil, el Mercosur, y el ALCA." *Foreign Affairs en Español* 1, no. 1 (Primavera): 95–112.
Domínguez, Jorge, ed. 1997. *Technopols: Freeing Politics and Markets in Latin America in the 1990s*. University Park: Pennsylvania State University Press.
Domínguez, Jorge. 1998. "The Americas: Found, and Then Lost Again." *Foreign Policy* 112 (Fall): 125ff.
Drake, Paul, ed. 1994. *Money Doctors, Foreign Debts, and Economic Reforms in Latin America from the 1890s to the Present*. Wilimgton, DE: Scholarly Resources.
Edwards, Sebastian. 2003. "Americas: How Chile Can Make the Most of Its U.S. Trade Deal." *The Wall Street Journal* (3 January).
Feinberg, Richard. 2002. "The Bush Administration and the Regionalist Option in the Americas." Paper presented at the Competing Regionalisms in the Americas Conference, Colegio de Mexico, Mexico City, March 14–15.
Fukuyama, Francis. 1989. "The End of History?" *The National Interest* (Summer): 3–18.
Gourevitch, Peter. 1989. "Keynesian Politics: The Political Sources of Economic Policy Choices." Pp. 87–106 in *The Political Power of Economic Ideas: Keynesianism across Nations*, ed. P. A. Hall. Princeton, NJ: Princeton University Press.
Hall, Peter A. 1989. *The Political Power of Economic Ideas: Keynesianism across Nations*. Princeton, NJ: Princeton University Press.
Hakim, Peter, and Michael Shifter. 1995. "United States-Latin American Relations: To the Summit and Beyond." *Current History* (February): 49–53.
Hausmann, Ricardo. 2003. "La crisis de esperanza de América Latina." *Foreign Affairs en Español*, 3(1) (Enero–Marzo): 67–77.
Hey, Jeanne A. K. 1997. "Three Building Blocks of a Theory of Latin American Foreign Policy." *Third World Quarterly* 18, no. 4: 631–57.
Hinojosa-Ojeda, Raúl. 2000. "Brazil and the United Status at the Gateway of the FTAA: A CGE Modeling Approach to Challenges and Options." In *Economia Brasiliera e os Processos de Integração Subregional e Hemisférico*. Brasilia: IPEA-Instituto de Pesquisa Econômica, Ministério do Planejamento e Orçamento.
Hirst, Monica. 2001. "La política de Brasil hacia las Américas." *Foreign Affairs en Español* 1, no. 3 (Otoño–Invierno): 141–56.
Iglesias, Enrique. 1992. *Reflections on Economic Development: Toward a New Latin American Consensus*. Washington, DC: Inter-American Development Bank.
Inter-American Development Bank (IDB). 2002. *Beyond Borders: The New Regionalism in Latin America. Economic and Social Progress in Latin America*. Washington, DC: IDB.
International Monetary Fund. 2002. *Direction of Trade Statistics Yearbook*. Washington, DC: IMF.

Lake, David A. 1983. "International Economic Structures and American Foreign Economic Policy, 1887–1934." *World Politics* 35, no. 4 (July): 517–43.
Lake, David A. 1991. "British and American Hegemony Compared: Lessons for the Current Era of Decline." Pp. 106–22 in *History, the White House, and the Kremlin: Statesmen as Historians*, ed. M. G. Fry. London: Frances Pinter; New York: Columbia University Press.
Latinobarómetro. 1996–2002. Various polls. www.latinobarometro.org
Lowenthal, Abraham. 2000. "Latin America at the Century's Turn." *Journal of Democracy* 11, no. 2 (April): 41–55.
Lowenthal, Abraham. 2001. "Estados Unidos y América Latina en el nuevo siglo." *Foreign Affairs en Español* (Mayo). www.foreignaffairs-esp.org
Mattli, Walter. 1999. *The Logic of Regional Integration: Europe and Beyond*. Cambridge, UK: Cambridge University Press.
Millett, Richard. 1994. "Beyond Sovereignty: International Efforts to Support Latin American Democracy." *Journal of Interamerican Studies and World Affairs* 36, no. 3 (Fall): 1–23.
Milner, Helen. 1987. "Resisting the Protectionist Temptation: Industry and the Making of Trade Policy in France and the United States during the 1970s." *International Organization* 41, no. 4 (Autumn): 639–65.
Moreno, Alejandro. 2002. "La opinión pública latinoamericana y Estados Unidos." *Foreign Affairs en Español* 2, no. 1 (Primavera): 86–99.
Otteman, Scott. 2002. "El Congreso estadounidense y el libre comercio en América Latina." *Foreign Affairs en Español* 2, no. 3 (Otoño–Invierno): 105–12.
Roy, Martín. 1999. "Canadá y el ALCA." *Nueva Sociedad* 162 (July–August):166–80.
Schoultz, Lars. 1998. *Beneath the United States: A History of US Policy toward Latin America*. Cambridge, MA: Harvard University Press.
Shifter, Michael. 2002. "A Shaken Agenda: Bush and Latin America." *Current History* (February): 51–57.
Smith, Peter H. 2000. *Talons of the Eagle: Dynamics of U.S.-Latin American Relations*. New York: Oxford University Press.
Thorp, Rosemary. 1998. *Progress, Poverty and Exclusion: An Economic History of Latin American In the 20th Century*. Washington, DC: Interamerican Development Bank.
Valdés, Juan Gabriel. 1995. *Pinochet's Economists: The Chicago School in Chile*. New York: Cambridge University Press.
Weintraub, Sidney. 2001. "Las posibilidades del libre comercio hemisférico." *Foreign Affairs en Español* 1, no. 3 (Otoño–Invierno): 61–66.
Weyland, Kurt. 2002. "Assessing the Political Sustainability of Latin American 'Neoliberalism.'" Paper presented at the conference "Reforms after Reforms in Latin America," Watson Institute of International Studies, Brown University, Providence, RI, November 1.
Yopo, Mladen. 1991. "Japan-Latin America: Taking Advantage of Mutual Space and Opportunities." *Journal of Interamerican Studies and World Affairs* 33, no. 1 (Spring): 59–86.
Zoellick, Robert. 2003. "Comerciar en libertad." *Foreign Affairs en Español* 3, no. 1 (Enero–Marzo): 39–48.

CHAPTER 5

The U.S.–China Peace: Great Power Politics, Spheres of Influence, and the Peace of East Asia

ROBERT S. ROSS

Introduction

East Asia in the post–Cold War era has been the world's most peaceful region. Whereas since 1989 there have been major wars in Europe, South Asia, Africa, and the Middle East and significant and costly civil instability in Latin America, during this same period in East Asia there have been no wars and minimal domestic turbulence. Moreover, economic growth in East Asia has been faster than in any other region in the world. East Asia seems to be the major beneficiary of Pax Americana.

Yet East Asia is the region where the United States is the least powerful, where it experiences the greatest constraints on its power and on its flexibility. In East Asia the United States does not enjoy hegemony. On the contrary, in East Asia the United States confronts its most formidable rival and potential great power challenger — the People's Republic of China (PRC). Thus, the paradox of East Asia is also the global paradox. Where America has been most powerful, there has been regional instability and war.

Where there has been great power rivalry and traditional balance of power politics, there has been peace and prosperity.

The explanation of this paradox lies in the power differential between the great powers and local powers. The United States can be the sole great power in the region, but due to distance and geostrategic obstacles, it may not possess sufficient dominance over smaller powers to compel compliance and establish order. Thus, it confronts challenges to its rule and the region experiences instability. This is frequently the case when establishing dominance requires the United States to project power onto the Eurasian mainland. This had also been the case in East Asia during the Cold War, where U.S. inability to project dominant power onto the mainland contributed to the protracted conflicts in Korea and Vietnam. But U.S. weakness is Chinese strength, such that China has overwhelming dominance on the mainland. The result is that China maintains a Pax Sinica on mainland East Asia and the United States maintains a Pax Americana in maritime East Asia. The bipolar peace of East Asia reflects the ability of China and the United States to dominate the local powers in their respective spheres.

The first section of this chapter examines the zone of Pax Americana. The second section examines the zone of Pax Sinica. The third examines the most contested area of East Asia — the Taiwan Strait — where the United States and China contend for influence and where there still exists considerable potential for instability. The concluding section examines the prospects for stability in an era of declining U.S. power in East Asia.

Pax Americana: Dominance at Sea

Pax Americana establishes its rule and imposes order in East Asia in the twenty-first century in just the same way that Pax Britannica established its rule in the eighteenth century — through sea power. But whereas Britain insisted that its national security required it to possess a two-power standard, whereby its naval power would be sufficient to contend with the world's next two largest navies at the same time, in the twenty-first century the United States possesses the world's only great power navy. Thus, the United States does not possess a two-power standard but a global standard. It can contest all of the world's navies simultaneously.

American naval supremacy is particularly well suited to establish order in maritime East Asia. The East Asian littoral is composed of a vast island chain that extends from Japan in the northeast to the Malaysian Peninsula in the southeast. The vast amount of water and the distance between the states enables the U.S. Navy to operate in secure waters. Moreover, the archipelago nature of many of the states, especially of Indonesia and the Philippines, but also of Japan and Malaysia, enables a naval power not only to dominate the sea-lanes but also to determine the security of the local powers. Equally important, with the important exception of Taiwan, the distance from the East Asian mainland to the maritime theaters makes it difficult for a land power to project power and exercise influence in the maritime region. This was the case for the Soviet Union and then Russia in the nineteenth and twentieth centuries, and it is currently the case for China.

The combination of U.S. naval power and the geopolitical characteristics of maritime East Asia enable the United States to establish a secure sphere of influence that extends from Japan in Northeast Asia to Malaysia in Southeast Asia. The Philippines, Singapore, Brunei, and Indonesia also lie in this zone of peace. This sphere of influence has existed since World War II, when the United States replaced all of the colonial powers, including Japan, as the region's sole great power. Today, this region is a more secure and stable U.S. sphere of influence than at any time since World War II.

During the Cold War, the Soviet Union engaged the United States in a global competition, which challenged U.S. authority in maritime East Asia. In the final decade of the Cold War the Soviet Union's nascent Pacific Fleet began to establish a presence in East Asian waters, suggesting the rise of naval power in East Asia. But now Moscow lacks the capital to maintain and purchase Russian naval vessels for its own defense, so that the Russian navy consists of dated vessels in need of repair. Thus, the Russian naval industry survives as an export industry. Seventy percent of Russian arms production is for export. Only through these exports can Moscow keep production lines open and maintain employment in its defense industry.[1]

The end of the Cold War did not enable the United States to expand its sphere of influence in East Asia, but it did enable the United States to consolidate it. In the aftermath of the Cold War, no great power candidate has emerged to challenge U.S. naval supremacy in East Asia. Japan had once been considered a rising power. It has acquired a formidable modern and growing surface fleet. But ten years of economic stagnation and the prospect of another five years of little or no growth have altered expectations of Japan's ability to became an independent great power. Although during the 1990s Japan's defense budget remained steady at 1 percent of its gross national product, relative to U.S. defense spending (and Chinese defense spending), Japanese defense spending has declined dramatically.[2] Moreover, whereas Japan's technological development had been rapid during the catch-up phase of development, its more recent efforts have not been able to match those of the United States.

The combination of the relative decline of Russian and Japanese power have served to enhance U.S. power in East Asia. Moreover, the United States has not stood still. It has enhanced its power in maritime East Asia through expansion of its military presence. It has plans to base three Los Angeles-class nuclear-powered attack submarines at Guam. The first such submarine arrived in October 2002.[3] The United States is also converting its Cold War Trident submarines equipped with strategic nuclear missiles to nuclear-powered guided-missile submarines (SSGNs), with plans to deploy these power-projection platforms in East Asia. These ballistic missile submarines will be able to launch as many as 154 precision-guided sea-launched cruise missiles.[4]

The United States is also improving its forward presence of air-power in East Asia. In August 2002 the United States began stockpiling conventional air-launched cruise missiles (CALCMs) at Andersen Air Force Base in Guam. This forward basing enables U.S. bombers to reload in East Asia rather than return to the United States for munitions. CALCMs permit the United States to target any adversary asset anywhere in the Western Pacific, as well as on most of mainland East Asia.[5] The United States is also considering expanding its aircraft presence in Guam.[6] Andersen Air Force Base provides much better coverage of Southeast Asia than Kadena Air Force Base in Japan.

Thus, in the aftermath of the collapse of Soviet power, U.S. hegemony in maritime East Asia has increased, providing even greater U.S. ability to manage regional politics and to keep the peace. This continues to be the case, despite the remarkable rate of Chinese economic modernization. The resources and technology required to establish an effective navy and challenge U.S. capabilities are formidable, and China has yet to develop even the foundations for such a challenge. Chinese recognition of the long-term inability to challenge U.S. capabilities is reflected in the decision to rely on dated Russian weaponry as the backbone of China's air and naval power for the next two decades. Russian surface vessels sold to China, including the Sovremmeni destroyer, significantly enhance Chinese absolute capabilities, but they cannot offer China sufficient relative improvement so that its navy can challenge the security of the U.S. Navy. Even when equipped with advanced missiles, the Sovremmeni lacks the range to be able to target U.S. aircraft carriers.

China's contemporary naval strategy is similar to that of the Soviet Union during most the Cold War. Faced with U.S. naval superiority, the Soviet Union focused on developing submarines in order to enhance its coastal defense ability against the U.S. naval forces. Now China is buying Russian technology to pursue the same strategy. Its interest in Russian

Kilo-class submarines reflects its concentration on developing an access-denial capability so as to compel the U.S. Navy to maintain its distance from the Chinese coast and from the most likely theater of a U.S.–China war, the Taiwan Strait. China has already contracted to purchase four Kilo-class submarines. If it purchases an additional eight submarines, as reported, its commitment to this strategy will be evident.[7]

Chinese development of submarine capabilities may well enhance its coastal security, but it will not yield power projection capability that can either challenge the security of the East Asian littoral states within the U.S. strategic envelope or the U.S. ability to determine the states' security. Submarine power will not enable China to determine the outcome of a war and, thus, the ability to risk a war with the United States. Indeed, relying on submarines, China cannot challenge the territorial integrity of the maritime states, independent of U.S. power. This knowledge creates the political environment necessary for the United States to maintain authority in maritime Asia. The Soviet navy, even though inferior to the U.S. Navy, was far more capable than the current Chinese navy. Yet Soviet power, even at its greatest, was unable to erode U.S. strategic partnerships in insular East Asia. Chinese capabilities cannot challenge U.S. supremacy in post-Cold War maritime East Asia.

U.S. economic power in East Asia reinforces U.S. military power and contributes to Pax Americana. Despite the growth of the Chinese economy, the United States remains the region's most important export market and the most important target of direct foreign investment. Thus, every country in the region depends on stable political relations with the United States for continued economic growth and high levels of employment. Japanese economic prosperity continues to depend on the U.S. market. Despite the size of the Japanese economy, Japan's domestic market is too small to sustain economic development for the world's second largest economy. Japan requires exports for growth, particularly exports to the United States. Although China is rapidly becoming a major Japanese export market, it will contend with the United States for trade influence over Japan, but it will not supplant it. Moreover, despite the recent upsurge in Japanese investment in China, for many years the United States will continue to be the location of the overwhelming share of Japanese direct foreign investment.[8]

Southeast Asia's maritime states are similarly dependent on the United States for economic growth, but for different reasons. First, these countries' overall dependency on trade has grown since the late Cold War era. This is the case even for the less developed countries, such as Indonesia and the Philippines. As these countries have abandoned import-substitution trade policies for export-driven economic growth, they have become more dependent on international markets for economic growth and political stability.

Second, with the exception of Singapore, these states' dependency on international markets is primarily a dependency on the United States. Because Malaysia, Indonesia, and the Philippines had not developed indigenous manufacturing facilities by the mid-1990s, their economies were not able to take advantage of Chinese economic reform to move production facilities to China and maintain competitively prices exports. Rather, U.S. and European multinational corporations based in these countries moved their facilities to China, seeking to take advantage of low labor costs and the large Chinese market. The result is that the Southeast Asian countries remain dependent on exports of low-cost commodities for continued growth, and their most important market is the United States. Japan has never been especially open to imports, even of low-cost goods. And European countries remain much less important to these countries than does the United States. China will become an in increasingly important market, especially as Beijing implements the trade liberalization measures of free trade agreement between China and the Association of South East Asian Nations (ASEAN). Nonetheless, China produces low-cost commodities itself rather than import them; China and the Southeast Asian economies are not complementary. Despite the growing importance of China to the ASEAN countries, the rate of increase is moderate, and in 2001 the value of ASEAN exports to the United States was twice the amount of its exports to China. At least until 2010, the United States will remain an important market for all of the ASEAN countries.[9]

This combination of overwhelming military power and significant economic power creates the conditions for U.S. political dominance. This is reflected in the military and economic policies of the littoral states. In the post–Cold War era, as the United States consolidated its power in maritime East Asia, the littoral states have moved closer to the United States; they have accommodated, in recognition that to do otherwise would jeopardize their security. Japanese bandwagoning began in the mid-1990s.

Thus, rather than develop its own military capabilities to provide for its security, Japan has recommitted itself to working with the U.S.–Japan alliance. The first indication of this trend was Japan's agreement to the 1995 revised treaty guidelines. These guidelines committed Japan to greater cooperation within the alliance, rather than seek an independent security posture. This trend has not only reduced Japan's long-term challenge to U.S. power; it has also enhanced U.S. ability to depend on Japan to expand its own regional military power. The implied contingency in the revised guidelines is U.S. use of Japanese facilities in a war with China over Taiwan. Tokyo has resisted Chinese pressure to declare that the alliance does not apply to a Taiwanese contingency. Since agreeing to the revised guidelines, Tokyo has expanded cooperation with the United States in the development of a missile defense system. Most recently, Japan has taken new steps to expand naval cooperation with the United States. It has deployed advanced Aegis-class destroyers and other naval vessels in the Persian Gulf region in support of the U.S. war against terrorism.[10]

The Southeast Asian countries have been equally responsive to U.S. power. In March 2001, Singapore completed construction of its Changi port facility. The opening ceremony was attended by military officials from the United States as well as Singapore. In all but name, Singapore has created a naval base for the United States. Changi can provide short-term support for a second U.S. aircraft carrier in East Asia, enabling extended stays in East Asian waters. In apparent recognition that the United States will be able to deploy a second aircraft carrier in East Asia for extended periods, the U.S. defense budget for fiscal year 2003 allocates funding for an increased carrier presence in East Asia.[11] Singapore has also signed a free trade agreement with the United States, in recognition of the importance of U.S.–Singapore ties to its economy.

The Philippines is expanding its military cooperation with the United States. Since September 11, 2001, U.S. forces have returned to the Philippines in significant numbers. Their role is not limited to carrying out joint counterterrorism operations with Philippine troops. In January 2003, 600 U.S. Marines arrived at Clark Air Field, the site of the former U.S. Air Force base in the Philippines, to conduct joint exercises involving patrol and reconnaissance techniques, helicopter missions, and ordinance identification.[12] Although Subic Bay and Clark will not again become formal U.S. military bases, continued U.S.–Philippine defense cooperation will contribute to U.S. forward deployment of military capabilities in East Asia. Moreover, it is not unlikely that U.S. aircraft carriers will return to Subic Bay.[13] The Philippines, following Singapore's lead, is also negotiating a free trade agreement with the United States.

As U.S. power in maritime East Asia has grown, regional peace has become more prevalent. Proving a negative is difficult; establishing why there has not been greater conflict in East Asia, why East Asia has experienced less conflict than in the past, is a dubious task. Nonetheless, there are suggestions that U.S. power is the source of regional stability.

In the 1960s domestic turbulence in Indonesian politics combined with the decolonization process on Indonesian borders to cause significant regional tension associated with Jakarta's "confrontation" policy.

The territorial dispute between the Philippines and Malaysia over Sabah was also a source of bilateral tension, and there were periodic disputes between Singapore and its larger neighbors, Indonesia and Malaysia. In the 1970s and 1980s cooperation replaced conflict as the local powers combined forces in opposition to a common threat. The U.S. withdrawal from Vietnam in 1973 and the subsequent decline in U.S. international activism, the unification of Vietnam in 1975, and the Vietnamese invasion of Cambodia in cooperation with the Soviet Union all challenged the security of the Southeast Asian countries. During the ten years of the Vietnamese occupation of Cambodia and its war against Pol Pot and the Khmer Rouge, the ASEAN nations shelved their bilateral conflicts in the interest of cooperating against the common and greater threat — Soviet–Vietnamese power.

Soviet power in East Asia is now only a memory. Vietnam lost its war against the Khmer Rouge and withdrew its forces from Cambodia. It is now focused on managing its economy and on maintaining domestic political stability. Moreover, China remains a conservative state, focused on cooperating with the international political and economic orders and on building its economy. The key counterfactual question is why, after the demise of the common threat, has conflict not returned to Southeast Asia? The answer lies in the consolidation of U.S. hegemony in the post–Cold War era.

From 1963 to 1965, when President Sukarno tried to use Indonesian opposition to the British creation of Malaysia to bolster his domestic legitimacy and maintain political power, he sought improved relations with China to compensate for deteriorated relations with the United States. This was the background to Indonesia's "new emerging forces" policy, which Sukarno offered as an alternative to participation in the U.S. political order and the "Beijing–Hanoi–Jakarta axis."[14]

In 1999, Indonesia faced a domestic leadership crisis very similar to the 1965 crisis, but the outcome was very different. In 1999, the leadership's legitimacy was significantly weakened, and it faced a separatist challenge from the island of East Timor. But in contrast to 1965, the Indonesian leadership in 1999 had no option but to work within the U.S. political order. It could not use the East Timor separatist movement as a scapegoat for the nation's problems and tolerate widespread violence against minorities, as it had done in with its Chinese minority in 1965, and lash out against its neighbors who were encouraging moderation. This is because it could not resist U.S. pressure by reaching out to an alternative great power, for China no longer offered itself as a counterweight to U.S. power.

Thus, when the United States organized an international coalition in support of independence for East Timor and encouraged Australian efforts to provide the peacekeeping force on East Timor while it moved its naval forces into the vicinity, Indonesian leaders had little choice but to comply. The potential costs of resistance to the United States were simply too high, including total international isolation and very damaging economic sanctions at the low end of the continuum and U.S. naval intervention at the high end. Indeed, the peaceful dismemberment of Indonesia and the eventual establishment of the independence of East Timor in 2002 exemplified the process of Pax Americana in East Asia. In contrast to its experiences in Kosovo and Iraq, the United States in the Indonesian case compelled another state to make the ultimate concession, acquiescence to a separatist movement, without having to fire a shot.

Pax Sinica: Domination on Land

Since the end of the Cold War and the emergence of the United States as the sole superpower, East Asia has been peaceful both at sea and on land. Yet the source of the mainland peace has not been U.S. power but rather Chinese power. Pax Sinica and Pax Americana together create East Asian peace.

The history of Cold War East Asian international politics is dominated by the wars in Korea and Indochina, which all reflected China's demand for hegemony along its borders. It achieved this objective in Northeast Asia in 1953 when the United States acquiesced to a divided Korea, in which China dominated the northern half through its relationship with North Korea. The history of Indochina was more difficult and costly for China, for the outside powers, and for the local states. Through a succession of wars, China used the local states to inflict high costs on outside powers, compelling them to leave the region. First, China benefited from Vietnamese efforts to oust the French from Indochina in 1954. From 1954 to the early 1960s, there were no foreign troops in Indochina or Burma, and China's borders were secure. But beginning in 1962, when U.S. troops first returned to South Vietnam, to 1973, when the United States left mainland Southeast Asia, China once again relied on Vietnamese troops to rid the region of a foreign great power presence. Then, in 1978, when the Soviet Union replaced the United States as the outside power in the region and cooperated with Vietnam to challenge Chinese border security, China relied on Cambodian troops to oust Soviet influence from Indochina. By 1989, Cambodian insurgents had defeated the Vietnamese occupation, the Soviet political presence in Vietnam and the other countries of Indochina had all but disappeared, and China had established hegemony throughout most of mainland East Asia.

Whereas the United States establishes hegemony as Britain did in the nineteenth century, through sea power, China establishes hegemony as it always has, through land power. China is now the uncontested land power on mainland East Asia. The United States tried to be an East Asian land power in the 1950s and 1960s, but it failed. It could not defeat Chinese forces on the Korean Peninsula, and it could not defeat Vietnamese forces in Indochina. It ultimately acquiesced to its limitations. It withdrew from Indochina in 1973, ceding to China the responsibility for containing Soviet power and ultimately dominance on mainland Southeast Asia.

From the mid-nineteenth century to the end of the twentieth century, Russia and the Soviet Union used land power to expand into East Asia. Yet this was a short-lived affair that reflected the anomaly of Chinese weakness. The distance and geography, as well as the severe weather, separating the Russian industrial and population centers from East Asia undermined Russian capabilities throughout this period. Thus, once Russia encountered even a minimal challenge, it retreated. It was able to pose only nominal resistance to Japan on land and sea during the 1904 Russo-Japanese war.[15] Once China regained its political and economic stability in the 1980s and 1990s, taking advantage of its favorable geography, it quickly came to dominate the Sino–Russian border in East Asia. Once Russia regains its footing, its ability to challenge China in East Asia will still remain limited. It will first have to manage the areas closer to home, including Central Asia and the Balkans. Then, even should it turn its attention to East Asia, it will have to contend with China's geostrategic advantages.

But China has not only benefited from the collapse of Soviet power; it has also modernized its forces. Just as the United States has not stood still since the end of the Cold War and has improved its regional maritime capabilities, China has enhanced its land power capabilities. The changes in Chinese ground force capability during the post-Mao era have been significant. These changes have not been expensive, and they do not reflect large acquisitions of advanced hardware. Rather, through improved training, education, and communication capabilities, selective allocation of advanced weaponry to key units, and through the demobilization of approximately two million soldiers, China has developed a disciplined and effective land army capable of carrying out increasingly sophisticated operations.[16] It domination of its periphery is thus all the more effective.

Growing Chinese economic power in mainland East Asia compliments its military hegemony. China is surrounded by less developed countries.

U.S. economic relations with these countries are nominal. They cannot afford to buy high-cost U.S. consumer goods, and the U.S. market is not interested in their low-quality consumer goods. Nor is there much U.S. direct foreign investment in these countries. The investment capital of the United States is going to China, not to China's neighbors. The United States is thus a nonfactor in the economies of these states. China, in contrast, is a key economic partner of all these states. Region-wide, the United States has less relative economic power in mainland Southeast Asia than Chinese relative economic power in maritime Southeast Asia.

China's low-cost consumer goods are very competitive in these countries; Chinese exports have penetrated these markets and play an important role in the economic and political stability of these countries. Vietnam's traditional bicycle industry, for example, has come under significant pressure from imports from China. More important, through trade, investment, and societal penetration by Chinese entrepreneurs, the economies of the three Indochinese countries, of Burma, and of northern Thailand have become significantly integrated into the Chinese economy. Thus, the economic prospects of each of these countries and the political fortunes of their governments depend not only on continued Chinese economic growth but also on good political relations with China.

Chinese hegemony has led East Asia's mainland states to accommodate Chinese power, just as East Asia's maritime states have accommodated U.S. hegemony. The first sign of bandwagoning in Southeast Asia occurred in 1975, in the wake of North Vietnam's final invasion of South Vietnam. Thailand understood that the United States was no longer a factor in the politics of mainland Southeast Asia and that it could either seek security through accommodation with a unified and very powerful Vietnam or turn to China for a strategic partnership. It chose the latter course and quickly distanced itself from Washington, demanding that the United States close its bases in Thailand and withdraw its troops. Chinese influence in Thailand grew through the 1980s in the context of Soviet–Vietnamese expansion. Thai resistance to the Vietnamese occupation of Cambodia depended on Chinese support, and the Thai and Chinese militaries closely cooperated throughout the ten-year war in Cambodia. In the post–Cold War era, Chinese strategic influence is reflected in Thai reluctance to accommodate U.S. requests for expanded military cooperation. Bangkok has turned down U.S. requests that it be able to forward position military supplies in Thailand to facilitate resupply during a war in the Persian Gulf.[17]

The next stage of accommodation to Chinese power occurred in 1989. As it became clear to Vietnam that Soviet power was a wasting asset and that it was losing both its counterweight to Chinese power and the economic assistance necessary to wage war, it sought a rapid and humiliating peace in Cambodia. By 1991 Hanoi had formerly accepted Chinese terms for an end to the war, including full Vietnamese troop withdrawal, the symbolic removal of the Vietnamese puppet Hun Sen leadership, and the inclusion of the Khmer Rouge in the immediate postwar coalition government. Rather than resist Chinese power, Vietnam accommodated it.[18]

Cambodian accommodation was equally rapid and significant. Immediately after the signing of the 1991 Paris Accords, Hun Sen traveled to Beijing and established Sino-Cambodian cooperation. Then Phnom Penh sent Chea Sim, a senior and erstwhile strong anti-Chinese leader, to Beijing.[19] Now that Vietnam had withdrawn from Cambodia, Phnom Penh experienced both diplomatic freedom and heightened danger from Chinese power. It responded by returning to its Cold War formula of accommodating Chinese power to ensure its security. For its part, China welcomed the Cambodian puppet government's about-face. Now that Vietnam had been defeated and the Soviet Union had collapsed, Chinese leaders did not care who ruled Cambodia, as long as he accommodated Chinese hegemony.

In the post–Cold War era, Vietnam and Cambodia have continued to accommodate Chinese power. Although Hanoi seemed to welcome the suggestion of Bill Clinton's administration that Secretary of Defense William Cohen visit Vietnam, the visit was difficult to arrange and was delayed. Vietnam was apparently responding to Chinese displeasure at the development of U.S.–Vietnam military ties. Rather than offend its powerful neighbor, Hanoi delayed until the proper moment. China and Vietnam have also made progress in demarcating their border. They signed a new border agreement in December 1999, and by 2003 they had completed removal of land mines and made major progress in surveying and demarcating the border.[20] In 2000 Hanoi and Beijing reached agreement to demarcate their territorial waters, including the economic zone and continental shelf in the contentious Beibu (Tonkin) Gulf.[21] From the 1960s to the late 1980s, in the context of growing Soviet political and strategic presence in Hanoi, Beijing and Hanoi held long and fruitless negotiations over the increasingly contentious border. But in the post–Cold War era, in the context of Chinese hegemony over Indochina, Beijing is willing to negotiate, and Hanoi, despite its apparent dissatisfaction with the negotiations, has had no choice but to reach agreement with China.[22]

Chinese influence in Cambodia has been equally prominent. Phnom Penh has looked to Beijing as it has managed the difficult issue of the prosecution of the Khmer Rouge leadership for genocide. Cambodia has faced international pressure to hold public trials under United Nations auspices. Because China shares with Phnom Penh an interest in keeping the United Nations out of Cambodian politics, it has enabled Cambodian leaders to resist international pressure, including U.S. linkage of economic assistance to Cambodian concessions, to hold Khmer Rouge leaders accountable for their atrocities. China has been the ultimate arbiter of Cambodian factionalism, rather than the United Nations or the United States.

Finally, accommodation is evident in Burma's China policy. Burma has relied on China for purchases of military jets, naval vessels, and various artillery equipment. In return, Burma has expanded military cooperation with China. Just as Japan and the maritime Southeast Asian nations, including Singapore and the Philippines, have accommodated U.S. power by offering the United States expanded naval and ground force access to their countries, Burma has accommodated Chinese hegemony by offering the Chinese navy access to its port facilities at Sittwe and thus improved access to the India Ocean. The Chinese navy may not be an imposing force, and Burma's facilities may be primitive, but the trends in Burma's China policy are nonetheless revealing.

On mainland Northeast Asia, the signs of Chinese power and influence are no less significant. During the Cold War Chinese influence over Pyongyang was limited by the Soviet Union's power presence in Northeast Asia and its contribution to North Korea's security and economy. When the Soviet Union collapsed in 1991, China emerged as North Korea's sole strategic and economic benefactor. China provides North Korea with enough food, energy supplies, and daily basic commodities to ensure a subsistence-level existence for the North Korean population and political and social stability. China also fulfills a basic deterrent function. Without the Chinese security guarantee, North Korea would be far more vulnerable to U.S. and South Korean use of force. The Pyongyang regime is thus totally dependent on China for survival. Without Chinese assistance, it would have already collapsed from either economic failure or from military defeat. North Korea's foreign policy and its nuclear weapons program may encounter Chinese opposition, but North Korean independence reflects Chinese reluctance to use its influence, not the absence of influence.

China's influence in South Korea, though not yet rivaling American influence, is also significant; China plays a critical role in South Korean security. Since the normalization of diplomatic relations between China and South Korea in 1992, economic relations have grown dramatically and have yielded China considerable influence. In 2001 China became South Korea's number-one target for direct foreign investment. As South Korean labor costs have risen, South Korean firms have moved their production facilities to China. Equally significant, in 2002 China and Hong Kong became South Korea's largest export market.[23] China now exercises greater economic leverage over South Korea than does the United States. Military trends are also important. The United States remains South Korea's most important strategic partner, reflected in the U.S.–South Korea Mutual Defense Treaty and in the bases and troops the United States has in South Korea. Nonetheless, South Korea has come to depend as much on China as on the United States to manage the North Korean threat; it relies on the combination of good relations with Beijing and Beijing's influence over Pyongyang and on the U.S. deterrent posture to avert war on the Korean Peninsula. Moreover, South Korean leaders must take into account China's improved land-based military capabilities and growing power on the Korean Peninsula, as well as the prospect of a united Korea in which Seoul will make foreign policy in the context of a common border with China.

These trends in Chinese power on the Korean Peninsula are reflected in the diplomacy in 2002–2003 over North Korea's nuclear weapons program. Efforts by the United States to rely on coercive diplomacy to obtain North Korean concessions failed, in part, because Washington could no longer compel South Korean compliance with U.S. policy. No longer solely dependent on the United States for its security, and sensitive to Chinese power, Seoul cooperated with China to seek a negotiated solution to the crisis. In the midst of the most serious Korean crisis since the Korean War, Seoul distanced itself from Washington and enjoyed closer relations with Beijing than with Washington. Despite considerable U.S. pressure, Seoul continued to advocate a high-level dialogue with North Korean leaders and, in cooperation with Beijing, opposed U.S. efforts to impose international economic sanctions on North Korea. North Korean leaders, observing the cracks in the U.S.–South Korea alliance and confident in China's strategic support, resisted U.S. pressure to abandon its nuclear program.

Most revealing was China's role as host for the 2003 U.S.–North Korea negotiations. Through the 1990s China had retained its influence in Pyongyang while benefiting from the early stages of South Korean bandwagoning. It has thus gradually assumed the responsibility of the great power arbiter of the North–South conflict. U.S. plans to remove its troops from the demilitarized zone and to reduce its overall troop presence in South Korea have not created this strategic transformation on the Korean Peninsula, but they will hasten it. The removal of the U.S. trip-wire force in the demilitarized zone and reduced U.S. military presence in South Korea cannot but diminish South Korea's confidence in the U.S. commitment to resist a North Korean attack. Seoul will respond to its heightened insecurity by working even closer with China to manage the North Korean threat.

Under Chinese hegemony, a Pax Sinica exists on mainland East Asia that poses a stark contrast to the violence of the Cold War. Coinciding with the post-Cold War Pax Americana in maritime East Asia, since 1989 and the resolution of the conflict in Indochina there has been peace on mainland East Asia. The traditional rivalries that contributed to the succession of wars in Indochina from 1945 to 1989 continue to exist. Cambodians do not trust Vietnamese intentions and remain wary of holding negotiations over the contentious border. For its part, Hanoi remains intent on establishing some influence over Cambodia, a potentially troublesome neighbor that has good relations with China, Vietnam's dangerous northern neighbor. Thai–Cambodian relations also remain difficult, reflecting power disparities similar to those between Vietnam and Cambodia. The violent anti-Thailand demonstrations in Phnom Penh in January 2003 and the ensuing, yet brief, Cambodian–Thai tension reveal ongoing Cambodian concern for Thai territorial ambitions and Thai impatience with Cambodian nationalism, as well as the potential for heightened Thai–Cambodian conflict. The conflicts on mainland Southeast Asia have not been resolved; the great power conflicts that overlaid them simply no longer exist. Chinese hegemony has replaced the succession of rivalries in Indochina between China and France, China and the United States, and China and the Soviet Union. Accompanying Chinese hegemony is peace.

Pax Sinica is also evident on mainland Northeast Asia. Tension between the United States and North Korea escalated in 2002–2003 over North Korea's nuclear weapons program, but relations between Seoul and Pyongyang have been better than ever before and have showed few signs of reversing direction. Confident that China seeks good relations with South Korea and that it will restrain North Korean aggression, the South Korean leadership sees the reduced threat of an unprovoked North Korean attack, whether or not North Korea possesses weapons of mass destruction. In this strategic context, a succession of South Korean leaders have pursued the "sunshine policy," despite U.S. misgivings. The result has been improved economic relations between North Korea and South Korea and greater communication between the two governments. As Chinese economic and strategic influence has grown since the early 1990s, the Korean Peninsula has become increasingly stable.

Taiwan and the Peace of East Asia

The Taiwan issue is emerging as the sole hot spot in East Asia. Whereas maritime East Asia and Indochina are stable and the political trends on the

Korean Peninsula seem to be moving in the right direction, conflict over Taiwan remains deadlocked. Taiwan and the mainland are significantly expanding economic relations, and negotiations to promote direct cross-strait trade are making progress. Nonetheless, the military situation remains tense. Beijing continues to deploy short-range missiles across from Taiwan and to purchase Russian military equipment in preparation for a possible war with the United States over Taiwan. Washington, also preparing for a war, continues to increase its air and naval forces in the Western Pacific, sell advanced weaponry to Taiwan, and expand military relations with Taiwan. Meanwhile, Taiwan–mainland differences over the "one-China" issue, the central issue have deepened as Taiwan's leadership seems increasingly committed to formal independence for Taiwan.

The Taiwan Strait remains a contentious region because it is the one region in East Asia where there are serious conflicts of interest and where each of the great powers exercises relatively equal and stable influence. First, China wants unification, and Taiwan wants independence. This is a nondivisible, zero-sum issue; resolution requires a winner and a loser. Second, neither China nor the United States exercises hegemony over the Taiwan Strait. Because Taiwan is both an island and close to the mainland, its security is subject to U.S. maritime capabilities and to Chinese land-based capabilities. In this context, peace cannot depend on the will of a single great power. Rather, it depends on the strategic relationship between the two great powers and their allies and whether any of the actors are likely to use war to pursue their interests. Ultimately, peace in East Asia depends on the deterrence dynamics across the Taiwan Strait.

Not all militarized relationships are the same. Some are more likely to lead to war than others. The deterrence dynamics in the Taiwan Strait are particularly strong. None of the actors in the Taiwan conflict consider war a viable instrument to challenge the status quo. There is robust deterrence in the Taiwan conflict, and continued peace in East Asia is likely.[24]

China's interest in using force to achieve unification is minimal. The status quo is not its preference, but Chinese leaders have endured Taiwanese political autonomy for more than fifty years. Moreover, China has much at stake in maintaining a peaceful East Asia. During the past twenty years, in the context of cooperation with the United States and its East Asian neighbors, China has modernized its economy and military and expanded its political influence throughout East Asia. Thus, to use force against Taiwan for unification, Chinese leaders must be convinced that the costs can be minimized. Yet just the opposite is true: Chinese leaders assume that the United States would intervene against Chinese forces in a mainland–Taiwan war and that the United States would inflict unacceptable costs on Chinese interests.

Threats by the United States to intervene in a mainland–Taiwan war are credible in Beijing. Chinese leaders believe that the U.S. willingness to defend Taiwan reflects a fifty-year security commitment and the attendant implications for the credibility of U.S. commitments to its other East Asian security partners and for a long-term U.S. regional presence. They recognize that the dispatch of two U.S. aircraft carriers to the vicinity of Taiwan during the 1996 Taiwan Strait confrontation further committed the United States to the defense of Taiwan. Subsequent and ongoing U.S. arms sales to Taiwan further signal to China the U.S. commitment to Taiwan. Moreover, Chinese leaders understand that U.S. domestic politics will constrain U.S. flexibility in a crisis, insofar as public opposition to communism and support for democracy will combine to encourage intervention in support of Taiwan.

Chinese leaders also assume that U.S. intervention would impose extreme costs to vital Chinese interests. Analysts from the People's Liberation Army (PLA) have studied U.S. military operations against Iraq in 1991, Serbia in 1999, and Afghanistan in 2001. They understand that the Chinese navy would be vulnerable to advanced long-range high-accuracy U.S. weaponry. A senior Chinese military officer has lectured his troops that China's likely adversary in a local war would possess high-tech equipment that could neutralize China's ability to rely on manpower to defeat the enemy. A civilian analyst has noted that in a war in China's coastal region the adversary could "make full use of its superiority in air and naval long-range, large-scale, high-accuracy weaponry."[25] A military analyst was more direct, explaining that not only would such superior capabilities seriously restrict China's ability to seize and maintain sea control around a "large island"; it would also pose a major threat to China's coastal political, economic, and military targets.[26] Experts at China's Air Force Command College have concluded that an aerial attack "revolution" has occurred and that a "generation gap" exists between the high-tech aerial attack capabilities of the United States and the "stagnant" air defense capabilities of less advanced countries, causing a "crisis" in air defense.[27]

Thus China cannot expect to win a war for unification and must expect that the potential military and civilian costs would be enormous. The economic costs would also be great, including diversion of scarce economic resources to military development in a prolonged postwar cold war economy and reduced access to global markets, investment capital, and technology. Moreover, military defeat and economic downturn would most likely mean the demise of the Chinese Communist Party. Thus, even should Chinese leaders believe that China could sink a major U.S. surface ship, such as an aircraft carrier, and inflict significant casualties on U.S. forces, given the good possibility and enormous potential costs of U.S. retaliation, such an asymmetric tactic cannot provide Chinese leaders the confidence to launch a war. Thus, the combination of the risk and cost of U.S. intervention and the low cost to Chinese interests of continuing to endure the Taiwan–mainland status quo creates robust deterrence of Chinese use of force for unification.

The other potential source of war is a Taiwanese declaration of sovereign independence, leading to mainland military retaliation and a possible U.S.–China conflict. But Taiwan has endured the diplomatic fiction of PRC rule over Taiwan for more than thirty years. The status quo is not its preference, but before declaring independence it must be convinced that the costs of revising the status quo are acceptable. Similar to the mainland's evaluation of the U.S. deterrent posture, Taiwan's assessment of the mainland's deterrent posture is that the Chinese retaliatory threat is credible and that the cost to Taiwan of war with the mainland is unacceptable.

The result of China's fifty-year commitment to unification is that the political legitimacy and survival of the Chinese leadership are attached to its commitment to resist Taiwanese independence. As one Chinese analyst argues, "No Chinese politician, strategist, or anyone else will dare to abandon the objective of making Taiwan return and the unification of the motherland."[28] Failure to respond to a declaration of independence would also challenge China's international reputation to use force to defend other vital Chinese interests, thus affecting its border security and the threat posed by independence movements around its periphery. Moreover, the mainland has developed a reputation for resolve regarding the Taiwan issue. Despite the risk of U.S. intervention and of a U.S.–China crisis, in March 1996, the PLA launched DF-15 missiles into coastal waters within the vicinity of Kaohsiung, Taiwan's major port city, to underscore its will to oppose Taiwanese independence and thus reverse the trend in U.S. policy toward Taiwan and in Lee Teng-hui's independence policy.

The cost to Taiwan of PRC retaliation would be massive. China's DF-15 missiles are not very accurate and possess minimal war-fighting capability. Nonetheless, PRC attacks on Taiwan would cause panic in Taiwan's society and punish its economy and political system. In 1996, when China amassed its troops across from Taiwan and carried out military exercises in the vicinity of Taiwan, the Taiwanese stock market fell by 25 percent.[29] Moreover, Chinese missiles are inexpensive and in close proximity to Taiwan, so that missile-defense systems cannot offset Taiwan's vulnerability to PRC missiles.[30] The mainland could also declare a blockade around the island. The mere announcement of such a blockade, regardless of PRC enforcement capabilities, would dramatically curtail commercial shipping to Taiwan. Finally, the mainland could directly retaliate against Taiwan's economic interests. In 2002 the mainland became Taiwan's most important export market. In the first seven months of 2002, Taiwanese exports to China grew by nearly 31 percent, whereas its exports to the United States fell by 6.5 percent. Moreover, in 2002 the mainland became the leading production center of overseas Taiwanese investors. Nearly 55 percent of Taiwanese overseas investment is located on the mainland, and Taiwan's largest corporations, including its high-tech manufacturers, are moving production to the mainland.[31]

Chinese military and economic retaliation against a Taiwanese declaration of independence and the ensuing international and domestic crisis would inevitably cause political instability on Taiwan. In a mainland-Taiwan war, not only would the Taiwanese economy suffer; the survival of Taiwan's democratic political system would be in jeopardy. Moreover, having started the war in an effort to achieve independence, the resulting economic and political instability could compel Taiwan to accept Beijing's demands for unification. Thus, the cost to Taiwan of mainland retaliation against a declaration of independence would be the loss of its economic prosperity, its democracy, and its long-term aspiration for sovereignty.

The mainland's deterrent capability is reflected in Taiwan public opinion. Since 1997, public opinion surveys have shown that support for an immediate declaration of Taiwanese independence has declined since the high of only 7.4 percent in mid-1998. The Taiwanese public understands that mainland retaliation would be both costly and likely. If there is a source of instability, it is the high-risk behavior of Taiwan's leader, Chen Shui-bian, rather than Taiwan's democratic politics or an emerging "Taiwan identity." Chen seems intent on moving Taiwan toward formal independence, despite the danger of war. Nonetheless, his challenge to the status quo remains constrained by both PRC power and U.S. pressure to maintain the status quo.[32]

Conclusion

East Asia is the world's most peaceful region. To achieve this result, the region experienced nearly forty years of uninterrupted war as well as two cold wars — first the U.S.–China cold war, then the Sino–Soviet cold war. The outcome of these cold wars is the current peaceful order in East Asia. After forty years of turmoil and violence, the two remaining great powers in East Asia — the United States and China — have ordered East Asia into two distinct spheres of influence. In each sphere, one great power holds sway and has ordered relations without the interference of the other great power. In the absence of great power rivalry, there is stability. The one exception is the Taiwan issue. In this case, the risk of war is posed by a great power rivalry that overlays a local conflict, which reflects unrealized Chinese and Taiwanese interests. Yet even this exception to the regional order is manageable. Mutual deterrence across the Taiwan Strait maintains stability.

East Asia is an exception to the post–Cold War trend of U.S. hegemony and Pax Americana. On the one hand, there is peace. On the other hand, there is not U.S. hegemony. Nonetheless, the sources of the East Asian peace suggest the sources of peace more generally. East Asia is peaceful because the power politics of East Asia, reflecting the pattern of military and economic influence, are conducive to peace. There are no region-wide functional international organizations in East Asia. ASEAN is the only subregional organization that approaches functionality. Although it has existed since the mid-1960s, its inclusion of Vietnam, Laos, and Cambodia occurred after peace came to Indochina, that is, after the demise of the Soviet Union and the emergence of Chinese hegemony. Broad-based ASEAN membership did not contribute to regional stability but reflected the prior emergence of regional stability.

Similarly, there is an absence of common ideologies and of U.S. or Chinese soft power in East Asia. China's political-economic system and ideology have little in common with the political-economic systems and ideologies of the two Koreas, of Thailand, or of any of the Indochinese countries. Similarly, there is little in common in the political-economic systems of the United States and of Singapore, Malaysia, and Indochina. U.S. culture, including its dominant religions, barely resonate in any of the cultures of East Asia.

There is peace in East Asia despite the absence of effective international organizations, common political and economic systems, soft power, and cultural affinity. But what East Asia lacks, other regions lack as well. U.S. political and economic institutions and U.S. culture are just as alien to much of the Balkans, the Middle East, and South Asia as they are to East Asian countries. What distinguishes East Asia from most of the world are the political sources of peace. The United States may be the only great power in every other region of the world, but it is not a constant military presence on the ground in these regions. It is a naval power not only in East Asia but also everywhere outside the Western Hemisphere. Thus, its power is neither constant nor omnipotent in mainland theaters along the entire perimeter of Eurasia. Nor has the United States created economic dependency in these regions, reflecting the backward economies and/or trade policies of the local actors or the politics of oil, which create mutual offsetting dependency relationships that limit U.S. power. The United States may not confront a challenger, but neither does it enjoy such military or economic supremacy over the local powers that it can impose a regional order.

In contrast, in their respective spheres of influence in East Asia, China and the United States possess omnipresent and even omnipotent military power. U.S. naval power is present and effective against the maritime countries; China's land power is present and effective against its neighbors all along its periphery. And both China and the United States possess significant economic leverage over their respective security partners. This combination of overwhelming economic and military supremacy allows each power to impose a peaceful order in its own sphere and together to establish a peaceful region-wide order. Not American hegemony, but a U.S.–China peace, reigns in East Asia.

That the peace of East Asia reflects the traditional politics of the great powers does not mean it is any less stable or less beneficial to the region. The fact that the region is at peace is sufficient to welcome the sources, no matter how Paleolithic they may seem. The challenge for the post–Cold War era is to apply the lessons of East Asia, including those of the Cold War, to other regions, and thus understand the political sources of enduring conflict and of prolonged peace.

Notes

1. *Christian Science Monitor*, June 27, 2003.
2. U.S. Department of State, *World Military Expenditures and Arms Transfers* (Washington, DC: U.S. Department of State, 2002), pp. 67, 79, 99.
3. U.S. Department of Defense, *Annual Report to the President and the Congress*, 2002, chap. 5; Nathan Hodge, "Navy Basing Subs in Guam," *Defense Week Daily Update*, October 1, 2002.
4. Owen R. Cote Jr., *The Future of the Trident Force: Enabling Access in Access-Constrained Environments* (Cambridge: Security Studies Program, Massachusetts Institute of Technology, 2002); U.S. Department of Defense, *Quadrennial Defense Review Report*, 2001, chap. 4; Robert Aronson, "SSGN: A 'Second Career' for the Boomer Force," Undersea Warfare 2, no. 2 (Winter 1999), http://www.chinfo.navy.mil/navpalib/cno/n87/usw/issue_6/ssgn.html.
5. Jim Mannion, "Pentagon Moves Cruise Missiles to Guam," *Space Daily*, http://www.spacedaily.com/news/missiles-00d.html.
6. Adam J. Hebert, "Footholds on the Asian Rim," *Air Force* 85, no. 11 (November 2002), http://www.afa.org/magazine/Nov2002/1102rim.asp.
7. On the Chinese navy, see Bernard D. Cole, *The Great Wall at Sea: China's Navy Enters the Twenty-First Century* (Annapolis, MD: Naval Institute Press, 2001). On PRC interests in additional Kilos, see John Pomfret, "China to Buy 8 More Russian Submarines," *Washington Post*, June 25, 2002, p. 15.
8. Japanese statistics on Japan's exports to the United States and China are at http://www.customs.go.jp/toukei/info/index_e.htm. Japanese statistics on Japanese direct foreign investment are at http://www.mof.jp/english/fdi/ 2001b_2.htm.
9. ASEAN trade statistics are at http://202.154.12.3/trade/publicview.asp.
10. See Yoichiro Sato, "Japan's Naval Dispatch Plans Expand the Envelope," *Pacific Forum/CFIA, PacNet*, no. 4A (January 24, 2003).

11. U.S. Department of Defense, *Annual Report to the President and the Congress*, 2002, chap. 5.
12. "U.S. Marines Arrive in Philippines," Associated Press, February 1, 2003.
13. U.S. Department of Defense, *Quadrennial Defense Report; Statement of Admiral Dennis C. Blair, Commander in Chief, U.S. Pacific Command*, before the House International Relations Committee, Subcommittee on East Asia and the Pacific and Subcommittee on Middle East and South Asia, February 27, 2002; Thomas E. Ricks and Walter Pincus, "Pentagon Plans Major Changes in U.S. Strategy," *Washington Post*, May 7, 2001, p. 1; James Dao, "Army to Move Some Weapons Out of Europe," *New York Times*, August 31, 2001, p. 16; *Straits Times*, June 4, 2002.
14. On confrontation and China, see J. A. C. Mackie, *Konfrontasi: The Indonesia-Malaysia Dispute, 1963-1966* (London: Oxford University Press, 1974); David P. Mozingo, *Chinese Policy Toward Indonesia, 1949-1967* (Ithaca, NY: Cornell University Press, 1975); Michael Leifer, *Indonesia's Foreign Policy* (London: George Allen & Unwin, 1983).
15. Donald W. Mitchell, *A History of Russian and Soviet Sea Power* (New York: Macmillan, 1974), pp. 204–210, 216–233; chaps. 11, 12.
16. On improvement in People's Liberation Army training, see June Teufel Dryer, "The New Officer Corps: Implications for the Future," *China Quarterly*, no. 146 (June 1996), pp. 315–35; Dennis J. Blasko, Philip T. Klapkis, and John F. Corbett Jr., "Training Tomorrow's PLA: A Mixed Bag of Tricks," *China Quarterly*, no. 146 (June 1996), pp. 448–524.
17. Elaine Sciolino, "With Thai Rebuff, U.S. Defers Plan for Navy Depot in Asia" *New York Times*, November 12, 1994, p. 1.
18. See Robert S. Ross, "China and the Cambodian Peace Process: The Value of Coercive Diplomacy," *Asian Survey* 31, no. 12 (December 1991).
19. See Xinhua, in Foreign Information Broadcast Service (FBIS), FBIS/China, July 13, 1992, pp. 13–14.
20. Xinhua, December 31, 1999, in FBIS, doc. no. FTS199911231000448; Agence France Presse (AFP), January 24, 2003, in FBIS, AFS doc. no. CPP20030124000012; Qin Jize, "Mines Removed along China–Vietnam Border," *China Daily*, January 25, 2003, in FBIS, Doc. No. CPP20030125000034.
21. Xinhua, December 24, 2000, FBIS, AFS doc. no. CPP20001224000072.
22. Note that Vietnam waited more than two and a half years before finally publishing the 1999 border agreement. See AFP, September 16, 2002, in FBIS, AFS doc. no. CPP20020916000099. On the course of the negotiations during the 1970s, see *The Indochina Tangle: China's Vietnam Policy, 1975-1979* (New York: Columbia University Press, 1988).
23. "China Becomes South Korea's Number One Investment Target," *China Daily*, February 2, 2002, http://www1.chinadaily.com.cn/news/ 2002-02-05/55641.html; "China Emerges as Biggest Export Market of South Korea," *People's Daily*, November 14, 2002, http://english.peopledaily.com.cn/200211/14/eng20021114_106796.shtml. Also see James Brooke, "Korea Feeling Pressure as China Grows," *New York Times*, January 8, 2003, p. W1.
24. This section draws on Robert S. Ross, "Navigating the Taiwan Strait: Deterrence, Escalation Dominance, and U.S.-China Relations," *International Security* 27, no. 2 (Fall 2002).
25. Zhang Wannian, *Dangdai Shijie Junshi yu Zhongguo Guofang* [Contemporary world military affairs and Chinese national defense] (Beijing: Junshi Kexue Chubanshe, 1999), pp.183–84; Chu Shulong, "Zhongguo de Guojia Liyi, Guojia Liliang, he Guojia Zhanlue" [China's national interest, national strength, and national strategy], *Zhanlue yu Guanli*, no. 4 (1999), p. 15.
26. Liu Yijian, *Zhi Haiquan yu Haijun Zhanlue* [Command of the sea and naval strategy], p.146. See also Zhang, *Dangdai Shijie Junshi yu Zhongguo Guofang* (Beijing: Zhonggong Zhongyang Dangxiao Chubanshe, 2000), p. 100. Chinese comparison of the Gulf War andthe war in Kosovo underscores that deserts do not provide the cover necessary to defeat information dominance. The implication for China's surface fleet is clear. See Zhao Zhongqiang and Peng Chencang, *Xinxi Zhan yu Fan Xinxi Zhan: Zema Da* [Information war and anti-information war: How to fight] (Beijing: Zhongguo Qingnian Chubanshe, 2001), pp. 42–44.
27. "Kongjun Zhihui Xueyuan Zhuanjia Tan—21 Shiji de Fangkong Geming" [Air Force Command College experts discuss—the twenty-first-century revolution in air defense], *Jiefang Junbao*, May 16, 2001, p. 9; Yu Kaitang and Cao Shuxin, eds., *Tezhong Kongxi Mubiao yu Dui Kang Lilun Yanjiu* [Theoretical research on special air-attack targets and counterattack]

(Beijing: Guo-fang Daxue Chubanshe, 2000); Wang Honqing and Zhang Yingyt, *Zhanyi Xue* [*Science of campaigns*] (Beijing: National Defense University Press), chap. 12; Wang Qiming and Chen Feng, eds., *Daying Gao Jishu Jubu Zhanzheng: Junguan Bidu Shouci* [*Winning high-technology local war: Required reading handbook for military officers*] (Beijing: Junshi Yiwen Chubanshe, 1997). See also Kenneth W. Allen, "China and the Use of Force: The Role of the PLA Air Force," photocopy.

28. Wang Yizhou, "Mianxiang 21 Shiji de Zhongguo Waijiao: San Xuqiu de Xunqiu ji qi Pingheng" [Chinese diplomacy facing the twenty-first century: The search for the three musts and their balance], *Zhanlue yu Guanli* [*Strategy and Management*], no. 6 (1999), p. 20.

29. Edward Gargan, "Long-Term Forecast for Taiwan Remains Upbeat," *New York Times*, March 22, 1996, p. 35; Sheila Tefft, "Taiwan Moves to Restore Shaken Investor Confidence," *Christian Science Monitor*, April 1, 1996, p. 9; Steven Mufson, "China-Taiwan Conflict 'In Remission, Not Resolved,'" *Washington Post*, April 22, 1996, p. 17.

30. James. M. Lindsay and Michael E. O'Hanlon, *Defending America: The Case for Limited National Missile Defense* (Washington, DC: Brookings Institution, 2001), pp. 123–30. On Taiwan's diminished interest in missile defense, see James Mulvenon, *Missile Defenses and the Taiwan Scenario*, report no. 44 (Washington, DC: Henry L. Stimson Center, 2002); *Lien-ho Pao*, July 27, 2002, in FBIS, July 29, 2002.

31. The 2002 trade statistics are from the Taiwan Board of Foreign Trade; Central News Agency, September 15, 2002, FBIS Doc. no. CPP20020915000025; Central News Agency, September 28, 2002, FBIS Doc. no. CPP20020928000044; Central News Agency, August 7, 2002, FBIS Doc. no. CPP20020807000167. The investment statistics are in Central News Agency, August 7, 2002, FBIS Doc. no. CPP20020807000167; Central News Agency, October 21, 2002, FBIS Doc. no. CPP20021022000004.

32. Chart of opinion polls commissioned by the Taiwan government retrieved from http://www.mac.gov.tw/english/POS/9108/9108e_1.gif. On Taiwan identity, see Chu Yun-han, "Taiwanese Nationalism and Its Implications: Testing the Worst-Case Scenario," *Asian Survey*, vol. 44, no. 4 (July/August 2004).

CHAPTER 6
Japan's Ambition for Normal Statehood

TAKASHI INOGUCHI

The Denial of Normal Statehood and the Embracing of Defeat

States in the international system have varying degrees of sovereign power, and sovereignty has many dimensions. The sovereign power of particular states can vary dramatically over time. Furthermore, many dispute the conventional Westphalian notion of sovereignty (Krasner 1999). Kenneth Waltz defines sovereignty as the ability to retain autonomy over the fate of one's state and singles out the possession of strategic nuclear forces as a fundamental means to this end (Alker, Biersteker, and Inoguchi 1985). On this view there are only two normal states: the United States and to a lesser extent the Russian Federation. The European Union has deepened its authority to coordinate economic policy among member countries since January 2001. The result is that its member states have lost the sovereign power to issue currency and exercise exclusive management of their national economies. In this sense there is no normal state in the European Union. Not adhering to such narrow definitions of itself as the above two, I define normal statehood in a conventional Westphalian manner. In other words, I refer to a state's basic authority and the extent to which it can exercise autonomy in the management of its economic and security affairs.

Normal statehood was denied to Japan in the period between 1945 and 1952 (Dower 1999). It is common for regime change to occur after comprehensive military defeat (Russett and Stein 1972). Japan surrendered unconditionally to the Allied Powers, led by the United States, to end World War II. The result was military occupation by the Allied Powers until Japan regained its formal independence in 1952. Since then, however, the United States has maintained a permanent military presence on Japanese territory under the auspices of the United States–Japan Security Treaty. Japan's new constitution, which was mostly drafted in 1946, abrogates the use of force in the settlement of disputes. The Security Treaty, drafted mostly in 1950, serves as a linchpin that sustains Japan in war and diplomacy (Inoguchi 2001). These initial institutional and spiritual constraints, established during the seven-year period of occupation, mean that Japan has not possessed normal statehood for more than half a century. In the following pages I will examine Japan's ambition for normal statehood as exhibited since the end of the Cold War. As the issue of normal statehood has been intermittently laid bare most clearly in Japan's alliance with the United States, this chapter focuses on the Japan–U.S. security alliance and Japan's internal and external adjustments to its changing environments.

First, in order to be clear about the range of "normalcy" Japan aspires to achieve, I will present the three models of "normal" partnership with the United States that might be possible for Japan to have. Looking at British, German, and French partnerships with the United States and examining the key features of their partnerships with the United States, namely, special relationship, regional enbeddedness, and autonomy, respectively, I will illustrate the intricate subtle complexity of Japan's yearning for normal statehood, which would be in congruence with its alliance with the United States.

Second, after specifying the range of normalcy to be examined, I will turn to three of those issues that have been brought up in Japan in relation to normal statehood, namely, the role of force, the recurring salience of history, and the exercise of leadership. These three concepts need to be examined closely, as they constitute parts of what are widely regarded as the conventional Westphalian conception of normal statehood. I will specify the relationships between the use of force, the recurrent salience of history, and the lack of leadership exercise, all of which are discussed in the Japanese context of yearnings for normal statehood.

Third, I will give three recent events, the naval operations in the Indian Ocean, the free trade agreement initiative, and the engagement with Pyongyang, that illustrate how the three parameters of the use of force, the recurrent salience of history, and the exercise of leadership have been interwoven into Japan's action and inaction as these three events unfolded.

Fourth, after all these examinations, I will reflect on the three parameters in the Japanese equation of normal statehood, with an eye at an emerging profile of Japan's normal statehood and partnership with the United States under the new Pax Americana.

Three Models of Normalcy (Inoguchi, 2004)

It is likely that the Pax Americana will endure for some time to come, like the Pax Romana (Nye 2002; Nau et al. 2002). As such, any discussion of the extent to which Japan can regain normal statehood must be located in the context of Japan's relationship with the United States (Armitage et al. 2000; Vogel 2002; Ikenberry and Inoguchi, 2003). Here, alliance has arguably been replaced by partnership (Friedman 2002). As Francis Fukuyama (1995) argues, fundamental differences in values and institutions have vanished since the end of the Cold War. In post–Cold War global politics, trust has gained increasing salience. When trust is ascertained, then partnership can be created. Befittingly, the key theme of the World Economic Summit in Davos in 2003 was trust. When I refer to the U.S.–Japan relationship, the idea of a transition from alliance to partnership should be kept firmly in mind. I have come up with the following three models, which I hope will be of use in surveying and illustrating the range of normal partnerships with the United States that it might be possible for Japan to consider. I will look in turn at the following models: (a) British, (b) German, and (c) French.

The British Model

The key idea is that of a special relationship. Japan conceives itself as having special bilateral relations with the United States. Slightly more than a decade ago Ambassador Mike Mansfield characterized the U.S. relationship with Japan as its "most important bilateral relationship—bar none." This phrase was often deployed as the defining concept of Japan–U.S. relations during the 1990s. Britain also conceives of itself as having a special relationship with the United States. In policy recommendations proposed by Richard Armitage, the U.S.–United Kingdom model was recommended as the best model on which to build a future partnership between Japan and the United States (Armitage et al. 2000).

Japan and the United Kingdom share some significant commonalities:

1. Both conceive of themselves as distinctive and somewhat distant from their respective continental neighbors.

2. Both have high levels of economic interdependence with the United States and are embedded in the American pattern of economic relations.
3. Both have significant alliance links with the United States.

Since 9/11 the United States has drawn on the cooperation of a very wide-ranging number of partners from the antiterrorist coalition, rather than on a few close allies noted for their special relationship with the United States. It is true that the United Kingdom and to a lesser extent Australia have been regarded as reliable allies by the United States on many occasions since September 11, 2001. Indeed, the United Kingdom and Australia are qualitatively distinguished from Japan, in that the former two can take military action without being subject to the same constraints as Japan. It sometimes seems as if the United Kingdom and Australia act like America's mercenaries. This has provoked senior Japanese diplomats to remark that Japan is not as small as the United Kingdom (whose population size is half of Japan's) and does not feel it to be quite as necessary to fall into line so unquestioningly. As such, they are suggesting that the U.S.–United Kingdom model might not be so appropriate to the governing of a U.S.–Japan partnership. Japan was mentioned as a reliable ally a couple of times in the fall of 2001, but not after that. Rather, Japan has been lumped together with other members of the coalition against terrorism, in which other partners such as China and Russia loom much larger, a fact that Japan finds mildly disturbing.

Yet the prospect of American war with Iraq drew an ambivalent response from Japan. This is why Japan was mostly silent about the prospect of war with Iraq until Japan gave a speech at the United Nations after France and Germany took a very different position with regard to the postponement of the UN inspections in Iraq. Japan has made explicit that its position is more tightly aligned with the United States. There is, of course, an element of contradiction in Japan's staying out of a war that is so clearly important to America and yet still aspiring to be recognized as its most important bilateral partner. It is true that sending Self-Defense Force (SDF) troops into Iraq would arouse opposition at home. But sending state-of-the-art Aegis destroyers into the Indian Ocean, if not into the much closer Persian Gulf, is also argued by some to be both a prudent and gallant strategy for Japan to adopt. There is also a contradiction between the deftness and decisiveness of the initiatives taken on the Korean Peninsula and the indecisiveness and ambivalence demonstrated over the issue of potential war with Iraq. What is more, Japan acted on the North Korea issue after little consultation with the United States at the last moment.

Presumably, North Korea wanted to extract concessions from Japan bilaterally, while Japan wanted to create a diplomatic success domestically.

The German Model

The key idea here is regional embeddedness. Germany has been concealing itself within regional and international institutions such as the European Union and the North Atlantic Treaty Organization (NATO), adroitly aligning its national interests to broader regional and international interests. With its technocratic competence, rule-based steadiness, and economic surplus deployed in pursuit of higher purposes, Germany has been quite successful in rehabilitating itself within a context where it does not regenerate old security concerns. This notwithstanding, Germany is also able to take initiatives that suit its own purposes within the broader context of European governance. This can be seen in the European Union's eastern expansion and in the introduction of the single currency (Eberwein and Kaiser 2001).

Japan and Germany share some significant commonalities:

1. Their past experience as revisionist powers. In the words of Hans-Peter Schwartz (1985), Japan and Germany have progressed from *Machtbesessenheit* (self-aggrandizement before 1945) to *Machtvergessenheit* (an abstention from power politics after 1945). This experience, combined with significant economic strength, renders both significant global civilian powers (Maull 1990/1991).
2. Their strong alliances with the United States, sustained by a substantial American military presence.
3. Their strong economic ties with and economic embrace of their respective regional hinterlands.

Despite its firm economic embrace of Asia, at least until the Asian financial crisis of 1997, Japan has not been characterized as being strongly embedded within the region. First, Japan's traditional approach has been to conceive of Japan as somehow external to Asia. Thus, "Japan and Asia" sits well, just as "Britain and Europe" sits well (Inoguchi 1995). Second, China, which does not necessarily share basic norms and values with maritime East and Southeast Asia, has been on the rise, both in terms of economic might and military power. If Japan is to embed itself with Asia, Japan has to reshape itself with the much deeper linkage and alignment with China, a possibility that Japan is not willing to take, given its predominant thinking with an emphasis on freedom, democracy, human rights, free trade and the market economy, and strong alliance with the United

States. Until 1997 Asia could be characterized as "in Japan's embrace" (Hatch and Yamamura 1996), but since 1997 can more aptly be characterized as "lured by the China market" (Inoguchi 2002), albeit arguably still in Japan's embrace. China's offensive to lure foreign direct investment and conclude a region-wide free trade agreement has intensified since its accession to the World Trade Organization. Third, Japan's way of handling its historical legacy has not always been to the liking of other countries in the region. Japan's adherence to an American-certified interpretation of its modern history has been solid but has in recent times been partially diluted, due to both the passing of time and the rise of nationalism. But Japanese nationalism should not be exaggerated. The Japanese are much less likely than other Asians to conceive of national identity as their primary source of identity. Ninety-six to ninety-eight percent of South Koreans and Thais depict national identity as their primary source of identity, but only 60% of Japanese do the same (Inoguchi 2002b).

In the war against terrorism in Afghanistan, Japan and Germany, like most others, did their best to support the United States by disregarding precedents, bending interpretations, and sending military personnel to the Indian Ocean and Afghanistan, respectively. With the prospect of an American war with Iraq increasing, Gerhard Schroeder proclaimed that Germany would not participate. On September 17, 2002, Junichiro Koizumi visited North Korea, one of the members of the "axis of evil," and concluded a communiqué with Kim Jong Il. In this communiqué Japan acknowledged historical issues and pledged to extend compensation once diplomatic normalization is complete, while North Korea undertook to demonstrate its peaceful intentions, declaring that it would not seek to develop and maintain missiles and weapons of mass destruction. (One month later, Kim Jong Il admitted to James Kelley, Under Secretary of State for East Asia and the Pacific, that North Korea had been developing nuclear weapons until recently, which is quite contrary to what Kim Jong Il said to Junichiro Koizumi.) Depending on your view, the actions of Schroeder and Koizumi could be interpreted in two ways. They could be interpreted as constructive attempts to reduce tension and facilitate peaceful accommodation with axis of evil countries or as maverick self-interested acts that undermine the focus and integrity of America's policy of seeking disarmament, and ultimately regime change, in axis of evil countries.

One should also bear in mind the fact that the greater a state's regional embeddedness, the less straightforward its process of preference ordering. This is especially so when domestic antimilitarism norms are so strong, and especially in countries where the legacy of war has played such a pervasive role in the construction of contemporary national identity. The

United States is concerned that if Germany and Japan become more regionally embedded, this will push their foreign policy preference-ordering still further out of kilter with American concerns. Schroeder's flat refusal, during the election campaign, to participate in the war on Iraq and Koizumi's blitz summit diplomacy in Pyongyang were both in broad disharmony with the evolving American campaign against the axis of evil (Iraq, North Korea, and Iran). The United States ascribes differing degrees of significance to NATO and the Japan–U.S. Security Treaty. After 9/11, the United States found Europe decreasingly problematic. Its policy toward Europe has become more benign, if only because of the lack of threat from Russia and from its strategic nuclear forces. Instead the United States finds the Middle East and East Asia much more problematic and volatile, with each region having the potential to destabilize the peace and stability of the entire world. Here lies the qualitative difference in anti-U.S. or pro-U.S. policies that Germany and Japan can take. It has a lot to do with the difference between Europe's and East Asia's strategic importance to the United States. In this view, Japan has less latitude to adopt anti-U.S. policy than Germany, because of the greater contemporary significance for peace and security of the East Asian region.

The French Model

The key idea here is that of autonomy. Japan is a close ally and partner of the United States. But this alliance has its roots in an ultimatum, an all-out war, complete disarmament, occupation, and regime change. Given Japan's economic performance since World War II, it is only natural that it should seek more autonomy. France has recently asserted itself against the United States, even if only in a practical way. It has accomplished this through Jacques Chirac's deft and adroit maneuvering in the debates surrounding the passing of the UN Security Council Resolutions permitting the use of force against Iraq. This French self-assertion is something of which Japan is quietly envious, but very apprehensive about its self-destructive nature with respect to helping to divide Europe, to make the United Nations less effective, and to enhance the influence of the United States (Keeler and Schain 1996).

Japan and France share some significant commonalities:

1. Both are close allies of the United States.
2. Both have a strong interest in peaceful and prosperous regional relations. Japan is sandwiched by China and the United States, as is France by the United States and the United Kingdom, on the one hand, and by Germany and Russia on the other.

3. Both seek to cultivate a diverse range of diplomatic partners from outside their immediate spheres of activity, using such concepts as comprehensive security and the Francophone group, respectively.

Gaullism is attractive to Japan, as it essentially boils down to an assertion of autonomy. Through its tight alignment with the United States, Japan has placed all of its diplomatic eggs in one basket. This excessive alignment has generated a significant body of dissenting argument suggesting that Japan should strive for greater autonomy. Akira Morita and Shintaro Ishihara famously published a book to this effect, entitled *The Japan That Can Say No*. Prime Minister Ryutaro Hashimoto, in a speech in Washington, DC, suggested that converting all the Japanese-owned U.S. government bonds back to Japanese yen might lead Americans to think again about taking Japan for granted. Eisuke Sakakibara, Vice Minister for International Affairs at the Ministry of Finance, was openly defiant when his idea of setting up an Asian Monetary Fund in the wake of the Asian financial crisis was flatly rebuffed by his American counterpart, Lawrence Summers. Summers wryly noted that he thought wrongly that Sakakibara was a true friend. When this author interviewed him in 1997, his office was dominated by a picture of a militant Islamic Mujahedeen fighter brandishing a sword. The alleged beauty of the French model is that, in the words of Jacques Chirac, France is a true friend, in the sense that true friends will often give you advice that you do not want to hear before ultimately offering you their support. He also noted that sycophants will not do this, alluding perhaps to Tony Blair's United Kingdom.

The problem with the French model is that the Japanese leadership style is poles apart from the French. Japanese elites have not produced a Jacques Delor, a Pascal Lamy, or a Jacques Attali. These men all exercise a strong leadership role in an articulate, confident, and adroit fashion. The Japanese political system, as an essentially decentralized consensus-oriented system, tends either not to create, or perhaps more importantly not to reward, such a leadership style at the highest level (Inoguchi 2002a). Potential Japanese Gaullists endure great frustration as a result. However, Koizumi's articulate message and decisive response in support of the war against terrorism and his dramatic Pyongyang summit are not inconsistent with the French model of leadership and a French preparedness to pursue initiatives that might upset the United States.

Viewed from the United States, France and Japan are different, and as such should not be expected to attempt to achieve similar levels of autonomy from the United States. The key intermediary variable is the perceived value to the United States of the roles they both play in their respective regions. France is critical to the aggregation of unity and stability in

Europe, with the United Kingdom psychologically semi-detached from the Continent and Germany hampered by the institutional and historical constraints placed on its foreign policy initiatives, especially in the absence of a countervailing Soviet threat. France is perceived to be sufficiently critical to unity and stability in Europe so that the United States is prepared to grant it considerable autonomy in its diplomatic affairs. One might argue that French Gaullist policy seeking the autonomy of not only France but also a greater Europe stretching to Estonia and Cyprus collides with the interest of the United States, of NATO, and to a lesser extent of Germany in Central Eastern Europe, the Baltic, the Balkans, and the East Mediterranean.

Japan's role in East Asia is very different. Other than Japan, there is no country that the United States can count on as a key stabilizing power. China does not share core values and norms with the United States and the other leading, largely Western, liberal democracies that manage the international system. Korea is too small for the United States to count on. The Association of South East Asian Nations (ASEAN) is not only too small but also too fragmented and vulnerable. Hence the degree of autonomy the United States can afford to give to Japan is measurably smaller.

Japan's Return to Normal Statehood?: Three Possible Indicators

I now examine closely three events that suggest that Japan is moving toward normal statehood at the beginning of the twenty-first century: (a) Japan's naval operations in the Indian Ocean, (b) Japan's free trade agreement initiative, and (c) Japan's engagement with Pyongyang.

Naval Operations in the Indian Ocean

The events of September 11, 2001, were, of course, a shocking surprise for Japan as well as the United States and all other civilized countries. Both the public and lawmakers in Japan gave emphatic support to President George W. Bush as he announced a war on terrorism. As *Le Monde* editorialized at the time, "Nous sommes tous Americains." Flowers were laid high in front of the United States Embassy in Tokyo to commemorate those killed in the attacks. Ambassador Howard Baker expressed his heartfelt gratitude to the people and the government of Japan for recognizing and sharing the deep sorrow and anguish of Americans.

The Japanese government, led by Prime Minister Junichiro Koizumi, took swift and effective action and dispatched warships to the Indian Ocean to "show the flag" of Japan in the joint antiterrorist war in Afghanistan in 2001. Japan's self-assigned tasks there were primarily to fuel the bomber aircraft of the United States and the United Kingdom.

By not placing warships directly in combat zones for combat purposes, which is forbidden by law, the Japanese government was able to make a contribution without arousing substantial opposition in the National Diet, or among the public. The Japanese government's obsession in the aftermath of September 11 was an avoidance of Japan's perceived failure in the Gulf War of 1991. Then, the Japanese government contributed an enormous amount of money to the war effort, without its role being significantly acknowledged in the relevant official statement by the United States government (Inoguchi 1991).

This time Japan was hailed in one of the State Department statements as one of America's most valuable and trustworthy allies, along with the United Kingdom and Australia. It must be noted, however, that one of the statements by the chairman of the Joint Chiefs of Staff after the Afghanistan campaign did fail to mention Japan as a war ally. Only after the State Department's intervention in the announcement of the statement did the chairman mention Japan. Aside from the Japanese government's obsession about the Gulf War "mistake," Japan's action represented "two steps forward" in attaining normal statehood; Japan's navy played a vital role in the Indian Ocean.

At the same time, "one step backward" can be detected in the final decision. At the highest level of decision-making, lawmakers, represented by former secretary general of the Liberal Democratic Party Hiromu Nonaka, a staunch antimilitarist, opposed the deployment of Aegis-equipped warships that could detect and prevent missile attacks from ten sources simultaneously. These are state-of-the-art weapons with which the United States, Japan, and Spain are equipped. Instead, warships equipped with Airborne Warning and Control Systems (AWACS) were deployed, whose major roles are submarine detection and the fueling of bomber aircraft. This notwithstanding, Japan's naval operations in the Indian Ocean marked a significant departure from the past. In Cambodia in 1991–1992, 250 SDF troops were sent for peacekeeping operations (Ikeda 1996). In the Gulf War of 1991, the SDF were sent to conduct postcombat mine-sweeping operations. In East Timor since 1999, 750 SDF troops were sent for peacekeeping and building operations. These are, of course, positive developments, but they do not come close to the Rubicon of engagement in military combat. In the war on terrorism, the SDF flirted with this Rubicon.

Another noteworthy feature of Japan's response is that opposition to Japan's naval operations was minimal, both at home and abroad. Ten years before, during the Gulf War, vehement opposition to Japan's potential military involvement was expressed in the National Diet. This opposition killed the government's move to send the SDF into the Persian Gulf during that war. But in 2001 domestic opposition was minimal. The response of Japan's neighbors to its dispatch of SDF forces was also mild. Normally South Korea and China vehemently oppose any kind of security-related activity by Japan. But this was not the case with regard to the war on terror. South Korea has been forging close ties with Japan and shares an antiterrorist commitment with both Japan and the United States. China also has radical Muslim dissidents who have been prepared to use violent methods of destabilization. Curiously enough, the Chinese media played down the reporting of the 9/11 attacks. Furthermore, the Taliban was phonetically translated into Chinese, *Ta-li-ban*, rather than *shenxueshi*, students of theology, the direct translation from Arabic. The latter might give readers the impression that the Taliban is some respectable entity. The Taiwanese media use *shenxueshi*. There are also Fa Lung Gong adherents, democracy activists, and a massive number of city-ward immigrants without a solid job and home, all of whom can be governed under the auspices of a tough solidarist stance on terrorism. China also has every reason to cultivate and maintain stable and friendly relations with Japan; the maintenance of a peaceful international environment is necessary as the leadership of the Chinese Communist Party strives to develop China into a powerful and wealthy country (Shambaugh and Yang 2003).

Article Nine of the Japanese Constitution has been de facto modified a number of times to suit the needs of Japan, through governmental reinterpretation during deliberations in the National Diet. There is another factor that could potentially contribute to the accelerated restoration of Japan's normal statehood. Major wars among states have been in steady decline (Mueller 1989). Thus the significance of conventional alliance politics seems to have been significantly reduced. Also, after 9/11 NATO has been de facto replaced by a new military alliance, NASTY (Nations Allied to Stop Tyrants), of which the United States, the United Kingdom, and Australia are core members (Friedman 2002). The likelihood of those nations less inclined to use force for international disputes or humanitarian interventions being associated with the normal state in the conventional Westphalian sense will decline in tandem with the overall decline in the incidences of the use of force in the world because the Westphalian abnormality will become perfectly normal. Finally, as a global civilian power (Maull 1990/1991), Japan has a legitimate role to play in places such as the Indian Ocean, East Timor, and Afghanistan.

Japan's Free Trade Agreement Initiative

Japan can be regarded as a champion of free trade for those who undertake it on a voluntary basis. This has been the spirit of the Asia–Pacific

Economic Cooperation forum (Garnaut and Drysdale 1994). It can be characterized as open, loose regionalism. No obligatory trade and market liberalization targets are imposed on member countries. As the newly industrializing countries of the Asia–Pacific region attempt to learn from the theory and practice of the developmental state, as exemplified by Japan in the third quarter of the twentieth century (Johnson 1983; Woo-Cumings 1999), it is perhaps natural to pursue the notion of open, loose regionalism (Japan, South Korea, China, Taiwan, and the ASEAN states). The aggregation of domestic sectoral interests and diplomatic deftness and dexterity has a lot to do with the exercise of leadership at the high level of the Japanese polity in a highly decentralized country. Since these issues are arguably the problem of internal power structures, one might as well not relate them to the issue of normal statehood. But as long as the Japanese debate concerns normal statehood, these issues are directly or indirectly related to the issues of normal statehood. Those emphatically arguing for Japan's attainting normal statehood point to these two major factors: (a) that Japan has been so accustomed to its free ride and dependence on the United States for its security and free market and (b) that Japan has attained so high a level of material wealth and been addicted to the postmaterialistic life of individualism, laissez-faire, and weak national identity and patriotism.

However, financial market globalization has deepened, and regional economic integration has emerged as the most appropriate way to absorb the impact of globalization on regional economies. It was natural for countries to seek free trade agreements within the Asia–Pacific regional economy. Furthermore, there has been a substantial increase in foreign direct investment in China, which has also proved itself able to competitively export manufactured goods. This has alarmed other Asia–Pacific countries and caused them to seek free trade agreements within the region. China's increased ability to attract foreign direct investment and competitively export manufactured goods means that unless regional free trade agreements can be concluded, other economies in the region will have their competitiveness reduced. The scramble for regional free trade agreements can be seen as an attempt to achieve two objectives: (a) to absorb the forces of globalization, especially the negative implications of the rise of China, and (b) to consolidate economic competitiveness vis-à-vis other regions.

Japan's desire for free trade agreements has intensified as its own economic surplus has visibly shrunk. This is due to structural rigidities within Japan and the fact that China has absorbed so much foreign direct investment, both within the region and from Japan. Japan's initial procrastination in undertaking regional free trade agreement initiatives led China to beat it to the punch, in the form of a China–ASEAN free trade agreement. Japan can be slow to pursue its free trade agenda. At home, Japan is unable to swiftly aggregate various sectors' tariffs and non-tariff barriers into a package of positions on each product. Abroad, it is unable to deftly aggregate various countries' preferences into a regional package. By contrast, in 2002 China was able to conclude such an agreement with ASEAN, although needless to say, its implementation will take some more years.

Concluding a regional free trade agreement requires two important attributes that are conventionally associated with the possession of normal statehood: (a) authority to claim domestic sovereignty over variegated domestic interests and (b) diplomatic deftness and dexterity to attract would-be members, come to grips with their various needs, and aggregate them harmoniously into a package. The problem is that the Japanese political system is decentralized, with local chieftains invariably acting as "kings of small things." These kings often effectively exercise a veto, by using the culturally acceptable excuse of forming and consolidating consensus (Inoguchi 1993). This facade of consensus and unity defies reality, which is revealed most glaringly at times when nation-level packages must be formulated, such as when there is the prospect of a fruitful regional free trade agreement. Japan's first bilateral free trade agreement was concluded with Singapore, principally because Singapore does not have a significant agricultural sector. This meant that it was not necessary for sectoral interests in Japanese agriculture to veto the free trade agreement. Normally, the conclusion of such an agreement would entail some compromise with Japan's uncompetitive agricultural sector. A free trade agreement with Korea has been talked about for more than a decade to no avail. More recently, a proposal has been put forward that instead of a Japan–ASEAN free trade agreement, bilateral free trade agreements should be brokered, such as the bilateral free trade agreement between Japan and Thailand. Sectoral protectionism within the Japanese polity has made Japan a very weak actor in the regional free trade game.

Second, diplomatic deftness and dexterity are not regarded as something with which the Japanese are amply equipped. Designing a package that could accommodate the needs of the 15-plus members of ASEAN is indeed a daunting task. That is why some want to proceed in a more piecemeal fashion through bilateral free trade agreements. More fundamentally, Japan's utmost priority does not seem to be trade liberalization but developmental facilitation and sectoral protection (*Asahi Shimbun* 2002). In the 1998 Asia Pacific Economic Community (APEC) negotiations, there was a clash between Japan and the United States over the U.S.-initiated early voluntary sector-specific liberalization scheme, through which the United States wanted to accelerate trade liberalization in fisheries and forestry. The United States regarded its initiative as being in harmony with the APEC spirit of respecting member countries' initiatives, but Japan vetoed it. On the U.S. view, Japanese priorities are less with trade liberalization than with developmental facilitation and enhancement of regional ties, along with sectoral protection. Japan's decentralized authority structure also undermines its diplomatic deftness. The Japanese political system has been far more decentralized and fragmented than one would imagine in view of the centralizing tendencies of the Meiji government and the war-mobilization operations of the early Showa government (Inoguchi 2002a). Globalization can diversify consumer preferences but also those of electorates and sections of the government. Isolated acts of diplomatic deftness are possible, as can be seen from Prime Minister Junichiro Koizumi's dramatic summit with Kim Jong Il in Pyongyang on September 17, 2002. But if the authority structure remains so decentralized, political leadership will be difficult to sustain. Those agencies that are not constrained by sectoral protectionism have started to use the World Trade Organization to undermine sectoral protectionism more consciously than before.

Engaging Pyongyang

Normal statehood can be resumed when the collective past is settled and when a collective identity is constructed. The history issue is part of the abnormal state of limited sovereignty. Standing tall in the commonwealth of nations has been more or less prevented for Japan because of its history. History comes into play in the sense that all countries are heavily influenced, and some even haunted, by their pasts. The United States, standing tall after the antiterrorist war, is arguably still haunted by Vietnam. Leading figures in the Bush administration have drawn lessons from Vietnam and from Hitler. When Hitler was on the rise, the West did not confront him or act in time to thwart the early development of his project of annexation and annihilation. When Vietnam became a major problem, the U.S. government was prevented by enemies within from completing its military and nation-building project to its satisfaction. But now that the United States is the only superpower and does not appear to face any genuine immediate challenge to its hegemony, the United States is able to attempt to mold the world to its taste and has adopted a new unilateralist and preemptive doctrine to this end.

Nevertheless, historical issues continue to prevent Japan from attaining normal statehood. Japan's modern history has been haunted by the legacy of its being the only non-Western nation to achieve modernization and achieve a rank on a par with Western powers by World War I. On the one hand, Japan wanted to achieve wealth and strength by learning from the West. On the other, Japan wanted to free itself from Western domination and place itself at the center of the rise of a powerful Asia. Japan did not appreciate the motives of Western powers in developing multilateral schemes for conflict prevention, confidence building, and arms control after World War I (Iriye 1962, 2002). All these schemes were simply regarded as new cloaks for the perpetuation of Western dominance. Therefore, Japan continued to extend its influence over proximate territories, even in the face of protests and warnings. This process culminated in the imposition of sanctions and all-out war in 1941. By 1945 Japan was bombed to ashes.

A majority of Japanese regard the events of the 1930s and 1940s as an aberration, a detour from the appropriate course of enlightenment and entrepreneurship that has enabled Japan to achieve its status as a rich country with a strong army (Inoguchi 2002b). The Allied Powers, led by the United States, reformed Japan's political structures during the occupation, 1945–1952, attempting to shape its history according to a Western view of acceptable standards. Americans initially wanted to deny Japan's history in much the same way that Germany wanted to deny its own immediately after defeat. In the German version, all modern German history led to the Third Reich, and an entirely new German history started in 1945. In contrast, Americans came to adopt a milder and more benign interpretation of modern Japanese history. It was conducive to the emerging demands of the Cold War world that Japan was conceived as an ally that had suffered an aberration (Reischauer and Fairbank 1973). The Japanese leadership welcomed this history, as it suited their preference of retaining the emperor as the symbol of Japan, the preference that has kept the history issue more difficult to deal with till today. Japan initially largely avoided these issues by not treating any twentieth-century history in textbooks. The outcome has been that the Japanese settlement of history has been placed in limbo since 1945.

Nevertheless, some aspects of the historical legacy have been addressed, in the diplomatic sphere at least. Diplomatic normalization took place with the Republic of Korea (ROK) in 1965, with the People's Republic of China in 1972 (Fukui 1977), and with the Soviet Union in 1957, albeit without the formal conclusion of a peace treaty (Hellman, 1970). As of December 2002, the only country that had not embarked on diplomatic normalization was the Democratic People's Republic of Korea. The problem is that the Japan–ROK Basic Treaty of 1965 covers the entire territory, including that of North Korea. Japan regards the ROK as the sole legitimate state entity on the Korean Peninsula. North Korea accuses Japan of colonialism, suppression, and exploitation during the colonial period and thereafter. North Korea regards Japan as serving the interests of the United States in keeping the Korean Peninsula divided and by posing military and economic threats. North Korea demands that on the eve of diplomatic normalization, Japan needs to acknowledge the wrongs of the past and to promise to pay a massive amount of compensation, which would be invested in economic recovery and development in North Korea.

Historical issues are not easy to resolve because they relate so fundamentally to questions of Japanese identity. Japan's sense of historical affiliation with Asia is weak. "Japan and Asia" sits more comfortably than "Japan in Asia" among the Japanese (Inoguchi 1995). However, with the passage of time the history issue will become less significant. When Secretary General Hu Yaobang of the Chinese Communist Party was asked when China might forgive Japan for its aggression and atrocities, he answered that it would take 85 years after the war. After all, he said, the Chinese had now forgotten the Boxer intervention of 1900–1901. Further, with the steady intensification of binding regional ties, historical issues will assume less relative significance.

The Issue of Normal Statehood

The Exercise of Leadership

By authority structure, I refer to the way in which decisions are made and how they are implemented. In the past half century Japan's authority structure has often been characterized as a system of decentralized consensus formation. The power structure is decentralized, preference aggregation through consensus formation is a lengthy process, and yet the decisions that are eventually implemented tend to be solid. This decentralized consensus-based authority structure has its origins in Japanese history. First, the fact that Japan did not experience absolutism in its early modern period meant that the structure of a fairly decentralized system was already established by the seventeenth century (Ikegami 1993; Inoguchi 2002a). There were, of course, influential centralizing aspects to the governance practiced through the Meiji Restoration of 1868. The Tokugawa system of ceding quasi-autonomy to about 300 domains was replaced by the Meiji system, under which quasi-autonomy was ceded to about 20 agencies at the center of government. The Imperial Constitution of 1890 placed the emperor at the apex of the state, but the essentially decentralized system of decision-making remained intact. Cabinet ministers representing each bureaucratic agency, including the army and the navy, had veto power vis-à-vis the prime minister, for instance. The 1952 Constitution (drafted largely in 1946) was refreshingly progressive in areas such as gender equality, freedom, and social policy. It reflected the ideas of the democratic grand coalition of the 1930s, which remained influential in the United States at that time. But the authority structure as prescribed in the new Constitution is not much different from that contained in its predecessor. There were, of course, some differences: the emperor lost his political stature and influence, the army and the navy were abolished, the Ministry of Home Affairs was disbanded and reconstructed into a several smaller agencies, and the prime minister was given slightly more power than in the Imperial Constitution.

Second, the waning of the developmental state in Japan, which was designed to coordinate the mobilization of resources during the initial period of industrial take-off, has also contributed to the recent decentralization of decision-making (Johnson 1983; Woo-Cumings 1999; Schaede and Grimes 2003; Inoguchi, forthcoming). This decentralization took place in the 1980s and 1990s when the United States wanted immediate and tangible concessions from Japan to help it address the economic difficulties it was then experiencing. It seemed to many Americans as if either nobody was in charge of Japanese decision-making or that there were too many leaders, each with a veto. This was a source of great exasperation to U.S. negotiators, who wanted deals and decisions made on the spot and imagined that these could be obtained by dealing directly with people at the highest level (Blaker et al. 2002). To the Americans' great dismay, the Japanese authority structure, especially in the twilight of developmental momentum, did not and does not seem to produce leaders in the American sense of the word.

The third explanation for Japan's decentralized decision-making structure is related to the second. Globalization has steadily permeated Japanese society, despite Japan's facade as a hierarchically bureaucratized structured society and despite Japan's hitherto predominantly domestic market orientation. It is true that in the past Japan has been internally comfortable and well integrated. This was achieved through social policy tailored to alleviate the plight of the disadvantaged and cartelized arrangements among sectors and between management and unions. But a society that was once well integrated is fragmenting, as is an economy that in the past was predominantly oriented to the domestic market, except for a tiny portion of competitive firms and sectors that contributed to the accumulation of foreign reserves.

As Renato Ruggiero, former director of the World Trade Organization, says, it is more difficult to govern an integrated world than a divided one. Consumption patterns diversify as global markets integrate. Previously unitary national markets fragment in the face of the intensification of globalization and the diversification of choice. There is no compelling reason to imagine that Japan will prove to be an exception to this rule. Indeed, the fragmentary implications of globalization have reinforced the centripetal nature of the Japanese authority structure (Inoguchi 2003).

Fourth, given the increased trend toward decentralization and fragmentation behind the facade of centralized government, a new trend has been emerging. The cozy entente among central bureaucracy, the Liberal Democratic Party, and big business has gone forever. When the center cannot hold, people at the grassroots level of society seek new kinds of leaders. They can be young and ambitious mavericks like Jun Saito, a former graduate student of political science at Yale, who won a seat in the vacuum created by Koichi Kato, former secretary general of the Liberal Democratic Party, who was forced out of office by scandals. They can be time-tested governors like Masayoshi Kitagawa, who clearly has an eye on the position of prime minister, after announcing that he would not seek a third term as governor of Mie prefecture. They can be highly visible public figures like Yasuo Tanaka, a well-known and independent-minded novelist, who has been elected twice as governor of the mountainous and scenic Nagano prefecture. This prefecture, like many others, has a perennial budget deficit, and political protagonists have split into two camps, one that is seeking more money from the central government for public works and one that is seeking to develop new industries based on a new lifestyle concept. Tanaka belongs to the latter camp.

Within the Liberal Democratic Party the trend is clearly for politicians and potential leaders to become more self-reliant, personally mobilizing district-level organizations by conversing with local people much more intensely. This strategy can be pursued through a variety of media, including more targeted and intensive use of the Internet and e-mail, appealing proactively to business for political donations, appealing to popular sentiment through television and media appearances, articulating a policy vision through participation in public symposia, and, finally, through volunteer activities (Inoguchi and Hotta, forthcoming).

The fifth point is more directly related to global forces, as globalization also requires astute, articulate, and agile leaders. The globalization of governance entails more integrated markets, the global diffusion of military weapons, and the global permeation of public elite culture as evidenced in the Davos World Economic Summit meetings (Berger and

Huntington 2002). Astute, articulate, and agile leaders must always be mindful of domestic audiences and yet must act globally — and decisively. Politicians must be shrewd, media literate, and able to appeal to a broad cross-section of public opinion through quality of performance.

All of these developments have been influencing Japan's authority structure. Whether Japan is capable of remolding its authority structure to make it more conducive to the exercise of leadership is something one needs to consider in light of the relative weight of these factors and the alchemy derived from a combination of them. Even a casual look at Koizumi's record yields mixed results. The decisiveness of his summit diplomacy with Kim Jong Il augurs well for those who hope that Japan can become a normal state. But the difficulties he has in acting decisively on economic reform issues augurs ill.

The Use of Force

The prohibition on Japan's use of force arose out of the project pursued by the Allied Powers during the period of Occupation (1945–1952). The aim of the Allied Powers was to disarm Japan, change the war-prone regime, and reshape Japan into a peace-loving country that would not make another attempt at aggression in East and Southeast Asia in defiance of the preferences of the West. This can be referred to as "putting the cap on the bottle" (Inoguchi 2001). A new constitution was drafted by the still vibrant remnant of the New Deal Coalition, interested in extending their own experiment in the United States to other parts of the world, most notably in Japan and in Germany (Zunz 2000). The drafters of the Constitution were interested in promoting freedom, democracy, free enterprise, trade unionism, and gender equality. And they were interested in remolding Japan as a disarmed, agricultural, and stable country in America's embrace. The bulk of the Constitution drafting was carried out in 1946. That is why the Preamble contains a passage on an aspiration to eradicate the use of force, and Article Nine refers to the abrogation of the use of force in settling international disputes. As the Cold War intensified in the Far East, however, the United States decided not to put the cap on the bottle after all. Instead the United States wanted Japan to be a stable, peaceful but robust country that could sustain the United States' Cold War strategy, in terms of securing military bases and ports, fueling and repairing aircraft and warships, and supplying food and comfort. The immediate outcomes of this policy shift were as follows: (a) Japan regained its independence and (b) the Japan–United States Security Treaty was concluded. The United States retained its military presence while pledging to defend Japan and to act as a deterrent to countries considering aggression against

Japan. In this scheme, the Constitution and the Security Treaty are complementary. The SDF were created incrementally, initially as police reserve forces. Their function was auxiliary to the United States Armed Forces in the Far East, other than in the prosecution of the initially very important role of maintaining law and order. This was a time when Japan was recovering from defeat and dealing with alarmingly strong left-wing forces.

The Constitution prohibits the use of force as a means of settling international disputes. Japan does have a number of territorial disputes with other countries in East Asia: with the Soviet Union/Russia (four southern Kurile islands), with South Korea (Takeshima/Dokdo island), and with China/Taiwan (Senkaku/Diaoyutai islands). However, the structure of the Cold War and the nature of Japan's security relationship with the United States made it effectively impossible for Japan to act unilaterally or aggressively with regard to any of these disputes. After the Cold War new contingencies have arisen that highlight the nature of this constraint on Japan's prosecution of a normal foreign policy. United Nations operations require member states to place troops in combat situations. As a result of the constraint on the use of force, the only operations in which Japan has been involved have been postwar peace-building and peacekeeping operations (Fukushima, forthcoming). Japan engages its peacekeeping and peace-building operations only on the basis of a UN Security Counsel resolution. Palestine, Kosovo, Rwanda, Cambodia, and East Timor are examples of such engagement. Japan's justification for participating at all is that even though the use of force is constitutionally forbidden, Japan's desire to promote peace is sufficiently strong to motivate it to participate in UN operations. After all, Japan is a self-appointed global civilian power. Japan's antimilitarism has been deep-rooted for the past half century (Berger 1997; Katzenstein 1996). Even in the recent past it has been common for a government not to expect to survive unless it moves within the parameters of prevailing antimilitarist public opinion and norms.

The Yomiuri Shimbun (2002) has regularly asked the following question about Constitutional revision since 1981: "Do you think that it is better to revise the Constitution now or that it is better not to revise the Constitution?" For the past five years those in favor of Constitutional revision have constituted a majority (52.3 to 60%). Since 9/11, those favoring the dispatch of the SDF for peacekeeping purposes, even during periods of military conflict, have constituted a majority, with 44.4% in favor and 25.8% opposed. Motives for advocating Constitutional revision differ from one person to another. The majority answer for the past decade has been that new problems have emerged in international relations that cannot be satisfactorily addressed due to the constraints embodied in the

Constitution. In parliamentary terms, the Liberal Democratic Party, the New Conservative Party, and the Liberal Party form the revisionist wing. The Komei Party argues for Constitutional revision, but places greater emphasis on other issues such as social welfare, the protection of privacy, transparency in governance, and reform of the electoral system. Although revisionists are in the majority in public opinion and in both houses of the National Diet, they have not been able to make a breakthrough. First, for Constitutional revision to occur, a two-thirds majority is necessary in both houses of the National Diet. Second, prolonged economic stagnation discourages the government from undertaking risky and burdensome initiatives.

Two significant new developments have complicated Japan's pacifist orientation. One is the increasing number of cases where the United States takes military action in an often unilateralist fashion. The 9/11 events precipitated this new trend. Given the overwhelming power of the United States and given the increased significance of failed states and rogue states in terms of their ability to disturb law and order in globalized politics, the United States defines its new mission as promoting freedom, democracy, and the free market on a global scale. In its predominantly military-oriented strategy, the traditional significance of allies seems to have been diluted by an overriding need to have as many close partners as possible, who give unstinting support and credence to U.S.-led military action, thereby legitimating it. In the antiterrorist war in Afghanistan there were two kinds of close partners: the United Kingdom and Australia, and China and Russia. The former two partners played two key roles. One is the extraordinary ease and speed with which troops were sent. In the words of critics, they were like mercenaries. The other is the articulation and legitimation of the logic behind the military strategy. Blair's passionate and eloquent speeches are evidence of this. So is Prime Minister John Howard's apt characterization of Australia's role: deputy sheriff. Both the troops and the words are indispensable. Britain committed far fewer troops to the war on terrorism in Afghanistan than Germany, which sent 10,000 troops. However, it is Britain, not Germany, that of all the partners gives the greater impression of closeness to the United States. China and Russia were close partners in this enterprise, because they both have domestic equivalents of Osama bin Laden and have every reason to legitimize their own suppression of dissident groups by enthusiastically endorsing Bush's war on terrorism.

The second development is the increasing number of cases where the Japanese believe that a material breach of their sovereignty has taken place. This includes North Korea firing missiles over the Japanese archipelago in August 1998 and the case of the North Korean ship that was chased over the Japanese Exclusive Economic Zones and sunk by Japanese Coastal Guard ships in 2001. It was long suspected, but only officially admitted at the September 2002 summit talk between Junichiro Koizumi and Kim Jong Il, that a number of Japanese nationals had been abducted by the North Koreans. North Korea revealed details of its nuclear program to the United States two weeks after misleading Japan at the above summit meeting. Chinese ships regularly measure the Japanese Exclusive Economic Zones, North Koreans engage in drug trafficking, and Chinese illegal immigrants commit an increasing range and number of crimes.

The Japanese have become increasingly liable to conceive of such issues as an affront to their national dignity and sovereignty. Accordingly, measures have been taken to address these affronts. For instance, Japan has responded to the North Korean nuclear threat by signing an accord with the United States, accelerating the projected completion of the missile defense program. Japan has responded to North Korean ships engaged in drug trafficking, abduction, and espionage activities by upgrading the military hardware placed on coastal guard ships and by increasing general levels of vigilance. The increase in crimes committed by often-illegal residents has been responded to in part by a steadily raising consciousness ofthe need to tackle such crimes. All of the above developments have caused right-wing nationalistic groups to agitate. Populist right-wing politicians have also responded. For instance, Tokyo Governor Shintaro Ishihara has called for a rhetorical war against North Korea, rather than the strategy of diplomatic normalization that is currently being pursued by the Japanese government.

One possibly new development in Japan's peacekeeping and peacebuilding operation is its increasing emphasis on Asia. Till recently, it was usually argued that the history issue hindered Japan from sending its troops to Asia. It was only in 1991 that Japan first sent 250 troops to Cambodia. Then in 1999 Japan sent 750 troops (its largest force) to East Timor. From 2001 onward Japan sent large numbers of government and nongovernment organization personnel to Afghanistan for its reconstruction. Its recent focus on Asia has to do with several factors. Since the Asian financial crisis of 1997, Japan has faced a decrease in government revenue that can be used for foreign policy purposes. Its global civilian orientation notwithstanding, its focus on its vicinity has become compelling. In addition, its history constraints have been loosening, with its neighbors becoming less vocal. South Korea and China since 1998 are most noteworthy.

The Historical Legacy

Aggression and the atrocities Japan committed before 1945 have made it prudent for Japan to play a low-key role in postwar international affairs. Japan waged war against all of the Allied Powers and several countries that had signed the Declaration of the United Nations. It is important to recall that the position of the United States government on the issue of Japan's historical legacy has changed dramatically. This occurred when it faced the need to prop Japan up instead of placing a cap on the bottle, as China became communist and the Korean War broke out. With the end of the Cold War historical issues have once more become salient. Discussions of Japan's historical legacy often seem to be a function of its economic success. The end of the Cold War came at a time of economic stagnation for the United States. Exploitation of the historical legacy became part of the peace dividend, encouraging some groups to express anti-Japanese sentiment, especially in the United States. Another twist to the story of the significance of Japan's historical legacy has occurred with Japan's prolonged economic stagnation in the 1990s, during which historical issues have once again become less salient.

In Japan, it is felt that the righting of wrongs has been overdone and that there have been more than enough apologies for the war. These twin sentiments have gained increased support in the past two decades. It is only in the past five years or so, however, that it has been possible for these sentiments to materialize in concrete fashion (Inoguchi 2002b). In 1998 the Japanese–Korean joint communiqué recorded what was regarded as a full apology for colonialism and military aggression on the Japanese side and a future-oriented posture about the bilateral relationship on the Korean side. Later in 1998 the Japanese–Chinese joint communiqué did not register as comprehensive an expression of Japanese repentance for aggression as China wanted. Yet associated agreements on Japanese official development assistance to China were not jeopardized because of this. More recently, each time Prime Minister Junichiro Koizumi has visited the Yasukuni shrine where the Japanese war dead, including war criminals, are buried, both Korea and China have registered moderate protest. But neither went very far in an attempt to halt this activity. In January 2003 Prime Minister Koizumi paid a visit to the shrine, and in response President Kim Dae Joon cancelled a planned meeting with Foreign Minister Yoriko Kawaguchi. But President-elect Roh Moo Hyong did meet her, and registered a protest, but went on to have substantial talks on other matters with her. The Chinese government did suspend some expendable high-level meetings as a diplomatic gesture, but on the whole it did not register a strong protest. At home, in 2001 the Ministry of Education approved what is regarded as a right-wing history textbook for junior high schools for the first time. Five other approved textbooks of history are regarded as center-right or centrist or center-left. But it should be stressed that only slightly more than 0.03 percent of Japanese junior high schools adopted this right-wing textbook. I suggest that this fact demonstrates the existence of a resilient antimilitarism.

Indeed, by the turn of the new century, critical references to the Japanese historical legacy have become more intermittent and less strident. This is not to say that there has been no criticism. However, it is undeniable that the historical legacy has become less of an issue. South Korea under President Kim Dae Jung has taken initiatives to consolidate its ties with Japan, ties that are qualitatively different from what has gone before. In 1998 Kim Dae Jung and Keizo Obuchi issued a joint communiqué announcing a new era for this important bilateral relationship. Jiang Zemin's China was very pragmatic but at times rhetorically vehement about Japan's ambivalent attitude toward its historical legacy, as exemplified in his speeches during his visit to Japan in 1998. China under Hu Jingtao seems set to take a course much milder than that pursued under Jiang Zeming. This has been suggested in a journal article authored by Ma Licheng, calling for a new strengthened relationship with Japan, which regards the Chinese accusation of Japan for its historical legacy, the Taiwan issue, or Japan's militarist revival as harmful (Ma Licheng 2002).

First, the passage of time is an important issue, and World War II will soon be a thing of the past to many people. Second, Japan's neighbors, the United States, China, and South Korea now have much more economic self-confidence vis-à-vis Japan. Recent travails notwithstanding, the United States remains proud of its new economy. China talks of 7% annual growth rates for the next two decades. South Korea has recovered from the nadir of the Asian financial crisis of 1997–1998, registering 5% to 6% annual growth. Third, the United States has become the only superpower, or even hyperpower, and has often flexed its muscles unilaterally. In order to reduce the possible negative impacts of the new Pax Americana, many countries in the rest of the world have attempted to forge larger regional groupings, as in the case of the European Union, and ASEAN plus Three.

At home, those who have personal experience of Japan's historical legacy have significantly reduced in number. Yet antimilitarism remains strong, as demonstrated by the latest version of the textbook controversy. Furthermore, each time the issue of the use of force has been discussed, the Japanese government has decided not to violate basic antimilitarist norms. In the Gulf War of 1991, Japan sent minesweepers to do the job only after the war was over. With regard to peacekeeping operations since the United Nations Transitional Authority in Cambodia (UNTAC) in 1991, Japan has participated in nonmilitary activities only. Japan sent large numbers of troops to East Timor, but only after a cease-fire was realized. Japan contributed to the war on terror in Afghanistan by sending warships to the Indian Ocean to detect and monitor ships and submarines operating in the region and to provide gasoline for American and British aircraft. Anticipating the vacuum to be created by the United States' entry into an anti-Iraq war in 2003, Japan sent an Aegis-equipped warship to detect and destroy missiles aimed at warships operating there. Japan's deployment of an Aegis-equipped warship in the Indian Ocean is the first instance where Japan has taken the risk of war casualties in its antimilitarist postwar history. Therefore it is safe to say that Japan has not forgotten about history, but it has modified its behavior. It now acts as a responsible global civilian power, committed to the causes of antiterrorism and peace-building within the constitutional and institutional framework entrenched in the Japanese Constitution since the occupation.

Conclusion

Having examined Japan's ambition for normal statehood in the preceding pages, let me speculate about what all this will add up to. It is helpful to consider the following two contingencies:

North Korea Going Decisively and Demonstratively Nuclear

What would Japan do if North Korea officially became a nuclear-weapon state? Would Japan go nuclear? My answer is probably not, unless some dramatically different situation were to arise (cf. Kamiya 2003). If Japan goes nuclear in response to developments in North Korea, this would be a source of concern for China, which has historically tended to regard North Korea as a useful buffer state. Should North Korea be threatened by Japan, China would start to view Japan in a more hostile light. Such was the case in 1931 when Japan's Kwantung Army crossed the Yalujiang (Amnokkang) into Manchuria (Ogata 1964). Such was also the case in 1951 when the UN forces came close to the Yalujiang and bombed Shenyang and other cities in China's Northeast, when China intervened in the Korean War (Whiting 1960). You might ask why Japan should be so concerned about what China thinks. The answer is that a stable relationship with China has been a sine qua non for Japan's prosperity. Some distance is advisable, but a mutually hostile relationship is clearly in neither Japan's nor China's interests. Japan should be careful that any nuclear strategy it might adopt could not be construed as hostile by Beijing. That would be difficult and potentially suicidal.

No less important to consider is the preference of the United States. Senator John McCain's and others' view in favor of the United States allowing Japan to go nuclear notwithstanding, the U.S. government is most likely to steadfastly continue its policy of nuclear nonproliferation, strictly applied to Japan as well. Otherwise Northeast Asia would be thrown into the domino effect of nuclear proliferation like the one that took place in South Asia in 2002, a scenario the United States is determined to suppress. Nevertheless, the voices arguing for the use of force for self-defense have been expressed at high levels, as well as among the public at large. Defense Minister Shigeru Ishiba expressed on February 13, 2003, "Our nation will use military force as a self defense measure if [North Korea] starts to resort to arms against Japan."

What the Japanese government has undertaken to cope with the nuclear threat from North Korea is limited, however. First is the increased reliance on the United States, which has been assuring that the Iraqi crisis will not dilute its commitment in Northeast Asia. Second, Japan has enhanced its commitment to develop missile defense with the United States in an accelerated fashion. Third, Japan has decided to deploy more Aegis-equipped warships. Fourth, it has heightened vigilance.

China Clearly Replacing the United States as Japan's Principal Trading and Economic Partner

What should Japan do if China becomes its most important trading and economic partner? A potentially worrisome trend is already emerging. From 2000 onward, during the process of recovery from the Asian financial crisis of 1997, Korea has been stepping up its economic interactions with China, in terms of both trade and foreign direct investment. By 2002, Korea's biggest trading partner was already China, with Japan a close second and the United States a distant third. In a similar vein, Japan's export drive to China has mitigated some of the negative side effects of economic stagnation.

In December 2002 Mainichi Shimbun (2003) asked the following questions: Do you want to maintain the Japan–United States Treaty? Or do you want to transform it into a Peace and Friendship Treaty? Or do you want to abrogate the Japan–United States Security Treaty? The percentage of respondents giving positive answers to each of the three options were, respectively, 37%, 33%, and 4%. Japan's export drive to China, which has been quite robust, especially in materials and machinery, is contributing to this unexpected rise in the number of people answering the second option in the affirmative. Another explanatory factor is the steady increase in negative sentiment about American unilateralism. Anti-Americanism was universal in anticipation of an American attack against Iraq (Pew Research Center 2002). Japan's anti-Americanism undisputedly registered a lower-than-global average, underlining the prudence and self-restraint shown by many Japanese. It may not be a coincidence that a steady rise in the China trade both in Korea and in Japan goes hand in hand with a rise in the kind of public opinion that bandwagons the cure of the China market or, to exaggerate, Finlandizes itself in anticipation of the possibly irreversible trend of China's rise. Since the second option implies the absence of U.S. military forces in Japan, the increased popularity of this option could indicate a trend that needs careful attention. But a rise in pro-Chinese public opinion does not necessarily have profound implications for Japan's security arrangements. Japan has a significant stake in the global economy, and given the basic lack of shared norms and values between Japan and China, it would be very difficult to argue that Japan would move substantially toward a pro-China position, because this would dilute and possibly unravel its institutional arrangements with and ties to the United States.

To sum up, Japan's ambition for normal statehood will not trigger a dramatic systemic change as long as these aspirations are anchored in its security alliance with the United States, on the basis of shared norms and values as well as on trust that is to be intermittently demonstrated as they, together with others, manage risks and difficulties that lie ahead. But Japan should also keep in mind Deng Xiaoping's warning that if Japan and China go to war, then at least half of heaven collapses. Japan's ambition for normal statehood in terms of its authority structure, its use of force, and its historical legacy will be best managed on the basis of this line of thinking.

In discussing Japan's ambitions for normal statehood, I might have exaggerated the limitations and slighted its accomplishments. As a mater of fact, Japan has accomplished a lot in an environment where there was a wide consensus and changes tended to be slow. In 1945 Japan registered the lowest per capita level in Asia, with the Philippines registering the highest. In 2003 Japan was among the top-ranking wealthiest nations. This is very impressive. In 1945 the Japanese Imperial Army was disarmed completely. In 2003 the Japanese SDF is the second largest in terms of budget and weapons. This is all the more impressive because Japan has build up its military power slowly but inexorably without alienating the United States.

Japan has won peace throughout its post-1945 history, with no one killed in combat. This is impressive indeed. Whether Japan, with its yearning for normal statehood increasingly visible, is able to navigate in the *terra incognita* of the new Pax Americana is yet to be determined.

Acknowledgments

For their comments and questions that led me to improve an earlier draft, I thank conference participants, especially Jorge Domínguez, Byung-Kook Kim, Richard Cooper, Ezra Vogel, and Shunji Shimokoji. Paul Bacon helped me to normalize my English. Permission granted to reproduce adapted portions of Inoguchi (2004) from openDemocracy.net.

References

Alker, Hayward R. Jr., Thomas J. Biersteker, and Takashi Inoguchi. 1985. "The Decline of the Superstates: The Rise of a New World Order?" Presented at the World Congress of Political Science, International Political Science Association, Paris, July 15–20.

Armitage, Richard et al. 2000. *The United States and Japan: Advancing Toward a Mature Partnership*. Institute for National Strategic Studies Special Report, October 11, 2000.

Asahi Shimbun. 2002. "Boueki Ruru Demo Nichibei no Rigai Tairitsu WTO kaigou" (Confrontation of interest regarding trade rule between Japan and United States in WTO Conference), October 19.

Berger, Peter L., and Samuel P. Huntington. 2002. *Many Globalizations: Cultural Diversity in the Contemporary World*. Oxford: Oxford University Press.

Berger, Thomas U. 1997. *Cultures of Antimilitarism: National Security in Germany and Japan*. Baltimore, MD: Johns Hopkins University Press.

Blaker, Michael et al. 2002. *Japanese Negotiating Behavior*, Washington, DC: United States Institute of Peace.

Cha, Victor. 2001. "Japan's Engagement Dilemmas With North Korea." *Asian Survey*, 41, No. 4: (July–August): 549–563.

Dower, John W. 1999. *Embracing Defeat: Japan in the Wake of World War II*. New York: New Press.

Eberwein, Wolf-Dieter, and Karl Kaiser, eds. 2001. *Germany's New Foreign Policy: Decision-Making in an Interdependent World*. New York: Palgrave.

Friedman, Thomas. 2002. "The New Club NATO." *New York Times*, November 17.

Fukui, Haruhiro. 1977. "Tanaka Goes to Peking." In *Policymaking in Contemporary Japan*, ed. T. J. Pempel. Ithaca, NY: Cornell University Press, pp. 69–70.

Fukushima, Akiko. "Adapting Peace Operations to the Context of the 21st Century: From Japanese Perspective." In *The Use of Institutions: The United States, Japan and Regional Governance*, ed. G. J. Ikenberry and I. Takashi. Forthcoming.

Fukuyama, Francis. 1995. *Trust: Social Virtues and the Creation of Prosperity*. New York: Simon & Schuster.

Garnaut, Ross, and Peter Drysdale, eds. 1994. *Asia Pacific Regionalism: Readings in International Economic Relations*. Sydney: Harper Educational.

Haenisch, Sebastian, and Hanns W. Maull, eds. 2001. *Germany as Civilian Power: The Foreign Policy of the Berlin Republic*, Manchester, UK: Manchester University Press.

Hatch, Walter, and Kozo Yamamura. 1996. *Asia in Japan's Embrace: Building a Regional Production Alliance*. Cambridge: Cambridge University Press.

Hellmann, Donald C. 1969. *Japanese Domestic Politics and Foreign Policy: The Peace Agreement with the Soviet Union*. Berkeley: University of California Press.

Ikeda, Tadasu. 1996. *Kambojia Whei Eno Michi* (Roads to Cambodian Peace). Tokyo: Toshishuppan.

Ikegami, Eiko. 1993. *The Taming of the Samurai*. Cambridge: Harvard University Press.

Inglehart, Ronald. 1977. *The Silent Revolution*. Princeton, NJ: Princeton University Press.

Inglehart, R. 1997. *Modernization and Post-Modernization: Cultural, Economic and Political Change in 43 Societies.* Princeton, NJ: Princeton University Press.
Inoguchi, Takashi. 1991. "Japan's Response to the Gulf Crisis: An Analytic Overview." *Journal of Japanese Studies,* 26, No. 2 (Spring): 257–73.
Inoguchi, Takashi. 1993. "Japanese Politics in Transition: A Theoretical Review." *Government and Opposition* 28, No. 4 (Autumn): 443–55.
Inoguchi, Takashi. 1995. "Distant Neighbors? Japan and Asia." *Current History,* 94, No. 595: 392–69.
Inoguchi, Takashi. 1999. "Peering into the Future by Looking Back: The Westphalian, Philadelphian, and Anti-Utopian Paradigms." *International Studies Review* 1, Issue 2 (Summer): 173–91.
Inoguchi, Takashi. 2001. "A North-East Asian Perspective." *Australian Journal of International Affairs* 55, No. 2: 199–212.
Inoguchi, Takashi. 2002a. *Gendai Nihon Seiji no Kiso* (The Fundamental Layers of Contemporary Japanese Politics). Tokyo: NTT Shuppan.
Inoguchi, Takashi. 2002b. *Japan's Asian Policy: Revival and Response.* New York: Palgrave Macmillan.
Inoguchi, Takashi. 2003. *Gendai Nihon Seiji no Fuhen to Tokui* (Contemporary Japanese Politics: Its Universal and Particularistic Characteristics). Tokyo: NTT Shuppan.
Inoguchi, Takashi. 2004. "An Ordinary Power. Japanese Style." http://www.openDemocracy.net/debates/article-2-95-1754.jsp/Feburary 26.
Inoguchi, Takashi. "Has the Japanese Model Ceased to Be a Magnet in Asia?" In *Parties, Leadership and Governance in East and Southeast Asia: A Comparative Study,* ed. I. Marsh, J. Blondel, and T. Inoguchi. Forthcoming.
Inoguchi, Takashi, and Hotta Zen'u. *Seijika no mittsu no kao* (Three Faces of Legislators). Forthcoming.
Iriye, Akira. 1962. *After Imperialism.* Cambridge, MA: Harvard University Press.
Iriye, Akira. 2002. *Global Community: The Role of International Organization in the Making of the Contemporary World.* Berkeley: University of California Press.
Johnson, C. 1983. *MITI and the Growth of Industrial Policy, 1925–1975.* Stanford, CA: Stanford University Press.
Kamiya, Matake. 2003. "Nuclear Japan: Oxymoron or Coming Soon?" *The Washington Quarterly* 26, No. 1: 63–75.
Katzenstein, Peter. 1996. *Cultural Norms and National Security: Police and Militarism in Postwar Japan.* Ithaca, NY: Cornell University Press.
Keeler, John, and Martin Schain, eds. 1996. *Chirac's Challenge: Liberalization, Europeanization, and Malaise in France.* New York: Palgrave.
Krasner, Stephen. 1999. *Sovereignty: Organized Hypocrisy.* Princeton, NJ: Princeton University Press.
Ma, Licheng. 2002. "Dui Ri guanxi xin siwei" (A New Thought on China's Relations with Japan). *Zhanglue yu Guanli* (Strategy and Management) (December).
Mainichi Shimbun. 2003. "*Yoron-tyosa tokusyu; Genjouiji-ron 37%, 'Yuukoujouyaku ni' 33%*" (Feature articles on public opinion poll; preservation of the status quo 37%, "change to the treaty of friendship" 33%). January, 4: 8–9.
Maull, Hanns. 1990/1991. "Germany and Japan: The New Civilian Power," *Foreign Affairs,* 69, No. 5 (Winter 1990/1991): 91–106.
Mueller, John E. 1989. *Retreat from Doomsday: The Obsolescence of Major War.* New York: Basic Books.
Nau, Henry et al. 2002. *At Home Abroad: Identity and Power in American Foreign Policy.* Ithaca, NY: Cornell University Press.
Nye, Joseph. 2002. *The Paradox of American Power: Why the World's Only Superpower Can't Go It Alone.* Oxford: Oxford University Press.
Ogata, Sadako. 1964. *Defiance in Manchuria.* Berkeley: University of California Press.
Pew Research Center. 2002. *What the World Thinks in 2000.* Washington, DC: Pew Research Center for the People and the Press. http://people-press.org/reports/display.php3?ReportID=165
Reischauer, Edwin, and John K Fairbank. 1973. *East Asia: Tradition and Transformation.* Boston: Houghton Mifflin.

Russett, Bruce, and Arthur Stein. 1981. "Consequences and Outcomes of International Conflict." In *Handbook of Political Conflict: Theory and Research,* ed. T. Gurr. New York: Free Press.

Schaede, Ulrike, and William Grimes, eds. 2003. *Japan's Managed Globalization.* New York: M.E. Sharpe.

Schwartz, Frank J. 1998. *Advice and Consent: The Politics of Consolidation in Japan.* New York: Cambridge University Press.

Schwartz, Hans-Peter. 1985. *Die Gezähmten Deutschen: von der Machtbesessenheit zur Machtvaergessenheit.* Stuttgart: Deutsche Verglas-Anstalt.

Shambaugh, David L., and Richard Yang. 2003. *Modernizing China's Military: Progress, Problems, and Prospects.* Berkeley: University of California Press.

Vogel, Steven, ed. 2002. *U.S.-Japan Relations in a Changing World.* Washington, DC: Brookings Institution Press.

Whiting, Allen. 1960. *China Crosses the Yalu: The Decision to Enter the Korean War.* Stanford, CA: Stanford University Press.

Woo-Cumings, Meredith, ed. 1999. *The Developmental State.* Ithaca, NY: Cornell University Press.

Yomiuri Shimbun. 2002. *Nihon no Seron* (Japanese Public Opinion), Opinion Poll Department: *Yomiuri Shimbun.*

Zunz, Olivier. 2000. *Why the American Century.* Chicago: University of Chicago Press.

CHAPTER 7

Brazilian Foreign Policy since 1990 and the Pax Americana

MÔNICA HERZ

Introduction

This chapter analyzes the relevant changes that have taken place in Brazil's foreign policy since the 1990s, with emphasis on the management of international security. The policy orientations and perspectives of the Brazilian decision-making elite toward themes relevant to the Pax Americana, such as nonproliferation, the regional international system, and collective security, shall be considered. During the period covered, Brazilian foreign policy was characterized by the acceptance of the core values and norms of the Pax Americana and by a drive toward greater participation and acceptance of international institutions on the global, regional, subregional, and bilateral levels. The positive approach toward the United Nations as an administrator of international security and a global forum for cooperation on many issues, acceptance of the Organization of American States' (OAS's) democratic paradigm, the attempt to work toward regional integration in the Southern Cone, and adherence to various international regimes are the clearest expressions of these changes.

Institutions, such as regimes, represent constraints on the behavior of actors, as liberal institutionalists would point out, but at the same time create opportunities and constitute the identities of actors, shaping their interests.[1] They frame behavior, but they also affect the properties of actors. Norms, identities, and interests are constructed in the process of interaction, as a result of social practice, consciously promoted strategies, or deliberate negotiations. The relation between Brazil and the institutions that are one of the building blocks of the Pax Americana will be the focus of this chapter. I focus on those institutions that are geared toward the management of international security because the posture of the Brazilian ruling elite toward these norms, regimes, and organizations expresses both the drastic changes in this country's foreign policy that marked the period in question and the tensions between the Brazilian perspective and the international order in the making.

In order to understand the Brazilian perspective toward international institutions and toward the United States in particular, it is relevant to analyze the change in the definition of threats that occurred during the period under scrutiny. I depart from the tradition, largely inaugurated by Barry Buzan, that incorporates sociological concerns and perspectives into the study of security.

Buzan suggests we embark on the analysis of the process that produces the "securitization" of issues henceforth presented as existential threats and handled through extraordinary means. The rhetorical structure is characterized by key components — "existential threats, emergency action, and effects on inter-unit relations by breaking free of rules."[2] In this context, issues related to the use of force are not the sole objects of security studies, but states remain the central actors of the system. The social construction of the idea of security involves the definition of threats and specifying referent objects, that is, what is being secured. The analysis that follows does not focus on the threat perceptions of the Brazilian elite as opposed to the "real" threats "out there." The threats are constituted by speech acts; discourse and behavior are considered. The assumption of the dichotomy between subjective and objective threats that influenced the literature since the days of Arnold Wolfers is abandoned.[3]

During the 1990s, the Brazilian decision-making elite pursued a foreign policy characterized by a strong drive toward conformity with international norms and rules. After a period of transition between a model that associated foreign policy and economic development, a drive to reshape the country's foreign policy can be observed. Only by the mid-1990s can a clear direction be detected. The elected governments would pursue a "strategy of insertion"[4] that covers the acceptance of international regimes, the growing participation in UN operations, a wider participation in commercial multilateral negotiations, and an emphasis on regional stability rather than subregional competition.

The relation between foreign policy and a wider project of economic development acquired a new contour in the 1990s, as the commercial dimension was stressed in the context of a clear shift toward neoliberal economic policies. In fact, the search for a wider international presence in the commercial sphere is the main focus of the strategy of insertion. A clear tendency toward globalization ties the views on security and multilateralism to interdependence as a feature of the international landscape.

On the other hand, the realist tradition (according to which international norms are created insofar as they express the interests of the most powerful states in the system, and international order may only be produced when there is a congruency between the structure of international institutions and the distribution of power) was one of the pillars of the Brazilian perspective on the international system.

In line with this view and as a consequence of the domestic process of democratization, the country's representatives have openly and repetitively supported the idea that democracy and liberalism have now become regimes that carry universal legitimacy. In spite of its role as mediator between countries that hold more particular views on issues related to the Western concepts of liberalism and democracy and the hegemonic positions of the great powers, the decision-making elite has accepted that a new international norm is being generated. In his 1995 UN speech, Minister Luiz Felipe Lampreia stated this position clearly: "The current configuration of international relations converges towards the two concepts that have inspired the revolution of the 90s: democracy and economic liberty with social justice. This is the main characteristic that will shape the century that approaches us and will assure liberty and prosperity for all of us."[5]

At the same time, a clear concern about the Brazilian participation in the international decision-making process can be detected. The argument against Brazil's marginalization, in spite of the socioeconomic realities and its relative position in the hierarchy of states, is that the country's cultural and ethnic diversity, the mixture of First World and developing country characteristics, the tradition of a coherent foreign policy and sophisticated diplomacy, and the peaceful nature of its international relations justify a more intense participation in the international decision-making processes.[6] This is increasingly seen as a main interest due to the reflection on the internationalization of power and authority crystallized in the growing web of international norms.

Participation in multilateral forums is the main answer to this concern. Thus, the Brazilian government has sought to actively participate in the debate on the regulation of international commerce and on the reform of the UN System, among other multilateral agenda items. President Fernando Henrique Cardoso was particularly keen on negotiating new forms of regulation of the international financial markets. The security of the South Atlantic was pursued through a partnership with South Africa, and Brazil led the negotiations between the European Union and MERCOSUL. The role of regional mediator, as in the case of the territorial dispute between Peru and Equator and the political crisis in Paraguay, matches this image to perfection. Thus, in the context of President Cardoso's mandate, we may observe a drive to take part in the process of internationalization of authority, which tends to be taken on by newly elected President Luis Inácio Lula da Silva.

The understanding that the contemporary international system is under the tension of centrifugal and centripetal forces and that there are no international institutions that should, in the foreseeable future, function as a "world government" leads the Brazilian decision-making elite to stress the necessity to protect the country's national sovereignty, in particular, and the concept of state sovereignty, both in its internal and external facets. After the impeachment of President Collor de Mello, the presence of a defensive position with regard to interventionism in matters such as human rights, ecology, drug traffic, and terrorism can be observed, responding to concerns of sectors of the decision-making elite, in particular the military establishment, although a return to the pre-1980s posture did not occur. After the mid-1990s the defense posture regarding the concept of sovereignty was encapsulated in some issues, while the acceptance of the internationalization of authority acquired deeper roots.

The defense of sovereignty is accompanied by efforts to affirm the legitimacy of the country as a main actor in international politics. Hence, a balance is struck between the acceptance of a growing web of international norms and conditions and the protection of state sovereignty. As Celso Lafer and Gelson Fonseca Jr. put it, "The current context demands … a double conceptual movement, discerning a perspective which is truly national for the understanding of the implications of globalization … that should be complemented by a global perspective for the forms of national insertion."[7]

The realist assumption functions as a tool both for understanding the international political system and for placing Brazil in the global and regional distribution of power hierarchy. Thus, as a medium power with unrealized capabilities, the country's foreign policy guidelines accept the norms generated at the core of the system and, at the same time, seek reasonable means to guarantee a wider participation in global forums, always stressing the universalistic and legalist principles that grant greater autonomy for a marginal player in world affairs. Significant hard power is not available at present, given the state of the Brazilian armed forces and of the Brazilian economy. In this context, the stress placed on international institutions permits the country to raise its influence in the international arena and protect its internal sovereignty. This posture has been adopted across issue areas: commercial negotiations in the World Trade Organization (WTO) context (previously the General Agreement on Tariffs and Trade); the attitude toward nonproliferation regimes, environmental regimes, and human right regimes; and patterns of behavior of the Security Council and the acceptance of the Western Hemisphere democratic paradigm. Even in the regional sphere, where the country does hold a prominent position, the presence of the United States underlies the importance of wide support of universalistic institutions.

At the same time, given the size of the country and its population and level of industrialization, there is a deeply embedded expectation that Brazil is to play a greater role in world affairs, as if there were a dissonance between the country's potential and real power. In fact, if we look at gross national product, diversity of commercial links, industrial development, institutional robustness of the state apparatus, or population and geographic features, we can easily understand the high expectations of the ruling elite. Nevertheless, the significant change that occurred during the 1990s is not the place the country occupied in the international hierarchy of power, but the interpretation by the ruling elite of the best road map for forwarding their understanding of the national interest.

In sum, while the decision-making elite has, during the past years, been steadily moving toward a deeper understanding of the complexity of the international system, both with regard to the process of economic, social, and cultural globalization and with regard to the growing role played by international organizations, in particular the UN, the defense of state sovereignty is one of the pillars of the position adopted vis-à-vis the international scenario. The concept is closely associated with the definition of threats to be discussed in this chapter and the criticism of the decision-making process in international forums in the context of a search for a balance between a legalist and universalistic approach and a realist understanding of international institutions.

One of the hallmarks of the period is a move toward more involvement and cooperation in Latin America.[8] The end of the rivalry between Brazil and Argentina, the proposal for the creation of a South American Free

Trade Accord,[9] the creation of MERCOSUL, and the initiatives associated with greater economic and physical integration with Andean and Amazonian countries are part of the scenario. In particular, MERCOSUL was part of a wider strategy of insertion that stressed Brazil's position as a medium power. Nevertheless, the country refrained from assuming a leadership role in the region in spite of the pressure exerted by other Latin American countries. This perspective is likely to change in the near future as indicated by President Lula's first international initiative, negotiating the formation of the group of friends "for" Venezuela.

The Acceptance of International Regimes

The "acceptance of the internationalization of authority" and "the concern with the exclusion of the country from the international stage," two trends that may be observed in the country's multilateral behavior, favored the acceptance of international regimes and the move toward cooperative security.

The first president to come to power by means of democratic elections in Brazil since the 1960s, President Collor de Mello, started his term in office as the Cold War came to an end. During this period, there was a concern with the removal of disputes that could interfere with the project of internationalizing and liberalizing the national economy. The policies toward environmental issues, nuclear nonproliferation, and intellectual property legislation changed, and the end of the Cold War was seen as an opportunity to deal with north–south issues in a more cooperative manner.[10] Subsequently, the Brazilian government has actively participated in the discussions that aim at the creation of international norms capable of tackling environmental issues, human rights, and nuclear nonproliferation.

Since 1972, when the Stockholm Conference was held, the Brazilian position has changed dramatically with regard to the constitution of international norms to protect the environment. During the 1970s and 1980s, the idea of incompatibility between development and environmental protection still prevailed. During the first civilian government after 21 years of military rule, led by President José Sarney, in spite of a defensive position on international pressure on the development of the Amazon region, several measures were implemented in order to generate an environmentally responsible image, such as monitoring the clearing of land by burning, suspension of incentives for agriculture and cattle raising in the region, and the creation of reservations for extravism (economic activity based on the extraction or picking/collection of natural products, such as wood, which are not cultivated). The next government, which hosted the

1992 conference, continued this effort of changing the Brazilian image. In this field, as well as in others, the decision-making elite tended to take an active part in multilateral initiatives and accept the norms established by the most successful regimes such as the protection of the ozone layer and the Antarctica regimes.[11] The attempt to put the debate on development at the center of the environmental agenda is expressed by the focus on sustainable development. During the 1992 Conference on the Environment, held in Rio de Janeiro, a balanced treatment of development and environmental protection was sought, the Brazilian government having supported the principles that environmental problems are global in nature and that there should be a differential responsibility in dealing with the problem, the richest countries assuming greater costs.

After the end of the authoritarian phase of the country's history, it was possible for the government to reestablish its role in the international debate on human rights. Hence, the Vienna Conference can be considered an important turning point. This process started in 1985, when the decision to adhere to the three treaties for the protection of human rights (the American convention and the two UN pacts on human rights) was made, these treaties having been ratified, however, only in 1992. In 1997, the jurisdiction of the Interamerican Court of Human Rights was recognized and the position of Secretary for Human Rights was created. At the second International Conference on Human Rights (Vienna, 1993), with Ambassador Gilberto Sabóia presiding over the report committee of the conference, the Brazilian representatives also stressed the relation between human rights and development,[12] in line with a wider tendency to treat human rights in political, social, cultural, and economic terms. Furthermore, the creation within the UN System of a program for technical, material, and financial assistance to national projects and institutions directly related to human rights and the strengthening of the rule of law was defended.

Substantial changes in Brazil's security policies occurred after the country returned to civilian rule in 1985. After decades of reluctance and open criticism of the way international security was managed by the super-powers, Brazil now abides by virtually all formal and informal norms, treaties, rules, and regulations that govern, however imperfectly, international security affairs.

Brazil has never been a proponent of radical reforms in the functioning of the international peace and security institutions, in particular the UN. Nevertheless, during the Cold War era, decision-makers in Brasilia believed that a condominium of great powers controlled and froze the global distribution of power. According to this view, the United States and the Soviet

Union reached an accommodation that was dangerous for international security and detrimental to the interest of the developing nations.

Traditional geopolitics associated with the East–West confrontation was substituted by a drive to take part in a globalized world defined by economic competition, deregulation, financial liberalization, expanded foreign trade, and investment. Initially motivated by the need for sustainable economic growth and access to international finance and investment, Brazil moderated its criticism of the main rules and regulations, and ended up conforming to the international security regimes.

The most significant step in this direction was the acceptance of the nonproliferation regime after the transition to democracy in the 1980s. In 1987, the Brazilian government acknowledged the "parallel" nuclear program (Brazilian Autonomous Program of Nuclear Technology), under military direction, and by 1991, the International Atomic Energy Agency was allowed to inspect formerly secret nuclear facilities.[13] The 1988 Brazilian Constitution allows for nuclear activities only for peaceful purposes and if approved by the national Congress. The decision to become a full member of the Treaty of Tlatelolco was made in 1994.[14]

In October 1995, Congress approved legislation on export controls of nuclear materials, allowing the country to apply for membership in the Nuclear Suppliers Group (NSG), the multilateral group whose purpose is ensuring nonproliferation of nuclear materials and technologies through export controls. Brazil was admitted as a full member of the NSG in April 1996 at the Buenos Aires plenary meeting.

On September 18, 1998, Brazil deposited the instrument of accession to the NPT.[15] Yet one should not forget that the nature of the NPT has always generated opposition from certain sectors of Latin American societies; the discriminatory nature of the regime and the need to move further toward disarmament are issues raised by nationalist parties, sectors of the military establishment, and scientists. In line with this perspective, Brazil takes part in the New Agenda Coalition (NAC).[16]

In 1991, two years before the chemical weapons treaty was signed, Brazil joined with Argentina and Chile in the Declaration of Mendoza. They pledged not to produce, buy, stock, use, or transfer chemical or biological weapons. The parties also agreed to establish appropriate inspection mechanisms on a national basis. Four other South American nations (Bolivia, Ecuador, Paraguay, and Uruguay) signed the declaration later. MERCOSUL (Southern Common Market) declared its geographic region and Bolivia and Chile free of arms of mass destruction and a "zone of peace" in July 1998 ("Declaration of MERCOSUL as a Zone of Peace," Ushuaia, Argentina).

Brazil's commitment to nuclear nonproliferation included delivery vehicles for weapons of mass destruction. In 1995, the country joined the Missile Technology Control Regime (MTCR) membership. Brazil also scrapped its ballistic missile programs, although Avibras produces and exports the SS-series of rockets (ranges varying from 30 to 80 km). In the Brazilian case, the will to acquire technology for its space launch vehicle also motivated the country to adhere to MTCR guidelines in December 1994.[17]

Brazil also belongs to the 1972 Convention for the Prohibition of Biological Weapons, the 1991 United Nations Register of Conventional Arms, the 1993 Convention for the Prohibition of Chemical Weapons, and the 1996 Comprehensive Test Ban Treaty. In relation to antipersonnel land mines, the Brazilian government announced that it had suspended the use or export of mines on an informal basis starting in 1984. Brazil acceded to the Convention on Certain Conventional Weapons in October 1995 and supported the Ottawa process that concluded as a convention banning antipersonnel land mines.

The UN and International Security

In 1907, when the country took part in the second Peace Conference in Haia, the dominant theme in the discourse of the Brazilian representatives was the relevance of the norms of international law and the negotiated resolution of conflicts. In that context the "Haia paradigms" were generated, and a tradition of searching for international recognition through the defense of the principles of a lawful international society based on universal principles and the support for the role of reason and mediation in solving international conflicts was born.[18] Subsequently, based on this approach, the country aspired to be a member of the Council of the League of Nations. At the end of World War II, once again Brazil put forward its candidacy for a permanent seat on the executive branch of the newly formed international organization. Nevertheless, a temporary seat with a two-year term was the result of the pressure exerted. The token participation in the war effort and the mild support received from President Roosevelt did not represent a significant leverage in this attempt.

In spite of the failure of these efforts, they did play an important role in embedding the image of the country as a potential significant player in international affairs and the view that multilateral universal forums should be a target of a policy of international insertion. This fraction of the cognitive map of the decision-making elite combines easily with its traditional elements, often referred to as the country's "permanent diplomatic stock": pacifism, noninterventionism, defense of the equal sovereignty of all nations, and respect for the international legal system.

After the end of the Cold War, the new relevance of the UN was perceived in the context of the strategy of insertion mentioned earlier. Having occupied a temporary seat in the Security Council in 1993–1994, 1998–1999, and having joined several committees and informal groups, Brazilian representatives took part in the debates on the reform of the UN System and in the discussions leading to new mechanisms of collective security.

With regard to the debate on the reform of the UN System, the Brazilian position has favored discussing procedures, rather than changing the rights of intervention of the organization. Hence, Brazilian diplomats were skeptical about some propositions in the 1992 report "An Agenda for Peace," particularly the view that the UN should exert a pacifying function, regardless of the positions of the parties involved.[19] On the other hand, the importance of reforming the Security Council so that its composition expresses the current balance of power and is capable of dealing with the uncertainties of the next century has been stressed. During the government of Itamar Franco, Brazil formally applied to become a permanent member of the Security Council, and Fernando Henrique Cardoso maintained the same posture. The 2002–2003 Iraq crisis opened a window of opportunity for the newly elected government of Luiz Lula Inácio da Silva to restate the Brazilian candidacy. The Brazilian argument has been that the composition of the Security Council should express changes in the international system, particularly the emergence of new powers in the developing world. A more representative Council would carry greater legitimacy and function more efficiently.[20] Moreover, Brazil would be a strong candidate due to the country's diplomatic tradition as a mediator and as an active member of the UN. After Japan, Brazil has been the country without a permanent seat on the Security Council that has taken part for the longest period (1946–1947, 1951–1952, 1954–1955, 1963–1964, 1967–1968, 1988–1989, 1993–1994, 1998–1999).

The country's role as a mediator and its traditional deference toward international norms and legality is seen as an important asset and mentioned repeatedly in the context of the Brazilian candidacy for a permanent seat on the Security Council. As Gelson Fonseca, once the Brazilian representative to the UN, writes, "One of the most salient features [of the Brazilian diplomatic style] is the capacity to undramatize the foreign policy agenda, reducing conflicts, crises and difficulties in the diplomatic practice, avoiding that these be exploited or enhanced by situational interests."[21]

Brazilian diplomats have expressed the view that the role played by the General Assembly must be renewed and that the Security Council should function according to well-established and transparent criteria.[22] According to Ambassador Ronaldo Sardenberg, designated the new representative to the UN in 2003, there is a growing "institutional imbalance" in favor of the Security Council, with grave consequences to the role played by the General Assembly of the UN. Furthermore, he referred to the dangers of the creation of a world "Jurassic Park," where coercion will be the main instrument of implementing decisions, in contrast to the use of diplomatic instruments.[23]

There has been serious concern about the abyss between the decisions made by the Security Council, in line with the policies proposed by the Western powers, and established criteria on the Security Council's authority.[24] In general, the official view has been that the organization should preserve its universal and representative credentials. Brazil should play a pivotal role in this context. As one diplomat put it, our "capacity to formulate and mobilize" is recognized by the international community, and Brazilian behavior is marked by preoccupation with the preservation of "democratic principles."[25]

The international conferences scheduled for the last years of the century were considered a relevant forum where states could be equally represented. The preparation for each of the conferences involved the foreign office, other parts of the state apparatus, and sectors of civil society. In each of these conferences, apart from other tendencies mentioned earlier, the country's representatives have been pivotal in allowing the best possible balance between the particular interests or features of national and religious cultures and universal ideals.

Regarding the redefinition and reactivation of the system of collective security, there is a clear preference for a revival of the collective security functions of the organization present in Chapters VI and VII of the UN Charter rather than the transference of this role to military regional organizations that lack universality.[26] The maintenance of a central role for the Security Council in the context of multilateral action is stressed,[27] and the transference of collective security functions of the UN to regional organizations, as occurred in Haiti, Yugoslavia, Liberia, Sierra Leone, and Georgia, generates significant concern.[28] In line with the legalist posture adopted by Brazil, the cooperation between regional organizations and the UN should follow the parameters established in Chapter VIII of the UN Charter. The NATO operation in Yugoslavia and the American and British intervention in Iraq were most clearly opposed, the contradiction between the unilateral use of force and the legal venues offered by the UN having been stressed.[29]

Hence we can observe a tendency to maintain a legalist and universalistic approach while favoring changes in the decision-making process regarding international security that would allow for a more prominent role for Brazil.

The revival of peace operations since the end of the Cold War places this practice at the center of the debate on the UN and collective security. The Brazilian military has taken part in peace and observation operations since the genesis of the process that transformed the original collective security project in the 1950s. The support for a collective security system is expressed in the country's participation in UN peace operations.[30]

After the end of the Cold War, as peace operations became more diversified and numerous, Brazilian participation increased, though not at the same pace as that of its Southern Cone neighbors, Argentina and Uruguay. These two countries have set up training facilities geared toward peace operations. The Brazilian armed forces are not ready to redefine their role, putting UN missions at the center of their objectives and strategies. Yet, joint military operations at the Argentine–Brazilian border that recreate peace operation conditions have taken place, in line with the notion of cooperative security, and troops, medical staff, police personnel, and electoral specialists have been sent to Africa, Central America, Europe, and Asia. Brazilian diplomats have also joined the Special Committee on Peace Operations of the General Assembly.

The country's role in Angola has been particularly significant since 1991, Brazil having contributed both in the verification missions (UNAVEM I and II, 1991–1997) and the observer mission (MONUA, 1997). In Africa, Brazilian forces were also present in Mozambique (UNOMOZ, 1992–1995), Uganda, Rwanda (UNOMUR, 1993–1994, UNAMIR), and Liberia (UNOMIL). The participation of Brazilian troops in UNOMOZ between 1992 and 1995 represented the first deployment of combat troops in a foreign country since the 1965 OAS intervention in the Dominican Republic. Brazil has been particularly active in Angola and Mozambique, partly due to linguistic and cultural affinities.[31] In Angola, in the context of UNAVEM I, Brazilian officers were the liaison between the Cuban and Angolan authorities and the opposing guerrilla leaders.

Brazil was also present in Central America, verifying the electoral process in Nicaragua (ONUVEM, 1989); verifying that the governments of Costa Rica, El Salvador, Guatemala, Honduras, and Nicaragua were complying with the Esquipulas II accords (ONUCA, 1990–1992); supervising the internal accords in El Salvador (ONUSAL, 1991–1995); and observing the human rights situation in Guatemala (MINUGUA, 1994).

In the Balkans, Brazil was part of the UN protection force (UNPROFOR, 1992–1995), the missions in Croatia (UNCRO, 1995–1996 and UNMOP, 1996), and the mission in Macedonia (UNPREDEP, 1995).

In Asia, electoral observers were present in Cambodia (UNTAC), and Brazilian troops joined the mission in East Timor (UNAMET). Brazil sent military police to East Timor, having promptly answered the Australian request for troops, though the size of the group did not express the support for the mission given by Ambassador Gelson Fonseca in the Security Council.

Doctrinal changes have tried to follow this new engagement. The white paper "National Defense Policy" of 1996[32] establishes the new foundations for a concept of national security. According to this document, one of the objectives of the national defense policy is participation in the international decision-making process. This context stresses the relevance of Brazil's contribution to the maintenance of international peace and security. Among the directives contained in the document, we find reference to Brazil's active contribution to "the construction of an international order based on the rule of law which should promote universal and regional peace and the sustainable development of humanity." However, the irresolute efforts of the military establishment and of the government to upgrade Brazilian participation in peace operations, particularly in the sphere of strategic planning and training, outlines the reaction against a move toward the redefinition of the role of the military in the new democratic context. For example, the preparation of troops takes place due to the decision to take part in an operation, whereas the UN favors standing schemes. The belief that the main role of the military lies in its dissuasive capability and the maintenance of territorial sovereignty and integrity is widespread.

At the same time, since the end of the Cold War, the changes in the scope and nature of peace operations have been met with considerable concern by diplomats and the military establishment, particularly the move toward resolutions based on Chapter VII of the Charter. The principles on which peace operations were based have traditionally been supported by Brazilian governments — the previous agreement of all the parts, impartiality, and minimum use of force. In contrast, the changes in the concept of intervention are seen with great concern.[33] As a temporary member of the Security Council, the country has not been supportive of the resolutions that involve the UN in coercive interventions. Indeed, the strategic orientation included in the 1996 "National Defense Policy" stresses the search for a pacific solution to disputes and the use of force only as a means of self-defense. Significantly, the government abstained from sending troops to the Persian Gulf War in 1991, in spite of the support for the collective security operation, as this was a clear case of aggression and a rupture of peace.

Ambassador Celso Amorim has written emphatically about this tendency, removing himself from the propositions in the *Agenda for Peace*. According to this former UN representative and present foreign minister

> ... it is necessary to acknowledge that the comparative advantage of the United Nations as a privileged forum for multilateral diplomatic conciliation can be found in the sphere of understanding and negotiation. The monitoring of cease fires, disarmed peace missions or even robust peace missions are the only means for the promotion of dialogue and understanding in situations where the lack of mutual trust undermines the generation of peace. In a context still marked by the militarizing bias of the Agenda for Peace to value diplomacy as such represents in the present Security Council an original position, to a certain degree, as odd as this may seem in light of the contents of the Charter. It is nonetheless an attitude which corresponds to Brazil's natural vocation.[34]

During 1993–1994, as a member of the Security Council, Brazil abstained from the vote on the proposal, which was not adopted, to lift the embargo on arms applicable to the regions of the former Yugoslavia; it did not favor peace enforcement in Somalia or Rwanda. Brazil also abstained from the vote on the intervention in Haiti.

When the Security Council adopted "for the first time in history" a Chapter VII resolution in connection with a Western Hemisphere country, Brazil abstained but strongly opposed in its discourse the interventionist measures, favoring an extension of the UNMIH (United Nations Mission in Haiti). The Brazilian representative quoted Article 2(b) from the OAS Charter, " ... the Organization has an essential purpose, 'to promote and consolidate representative democracy with due respect for the principle of non-intervention.'"[35] While discussing the situation prevailing in and around the safe area of Bihac, the Brazilian representative expressed concern about the move toward the use of force in the context of UN operations: "We reiterate our reservation on the use of the expression 'all necessary measures,' which seems to have become a standard expression of the Council associated with military force to the detriment of diplomatic efforts."[36] In the case of the intervention in Rwanda, it was mentioned that the party closer to victory opposed the presence of French troops.[37] As stated by Ronaldo Sardenberg, then the Brazilian representative at the UN, in the context of a Security Council debate on Somalia, "It has been rightly pointed out that the United Nations cannot impose peace in Somalia or anywhere else if the parties involved are not willing to make peace themselves."[38]

The imposition of sanctions under Chapter VII is usually supported, given the necessary restrictions on the consequences for the civilian population. In the case of the war in Angola, Brazil strongly supported the imposition of sanctions against the National Union for Total Independence of Angola (UNITA) since this organization did not comply with the peace accords and did not accept the result of the 1992 elections.[39]

In addition, the move toward a wider range of activities and functions in the context of UN peace operations is viewed positively by the Brazilian ruling elite.[40] The landmark resolution 687 (April 3, 1991) that represented an expansion of Security Council responsibilities in the sphere of disarmament and nonproliferation was supported by the Brazilian representative. Nation building activities are widely endorsed.

Brazilian diplomats have expressed their concern about the lack of impartiality and previous consent observable in some UN operations. For example, Ambassador Augusto de Araujo Castro, in the context of a debate of the Special Committee on Peace Operations, stressed that successful operations have in common the establishment of a previous political agreement and the consent of the parties involved. In his words, "...these practices promote the confidence in the impartial authority of the United Nations...."[41] When supporting measures that could include the "halting of inward maritime traffic, with the exclusive purpose of enforcing the sanctions related to oil and arms" in Haiti, the Brazilian representative stressed that this should not constitute a "precedent" and that the "explicit request by the legitimate government of Haiti" was paramount.[42]

A supplementary theme that reoccurs in the discourse of Brazilian diplomats is the need to define the mandates of the operations in a clear manner, in accordance with the Charter. The definition of clear mandates by the Security Council is a basic condition for the legality of peace operations. Taking part in a debate in the General Assembly in 1993, Minister Edgard Telles Ribeiro mentioned the responsibility of the Council in this respect, emphasizing the possible conceptual confusion between humanitarian assistance, development assistance, and peace maintenance.[43] In the case of resolution 688, the government did not make troops available for implementation since the resolution represented a move toward *ad hoc* changes of international norms. A critical view of the move toward exceptions, which contradict established norms of nonintervention, was the justification put forward by the Brazilian mission.[44] When resolution 737, submitted by France on the Rwanda crisis, was debated, Brazil did not endorse the resolution, considering that the simultaneous maintenance of a peacekeeping and a peace-enforcement operation in the same country would be detrimental to humanitarian efforts.[45]

Definition of Threats

The definition of threats in the Brazilian case is affected by a historical legacy marked by the peaceful definition of borders and the concern with large parts of the country where the presence of the state has been fragile. Brazil developed a diplomatic culture based on the peaceful resolution of disputes, in favor of mediation and negotiation. The Paraguayan War was the last militarized territorial dispute that Brazil was engaged in, and the territorial borders were negotiated by the Rio Branco Baron during the nineteenth century.

Brazil's security policies of the past decades might be compared with those of similar nations in territorial and economic terms such as China or India. In contrast to the two Asian nations, however, Brazil has not been shaped in recent decades by disputes, conflicts, and wars; therefore, it did not invest human and material resources in the preparation for war on the same scale as those nations trapped in acute regional conflicts. Moreover, Brazil's international relations were shaped by a tradition of peaceful resolution of conflicts through diplomacy and negotiation, which left a decisive mark in nation and state building. It also contributed to forging a Brazilian self-image as a peaceful and law-abiding nation. In addition, one may observe a lack of serious ethnic or religious rivalries, which is quite unique among large developing nations.

For a very long time, the Brazilian ruling elite considered Argentina the greatest external menace to its security. The two nations were at war between 1825 and 1828 and finally signed the treaty of Montevideo, which recognizes the independence of Uruguay. The creation of a buffer state between the countries did not end the competition for political and military hegemony in the region or for access to Bolivian, Paraguayan, and Uruguayan markets and resources. During the 1960s and the 1970s, the exploration of hydroelectric power fueled the rivalry. Argentina did not accept the treaty between Paraguay and Brazil, which allowed for the construction of the Itaipu dam, this dispute having been resolved in 1979. Relations with Argentina remained competitive and unfriendly for most of the twentieth century, but force was never used between the two neighbors. Since the southern corner of the country was perceived as a main source of threat, defense policies reflected this reality.

Only during the 1980s did the relation change substantially in the context of redemocratization in both countries and growing contacts between the military establishments. Significantly, since the mid-1980s, an informal system of nuclear inspections has been in place. Finally, in 1991 the two countries signed a trilateral agreement with the International Atomic Energy Agency (IAEA) that puts all nuclear installations in both Brazil and Argentina under the supervision of the IAEA. Between 1985 and 1988, a nuclear regime was built, laying the institutional foundations for verified nuclear nonproliferation in the 1990s. Argentina and Brazil engaged in nuclear confidence-building measures and sought to integrate their national nuclear programs. The Argentine–Brazilian Agency for Accounting and Control of Nuclear Materials was created in 1991[46] in order to control the application of the Common System of Accounting and Control. During the 1990s, Argentina and Brazil, along with South Africa, became examples of proliferation "rollback."[47]

The perception of mutual menace has to a large extent receded today. Indeed, although security issues have not been part of the multilateral process of regional integration, contacts between the military establishments of Argentina and Brazil have been taking place, and the strategic and military aspects of regional integration have been discussed.

Nevertheless, one cannot forget that during the 1990s the differences between the foreign policies and economic strategies of the two countries were wide and often generated low levels of tension. Regarding relations with the United States, in particular, and the nature of the new international order, differences remained significant during the period, Argentina having sought a tight alliance with the United States. In the commercial sphere, the conflict of interest between the two countries increased and divergent views on the convertibility of the currency impeded the move toward greater economic integration.

The vast Amazon region, which consists of 61% of the country, and its porous borders became a main concern of the ruling elite during the twentieth century, and since the 1980s the focus on the region has systematically increased, troops having been transferred accordingly. The surveillance of the South Atlantic coastal area is another key objective. The region's fledgling infrastructure, the relations between local power and the federalist system, and the characteristics of the environment explain the absence of effective state sovereignty in the region. Several threats are defined under the heading of lack of control, such as disrespect for the borders, illegal or predatory economic activities, drug trafficking, invasion of national territory by insurgent movements or the armed forces of neighboring countries fighting against insurgencies, and the presence of international NGOs. Illegal activities include mining, logging without proper registration, deforestation, smuggling, and nonstop border crossing by planes carrying illegal cargo.

The redefinition of threats to the state allowed for the armed forces to find a new role in the post–Cold War environment. The democratization of the country and the end of the rivalry with Argentina opened a debate on the role of the armed forces and the contours of the country's security policy. The growing threat perception emanating from the Amazon region, the strong corporate identity of the armed forces, and the effectiveness of a discourse on the defense of national sovereignty permitted a vague definition of a security policy and the continuous allocation of resources for the military establishment. At the same time, a clearly delineated defense policy was not generated, and resources have been allocated in the absence of an acceptable planned strategy.

On average, military expenditure during the 1990s amounted to 1.3%[48] of GDP, and a modest effort to modernize the armed forces was made, a rapid reaction force having been created (FAREB, força de ação rápida do Exército Brasileiro). The army remains relatively small (300,000 personnel), considering the size of the country, but Latin America is the region with the lowest conflict level in the world, and even under military rule, the armed forces restricted their own budgets in favor of public investment and the industrialization plan. The military operates on a tight budget with limitations on procurement, operations, and training. It does have long-term plans for modernization, but the lack of a debate in the public sphere on the role of the military and budget restriction have not allowed a proper replacement and update plan to be generated.

The projects entitled Amazon Protection System (SIPAM) and Amazon Surveillance System (SIVAM) were set up by the federal government to deal with this perceived threat. The projects aim to produce information, particularly on biodiversity and illegal activities, generate a strategic and integrated governmental action, stimulate development, and enforce sovereignty.[49]

The move toward greater integration of the Amazon countries can also be understood in this light. Special attention has been given to initiatives for road and power integration. The completion of the surfacing of the Manaus–Boa Vista–Caracas highway and the Brazil–Bolivia gas pipeline are examples of this policy. An accord between the Andean Community and MERCOSUL is being negotiated. In 1995, the countries that had originally joined the Amazon Cooperation Treaty in 1978 (Brazil, Bolivia, Colombia, Ecuador, Guyana, Peru, Surinam, and Venezuela) decided to create a permanent secretariat based in Brasilia.

In contrast to the 1980s, when the pressure exerted by NGOs and international organizations was perceived as a threat to national sovereignty in the region, today the role played by transnational crime is increasingly seen as a major threat. The connection between urban violence and the activities of these transnational actors has been incorporated into the wider debate on significant social problems faced by the country. In 2001, Luiz Fernando da Costa was captured in Colombia and extradited to Brazil. This event had a huge impact on the perception of the links between domestic violence and transnational criminal organizations.

Moreover, this perception of threat acquires new contours in view of the Colombian conflict. The American involvement in the conflict, the presence of fighting parties across the border, and the effect on regional stability have been the main concerns of the Brazilian government. The transfer of combatants and drug-related activities to Brazil and the ecological consequences of eradication operations are the main themes discussed by members of the government, the military, and society in general. Thus, enhancing the presence of the state in the area acquired new urgency. In this context, Plan Cobra (Colombia–Brazil) seeks to reinforce Brazilian military and police forces along its Amazon border with Colombia. The armed forces, the Brazilian Intelligence Agency, and the federal police take part in this plan.

The Cardoso administration introduced the terrorist threat to Brazil's international discourse, although on the periphery of the foreign policy agenda. Terrorism has been defined as a crime, and domestic legislation establishes that the lifting of secrecy from the operations of financial institutions may occur if such a crime is detected. At the time of writing, Brazil had ratified nine of the twelve conventions dealing with this issue. In 2001, the Brazilian government signed the Convention for the Suppression of the Financing of Terrorism and issued decrees for enforcing resolutions 1333 (2001) and 1373 (2001) of the UN Security Council. In a speech during the opening debate of the 56th UN General Assembly in November 2001, President Cardoso stressed the connection between drug trafficking, arms smuggling, and terrorism.[50] In this context, more attention has been given to the triple frontier, an area where, according to the American government, terrorist activity takes place. In 1996, Brazil, Argentina, and Paraguay created the Tripartite Command for the Triple Frontier to coordinate police action and intelligence gathering in the region. Nevertheless, the Brazilian government publicly denies any knowledge of terrorist activity in this region.

The shift from the previous threat definition focused on Argentina to the lack of control over the Amazon region has direct repercussions regarding the acceptance of U.S. hegemony in the region. The entanglement between Andean security and Amazon security, the different views on the war on drugs, and the wider U.S. military presence in neighboring countries tends to generate tension between the policy orientations of the two major players in the Americas. At the same time, the coincidence in the definition of threats in terms of control of transnational illegal activities creates room for increasing cooperation.

Relations with the Regional Hegemon

The general pattern of relations between Brazil and the United States in the 1990s sustained the positive approach toward the Pax Americana both in terms of world order and regional order. It also allows for an understanding of the areas of tension regarding the shape of multilateralism and the specific policies toward Latin America.

The special relation with the United States changed after the mid-1970s in the context of the diversification of economic relations, the search for new suppliers of assistance and material or developed armament, the development of projects for defense-related industries, and a more independent foreign policy. Henceforth, several contentious issues would mark the bilateral agenda, such as trade issues, nonproliferation, environmental protection, human rights violations, territorial waters, access to sensitive technologies, and intellectual propriety regulations. In fact, the special alliance between the United States and Brazil endured only until the early 1960s. After this period the United States was no longer the focal point for Brazilian foreign policy.

The nationalization of the concept of security since the 1970s involved a process of detachment from the inter-American security system. The definition of an arms export policy by the Geisel government, the nuclear agreement signed in 1975 with Germany, the unilateral abandonment of the 1952 military accord with the United States in 1977, and the development of a parallel nuclear program are part of this movement.[51] The 1980s can be depicted as a period marked by the debt crisis, the aggravated nature of disagreements about the environment, and the need to liberalize the economy at the same time that a relative rapprochement in military relations was taking place.

The 1990s were characterized by significant changes in the relations between the United States and Latin America. The lack of a clear hemispheric policy; the stress on the universalization of the neoliberal model; and a limited, although emerging, multilateral perceptive[52] could be observed. After a period dominated by the effects of the second Cold War on the continent, the initiatives of the first Bush administration concentrated on straightening economic links, the negotiations of the North American Free Trade Area, and the launching of the Initiative for the Americas. The changes that took place were paradigmatic; a coercive and ideological policy was substituted by a perspective that emphasized cooperation, greater investments, and commerce. The two following administrations under the leadership of Bill Clinton maintained similar objectives. The negotiation of the Treaty for Free Trade of the Americas would be the next step in this process. The U.S. government concentrated on two strategic issues during the period: the promotion of neoliberal reforms and the war on drugs.

During the 1990s, the negative agenda that had marked U.S.–Brazil relations during the 1970s and 1980s was set aside, and adjustment of policies in the economic, security, human rights, and environmental spheres led to better relations. The decade began with liberal reforms under the aegis of International Monetary Fund standards. Fernando Collor de Melo applied economic measures in line with the "Washington Consensus," and Fernando Henrique pursued a set of economic reforms according to this same framework. Although the presidency of Itamar Franco (1992–1994) was an exception, the acceptance of international regimes and the neoliberal economic model facilitated the rapprochement between the two countries. In fact, during the eight-year presidency of Fernando Henrique, this became a priority, linked to a review of Brazil's international insertion. The project for the creation of a South American Free Trade Association was shelved. At the 1994 Summit of the Americas, an agreement was reached to work toward the creation of a hemispheric free trade area by the year 2005. As we have seen, the posture regarding international regimes in different spheres changed dramatically.

Nevertheless, Brazilian policy choices are distant from the automatic alignment of previous periods. As Maria Regina Soares puts it, "Diplomats begin with the premise of U.S. power, especially within the hemisphere, a premise that calls for a nonconfrontational strategy. However, in their scenarios for a new world order, they stress multipolarity and the opportunities it affords for Brazil's international ascent."[53]

In the regional sphere, the convergence and disagreements between the two countries can be most clearly pinpointed. While Brazil accepted the expressions of the norms of the international order in the Americas in terms both of the liberal economic paradigm and the democratic paradigm, disagreements centered on mechanisms for regional integration and the nature of the process of reform of the inter-American security system.

There is significant resistance to a free trade area among several relevant political actors in Brazil, and the divergences regarding the timetable for negotiations and the scope of an agreement have been made clear by Brazilian diplomats. Brazil favors negotiations between blocs, and the United States supports country-to-country negotiations. While Brazil would like to deal first with agricultural subsidies, dispute settlement arrangements, and technical norms, the access to markets, intellectual property, and government procurement take precedence for the United States. The rejection of the proposal to create a Free Trade Area of the Americas remained a contentious issue until the shift toward a more intense dialogue on this issue after Celso Lafer became the foreign minister. The failures of negotiations with the European Union, difficulties encountered within the WTO to limit protectionism, and the stagnation of MERCOSUL has prompted the Brazilian government to stress the need to become a main interlocutor of the United States.[54] Conversely the newly elected government has announced it will prioritize negotiations within South America and be particularly demanding in negotiations for the formation of the Free Trade Area of the Americas.

The construction of the American democratic paradigm throughout the 1990s, finally leading to the adoption of the 2001 Democratic Charter, was supported by Brazilian representatives. The concept of cooperative security was incorporated by the Brazilian decision-making elite, the confidence-building agenda having received wide support. As we have seen, the participation in peace operations was embraced. On the other hand, although the debate on the reform of the inter-American security system was stillborn, a clear split regarding the role to be played by the OAS can be observed. The OAS is widely viewed with great skepticism, and the prospect of a standing force allocated under the OAS or some other pan-American regional control is not acceptable to the Brazilian decision-making elite. In the absence of an external threat to the hemisphere, the Inter-American Defense Treaty/OAS mechanism can with greater ease be depicted as an instrument of U.S. control of the security policies of the countries in the region.

However, Brazil has supported the work of the Inter-American Commission of the OAS for Drug Abuse Control, created in 1986 and has taken part in the Multilateral Evaluation Mechanism (MEM)[55] in place since 1999. Other spheres of cooperation such as de-mining efforts and election monitoring by the Unit for Promotion of Democracy were endorsed by the Brazilian state.

While the rationale guiding the U.S. security policy in the hemisphere was traditionally based on the perception of extra-hemispheric threats, after the Cold War threats emanating from the region itself acquired growing relevance. The new threats that mobilized attention in Washington were illegal migrations; drug traffic; and loss of control by the state of the flow of arms, drugs, and people.

As mentioned earlier, the definition of threats by the Brazilian decision-making elite focused on the situation in the Amazon region during the period in question and tended to progressively incorporate the presence of transnational criminal organizations. This generated prospects for cooperation, given the convergence in the definition of threats, but also created conditions for tensions to arise, as the strategies adopted by the two countries acquired different tones.

In 1995, a new agreement for cooperation in counternarcotics was signed. The State Department's International Narcotics Control program works to improve the Federal Police's intelligence and investigative capabilities. The U.S. Drug Enforcement Administration (DEA) cooperates with the Federal Police in several counternarcotics efforts, particularly training and information sharing. DEA agents also teach at the Federal Police School outside Manaus. On the other hand, there is no coordination of interdiction efforts between the Brazilian and U.S. agencies as occurs with Bolivia, Colombia, and Peru.

In respect to Plan Colombia, the Brazilian government has manifested its concern regarding the safety of its northern border. Stating the principal of noninterference, the Brazilian government has opposed any direct involvement in the Colombian crisis. In contrast to other conflicts and crisis in which Brazil was willing to play a role, in this case the standard attitude of the ruling elite has been to stress the domestic nature of the conflict. The lack of a clear legal framework or multilateral forum within which diplomatic efforts could be pursued, the emphasis given by the Colombian government on bilateral cooperation with the United States, and the absence of a peace process that could be endorsed explains the present posture of the Brazilian government. In particular, the presence of American troops in Latin America generates concern, the militarization of the Colombian conflict has been widely criticized, and the spread of U.S. bases in the region did not include Brazilian territory, although the 1996 space agreement guarantees special access to the Alcântara base in northeastern Brazil.

In a nutshell, the role Brazil should or could play in the Western Hemisphere is the main source of tension between the two countries. On one hand, the United States expects greater leadership from the Brazilian government, but on the other hand, the level of autonomy and specificity the Brazilian decision-making elite pursues is not recognized by the U.S. state.

The response from the Brazilian side is to search for protection in the realm of legality and hold back from a more active regional foreign policy.

Conclusion

During the 1990s, Brazil adapted to the changes in the international system, accurately evaluating the constraints imposed by the institutions created, bolstered, or reformed during the period. At the same time, a new identity and new interests of the state were generated, in line with the pillars of the post–Cold War order. A regime-abiding, cooperative, and democratic actor emerged in the process. The image of a peaceful and stable nation suited the concern with the flow of international investment.

Domestic and regional transformations that coincided with the end of the Cold War set the conditions for these developments to take place. At the same time, relations with the United States moved toward a positive agenda, facilitating the acceptance of the hegemonic position of this northern neighbor.

Successive administrations gradually designed a new foreign policy. Largely under the leadership of President Fernando Henrique Cardoso, the Ministry of Foreign Relations was able to reshape the country's foreign policy, internalizing new concepts and perceptions. At the same time important elements of continuity can be detected. The universalistic and legalist tradition that dates back to the beginning of the twentieth century acquired new strength and different means of expression. The new security policy, concentrating on the threats to the northern border and participation in the administration of international security in the context of multilateral institutions, has historical roots as well. Apart from the Amazon region, the definition of threats to the state also includes an array of tendencies detected in the international scenario toward the redefinition of the concepts of sovereignty and nonintervention. In this context, the defense of international legality has been securitized.

The insulation of the Ministry from the democratic process, in spite of the gradual incorporation of the congress into the debate on foreign policy, allowed this process to take place without the necessary public debate.[56] Thus, in spite of positive signs regarding the democratization of the foreign policy decision-making process, as expressed in the publication for the first time in history of a document on defense policy in 1996, the tenets of the country's foreign policy have yet to hold wider public support.

As we have seen, hegemonic concepts regarding the administration of international security, the decision-making process within the UN, and other issues are not entirely accepted by Brazilian representatives.

In addition, the debate on the nature of international order is ongoing. Given the perspective of the Brazilian decision-making elite regarding multilateral institutions, based on a strong emphasis on legality and universality, there should be a strong connection between the foreign policy orientation emerging from Washington and Brazil's position toward the Pax Americana. The American policy toward multilateral universalistic institutions is a significant variable in determining the Brazilian attitude vis-à-vis the American hegemonic order.

Divergence between the United States and Brazil regarding regional security, regional integration, and other subjects is a potential source of tension. As the major player in the hemisphere, apart from the United States, Brazil is the only country that can persistently pursue a policy geared toward balancing American power. In line with the realist perspective, Brazilian foreign policy has pursued a balancing policy only in the economic realm and, up to the time of writing, unsuccessfully. The difference between the two countries regarding regional integration are the result of this policy orientation. Regarding the security sphere, it is clear that a balance of power approach is not feasible and the protection generated by international institutions is the only option available to guarantee a degree of autonomy. Thus, in the case of the Colombian crisis, the main resource used has been the institution of state sovereignty.

The Brazilian state has been seeking a greater role in the international sphere, but the search for alternative coalitions is limited, and up to Luis Inácio Lula da Silva's election there has been a great reluctance to play a major role in generating regional institutions or contributing to managing international regional relations. The mobilization of resources geared toward the commercial sphere, the fear that the concept of sovereignty and nonintervention are under threat, and the concern about U.S. control of regional institutions, particularly the OAS, explain this behavior. The realist pillar of the country's foreign policy, allied to a sophisticated diplomatic tradition, leads decision makers to choose carefully the issues and spheres of engagement. Very often silence is seen as an asset in the context of a distribution of power where Brazil is not placed in a comfortable position. This stance is under increasing pressure, given the regional security crisis and the need to generate flexible but effective coalitions.

Domestic constraints also explain the choice of a low-profile foreign policy, given the lack of interest in international affairs among the population in general and the cultural, political, and economic elite in particular. It is thus difficult to mobilize significant resources for international engagement. The urgency in dealing with economic and social problems has always been at the forefront of the public debate. This is most obvious in the security sphere, where investment in the modernization of the armed forces has been low, and the general guidelines for a post–Cold War security policy produced in the 1990s have yet to generate a well-defined defense policy. Regarding the most pressing crisis in the region, apart from enhancing the presence of the state on the border region, the government has supported the diplomatic peace process and stressed the continuing relevance of the principle of nonintervention.[57] Brazil did not become a member of the Commission of Facilitators of the Peace Process composed of Canada, Cuba, Spain, France, Italy, Mexico, Norway, Sweden, Switzerland, and Venezuela and has not used multilateral forums to raise this issue.

The Brazilian ruling elite chose to accept the Pax Americana in the 1990s both as a regional order and as an international order. The road ahead will be delineated largely by the tendencies of the new century, the main questions being the role international institutions will play and the options for new coalitions opened by the winds of international politics.

Notes

1. This perspective can be found in Peter J. Katzenstein (ed.), *The Culture of National Security: Norms and Identity in World Politics* (New York: Columbia University Press, 1996).
2. Barry Buzan, Ole Waever, and Jaap de Wilde, *Security: A New Framework for Analysis* (London: Lynne Rienner Publishers, 1998), p. 26.
3. Arnold Wolfers, *Discord and Collaboration. Essays on International Politics* (Baltimore, The Johns Hopkins University Press, 1962).
4. Celso Lafer and Gelson Fonseca Jr., "Questões para a Diplomacia no Contexto Internacional das Polaridades Indefinidas (notas analíticas e algumas sugestões)," in *Temas de Política Externa Brasileira II*, ed. G. Fonseca Jr. and S. H. Nabuco de Castro (Rio de Janeiro: Paz e Terra, 1994), pp. 31–46.
5. Luiz Felipe Lampreia, Speech at the 1995 session of the General Assembly of the United Nations, in Fundação Alexandre de Gusmão, *A palavra do Brasil nas Nações Unidas 1946–1995* (1995).
6. For example, Roberto Abdenur, "A Política Externa Brasileira e o 'Sentimento de Exclusão'" in *Temas de Política Externa Brasileira II*, ed. G. Fonseca Jr. and S. H. Nabuco de Castro (Rio de Janeiro: Paz e Terra), pp. 31–46.
7. Celso Lafer and Gelson Fonseca Jr., "Questões para a diploamacia no contexto intenracioanl das polaridades indefinidas," in *Temas de Política Externa Brasileira II*, ed. G. Fonseca Jr. and S. H. Nabuco de Castro (Rio de Janeiro: Paz e Terra), pp. 49–77.
8. Raúl Bernal-Meza, "Las Políticas Exteriores de Argentina y Brasil durante los anos 90: Coincidencias e diferencias," *Carta Internacional*, no. 88 (June 2002), pp. 7–10; Raúl Bernal-Meza, "Políticas Exteriores Comparadas de Argentina y Brasil hacia el Mercosur," in *O Mercosul no limiar do século XXI*, ed. M. Costa Lima and M. de Almeida Medeiros (São Paulo: Cortez Editora/CLACSO), pp. 42–52.
9. The proposal for the creation of this free trade area was made in 1994 largely as an alternative to the American proposal for the creation of the Free Trade Area of the Americas.
10. See Monica Hirst and Letícia Pinheiro, "A Política Esterior do Brasil," *Revista Brasileira de Política Internacional* 38, no.1 (1995/1): 5–23.
11. On this theme see Leila da Costa Ferreira and Eduardo Viloa, eds., *Incertezas de Sustentabilidade na globalizacão* (Campinas: Editora da UNICAMP, 1996).
12. See Antonio Augusto Canssdo Trindade, "A proteção internacional dos direitos humanos no limiar do novo século e as perspectivas brasileiras," in *Temas de Política Externa Brasileira II*, G. Fonseca Jr. and S. H. Naabuco de Castro, eds. (Rio de Janeiro: Paz e Terra, 1994), pp. 168–87.

13. It should be noted that Brazil never engaged in the research necessary to develop deployable weapons. Regarding the competition between Brazil and Argentina, Brazilian military and diplomatic thinking was based on the notion of latent technological deterrence. Michael Barletta, 1997, *The Military Nuclear Program in Brazil*, Center for International Security and Arms Control.
14. Despite being the original proponent of the idea of a Nuclear Weapon-Free Zone, Brazil did not become a contracting party of the 1967 Treaty of Tlatelolco until 1994. For a discussion of the Brazilian position see Paulo S. Wrobel, "Brazil and the NPT: Resistance to Change?" *Security Dialogue*, 27, no. 3 (September 1996): 337–47.
15. Celso Lafer, "As novas dimensoes do desarmamento: os regimes de controle das armas de destruicao em massa e as perspectivas para a eliminacao das armas nucleares," in *O Brasil e as Novas Dimensoes da Seguranca Internacional*, G. Dupas and T. Vigevani, eds. (Sao Paulo: Editora Alfa-Omegs, 1999).
16. On June 9, 1998, Brazil, Mexico, Egypt, South Africa, Sweden, New Zealand, Ireland, and Slovenia published a ministerial declaration called "Toward a World Free of Nuclear Weapons: The Need for a New Agenda."
17. Dinshaw Mistry, "Ballistic Missile Proliferation and the MTCR: A Ten Year Review," paper presented at the International Studies Association Conference, March 19–23, pp. 10–11. See also Wyn Q. Bowen, "Brazil's Accession to the MTCR," *The Nonproliferation Review*, 3, no. 3 (1996).
18. Luiz Felipe de Seixas Corrêa, "Íntrodução, Fundação Alexandre Gusmão," in *A Palavra do Brasil nas Nações Unidas: 1946–1995* (Brasilia: FUNAG, 1995), p. 17.
19. See, for example, Flavio Helmold Macieira, "O Brasil e as Nações Unidas em 1994," *Trevista Brasileira de Política Internacional*, no. 37 (1994): 121–33.
20. Celso Amorim, "O Brasil e o conselho de Segurança da ONU," *Política Externa*, no. 3 (March–May 1995). Celso Amorim, "A Reforma da ONU," *Estudos Avançados - série Assuntos Internacionais*, 43 (São Paulo: Instituto de Estudo Avançados/USP, March 1996).
21. Gelson Fonseca Jr., *A Legitimidade e Outras Questões Internacionais* (Rio de Janeiro: Paz Terra, 1998).
22. For example, see Ronaldo Mota Sardenberg (Secretary for Strategic Issues of the Presidency), "Conselho de Segurança: equilibrío e representatividade," *Carta Internacional*, no. 32 (October 1995): 8.
23. Ronaldo Sardenberg (Ambassador to the United Nations at the time), "Conselho de Segurança pode legitimar 'Jurassic Park' mundial," *Carta Internacional*, no. 6 (August 1993): 2.
24. Ronaldo Mota Sardenberg, "O Brasil na presidência do Conselho de Segurança das Nações Unidas," in *Temas de Política Externa Brasileira II*, ed. G. Fonseca Júnior and S. H. Nabuco de Castro (Rio de Janeiro: Paz e Terra, 1994), pp. 135–45.
25. Flavio Helmold Macieira, "O Brasil e as Nações Unidas em 1994," R*evista Brasileira de Política Internacional*, no. 37 (1994): 121–33.
26. See, for example, Lauro Soutello Alvez (advisor to the Department of International Organisations of the Ministry of Foreign Affairs), "O Brasil e as operações de paz da ONU," *Carta Internacional*, no. 37 (March 1996): 3.
27. See Celso Amorim, "O Brasil e as Novas Dimensões da Segurança Internacional," Paper presented at the Instituto de Estudos Avançadas da USP, September 11, 1998.
28. See, for example, Lauro Soutello Alvez (advisor to the Department of International Organisations of the Ministry of Foreign Affairs), "O Brasil e as Operações de Paz da ONU," *Carta Internacional*, no. 37 (March 1996): 6–7.
29. See speeches by President Fernando Henrique Cardoso and Minister Luiz Felipe Lampreia at the Instituto Rio Branco, Brasília, April 30, 1999.
30. See Ivan Cannabrava, "O Brasil e as Operações de Manutenção da Paz," *Política Externa*, 5, no. 3 (December 1996): 28–45.
31. This is not due to the presence of a lusophone orientation in Brazilian foreign policy.
32. *Parcerias Estratégicas*, 1, no. 2 (December 1996): 12.
33. See, for example, Ronaldo Sardenber's statement in the context of the discussion on the situation in Somalia. Security Council Meeting 3385, May 31, 1994. "Time has proved right those delegations in the Council which, like my own, have consistently maintained that this body should, to the fullest extent possible, seek to avoid the application of the extraordinary

powers for enforcement action conferred upon it in chapter VII of the United Nations Charter."

34. Celso Luís Nunes Amorim, "Entre o desequilíbrio unipolar e a multipolaridade: o Conselho de Segurança da ONU no período pós-Guerra Fria," in *O Brasil e as Novas Dimensões da Segurança Internacional*, ed. G. Dupos and T. Vigevani (São Paulo: Alfa-Omega, 1999): 98.
35. See Security Council Meeting 3413, July 31, 1994.
36. See Security Council Meeting 3461, November 19, 1994.
37. S/PV.3392, June 22, 1994.
38. See Security Council Meeting 317, November 18, 1993.
39. See Security Council Meeting 277, September 15, 1993.
40. See, for example, the Brazilian participation in the debate on the UN role in Somalia and support for resolution 665 (1993); Security Council Meeting 280, September 22, 1993.
41. Observations made by the Brazilian representative to the UN, Ambassador Luiz Augusto de Araujo Castro, Special Committee on Peace Operations, April 28, 1992.
42. See Security Council Meeting 293, October 16, 1993.
43. Intervention of Edgard Telles Ribeiro, General Assembly, debate on the revision of peace operations, November 29, 1993.
44. Quoted in Antonio de Aguiar Patriota, *O Conselho de Segurança após a Guerra do Golfo: A Articulação de um Novo Paradigma de Segurança Coletiva* (Brasília: Fundação Alexandre de Gusmão, 1998).
45. See Security Council Meeting 3392, June 22, 1994.
46. The agency was established by the Treaty of Guadalajara (Agreement for the Exclusively Peaceful Use of Nuclear Energy, July 18, 1991), which prohibits the testing, manufacture, acquisition, possession, and deployment of nuclear weapons.
47. Lewis Dunn, "On Proliferation Watch: Some Reflections on the Past Quarter Century," *The Nonproliferation Review*, V, no. 3 (Spring–Summer, 1998): 22.
48. According to SIPRI, accessed March 22, 2002: www.sipri.se
49. SIVAM consists of the infrastructure of technical and operational resources (sensors of various types such as fixed and mobile radar, stations for gathering environmental, weather, and other data) aimed at collecting, processing, compiling, and providing data that are of interest to the organizations that make up SIPAM (public institutions within the municipal, state, and federal structure, such as universities and agencies for environmental protection and the prevention of illegal activities). SIPAM consists of the systemic organization whose links are the various federal, state, and municipal agencies that carry out governmental activities in the Amazon region and whose objective is to integrate, evaluate, and provide data needed for the performance of general and coordinated activities in the Amazon region. From www.mre.gov.br, accessed December 23, 2002.
50. Statement by Alberto Mendes Cardoso, Head of the Brazilian Delegation to the Inter American Committee on Terrorism, January 30, 2002, OEA/Ser.L/X2.2 CICTE/doc.8/01.
51. Amado Luiz Cervo and Clodoaldo Bueno, *História da Política Exterior do Brasil* (São Paulo: Editora Ática, 1992).
52. Lars Schoultz, William C. Smith, and Augusto Varas, "Introduction," in *Security, Democracy, and Development in U.S.–Latin American Relations*, ed. L. Schoultz, W. C. Smith, and A. Varas (Miami: North-South Center Press, 1994).
53. Maria Regina Soares de Lima, "Brazil's Alternative Vision," in *The Americas in Transition: The Contours of Regionalism*, G. Mace and L. Bélanger (Lynne Rienner), p. 7
54. Raul Bernal-meza, "A política exterior do Brasil: 1990–2002," *Revista Brasileira de Política Exterior*, 45, no. 1 (2002): 36–71.
55. The program follows the progress of individual and collective efforts of all the countries, indicating results achieved as well as obstacles faced by each of them. See www.cicad.oas.org/en/
56. For a discussion on the role Congress plays in shaping Brazilian foreign policy see Leticia Pinheiro, "Os véus da transparência: política externa e democracia no Brasil," *IRI-Textos*, no. 25 (2003): 1–30.
57. Marco Cepik, "A Política Externa de Lula: desafios do primeiro ano e a questão colombiana." Paper prepared for the International Crisis Group, Bogota/Brussels.

CHAPTER 8

Cuba and the Pax Americana: U.S.–Cuban Relations Post-1990

JORGE I. DOMÍNGUEZ

Introduction

Their world crumbled. In 1989, Cuban leaders watched the dominoes tumble in Eastern Europe as one after another of Europe's communist regimes came to an end. In 1991, the Soviet Union collapsed. Cuban–Soviet relations had been deep and multifaceted, built not on the back of occupying Soviet military forces, as in Eastern Europe, but on a genuine partnership. Cuba was the Soviet Union's best ally during the Cold War.

Cuba differed from the four surviving East Asian communist regimes: China, Laos, North Korea, and Vietnam. Unlike all four, and alone among all Soviet allies during the Cold War, Cuba deployed hundreds of thousands of troops far from the homeland to fight in four wars from the early 1960s to the late 1980s (one in North Africa, two in Angola, and one in East Africa). In contrast, East Asian communist governments fought wars only with neighboring countries. Cuba also deployed tens of thousands of military and civilian advisers, including teachers, health care personnel, sports coaches, and others through dozens of countries — a degree of voluntary globalization far beyond that practiced by the East Asian communist governments, relative to the size of their respective populations. Castro's Cuba was also a sustained multilateralist. Unlike China, Vietnam, or Korea, Cuba belonged to the UN uninterruptedly. Cuba was an active and influential member of the UN family of organizations to an extent that none of the East Asian communist governments — not even China — had been. Cuba served as president of the Nonaligned Movement for several years starting in 1979. Cuba sustained diplomatic relations with a large number of countries and trade relations with a significant number including most major U.S. allies. In these respects, Cuba is especially unlike North Korea and Laos, which have long operated at the far edge of the international system, practicing autarchy. Cuba has been the single most internationalist communist regime.

The legacies of Cuba's past international behavior and the sudden implosion of the world that Cuban leaders had known shaped its government's response to the new unchallenged U.S. primacy in military force, worldwide predominance in political power, dynamism in global economic reach, missionary zeal in propounding its ideological creed, and combating international terrorism. Unlike North Korea, Cuba would not hunker down in a metaphorical cave and shout threats at the world beyond its boundaries.

At home, Cuba adjusted sufficiently to ensure its authoritarian political regime's survival, though not to sustain its people's standard of living or even to recover lost past economic gains. (Analysis of the domestic adjustment strategy is beyond the scope of this chapter.) Internationally, it designed four strategies to cope with the United States:

1. It made a neorealist diagnosis of the post-1990 international system, designing a foreign policy in the expectation that other governments would balance U.S. power as it pertained to Cuba. It drew on its legacy of deterring the United States effectively. It built on its long experience as an activist multilateralist to enlist international support.
2. It designed an international strategy to diversify political risk in its international economic relations. Unlike in its past, it would avoid concentrating its international economic activity on one country.
3. It would actively seek instances of cooperation with the United States, especially over shared security interests, to address U.S. concerns and build some support against U.S. military action within U.S. military and coast guard services.

4. It would exercise "soft power," promoting internationally the attractive qualities of Cuban society in order to develop a constituency abroad, especially in the United States, friendly to Cuba and its people.

Security tensions did arise in U.S.–Cuban relations in the aftermath of the September 11, 2001, terrorist attacks on New York and Washington, but, on the whole, both governments managed bilateral relations professionally and even expanded certain areas of bilateral cooperation after September 11.

Internationally Induced Adjustments in Cuba

The end of the Soviet Union and communist Europe knocked down three pillars that had supported Cuba's political regime.

Military support. The Soviet Union had dissuaded the United States from invading Cuba. The Soviet Union had also transferred vast quantities of weapons to Cuba free of charge from the immediate aftermath of the 1962 missile crisis to the end of the 1980s and provided politico-military cover and substantial resources to enable Cuba to engage in a global foreign policy, even deploying hundreds of thousands of troops to African wars in the 1970s and 1980s. Cuba's political regime could not have survived in the 1960s without Soviet support, nor played such a major international role in the decades that followed.

Economic support. The Soviet Union paid a very high price for Cuba's sugar and sold Cuba petroleum at a discount. It provided huge loans at low interest rates to finance perpetual bilateral trade deficits, and it postponed indefinitely the collection of principal and interest on those loans. The USSR also provided development credits for specific projects as well as manifold opportunities for advanced training for Cuban military and civilian personnel. The best measure of the worth of this support is what happened to the Cuban economy once these subsidies stopped in 1990. From 1989 to 1993, gross domestic product (GDP) per capita fell 37 percent. Imports dropped 75 percent, while exports plunged 79 percent.[1]

Ideological support. "Condemn me; it does not matter. History will absolve me."[2] Thus Fidel Castro argued in the peroration of his edited trial-defense speech following his attack on the Cuban army barracks at Moncada on July 26, 1953 — his first major statement to the people of Cuba. Castro believes that he has a historic mission and that he has been on the forefront of the march of history. "In America and in the world, it is known that the revolution will be victorious," said the text he crafted in 1962 as the topic sentence for the so-called Second Declaration of Havana.[3] This faith in the ever-growing strength of communist regimes was enshrined in Cuba's 1976 Constitution (Preamble and Article 12, paragraph f), drafted at the apogee of the regime's consolidation.[4] The collapse of the Soviet Union and the communist world in Europe shattered this ideological vision and the Cuban leadership's confidence that the future was theirs.

Worse still, the United States emerged militarily unchallenged in the international system. For President Fidel Castro, the United States is more than a simple adversary. As he told the second congress of the Cuban Communist Party in December 1980: Across the centuries, "the United States has been the sworn enemy of our nation… Imperialism has never stopped attacking our Cuban national spirit, putting it to the test."[5] The need for Cuba to confront the United States, moreover, was also a personal challenge for him. As he wrote on June 5, 1958, still a rebel in the mountains, to his long-time close associate Celia Sánchez, "the Americans will pay very dearly for what they are doing." After the victory that he expected in the revolutionary war, "a much longer and bigger war will begin for me: the war that I will make against them."[6]

The international change at the start of the 1990s produced cumulative losses for Cuba's leaders. Cuba was newly vulnerable to U.S. and other pressures. The defense of Cuba would have to rely more on nonmilitary means. Market-oriented economic policies would no longer be resisted but welcomed to generate the resources to rescue the regime. And the search was on for new means of ideological and political legitimation. The Cuban government responded through its own version of structural adjustment. The leaders felt compelled to change. Cuba had been too dependent on an international system that no longer existed.

Military adjustment. Cuba's global military deployments ended nearly instantaneously as the Cold War wound down in Europe, ending Soviet backing for Cuba. In September 1989, Cuba completed the repatriation of its troops from Ethiopia. In March 1990, all Cuban military personnel in Nicaragua were brought home. In May 1991, the last Cuban troops were repatriated from Angola. Also in 1990 and 1991, Cuba brought back its troops and military advisers from other countries. By fall 1992, Cuba had suspended its military backing for revolutionary movements in other lands. Also in 1992, the last Russian ground troops departed; they had been stationed in Cuba since the 1962 missile crisis. In 2002, Russia shut down its electronic intelligence center at Lourdes, Cuba.[7] From 1989 to 1996, the military and internal security budget in nominal pesos fell 74 percent. Cuba also lost the off-budget free weapons transfers from the Soviet Union. For those same years, the military budget's share of the total budget dropped from 9.1 to 3.9 percent, bearing a greater burden of adjustment than the civilian economy.[8]

Economic adjustment. The budget deficit fell from 33 percent of GDP in 1993 to 7.4 percent in 1994 and 3.5 percent in 2000.[9] Sugar had been Cuba's long-time prime foreign exchange earner. In 2000, revenues from sugar amounted to $453 million, while international tourism revenues were worth $1.8 billion. Revenues from international tourism had become the main source of foreign exchange. The second most important source of foreign exchange was international transfers, valued at $842 million in 2000 — nearly all of it remittances from Cuban Americans.[10] In 2002, the government shut down 45 percent of Cuba's sugar mills; their inefficiency was hopeless.[11] Cuba was en route to becoming just one more Caribbean archipelago dependent on sunshine and its diaspora for its welfare.

Political adjustment. Cuba's downsizing of its armed forces was also a political adjustment, highlighting civilian supremacy. Cuba's economic strategy reorientation implied another political adjustment. Despite grumbling from many long-time cadres, the government adopted policies to welcome direct foreign investment and establish cordial relations with the Cuban diaspora to generate remittances. Generational replacement was a third political adjustment. Cuba's most important leaders belong to the Political Bureau of the Communist Party of Cuba. From 1965 through 1980, no member had been dropped from the Political Bureau. Yet after the 1991 Fourth Party Congress, two-thirds of the Political Bureau members were new. At the conclusion of the 1997 Party Congress, only six of the twenty-four Political Bureau members had belonged to this entity prior to the collapse of the Berlin Wall. The median birth year of the 1997 Political Bureau was 1943.

Ideological adjustment. The Fourth and Fifth Party Congresses and the new 1992 Constitution justified the economic policy reorientation to save the Cuban nation from doom. The new Constitution and new laws provided a measure of property rights to foster international investment. References to the Soviet Union and the international socialist community were purged from the Constitution. The state would no longer be atheist, though it would remain secular. Religious believers were welcome in the communist party. Fidel Castro's personal leadership role was emphasized in ways not observed since the 1960s. These ideological adjustments could not prevent a substantial erosion of support for the political regime, however.[12]

Cuba's adjustment enabled Castro's authoritarian regime to survive. It promoted enough globalization and domestic political change to build the basis for a new, albeit much less strong, political order. It ceased to challenge the United States militarily while remaining capable of inflicting damage on an invasion of the homeland. Its government would not join the ranks of those in Panama, Haiti, Iraq, Afghanistan, or the former Yugoslavia, all of which came to be occupied by the U.S. military after the fall of the Berlin Wall in 1989. Cuba's domestic adjustments were also limited. Cuba has not yet returned to the GDP level it had in 1985. The standard of living of its people has deteriorated greatly. And there has been no democratic transition. This last fact has been at the core of U.S.–Cuban contention since 1990.

A Multilateralist Cold Warrior

Fidel Castro's regime did not survive for so many decades by being reclusive or defensive. The Cuban government designed an effective international strategy for the post-1990 period. This was not a master plan born in an instant of political creativity. Rather, it resulted from a proactive approach to problem solving. Some pre-1990 legacies mattered. One diplomatic legacy was engagement in the international system and in nonfinancial multilateral institutions, especially the UN system. Multilateralism is a weapon of the weak. (Cuba did not belong to the International Monetary Fund, the World Bank, or the Inter-American Development Bank.) Another legacy was well-established diplomatic and trade relations with many countries. The Cuban government also held two key foreign policy assumptions:

1. The political regime's survival was the fundamental goal. Economic or social performance would be secondary to that goal. Relations with others would be sacrificed if they conflicted with the primacy of survival.
2. The U.S. government could be trusted to blunder in its relations with Cuba. At some point its actions would alienate U.S. allies, lead them to oppose U.S. policies toward Cuba, and reactivate the waning flames of Cuban nationalism.

The key characteristics of the political regime that the leadership endeavored to preserve were the preeminent roles of President Fidel Castro and Vice President Raúl Castro; a "hard shell" conception of sovereignty to ward off external influence over the political regime, especially respect for human rights; a single-party political system with state ownership and operation of all mass media; the communist party's leading role, namely, across all sectors of human endeavor its right to vet all key administrative and managerial appointments, set the main lines of policy, and demand deference to centralist principles; and high priority to provide educational and health-care services to the entire population.

The government's most effective strategy was to act upon the second proposition listed above. This is an essential building block of the neorealist school of international relations. From 1990 to the start of the Second Iraq War in 2003, the extent of such international balancing behavior to contain the power of the United States had been extraordinarily limited. The case of U.S. policy toward Cuba fit that proposition, however, even for the 1990s. The premier neorealist scholar, Kenneth Waltz, has written about the international system after the end of the Cold War, arguing that "the response of other countries to one among them seeking or gaining preponderant power is to try to balance against it. Hegemony leads to balance, which is easy to see historically and to understand theoretically." In the post–Cold War world, Waltz averred, "that is now happening, but haltingly so because the United States still has benefits to offer and many other countries have become accustomed to their easy lives with the United States bearing many of their burdens."[13]

In general terms, the Cuban government and communist party also had empirical reasons to expect such U.S. behavior even if they could not have predicted its timing or the specific actions involved. The United States had relentlessly opposed the Cuban government during the preceding decades. Except for a brief interlude during the Ford and Carter administrations in the 1970s, U.S. policy toward Cuba had had a strong ideological anticommunist component. In the aftermath of the Cold War, the United States sought to enlarge the world of democracies, fostering regime change in Cuba. The United States had an even longer history of behaving imperially, at times arrogantly, toward Cuba and its people; Cuban leaders expected this pattern to recur as the United States savored its triumph in the Cold War. Moreover, since the start of the 1980s Cuban–American lobbying organizations had become much stronger and sought to toughen U.S. punitive policies toward the Cuban government.[14] The Cold War had not ended in the Caribbean. The legacy of U.S.–Cuban adversarial relations lingered.

The United States performed its role as expected and quickly. In 1992, the U.S. Congress enacted the Cuban Democracy Act (sponsored by then U.S. Representative Robert Torricelli) to prohibit subsidiaries of U.S. firms located in third countries from trading with Cuba. In 1996, the U.S. Congress approved the Cuban Democracy and Solidarity Act (better known as Helms–Burton), which sought to stop direct foreign investments in Cuba and to impose substantial financial penalties on those firms that had already done so. The law angered a number of U.S. allies that opposed the extraterritorial reach of U.S. law even if they agreed with the United States in their opposition to the Cuban regime.

Building on the legacies of a successful foreign policy during the Cold War, the Cuban government mobilized its diplomats in the UN General Assembly and other UN organizations, the Iberoamerican summits, and the Association of Caribbean States (ACS). Cuba's UN activism drew on decades of hard work by its diplomats and the gratitude of many African states that had received Cuban assistance on generous terms in decades past.[15] Membership in Iberoamerican summits was a culmination of long and sustained Cuban engagement with Spain and Mexico — the leaders in founding the Iberoamerican summits and hosts of the first two summits — and to a lesser extent also with other Latin American countries. ACS membership was a legacy of Cuba's political relations with Anglophone Caribbean countries since the early 1970s, even though the ACS itself was founded in the 1990s.[16] Thus unlike most governments that believe in neo-realist international politics, Cuba acts pragmatically through nonfinancial multilateral institutions. Its armies can no longer contain the United States; its diplomats may.

In the UN, one measure of broad and growing opposition to these U.S. laws has been the vote in the UN General Assembly on a Cuban motion to condemn U.S. economic sanctions on Cuba. Cuba's diplomatic corps has worked worldwide over the years to build support for Cuba's position. In 1992, this Cuban motion received the votes of 33 percent of all UN members. In 1994, it got 54 percent. In the aftermath of the enactment of Helms–Burton in 1996, the Cuban motion garnered support from 73 percent of U.N. members. In 2001, at the apogee of U.S. power during the war on the Taliban regime in Afghanistan, 88 percent of UN members voted for the Cuban resolution.[17]

The European Union (EU) illustrates how U.S. allies balanced against U.S. policy. In the early 1990s, the European Parliament condemned the Cuban Democracy Act, yet it also called for Cuba's democratization. In 1993, the European Commission approved its first program of humanitarian assistance to Cuba. Yet the Commission refused to sign a formal "cooperation agreement" with Cuba — the only Latin American country with which it still lacks such an agreement. Beginning in 1995, the EU fashioned a comprehensive policy toward Cuba, a "common position" approved in December 1996 — the first time that the EU adopted such a mechanism in its relations with a Latin American country. The EU opposed U.S. policy toward Cuba as embodied in the Helms–Burton and Torricelli Acts. It also supported Cuba's democratization. It would continue humanitarian assistance. Consistent with this policy, the EU invited Cuba as an observer to participate in the renegotiation of the Lomé Convention that was about to become the Cotonou Convention. Through these means former European colonies in Africa, Asia, the Caribbean, and the Pacific Ocean receive certain EU preferential trade treatment and economic assistance. Yet the EU's insistence that only a democratic Cuba could join the Cotonou Convention led Cuba in April 2000 to withdraw its request to join the Cotonou system.[18] The Cuban government accorded primacy to its survival as an authoritarian regime; it would reject democratizing pressures from the EU (and others).

Parallel to those Cuba-specific actions, the EU contested the Helms–Burton Act, litigating before the World Trade Organization (WTO) while also negotiating with the United States. On May 18, 1998, the EU agreed to discontinue its complaint against the United States before the WTO and to discourage investment in certain properties of doubtful title in Cuba. The United States pledged that the president would henceforth exercise his lawful right under the Helms–Burton Act to suspend every six months the enforcement of Title III — the guts of the Act, applying to direct foreign investments in Cuba. The White House also agreed to seek a congressional amendment to Helms–Burton to eliminate its Title IV, which mandated the denial of U.S. visas to executives (and their families) whose non-U.S. firms invested in Cuba.[19] At the time of signing, the United States did not believe that the EU would discourage investments in Cuba and the EU did not believe that the U.S. Congress would repeal Title IV. Nonetheless, the result of this negotiation killed Helms–Burton de facto. President George W. Bush's administration honored this agreement, regularly suspending Title III and keeping to a minimum the enforcement of Title IV on Europeans.[20] In U.S.–EU relations, Cuba was a cheerleader for the EU's neorealist balancing but not a direct participant. In the end, the EU neutered Helms–Burton and saved Cuba from potential risks.

Cuba played a more active role to break out of its isolation in the Americas. Iberoamerican summits have been held every year since 1991; the Spanish-American countries, Spain, Brazil, and Portugal, attend them. President Castro has attended them as well and hosted one in Havana. These summits regularly approve ringing endorsements of pluralist democracy, which Castro signs without blushing. Through these summits, the Cuban government widens its political relations and obtains a modicum of additional international legitimacy, even before its own people: Cuba does not stand alone, despite the differences between its domestic politics and those of other countries at the summit. Moreover, Cuba's active participation in these summits undermines U.S. attempts to isolate Cuba. The Latin American governments thus also exemplified neorealist balancing against U.S. policy.

The Cuban government's most successful efforts to undermine U.S. policy have taken place in the Anglophone Caribbean. Cuba first had to end its own Cold War in the Caribbean. From 1979 to 1983, Cuba provided substantial support to the New Jewel Movement — a self-styled Marxist–Leninist party — government in Grenada. In 1983, U.S. troops invaded Grenada, overthrew that government, and installed one more to its liking. Cuban–Grenadan relations were suspended. In May 1992, Cuba took the initiative to recognize and establish diplomatic relations with Grenada. A month later, the Caribbean Tourism Organization admitted Cuba as a member. In December 1993, the Caribbean Community (CARICOM) signed a cooperation agreement with Cuba, notwithstanding severe U.S. pressure on CARICOM to require Cuba to democratize and respect human rights (the accession clauses that the European Union requires of Cuba for access to the Cotonou Convention). Cuba objected to such a requirement, and CARICOM did not insist. The Association of Caribbean States was founded in 1994, with Cuba as a charter member. Anglophone Caribbean governments are among Cuba's staunchest allies in the post–Cold War world, defying U.S. pressures in international organizations.[21] In the late 1990s and early 2000s, Cuban relations with Haiti, the Dominican Republic, and Suriname also improved.

Cuba had no alliances, however. Communist Asia did not replace Communist Europe, rescuing Cuba for an ideological cause, though Cuba's political relations with Asian communist governments were good and trade with China was important. The People's Republic of China was unwilling to replace the Soviet Union as Cuba's patron.

For small, threatened countries, neorealist multilateralism is the best they can do. Multilateral institutions served as key arenas for Cuba's international activity and means to mobilize the support of other governments. Because Cuba's approach to multilateralism was neorealist, it did not foster a liberal institutionalist agenda; that is, Cuba did not seek to vest institutions with greater powers to shape domestic rules within countries, and it sought to stop any multilateral efforts that would constrain Cuba's freedom of action. Cuba's approach to multilateralism was fully within the clash of forces to be expected from an anarchic international system.

Cuba unfurled the flags of sovereignty and nonintervention in the domestic affairs of countries. Its government's top goal — to avoid domestic political regime change — was a goal that both neorealists and multilateralists understand well. Cuba's neorealist multilateralism parried U.S. pressures. This strategy, however, could not address Cuba's most important vulnerability in the post-1990 world, namely, the authoritarian character of its political regime. Cuban leaders resisted domestic regime change. As a result, relations with the EU and all countries in the Americas, including the United States, remained distant and, at best, formally correct.

Defensive International Economic Links

As the 1990s opened, Cuba designed a strategy to prevent the United States from manipulating its new economic vulnerability to accelerate domestic regime change. In 1986, Cuba had defaulted on its international debt to market-economy countries and remained unable to work out a rescheduling; as a result, it received no new long-term lending. For political reasons, it obtained no "soft" loans other than $9.8 million from the People's Republic of China in 2000.[22] It relied on suppliers' credits at a high margin over LIBOR (London Interbank Offered Rate). Foreign direct investment developed the international tourism sector effectively, but the monetary value of such investment was modest. Cuba's international economic strategy did not generate a vigorous recovery or renew economic growth. In 2000, on the eve of the economy's new slowdown, GDP in constant prices remained 18 percent below its 1985 level.[23]

On the other hand, since 1990 Cuba has diversified its international economic partners. In 1989, the Soviet Union purchased 60 percent of Cuban exports and supplied 68 percent of its imports. In 2000, Russia remained the most important buyer of Cuban exports, but it only took 18 percent. Spain was the main supplier of Cuban imports, but it accounted for just 16 percent. In none of the six international economic partnerships recorded in Table 8.1 — exports, imports, international tourism, financial debt, foreign direct investment associations,[24] and international donations — does Cuban dependence on a single partner exceed 27 percent. The lead partner is different in all but one category. Eleven different countries or entities occupy the eighteen slots in Table 8.1.

These outcomes did not occur by chance. The Cuban government no longer manages all international economic transactions, as it did prior to 1990, but its state enterprises continue to control all foreign trade and international tourist partnerships directly or through association with international firms. The government gives prior approval to all foreign investment deals, and only the government incurs international debts.

Table 8.1 Cuba's Main International Economic Partners at the End of the Twentieth Century

	First Partner (percent)	Second Partner (percent)	Third Partner (percent)
Exports[a]	Russia (18)	Canada (16)	Netherlands (12)
Imports[a]	Spain (16)	Venezuela (13)	Italy (8)
Tourism[b]	Canada (17)	Germany (11)	Italy (10)
Financial Debt[c]	Japan (19)	Argentina (14)	Spain (11)
Direct Investment Associations[c]	Italy (27)	Spain (20)	Canada (11)
International Donations[a]	Spain (27)	United States (14)	European Union (7)

[a]Refers to 2000.
[b]Refers to 1999. The order of countries remained the same in 2000–2001, however.
[c]Refers to 1998.
Sources: Exports and imports from http://www.odci/gov/cia/publications/factbook/geos/cu.html; tourism from http://www.cubagob.cubaweb.cu/des_eco/turismo.htm; financial debt and direct investment associations from Comisión Económica para América Latina y el Caribe, *La economía cubana: Reformas estructurales y desempeño en los noventa* (Mexico: Fondo de Cultura Económica, 2000), Tables A42, A44, A111. International donations, worth $79.2 million in 2000, retrieved from Cuban Foreign Ministry's web site. http://www.cubaminrex.cu/boletin/inveextranj_colab_asistec.htm. On tourism, see also http://www.cubaminrex.cu/boletin/datos-turismo.htm.

Mindful of a legacy of dependency on a single country (Spain in colonial times, the United States from 1898 to 1960, and the Soviet Union from 1960 to 1990) and a single product (sugar), Cuban officials worked hard and with stunning success to diversify international economic partnerships since 1990.[25]

Cuban officials do not worry much that any one of the governments in Table 8.1 would punish Cuba, but rather that excessive reliance on one partner might cause a problem. First, the U.S. government could affect the policies of any one of Cuba's partners. Second, any one of these countries could suffer an economic crisis that might adversely affect Cuba. A diversified portfolio of international economic partnerships provides some insurance against both risks. These were not abstract concerns.

The Russian government's decision to close the electronic intelligence center at Lourdes, Cuba, exemplifies the first risk. The Soviet Union had established the facility in 1964; Cuba supplied services free of charge. In 1992, the Russian Federation negotiated an agreement with Cuba to retain the Lourdes center but pay for rent and services from the Cubans. Russia paid $90 million in 1992, $160 million per year in 1993–1995, and $200 million per year from 1996 to 2000. Russian President Vladimir

Putin publicly toured the Lourdes center during his visit to Cuba in December 2000; he stated Russia's continuing interest in operating the facility. In mid-October 2001, however, Russia announced that it would close the Lourdes center and stop payment for rent and services.[26] In the aftermath of the September 11 terrorist attacks on the United States, Russia gave priority to its antiterrorist cooperation with the United States. This Russian decision had mainly an economic impact on Cuba because Russia had stopped supporting Cuba militarily a decade earlier.

The crisis of Venezuelan President Hugo Chávez's government in 2002–2004 exemplifies the second problem, namely, the effect on Cuba from a partner's crisis. Nearly all of Cuba's imports from Venezuela had been petroleum products. In late 2002, the anti-Chávez two-month-long strike in Venezuela's oil industry compelled Cuba to enact emergency energy conservation measures, drastically cutting back oil supplies for public transportation and household consumption.[27]

Cuba's defensive international economic strategy in the 1990s was the most successful in its history. It diversified political risks in its international economic transactions. It made it less likely that the United States could injure its economy. It limited the damage from troubles that might arise in Cuba's bilateral economic relations with any one partner. This strategy, however, did not generate a full economic recovery, much less growth. Cuba's leaders remained unwilling to adopt deeper market-oriented economic reforms and were thus unable to reap their benefits.

Cooperating with the United States

Well before 1990, the Cuban government had found areas of cooperation with the United States and reached agreement. In the 1990s, this strategy served two purposes. First, it addressed issues that mattered to both governments, such as migration, drug trafficking, terrorism, and relations around the U.S. naval base in Cuba's Guantánamo province. Second, given such responsible Cuban behavior, its government hoped to persuade U.S. officials that it was not a "rogue" state, much less a charter member of an "axis of evil."

The first U.S.–Cuban security agreement was signed in March 1973 (during the Nixon administration) to prevent air piracy over the Straits of Florida, thereby stopping the local air piracy crisis that had erupted after 1968. In 1977 (during the Carter administration), Interests Sections were established in the respective capital cities, operating as de facto embassies to facilitate agreements and reduce the likelihood of accidental conflict. Also in 1977, the two governments delimited their maritime boundaries. In 1984 (during the Reagan administration), a bilateral migration agreement permitted the repatriation of Cubans who had entered the United States illegally and, for the first time since 1960, permitted Cuban emigration to the United States within the framework of law in both countries. In the late 1980s, Cuba also cooperated actively with the United States to settle the military crisis in southern Africa, advancing their joint interests.[28]

Significant steps toward broader and deeper cooperation took place during the Clinton administration and were sustained during the second Bush administration. Migration agreements signed in 1994 and 1995 greatly reduced illegal Cuban migration. The U.S. Coast Guard would return to Cuba those Cubans picked up in the high seas, intending to enter the United States without documents; the United States also took steps to facilitate lawful Cuban immigration well beyond the terms agreed to in the 1980s.[29] Most aspects of U.S.–Cuban migration relations would henceforth receive routine treatment. The coast guards of both countries came also to collaborate in search and rescue missions at sea, especially useful during the 1994 migration crisis.

In 1993, the U.S. and Cuban armed forces began to develop confidence-building measures in and around the U.S. naval base located in Cuba's province of Guantánamo. U.S. and Cuban forces started to notify each other in advance of military movements. The highest-ranking military officers from both sides established regular and periodic communication. These relations would be helpful during the 1994 migration crisis and its aftermath when, for several months, the United States held several tens of thousands of would-be illegal migrants at the base (eventually most were allowed to enter the United States). At that time, meetings between the respective top military commanders took place every six weeks; lower-level technical meetings took place more frequently. The highest-ranking U.S. officer participating in these meetings was General John Sheehan, Commander-in-Chief of the U.S. Atlantic Command.[30]

In 1998, the U.S. Defense Intelligence Agency (DIA) published a finding that Cuba did not represent a significant military threat to the United States or to any of its neighbors. Its military capacities and intentions were limited to the defense of the homeland.[31] That formal finding facilitated military cooperation between Cuba's Eastern Army and the U.S. armed forces at the Guantánamo base. Computer connections were set up between the two forces to facilitate communication and prevent a military accident. Collaborative plans were developed to facilitate civil and military aviation over the Guantánamo naval base air space.[32]

In the mid-1990s, the U.S. and Cuban coast guards also began to cooperate on an ad hoc basis to combat drug trafficking. The U.S. Coast Guard would supply the information; Cuban *Guardafronteras* would arrest criminals in Cuban space. The U.S. Federal Bureau of Investigation started to inform Cuba about terrorist activities of some Cuban-origin persons in the United States.[33] U.S.–Cuban cooperation over drug trafficking received a boost in October 1996 when the coast guards of both countries collaborated in the interdiction and arrest of the *Limerick*. Approximately 1.7 tons of cocaine were found aboard this vessel. Bilateral cooperation expanded thereafter.

In May 1999, U.S. drug czar General Barry McCaffrey, former Commander-in-Chief of the U.S. Southern Command, declared that Cuba was not an accomplice of drug traffickers. Drug trafficking through Cuba represented only 9 percent of all traffic in the Caribbean's Bahamas–Cuba–Jamaica area. McCaffrey noted that Cuba made substantial efforts to combat drug trafficking and that it could not do more principally because it lacked the necessary equipment for effective interdiction. He acknowledged Cuban initiatives to cooperate with the United States to combat drug trafficking.[34] In October 1999, Cuba and the United States reached agreement on technical measures to improve cooperation, establishing telephone and fax communication and coordinating the radio frequencies of the respective coast guards. Procedures were approved to coordinate future joint boarding parties involving U.S. and Cuban forces. Drug trafficking through Cuba fell following this agreement.[35]

In the 1990s, the worst incident in U.S.–Cuban relations occurred on February 24, 1996, when the Cuban Air Force shot down over international waters two unarmed civilian aircraft that had previously penetrated Cuban air space without authorization. The President of the United States considered military retaliation but settled, instead, for accepting the enactment of the Helms–Burton Act, which he had hitherto opposed.[36] To prevent future incidents between the two countries that might be provoked by militant Cuban exiles, the two governments ordered their coast guards to cooperate to contain conflict on the high seas. Whenever a group of exiles organizes a flotilla to sail toward Cuban waters to organize a protest, the two governments activate stand-by procedures. The U.S. Interests Section in Havana coordinates meetings between officials of both governments. High-ranking U.S. Coast Guard officials travel to Havana to work with their Cuban counterparts in minute detail — the location of the flotilla and the Cuban and U.S. forces, the equipment that each will have, and the means for instant communication. On the day of the flotilla's protest, a U.S. officer is posted to Havana to facilitate communication with Cuban officers.[37] Since 2000, a U.S. Coast Guard Commander has been posted permanently to the U.S. Interests Section in Havana to foster cooperation over migration, drug traffic interdiction, and the enforcement of law at the maritime border.

U.S.–Cuban Security and Other Issues after September 11, 2001

U.S.–Cuban security cooperation continued on various issues after the September 11, 2001, terrorist attacks on the United States. Certain elements of such cooperation actually deepened while new fissures appeared. On September 11, the Cuban government made four decisions to signal its solidarity with the United States:[38]

1. It firmly condemned the attacks on New York and Washington.
2. It offered to deploy health care personnel to assist in caring for the wounded.
3. It opened its blood banks, noting that at such times especially rare blood types may be unavailable.
4. It opened its airports for emergency landing by U.S. or other aircraft.

President Castro and Cuban officials recalled that Cuba had been the target of numerous terrorist attacks during the preceding four decades (delicately omitting that, in the 1960s, the U.S. government sponsored many such attacks). The United States took no formal notice of any of these Cuban actions and instead focused on the subsequent Cuban criticism regarding U.S. policies toward Afghanistan and Iraq.

Further bilateral security cooperation developed when the United States decided to bring prisoners of war from the Afghan war to be detained at the U.S. base in Guantánamo. The U.S. government did not consult Cuba in advance but, prior to the deployment of prisoners, it provided "ample and detailed information on the steps that would be taken to accommodate the prisoners there and ensure that the security of our people is not in any way jeopardized," as the Cuban government put it. Cuba affirmed that "we shall not set any obstacles to the development of the operation" deploying the prisoners to the U.S. base. "The Cuban authorities will keep in contact with the personnel at the American naval base to adopt such measures as may be deemed convenient to avoid the risk of accidents...." Noting increased U.S. military deployments to the base for this purpose, the Cuban government decided not to respond in kind: "Cuba will make every effort to preserve the atmosphere of détente and mutual respect that has prevailed in that area in the past few years," pledging also its willingness "to cooperate with the medical services required as well as with sanitation programs in the surrounding areas."[39] There has been subsequent effective and continuing medical collaboration across the U.S.–Cuban land boundary to control a malaria outbreak at the base and a dengue outbreak in eastern Cuba. Cuban and U.S. officers have met approximately once a month and continue to provide advance notification to the other side of any unusual military maneuver.[40]

Moreover, in the late fall of 2001 the Bush administration changed some rules governing the U.S. trade embargo on Cuba to permit U.S. agricultural and some medical exports to Cuba. In 2002, U.S. exports to Cuba were worth approximately $114 million, the first time since 1990 that U.S. exports to Cuba exceeded $10 million in any one year. Also in 2002, Cuba signed contracts with U.S. firms worth over $200 million, covering both past and prospective deliveries. The United States accounted for about 2.3 percent of Cuba's imports, becoming Cuba's tenth most important supplier of imports.[41] Well over one hundred thousand U.S. citizens visited Cuba lawfully in 2001 when the United States became Cuba's principal partner for international academic and cultural exchanges.[42]

The U.S.–Cuban negotiations that permitted this significant break of U.S. trade embargo policy toward Cuba also called attention to Cuba's diplomatic skill. In early November 2001, Hurricane Michelle devastated parts of Cuba. On the afternoon of November 7, in a respectful letter the U.S. State Department communicated its sorrow for the effects of the hurricane and offered humanitarian assistance. On the evening of November 7, the White House spokesman, employing undiplomatic language, seemed to condition U.S. humanitarian assistance: it would be delivered only through international organizations and other intermediaries, provided assurances were given that the Cuban people would benefit, not Castro's regime. The Cuban government deliberately ignored the White House statement and, also in respectful diplomatic language, responded only to the State Department communication. Cuba politely declined the humanitarian assistance but proposed, instead, to be allowed to buy U.S. foods and medicines purely on a cash basis. The Cuban proposal became the basis for the agreement.[43]

Also known as Trollope's Ploy, this negotiating tactic has an honorable pedigree. President John Kennedy employed it during the Cuban missile crisis, ignoring a message from Prime Minister Nikita Khrushchev that he did not like and accepting a Khrushchev message that he did like, thereby opening the way to a settlement of the crisis. In November 2001, Cuba employed the same tactic to considerable success.[44]

Nevertheless, after September 11 three issues complicated U.S.–Cuban security relations: terrorism, weapons of mass destruction, and espionage.

Terrorism. For many years, the U.S. Department of State has included Cuba on the list of states that sponsor terrorism. Cuba harbors at least 20 Basque Euskadi ta Askatasuna (ETA) members. It also provides "some degree of safe haven and support to members" of Colombian guerrilla groups, the Revolutionary Armed Forces of Colombia (FARC) and the Army of National Liberation (ELN). Cuba has long permitted numerous U.S. fugitives to live there. In 2001, the State Department added the prolonged stays in Cuba in the 1990s and thereafter of cadres from the Irish Republican Army (IRA) and the Chilean Manuel Rodríguez Patriotic Front (FPMR).[45]

Weapons of Mass Destruction. Speaking on May 6, 2002, before the Heritage Foundation, U.S. Undersecretary of State John Bolton affirmed, "The United States believes that Cuba has at least a limited offensive biological warfare research and development effort. Cuba has provided dual-use biotechnology to other rogue states. We are concerned that such technology could support BW programs in those states."[46] A political storm followed because former President Jimmy Carter was visiting Cuba at that time. Prior to his trip a few days earlier, Carter had been briefed by U.S. officials who made no mention of this subject; Carter wondered publicly whether this was an effort to undermine his trip and to cater to a highly ideological conservative audience.

On May 13, U.S. Secretary of State Colin Powell made a rather different affirmation:

> We do believe that Cuba has a biological offensive research capability. We didn't say that it actually had such weapons, but it has the capacity and the capability to conduct such research. This is not a new statement; I think that it is a statement that has been made previously. So Undersecretary Bolton's speech ... wasn't breaking new ground as far as the United States' position on this subject.[47]

Powell's remarks undercut Bolton's. First, Bolton spoke of an actual "effort," whereas Powell referred only to Cuba's capability. Indeed, for years Cuba has had impressive biotechnology facilities and it exports many pharmaceutical and other biotechnical products. Second, by underlining that there was nothing new in Bolton's remarks, Powell admitted that there had been no change in Cuba's behavior.

Espionage. In the same speech addressing Cuba's possible biological warfare "effort," Undersecretary Bolton challenged the accuracy of the 1998 DIA finding that Cuba did not represent a significant military threat to the United States. Bolton reported that one of the drafters of that DIA finding, Ana Belén Montes, the DIA's senior Cuba analyst, was a Cuban spy. (Montes was subsequently arrested and pled guilty to espionage.) In addition, in 2001, several Cuban spies were arrested in southern Florida; five of them were tried, convicted, and imprisoned for spying on U.S. installations.

Cuba's Responses. The Cuban government acknowledges that some alleged terrorists or revolutionaries reside in Cuba. There are also U.S. fugitives, pending an agreement between the two governments on an extradition treaty. Cuba has offered to sign such a treaty; the United States has refused. More generally, in 2002, Cuba proposed to sign agreements with the United States to foster cooperation over migratory issues and to combat terrorism and drug trafficking; on June 13, 2002, the U.S. government declined.[48]

ETA members received asylum in Cuba in the 1980s in response to a request from the Spanish government, which wanted ETA terrorists out of Spain. The IRA and FPMR members accused of engaging in terrorism were no longer in Cuba. Cuba admits that it once supported FARC and ELN Colombian revolutionaries but denies that it currently supports violent actions on their part.[49] Cuba has also hosted several informal and formal meetings between Colombian officials and the ELN and the FARC to facilitate an end to the decades-old Colombian civil war. Cuba has worked with various Colombian presidents, including incumbent President Álvaro Uribe, on this aspect of the peace process. Cuba has supported an active role for the U.S. government in this peace process.[50]

The Cuban government claims to be responsible regarding weapons of mass destruction. In the early 1990s, it shut down and mothballed the unfinished nuclear power plant whose construction had begun during the Cold War with Soviet financing and technical assistance. That facility complies with International Atomic Agency regulations and is the object of routine international inspection.

Cuba denies that it is making any "effort" to develop biological weapons, challenges the U.S. government to provide evidence, and has opened its biotechnology labs to visits from scientists the world over, including the United States, and from regulatory agencies of countries to which it exports its products. Cuba complies annually with its obligations under the Convention on Biological and Toxic Weapons through reports to the UN on confidence-building measures. Cuban scientists hold over 500 patents registered abroad, for which pertinent documentation had been submitted.[51]

Cuba acknowledges that it engages in espionage activities in the United States just as the United States engages in espionage activities in Cuba.

It specifically denies, however, that its spies caught in southern Florida had targeted U.S. installations. It has decorated them as Heroes of the Republic of Cuba for spying on, and attempting to foil efforts by, some Cuban-American groups in combat with the Cuban government.[52]

In the aftermath of September 11, Cuba also emphasized its role as a good international citizen. It signed all twelve UN conventions on terrorism as well as the Iberoamerican declaration on terrorism at the 2001 summit. It reversed the policies it first adopted in the 1960s and, on September 14, 2002, signed and ratified the Nuclear Nonproliferation Treaty and the Treaty of Tlatelolco (in 1995 Cuba had signed but not ratified the latter treaty, which bans nuclear weapons in Latin America).[53]

Cuba managed reasonably well the most problematic issues in the post–September 11 bilateral security environments. It continued its cooperation over migration, search, and rescue on the high seas, and drug traffic interdiction, offering to expand collaboration on the last. Since the mid-1990s, it has not supported terrorist or revolutionary groups besides permitting some of their members to reside in Cuba. In the 1990s, it got political credit outside the United States for its role as peacemaker in settling the civil wars in Nicaragua, El Salvador, and Guatemala and for its ongoing efforts on Colombia's wars. Its biotechnology laboratories have been the object of respect, not fear, among international scientists.[54] In turn, U.S. accusations regarding Cuban relations with terrorist groups and the possible production of biological weapons have been seen, even within the United States, as being motivated more by ideological demons than by Cuban actions. Polemical U.S. declarations aside, Cuba has not been the object of new U.S. military threats. On the contrary, the practical collaboration between the United States and Cuba continued during the second Bush administration over security issues, and even some bilateral trade developed.

Cuba's International Strategy: "Soft Power"

U.S. worldwide influence, Joseph Nye has argued, depends not just on U.S. military and economic power but also on the attractive qualities of U.S. society, its way of life, its means of organizing public and private life, its popular music, television, Hollywood films, fashions, the intellectual clout of its universities, the dynamism of its religious missionaries, and so forth. Cuban scholar Carlos Alzugaray has argued that Cuba has some soft power as well.[55]

The Cuban government invests actively in its soft power. It policies are closer to those of governments of France that over the years have promoted the spread of the French language and culture to secure a leading role for France in the world. The Cuban government does not have a laissez-faire attitude toward intersocietal relations. Its artists, athletes, and physicians cannot leave Cuba without an exit permit. Most travel abroad only as part of explicit agreements that the Cuban government has signed and often as part of clearly identified policies. The Cuban government understands that its soft power is about *power*, not just about good feelings.

Some of Cuba's soft power dates from the Cold War years. Cuba defied the United States in the 1960s. For many Latin Americans, not just for leftwingers, the Cuban Revolution exemplified courage, creativity, liberation, the opening of new vistas, and a praiseworthy Latinamericanist affirmation facing the United States. Cuba's defiance drew from the deep well of a long-lived Latin American tradition, culturally and politically at odds with the United States. Cuban soft power in the twenty-first century retains some of those themes but it gathered some appeal even within the United States.

Cuban athletes impressively win many medals in the summer Olympics and in the Pan American games. The *Buenavista Social Club* film had a considerable impact on a segment of the U.S. public, charmed by its characters and their music. Cuba sends its orchestras and smaller musical groups on international tours, including U.S. tours. Cuba welcomes international visitors to large-scale art exhibits, each time with greater participation from U.S. art collectors. The subtle political message is, Could Cuban art be so attractive and its popular music so much fun if its government were so bad? The Cuban government actively regulates, promotes, and distributes the products of Cuban artists and musicians.

The development of international tourism in Cuba generates the funds to enable the Cuban economy to recover and also brings millions of foreigners to see for themselves how great Cuban society is. Canadians, Europeans, and Latin Americans have already visited Cuba in large numbers.[56]

Cuba's soft power became better known and thus more effective in the United States as a result of a U.S. government liberalization of its visa rules late in the Clinton administration and continuing through most of the second Bush administration, unleashing a soft power battle between the two governments. Because U.S. soft power had had a pervasive and deep penetration in Cuba for centuries, in the 2000s Cuba seemed to be gaining more from its soft power offensive in the short term, making it less likely that the U.S. government would obtain sufficient domestic support for more aggressive policies against the Cuban government. Perhaps for that reason, in 2004 the Bush administration prohibited most of these cultural and academic exchange programs.

Cuba continued to develop its medical diplomacy as one element of its soft power, hoping for influence in parts of the developing world. In 2001, 2,146 Cuban medical doctors and other health care personnel were posted in 14 countries. At the end of the 1990s, Cuba founded a new medical school to train Latin American medical doctors; in 2001, this school had 3,460 students from 23 countries. In 2000–2001, there were 11,366 international scholarship students from 89 countries in all Cuban universities. This policy has been especially effective in the Anglophone Caribbean, whose governments have sought but failed to receive U.S. health care assistance.[57]

Conclusions

In the 2000s, Cuba has no allies. It does not belong to the international financial institutions. Its authoritarian domestic political regime has turned it into a pariah in Latin America and causes continuing friction with the United States, Canada, and the EU. The character of its domestic regime is the Cuban government's principal international liability. In the 1990s, this government was compelled to adjust to the changes in the international system and the rise of unrivaled U.S. hegemony. It felt the heavy cumulative weight of the loss of its international military, economic, ideological, and political support. It adjusted successfully to permit the survival of the political regime — yet without the ideological fervor that once had buttressed it. It did not succeed in reactivating the economy or returning the welfare of its people to the levels that prevailed in the mid-1980s. Cuba is a poster child for the meaning of constraint in the international system of the twenty-first century.

Yet Cuba also exemplifies how a talented and committed political leadership can exercise a wide range of choice under very adverse international circumstances. To respond to the rising power of the United States in the 1990s, the Cuban government developed a four-pronged international strategy. It behaved as a neorealist multilateralist, taking advantage of U.S. hegemonic blunders as Washington tried to impose on its allies its preferences in Cuba policy. It fashioned a defensive international economic strategy to diversify risk. It constructed a web of cooperative bilateral agreements with the United States to advance shared interests. And it deployed its soft power creatively. The Cuban government's coping strategies worked well even with less bridled U.S. power after the September 11, 2001, terrorist attacks.

The Pax Americana is not the international system that President Castro and his older associates would have chosen for the waning years of their rule, but they showed, in the twilight of their careers, an unusual skill — unparalleled by any other authoritarian regime in the post–Cold War international system — to advance their interests and preferences beyond the boundaries of their very small country, notwithstanding the overwhelming power of the United States.

Acknowledgment

This paper was written for the International Conference on East Asia, Latin America, and the New Pax Americana, held at the Weatherhead Center for International Affairs, Harvard University, on February 14–15, 2003, sponsored by the Weatherhead Center and Korea's East Asia Institute. I am grateful to the Center for continuing research support.

Notes

1. Computed from Banco Nacional de Cuba, *Economic Report, 1994* (Havana: Banco Nacional de Cuba, 1995), 4, 11.
2. Marta Harnecker, *Fidel Castro's Political Strategy: From Moncada to Victory* (New York: Pathfinder, 1987), 152.
3. Fidel Castro, *Obras escogidas, 1953–1962*, vol. 1 (Madrid: Editorial Fundamentos, 1976), 131.
4. *Constitución de la República de Cuba* (Havana: Departamento de Orientación Revolucionaria, 1976).
5. *Granma Weekly Review*, December 28, 1980: 13.
6. Cited in the memoirs of the first Soviet envoy to Cuba, Aleksandr Alexeev, "Cuba después del triunfo de la revolución: Primera parte," *América Latina*, 10 (October 1984): 63.
7. http://www.cubaminrex.cu/informacion/DECLARCOFICIALesp.htm (December 28, 2001).
8. Budget calculations from Comisión Económica para América Latina y el Caribe, *La economía cubana: Reformas estructurales y desempeño en los noventa* (Mexico: Fondo de Cultura Económica, 2000), Tables A.13 and A.14. Hereafter CEPAL.
9. Calculated from Oficina Nacional de Estadísticas, *Anuario estadístico de Cuba, 1996* (Havana, 1998), 98, 99; and Oficina Nacional de Estadísticas, *Anuario estadístico de Cuba, 2000* (Havana, 2001), 105; hereafter *Anuario 2000*.
10. *Anuario 2000*, 128, 137; CEPAL, Table A.30.
11. See remarks by Cuba's Minister for Economy and Planning, José Luis Rodríguez, before the National Assembly on 21 December 2002, *Granma*, December 23, 2002.
12. See analysis by Cuban scholar Juan Valdés Paz, "El sistema político cubano de los años noventa: Continuidad y cambio," in *Cuba construyendo futuro: Reestructuración económica y transformaciones sociales* (Madrid: El Viejo Topo/Fundación de Investigaciones Marxistas, 2000), 245, 247.
13. Kenneth Waltz, "The Emerging Structure of International Politics," in *The International System After the Collapse of the East-West Order*, ed. A. Clesse, R. Cooper, and Y. Sakamoto (Dordrecht: Martinus Nijhoff, 1994), 169.
14. For discussion, see Jorge I. Domínguez, "U.S.–Cuban Relations: From the Cold War to the Colder War," *Journal of Interamerican Studies and World Affairs*, 39, no. 3 (1997): 49–75.
15. Jorge I. Domínguez, *To Make a World Safe for Revolution: Cuba's Foreign Policy* (Cambridge, MA: Harvard University Press, 1989), 171–176.
16. Ibid., Chapters 7, 8.
17. Computed from *Granma*, November 28, 2001.
18. Instituto de Relaciones Europeo-Latinoamericanas, "40 años de revolución en Cuba: ¿Transición hacia dónde?," *Dossier*, 68 (Madrid: 1999), 38–39, 43; and the Cuban Foreign Ministry's web page http://www.cubaminrex.cu/politicaregional/REGAmeLat.htm.

19. Joaquín Roy, *Cuba, the United States, and the Helms-Burton Doctrine: International Reactions* (Gainesville: University Press of Florida, 2000), 151–155.
20. President Bush's official waivers make explicit mention of the U.S.–EU agreement. Retrieved from http://usembassy.state.gov/bogota/wwwshb04.shtml.
21. John Walton Cotman, "Cuba and the CARICOM States: The Last Decade," in *Cuba's Ties to a Changing World*, ed. D. R. Kaplowitz (Boulder, CO: Lynne Rienner, 1993); Canute James, "Caribbean Community, Cuba Sign Controversial Trade Pact," *Journal of Commerce*, December 15, 1993.
22. http://www.cubaminrex.cu/boletin/invextranj_colab_asistec.htm.
23. CEPAL, Table A.2. Drawn also from http://www.cubagob.cubaweb.cu/des_eco/mep/cuba2000.htm.
24. There are few reliable data on direct foreign investment. The evidence presented refers to the number of associations, that is, investment contracts between international firms and the Cuban government. The rank order of the value of investments, however, is Canada, Spain, and Italy, but the Cuban government does not publish the pertinent statistics.
25. For a good summary of the history of Cuban dependence in the second half of the twentieth century, see William M. LeoGrande and Julie M. Thomas, "Cuba's Quest for Economic Independence," *Journal of Latin American Studies*, 34 (2002): 325–363.
26. http://www.cubaminrex.cu/informacion/DECLARCOFICIALesp.htm (December 28, 2001).
27. See report of Cuba's Economy Minister José Luis Rodríguez to the National Assembly on December 21, 2002, *Granma*, December 23, 2002.
28. Domínguez, *To Make a World Safe for Revolution*, 226–227, 245–246.
29. *Granma Internacional*, September 28, 1994: 10; *Granma*, August 31, 1999.
30. *CubaInfo*, 8, no. 9 (July 11, 1996): 2–3.
31. U.S. Defense Intelligence Agency, "The Cuban Threat to U.S. National Security," June 1998, http://www.defenselink.mil/pubs/cubarpt.htm.
32. Hal Klepak, *Confidence Building and the Cuba–United States Confrontation* (Ottawa, Canada: Department of Foreign Affairs and International Trade, International Security Research and Outreach Programme, 2000): 21–22.
33. *CubaInfo*, 7, no. 16 (December 20, 1991): 1.
34. "Cuba Cooperating to Combat Drug Trade, U.S. Official Says," *The New York Times*, May 8, 1999: A3; U.S. Executive Office of the Presidency, Office of National Drug Control Policy, "Testimony of Barry R. McCaffrey, Director, Office of National Drug Control Policy before the Senate Committee on Armed Services, Subcommittee on Emerging Threats and Capabilities, the Department of Defense's Role in U.S. Drug Control Policy," April 27, 1999: 22.
35. Peter Kornbluh, "Cuba, Counternarcotics, and Collaboration: A Security Issue in U.S.–Cuban Relations," *Cuba Briefing Paper Series*, 24 (Washington, DC: Georgetown University, 2000): 8–10.
36. Confidential interviews, Washington, DC, 1996.
37. Confidential interviews, Miami, FL, February 1998.
38. Drawn from President Fidel Castro's remarks on September 11, 2001. http://www.cubaminrex.cu/informacion/discursofidel11septiembre.htm. See also Cuban Foreign Minister Felipe Pérez Roque's response in http://www.cubasource.org/chronicles/sep01.htm.
39. Government of the Republic of Cuba, "Statement by the Government of Cuba to the National and International Public Opinion," January 11, 2002, courtesy of the Cuban Interests Section in Washington, DC.
40. Carol Rosenberg, "U.S., Cuba Talk about Malaria," *The Miami Herald*, February 22, 2002.
41. U.S. Census Bureau, "U.S. Trade Balance with Cuba," http://landview.census.gov/foreign-trade/balance/c2390.html; http://www.odci.gov/cia/publications/factbook/geos/cu.html. *The Economist*, (January 4, 2003): 28, reported U.S. exports to Cuba worth $165 million in 2002. Retrieved also from the Cuban Foreign Ministry's web site http://www.cubaminrex.cu/politicaregional/amenorte3.htm.
42. Discussion with Cuban Ambassador Dagoberto Rodríguez, Chief, Cuban Interests Section, Washington, DC. *The Economist* (January 4, 2003): 4, claims that twice that number visited in 2001.

43. "Información del Ministerio de Relaciones Exteriores," http://www.cubaminrex.cu/informacion/infominrex8nov.htm; *Granma*, 20 December 2001.
44. For a discussion of Trollope's Ploy during the 1962 Cuban Missile Crisis, see Graham Allison, *Essence of Decision: Explaining the Cuban Missile Crisis* (Boston: Little, Brown, 1971), 227.
45. U.S. Department of State, *Patterns of Global Terrorism 2001* (Washington, DC), 63–64.
46. John R. Bolton, "Beyond the Axis of Evil: Additional Threats from Weapons of Mass Destruction: Remarks to the Heritage Foundation," May 6, 2002, http://www.state.gov/t/us/rm/9962.htm.
47. http://www.state.gov/secretary/rm/2002/10113.htm.
48. http://www.cubaminrex.cu/politicaregional/amenorte3.htm.
49. Discussion with Cuban Ambassador Dagoberto Rodríguez, Chief, Cuban Interests Section, Washington, DC.
50. For one example of Colombian government negotiations in Havana with the ELN, see *Granma*, February 1, 2002.
51. "Response from Dr. Fidel Castro Ruz, President of the Republic of Cuba, to the Statements Made by the United States Government on Biological Weapons," May 10, 2002, courtesy of the Cuban Interests Section, Washington, DC.
52. *Granma*, December 30, 2001.
53. Nidia Díaz, "Cuba y el desarme mundial: un paso trascendental por la paz y el multilaterilsmo," on the web site of the Cuban Foreign Ministry http://www.cubaminrex.cu/enfoques/cuba%20y%20el%20desarme%20nuclear.htm.
54. See, for example, Julie M. Feinsilver, *Healing the Masses: Cuban Health Politics at Home and Abroad* (Berkeley: University of California Press, 1993), chapter 5.
55. Joseph Nye, *Bound to Lead: The Changing Nature of American Power* (New York: Basic Books, 2000); Carlos Alzugaray, "La política exterior de Cuba en la década de los 90: intereses, objetivos y resultados," Paper presented at the International Congress of the Latin American Studies Association, September 2001.
56. Some of Cuba's international tourism industry, more controversially, seems to promote sex tourism. See, for example, Jeff Cohen, "Cuba Libre," *Playboy* (March 1991): 69–74, 157–158.
57. See Feinsilver, *Healing the Masses*, chapter 6. Drawn also from the Cuban Foreign Ministry's web page http://www.cubaminrex.cu/cooperacion/resultadosgenerales.htm; http://www.cubaminrex.cu/cooperacion/coopera_becas.htm; and Domingo Amuchástegui, "Cuba's Reengagement with the Caribbean: Setbacks and Successes," *Cuba Briefing Paper Series*, 22 (Washington DC: Georgetown University, 1999), 7.

CHAPTER 9

To Have a Cake and Eat It Too: The Crisis of Pax Americana in Korea

BYUNG-KOOK KIM

Introduction

"The global order should be driven by *myongbun*,[1] not force.... Unfortunately, power still prevails in international politics. In domestic affairs, too, realism dominates over idealism." After appraising international and domestic politics in such a solemn way, President Roh Moo-hyun recollected his lifelong struggle against realpolitik: "As a politician I have always followed *myongbun*. That is why I was frequently criticized as too idealistic. Some even questioned my ability as a politician, but my ideals would not let me do otherwise.... I lost several elections as a price for upholding my *myongbun*." Then followed a dramatic twist in his logic.

> And it is *I* who calls for dispatching military troops to Iraq. I do so because our nation's fate rests on it. I chose defeat in elections because it risked only my personal life. As President, my choice can no longer be only my personal choice.... Rather than driving our relationship with Washington into a discord by holding onto my personal *myongbun*, I respect our obligation as its military ally and stand by Washington when it is in a difficult time.[2]

The speech was politically brilliant. Roh Moo-hyun was hard-pressed to come up with a rationale to dispatch troops in order to mend fences with a "hawkish" George W. Bush and preempt Korea's conservative establishment from capitalizing on his alleged anti-Americanism, but without hurting his moralistic image, which had won him massive support from Korea's younger nationalist progressive voters in his 2002 presidential election only three and a half months before. This speech delivered before National Assembly Members on April 2, 2003, helped Roh Moo-hyun come out ahead in his two-level game to nurture close ties with George W. Bush without alienating his progressive domestic political constituency. Bush telephoned two days later to thank him for the dispatching of army engineers and medics while also pledging to peacefully solve Pyongyang's nuclear threat through close consultation with Roh Moo-hyun.[3] Remarkably, this did not cause irreparable damage to his moralistic image nurtured through the unambiguous antiwar stand he took during his campaign. By describing his decision as based on "realism," Roh Moo-hyun denied Bush any legitimacy in invading Iraq and even implicitly blamed him for bullying Korea into supporting an unjust war. This was exactly how Korea's progressive forces interpreted his choice.[4]

Roh Moo-hyun ironically escaped from becoming a primary target of public outcries also because he was uniquely positioned within Korea's increasingly polarized ideological terrain. A dark horse in Korea's presidential election in a two-way race with Lee Hoi-chang, with a support level that danced wildly throughout 2002 in public polls,[5] Roh Moo-hyun not only faced an unruly National Assembly with conservative Hannara Party politicians in the majority, but also headed a minority *sinjuryu,* or "new mainstream," within his own New Millennium Democratic Party (NMDP). He could only propose — not guarantee — a troop dispatch. This weakness, however, became his strength because he knew the Hannara Party could only say yes, given its pro-American conservative stand on military security issues. As expected, Hannara's National Assembly members voted 118 yeas against 22 nays and 5 abstentions, whereas NMDP deputies split into 49 pros, 43 cons, and 4 abstentions. Those 43 NMDP votes against troop dispatch, moreover, largely came from Roh Moo-hyun's new mainstream,[6] which again helped redirect antiwar NGOs' anger and frustration to Hannara rather than Roh Moo-hyun.

What brought such a complex two-level game into play in Korea? How and why did its security interest in maintaining a robust alliance with Washington come into conflict, if not collision, with domestic political pressures? Was it only Seoul whose domestic and international political preferences changed to make alliance management an arduous task, or was

Washington too a source of trouble? How did Roh Moo-hyun strive to balance his domestic political requirements with national security interests? Was he scheming for a "double play" designed to blame Hannara and U.S. policymakers for unpopular policies, as his critics claimed,[7] or was he genuinely balancing anti-American public sentiments and U.S. political pressures? To systematically analyze his policy dilemma, the first section of this chapter lists major issues or problems in Korea's military alliance system, as it saw since it made a democratic breakthrough in 1987, and traces how its Ministry of National Defense (MND) held down societal demands to a level acceptable to its U.S. counterpart, the Department of Defense (DoD), until 2002. The second section follows up with a story of how such a tight control on agenda formation and negotiation processes by Korea's security community abruptly broke down in 2002. Then it analyzes U.S. responses to contain — if not retaliate against — anti-American sentiments by linking basic rights issues with military security and military security issues with economic risks. The third section summarizes implications of Pax Americana in Korea.

A Crisis of Success

By any standard, Korea constituted a story of U.S. foreign policy success. In less than four decades, it underwent a transformation from a classic client state living on U.S. aid into an Organisation for Economic Co-operation and Development (OECD) member with a dynamic information technology industry. Politically, too, Korea stunned even its own people by dismantling repressive Cold War political taboos one after another to strengthen basic civil rights and to make free and fair elections its "only possible game in town" since it made a democratic breakthrough in 1987. Militarily, Korea triumphed over Pyongyang as well, equipping its armed forces with high-tech U.S. weapons and advanced organizational know-how. Such a triple economic, political, and military success, however, ironically became a catalyst for discord rather than harmony with its U.S. ally by 2002, if not earlier. With Pyongyang hopelessly entrapped in a regime crisis and timidly making an overture for dialogue with Seoul, many thought Korea no longer had a clear military *jujok,* or "primary enemy."[8] The changed view on Pyongyang inevitably made Koreans heatedly debate over U.S. Forces in Korea (USFK): what raison d'être it had; whether it needed be restructured, if not reduced or even withdrawn; how socioeconomic costs for supporting it should be shared between Seoul and Washington as well as among Koreans; and who should exercise wartime command.

This debate obviously acquired a political aspect only because democratization deepened in Korea. By guaranteeing basic civil rights, democratization enabled more people to engage more openly in struggles for political power and to experiment with new ideas and values, many of which were previously thought of as ideological heresies. Wherever and whenever U.S. military troops became an issue, an NGO sprang up, networked with already existing activist groups into a broad but loose political coalition, and launched its own small media campaign by setting up a web site on Korea's burgeoning Internet, uploading defiant ideas onto other Internet sites and urging "Netizens" to join in its civic protest. Society was ready to listen not only because democratization had made it more open toward unorthodox ideas, but also because economic prosperity and military modernization imbued it with a strong nationalist urge. As seen by many critics, Korea's security system was outdated, giving U.S. military troops too many privileges with too little accountability. The Status of Forces Agreement (SOFA), which enumerated U.S. military troops' legal rights and responsibilities over diverse issues including facility and land grant, tax and custom duties, and criminal jurisdiction, was signed in 1966 when Korea — economically too poor and militarily too weak — was ready to limit its peoples' basic rights as well as compromise its state's sovereign rights in order to facilitate the U.S. military presence. Now Korea was on par with major nations in economic power and it deserved a more equal alliance system.

Military Security Constraints

The alarmist view's warning of a spread of anti-American sentiments notwithstanding, Korea in 2002 debated not over whether U.S. military forces should withdraw, but over what constituted equality in a bilateral relationship with America and how that equality could be achieved.[9] It could not be otherwise because in spite of Korea's rapid integration into China's economic orbit since diplomatic normalization in 1992, siding with Chinese militarily was not an option, given China's authoritarian regime and security alliance with Pyongyang. Realigning with Japan, too, was unattractive, not only because Koreans remained unforgiving toward its colonial atrocities, but also because Japan was a second-rate military power, incapable of defending itself without U.S. aid. Then there was Pyongyang, whose massive artilleries lined up along a 155-mile-long armistice line could "put Seoul on fire," to quote its threat during a nuclear crisis in 1994, even when its people starved. These tight geopolitical constraints gave Seoul no option other than striving to upgrade its security alliance with Washington into an equal partnership. The issue was how to ensure a U.S. military presence, but with a minimum of sociopolitical and economic cost.

The question had no easy answer because with political democratization, economic growth, and Pyongyang's regime crisis, Korea's understanding of what constituted the costs of supporting a U.S. military presence and whether they were fair continuously altered. Moreover, once Korea calculated its costs, it also had to take into account any risk that Washington might opt for a staged military reduction cum force restructuring if Korea insisted on cost reduction. To make its search for equality even more complex, this risk — like its own perception of costs — was a variable rather than a constant. The East Asia Strategic Initiative (EASI), unilaterally drawn by Washington under Defense Secretary Richard Cheney's leadership in 1990, had envisioned a gradual reduction of U.S. troops from Korea in three stages before a crisis over Pyongyang's nuclear development program abruptly disrupted it in 1992.[10] This was followed up by a de facto policy reversal with a Nye Report in 1995 that called for a continuous forward U.S. military deployment in East Asia,[11] but even then Cheney's second stage, which called for Washington's withdrawal of military troops except two army brigades and one air force unit over a period of three years, always remained an option if a new global or regional strategic situation arose or if EASI's architect or like-minded people returned to power in Washington. To make Korea even more anxious, Cheney's second stage would dissolve the U.S.–Korea Combined Forces Command (CFC), a symbol of U.S. military commitment, in line with the transfer of wartime operational command to Korea. That danger held Korea back from aggressively demanding compensation for whatever cost it thought it bore to support U.S. military troops — until 2002.

Korean society feared so because it thought it was only the U.S. Second Division deployed in between Seoul and Korea's armistice line that deterred Pyongyang from waging another civil war. The unit served as a "human tripwire," automatically forced into combat if Pyongyang attacked, given its geographic location. By making it impossible for Pyongyang to reach Seoul without running over the U.S. Second Division, Seoul hoped to make credible before Pyongyang as well as its own people America's pledge to intervene in war with up to 690,000 soldiers shipped and flown in from Japan and elsewhere within ninety days,[12] even if the U.S. public wavered over war support.[13] The U.S. war entry would be unavoidable once Pyongyang caused U.S. GI casualties in its military campaign. The EASI's second stage threatened precisely this deterrence mechanism. Were it implemented as Cheney originally planned, Seoul surely would have fallen into panic. With its massive artilleries forward-deployed only thirty miles from Seoul and its fighter planes poised to strike Seoul within a mere six minutes, Pyongyang could lull itself into thinking it could take Seoul through a blitzkrieg before U.S. troops arrived and present its military occupation of Seoul as a fait accompli before U.S. policymakers.[14]

Accordingly, Seoul was careful not to provoke Washington into reviving EASI when it urged U.S. actions to correct socioeconomic costs arising from and built into their alliance system. The seemingly most intractable issue, operational command, ironically resulted in only a few open political clashes. The CFC formally abided by what it called a "binational principle" in organization in order to make credible its pretension for equal partnership, placing a GI as a deputy if a Korean soldier was in charge and vice versa throughout its command hierarchy. The reality was, however, thorough U.S. control through interlocked command posts.[15] The USFK commander simultaneously performed three other roles, sitting in at a bilateral Military Committee (MC) responsible for drawing up military strategies and tactics, but also heading the CFC, which took orders from the MC. The structure assured that he could execute what he helped devise as a MC member. The same was also true for his role as a peacekeeper. As United Nations Commander (UNC), responsible for guarding Korea's 1953 armistice agreement, he ordered the CFC to carry out any measure he thought was necessary to stop Pyongyang from violating provisos of the armistice agreement. The USFK Commander not only interpreted the armistice agreement, but also executed his interpretations, thereby de facto defining what Korea could do whenever its northern foe engaged in military provocation.

This lopsided command structure repeatedly became a domestic political issue with democratization, only to fade away rapidly as an agenda for bilateral talks. The initial proposal for change ironically came from Cheney in 1990, who was then busy drawing up a global strategy to restructure U.S. military forces according to new requirements of the post–Cold War era. As already noted, he prepared EASI for East Asia, which translated into a plan for a three-stage U.S. troop reduction from Korea. To make way for the second stage, which planned for reducing U.S. military presence by 6,500 soldiers between 1993 and 1995, Cheney proposed to transfer peacetime operational command in February 1990, only to see the MND engage passively in — if not delay or avoid — any substantive talks, lest an agreement on peacetime operational command lead not to U.S. military reduction but to complete withdrawal. Then, in 1992, the two allies' positions reversed, with Seoul demanding peacetime operational command, and Washington opposing any immediate transfer because it allegedly could weaken U.S. congressional support for the CFC and USFK, undermine the UNC's authority, and encourage the intervention of Korean military troops into politics. The real reason for the policy reversal on peacetime operational command, however, was Cheney's decision to halt EASI's second stage in November 1991 after U.S. intelligence reports warned against Pyongyang's nuclear development program.[16] The second stage of troop reduction postponed indefinitely in Washington, Seoul could claim peacetime operational command without fearing its transfer escalating into a complete U.S. military withdrawal. That 1992 was a presidential election year helped, too. The recovery of sovereignty, however limited, made a good campaign issue for Kim Young-sam.

The transfer was eventually agreed to in November 1993, three and a half year since Cheney initially proposed it and two years after he froze EASI's second stage. The MND celebrated it as a moment of regaining sovereignty. The transfer, however, could be only partial, given tight geopolitical constraints. Very limited in its military intelligence capability, Seoul agreed to have the USFK monitor Pyongyang's troop deployment and war preparedness through satellites and advanced reconnaissance planes, as well as oversee joint military exercises during peacetime. This intelligence dependence also swayed Seoul into continuing the USFK Commander's authority to formulate military strategies, as well as recommend to the CFC the issuing of a DEFCON to put troops on alert. For some progressive NGOs, such a command structure still looked too severely limiting of Korea's sovereignty. To others, it even looked dangerously too trusting of Washington's intentions because based on press reports on possible U.S. sanctions against Pyongyang in retaliation against its nuclear and missile development in 1994, 1998, and 2002, top U.S. policymakers seemed ready to drag Seoul into war against its wish in pursuit of nuclear nonproliferation and antiterrorism.[17] The overwhelming majority, by contrast, accepted these limitations on Korea's peacetime operational command as a price for tying down U.S. troops.

Mirroring this *juryu*, or "mainstream," opinion on military strategic issues and the U.S. role was Korea's silence on the USFK's wartime operational command. To be sure, after winning his presidential bid in December 2002, Roh Moo-hyun in a bold moment revealed his hope for sharing wartime operational command, as well as jointly setting strategic military goals, agendas, and plans with Washington.[18] However, once Donald H. Rumsfeld, in his capacity as U.S. Defense Secretary, expressed his "sympathy" with Roh Moo-hyun's hope for an equal partnership and identified U.S. troop relocation cum downsizing as his starting point for discussion,[19] Roh Moo-hyun backtracked. When Rumsfeld showed his seriousness by sending in a DoD delegation for a bilateral talk on U.S. military troop relocation in April 2003, Roh Moo-hyun adopted a delay tactic like Roh Tae-woo did when Cheney proposed transferring peacetime operational command in February 1990. He proposed to talk about troop relocation only after Pyongyang's nuclear threat was resolved, when Rumsfeld's people showed interest in Osan and Pyongtaek in the south of the Han River, far away from the armistice line, as a new home for the U.S. Second Division.[20] Roh Moo-hyun was simply learning what his predecessors already knew: Do not go too far in demanding an equal alliance, lest Washington respond with its own demand for equal burden sharing and end its Second Division's role as a human tripwire through troop relocation.

Domestic Politics and U.S. Security Goals

What politically troubled Seoul more during its contentious reformist era ushered in by its triple economic, democratic, and security success was a rising discord over SOFA.[21] Economically prosperous, society eagerly imported from abroad new "postmodernist" views on human rights, which increasingly made it look at SOFA as a basic rights issue rather than a military security issue and criticize SOFA for its infringing on the rights of the Korean people. Unlike the authoritarian era, moreover, people acted on their normative critique because with political pluralization, enabling more people to more actively test new political ideas without prohibitively high transaction costs,[22] criticizing SOFA was no longer looked upon as an ideological taboo. The security constraints held society back less from voicing its views on SOFA, too, because it interpreted Washington's pledge to maintain a military presence as long as Koreans "desired" and thought it "necessary"[23] as enabling Korea to define SOFA issues as basic rights issues without risking its military security interests too much. Korean society was right from *its* perspective. To demand a SOFA revision to protect local villagers' basic rights while politically backing the continued presence of USFK troops was not illogical or contradictory in itself. As Roh Moo-hyun once said, "Demanding a SOFA revision *by definition* assumes continuous U.S military presence."[24] There would be no SOFA to revise if there were no U.S. troops.

However logical society thought it was when unlinking SOFA from military security issues, it clearly underestimated U.S. resistance. Washington thought it could not but oppose a SOFA revision if it compromised GIs' basic rights as U.S. citizens. Consequently, what started as a talk on GIs' legal rights and duties could be transformed into a security issue, with Washington reviewing troop relocation cum downsizing among other things as a measure to protect GIs from getting into trouble with local legal authorities if Korea requested the exercise of primary jurisdiction to try under Korean laws any bodily harm or property damages U.S. GIs caused to campside townspeople while in a military drill or public duty. The problem was particularly grave in Korea, compared with other U.S. allies, because towns had rapidly grown around and even in between U.S. military camps and training grounds,[25] increasing GIs' exposure to accidents during military drills. Moreover, for many campside towns, military drills impinged on local peoples' property rights and threatened their economic livelihood, as many villagers were prohibited from tilling their land inside U.S. training grounds during a military drill, with no compensation by Korean or U.S. military authorities. Environmental damages, too, periodically pitted U.S. troops against local villagers and their NGO allies.[26] The question was how to deal with safety, property rights, and environmental issues arising from having a large U.S. military presence in Korea's densely populated and thoroughly urbanized social setting without precipitating in Washington a serious concern over its GIs' interest.

The strategy Korea's authoritarian regime adopted to deal with safety, property rights, and environmental issues before 1988 was one of "benign neglect," if not "free riding." Fearing state repression, most campside towns in fact remained silent, misleading society into a belief that all was well. Very few like Nogeunli's villagers petitioned for justice since 1960,[27] only to see Korea's authoritarian regime brush aside their plea, or worse, slur them as leftist anti-Americans instigating political unrest and alliance discord. The general public was a de facto accomplice in this not only because it too lacked interest in protecting campside townspeople's basic rights, but also because it was a free rider enjoying military security without equally sharing the cost of the U.S. military presence with campside townspeople. The safety, property rights, and environmental problems caused by U.S. military installations were not its problem. When U.S. soldiers wronged local villagers, Korea's powerful media typically preached prudence and endurance without proactively searching for workable remedies. They did not or could not do so because they believed any serious search for remedies would end up with U.S. troop relocation with or without downsizing, which would only allow the U.S. Second Division to end its unwanted tripwire role. Nor would society and state elites seriously propose material compensation for campside townspeople due to Korea's severe resource constraints.

The search for a remedy accordingly began in earnest only after 1988. The general public could not but sympathize with what they, too, increasingly judged as a legitimate demand for basic rights. Even if society felt otherwise in its inmost heart, it could not preach "prudence" before campside townspeople because they would not allow their grievances to be silenced any more. The Maehyangli village began its lonely struggle to close down a nearby Kooni Fire Range in 1988.[28] The "National Campaign for Eradication of Crime by U.S. Troops" formed in 1992 to pressure a legal action against crimes committed by GIs, only to expand continuously its mission, soon becoming a watchdog over environmental pollution, a spokesperson for campside towns' safety and property rights, and an advocate of SOFA revision.[29] Radical NGOs in eleven major campside towns also came together to form a committee to recover lands from U.S. military troops in 1997.[30] The mainstream NGOs with a more general organizational mission, larger institutional structures, and more professional reputations soon joined in to lend their legitimacy to this protest against U.S. troops.[31]

Even before a rapid rise in NGO activism against U.S. military troops, however, the MND and DoD moved along two paths to reform their alliance. The allies jointly announced a "basic plan" for relocating the huge U.S. Yongsan military base from Seoul in May 1989. Then, in January 1991, they amended SOFA after negotiating for two years. The two allies, however, had dissimilar reasons. The U.S. developed a keen interest in both troop relocation and SOFA talks because it was reevaluating its global strategic options in a vastly altered post–Cold War era, which eventually culminated in EASI. For its top foreign policymakers, then, relocating the Yongsan Army Base and revising SOFA were part of its globally conceived strategy to reduce U.S. military commitment worldwide and persuade its allies to take a greater burden-sharing role in global military security. The Korean state, by contrast, had an inward looking view, interested in relocating the Yongsan Army Base and revising SOFA only as a measure to reduce the sources of domestic political discord over U.S. troops. Tougher SOFA provisions, it reasoned, would preempt many crimes as well as force GIs to diligently follow their safety rules, regulations, and ethics code. Relocating the Yongsan Army Base would likewise upgrade President Roh Tae-woo's (1988–1993) public image not only as a democratic but also as a nationalist.

As already noted, however, EASI was interrupted before it got to its second stage, due to intelligence reports on Pyongyang's nuclear development project. This change inevitably figured into both troop relocation and SOFA issues. The USFK indefinitely postponed its plan to relocate its Yongsan Army Base partly because Korea could not come up with funds to build a similar installation outside Seoul, but also because its strategic raison d'être for relocating the Yongsan Army Base faded away with Cheney's decision not to proceed with EASI's second stage.[32] The DoD and MND managed to revise SOFA in 1991, but only in a minor way. The two allies deleted their 1967 highly unpopular SOFA article requiring Korea to automatically waiver its right to claim jurisdiction over criminal cases, but still agreed to have Seoul waive this right if Washington requested.[33]

The troop relocation and SOFA issues accordingly lingered on as a political issue as Korea's triple economic, political, and military success continuously deepened after 1991. To prevent a further deterioration of Korean public sentiments, Washington began talks for another SOFA revision in 1995, only to see a prolonged deadlock with Seoul on which of the SOFA provisos to change. The talks picked up only after three incidents seriously increased anti-American sentiments in 2000. A U.S. soldier murdered a female bar worker in February, causing a public outcry for justice. Then, in May, a U.S. fighter plane accidentally dropped bombs on Maehyangli's nearby sea, again raising public concern over campside townspeople's safety and property rights. Finally, a U.S. civilian facility leaked a poisonous liquid into the Han River and subsequently tried to cover it up in May.[34] That Kim Dae-jung held a summit meeting with Kim Jong Il in June, resulting in a joint declaration to "resolve independently Korea's unification issue" based on their unification strategies' "commonalities,"[35] gave an added impetus to anti-American protests because with society believing in its imminent peace with Pyongyang, NGOs could politicize the alleged political and social costs of the U.S. military presence without being accused of undermining military security.

Then there was an equally critical change in U.S. global geopolitical calculation, which also encouraged the DoD to pick up its talks on troop relocation, and SOFA with the MND. In May 2000, the U.S. Joint Chiefs of Staff forecasted future wars as "asymmetric" in character, with its enemy focused on building "niche capabilities" to hit America where it was vulnerable with asymmetric ways and means such as a terrorist attack with biological, chemical, and even nuclear weapons; they envisioned such an attack making U.S. military services "interoperable," supporting each other as a truly "joint force" through a systematic use of information technology in its weapons as well as command system.[36] Eight months earlier, the U.S. Commission on National Security (USCNS) similarly saw information technology as a key component in designing any future U.S. military strategy and force structure, but for a more political reason. The pressures to reduce U.S. forward-deployed troops in Europe and Asia, it argued, will increase at home and abroad with the rising fiscal austerity as well as the perception of a reduction in the danger of a major war with the coming of the post–Cold War era.[37]

The National Defense Panel (NDP), with Richard L. Armitage as a key member, was much more precise and bold in articulating new ideas on military security. Foreseeing a world where traditional deterrence policy may not deter "nuclear, chemical or biological attacks by a rogue state against U.S. allies," it called for fully exploiting information technology to build up power to "detect, identify, and track far greater numbers of targets over a larger area for a longer time than ever before." The U.S. "will need greater mobility, precision, speed, stealth, and strike ranges while [it] sharply reduce[s] [its] logistics footprint."[38] According to this view, Washington should overhaul its Cold War strategy to build an armed forces capable of simultaneously engaging in two regional theaters of war, presumably against Pyongyang and one or another Middle East rogue state. That military strategy simply invested too many resources on what was a too unlikely contingency, and, in doing so, prevented U.S. policymakers from preparing for future asymmetric strategic requirements through comprehensive force restructuring. Moreover, it made Washington concentrate massive troops in a few fixed bases when what was required was "numerous small, dispersed supply points" from which ground, sea, and air forces rapidly and flexibly moved in and out to form one genuinely interoperable joint force in varying sizes.[39]

Propelled by both Korean domestic political pressures and U.S. military strategic rethinking — like 1988 to 1991, but with a much greater force — the two allies' talks on SOFA and troop relocation rapidly progressed. With Armitage and like-minded Republicans in power in Washington, the DoD and MND amended SOFA in January 2001 and signed a Land Partnership Plan (LPP) in March 2002. The two documents made much progress but still fell short of satisfying Korean NGOs' demands. The SOFA's agreed minutes newly established an article on environmental protection, only to be criticized by NGO activists as merely "declaratory" in character, without any provisos outlining USFK's responsibilities to clean up as well as compensate for environmental damages. Another set of amendments enabled Korea's legal authorities to take a GI into custody even before trial if there existed "adequate cause" to believe the GI committed a major crime and if there existed "necessity" for pretrial custody to preserve evidence, to prevent an escape, or to protect victims and witnesses. But, in another paragraph, Korea agreed to "give sympathetic consideration" to a formal request by U.S. military authorities to "forgo or postpone pretrial custody... in special cases where an accused was ill, injured or pregnant."[40]

The LPP likewise alleviated Korea's security worries by pledging to relocate U.S. troops only gradually over a decade, but it included thirteen U.S.

military bases in Paju, Dongduchon, and Uijongbu in its land release package, thus signaling Washington's intention to relieve the U.S. Second Division of its human tripwire role. To reduce campside towns' grievances, the LPP planned to cut down U.S. military installations by 43.9 percent and land use by 55.3 percent until 2011, but excluded Maehyangli's Kooni Fire Range from its list of land return. The Yongsan base likewise remained a subject for discussion, as it had been for fourteen years, because Washington and Seoul disagreed on its relocation cost. To deter U.S. congressional criticism, moreover, the LPP split its total costs between Seoul and Washington by the ratio of 46:54. To minimize political opposition in Korea, the LPP was publicly sold as a self-financing scheme, with Seoul to recoup its expenditures in land purchase for new U.S. bases through selling the closed down U.S. bases in Korea's lucrative real estate markets, presumably at profit.[41] As expected, the LPP drew criticisms from Korean NGOs as "unfair" or "infeasible."[42] The defense establishment in Seoul as well as Washington, however, had much to celebrate in early 2002, for they had, after all, succeeded in jointly revising SOFA and drawing up a long-term road map for U.S. troop relocation with the goal of putting the alliance on a more secure social and political basis. Or so they thought — until anti-American protests swept society after June 2002.

After the Election

The MND's ability to politically isolate progressive NGOs and campside townspeople from society to draw up a proposal acceptable to its U.S. counterpart suddenly broke down after June 2002. The NGOs surprised Korea's defense ministry and security community with their success in mobilizing middle-class groups for protests against SOFA on an ever larger scale over a prolonged period.[43] The political right led by the Hannara Party changed in a subtle but critical way, too, openly criticizing SOFA while reiterating its traditional pro-American Cold War stand on military security issues. Previously, when tension arose over social and economic issues with U.S. policymakers, the Hannara Party and its predecessors typically became a spokesperson for Korea's security community, toning down its demands for SOFA revision and even keeping a low profile in — if not staying out of — the MND's talk with the DoD, lest an open dispute with U.S. policymakers over social and economic issues inadvertently provoked anti-American sentiments with dire military security consequences. By contrast, as 2002 proceeded, the Hannara Party took a critical view of SOFA even more frequently and unambiguously than an allegedly more progressive NMDP.[44] The catalyst for such a rapid spread of anti-American sentiments was the deaths of two schoolgirls in Hyochonli on June 13.

The MND no longer appeared capable of securing political support from even state agencies for its balancing act between military security and other interests. The defense ministry worked to resolve the disputes over the deaths of the two schoolgirls as quietly and quickly as possible, only to see state prosecutors in Uijongbu side with NGOs and Hyochonli campside townspeople in demanding Korea's primary jurisdiction to try Sergeants Fernando Nino and Mark Walker, whose armored vehicle ran over the two teenage girls during a military exercise. The police likewise saw Uijongbu's district court dismiss its warrant to arrest two Internet news reporters for breaking into a U.S. military base to film NGO protests. The National Human Rights Commission (NHRC) made an even more unexpected move, asking the U.S. Second Division Commander to answer in writing a charge brought by those two reporters against U.S. military guards for assault and unlawful detention. When the U.S. Second Division refused to reply, the NHRC levied ten million won as a penalty for its refusal and looked for a way to make payment compulsory, only to discover it had no legal authority to do so under both Korean laws and SOFA provisos.[45] When a U.S. military court found Nino and Walker not guilty of negligent homicide in November 2002, even middle-class groups began joining political rallies to protest the unfair ruling and to force another SOFA revision to ensure Korea's primary jurisdiction over any similar future legal disputes involving GIs.[46]

Two Surprises

The causes of such a rapid and sweeping breakdown in Korean political authorities' ability to maintain a robust military alliance with Washington by toning down societal demands for SOFA revision were many. The Hyochonli tragedy responsible for bringing back SOFA revision as a national political issue was made for headline news. The two girls' deaths surely grieved and angered society, but without rebellious NGOs and Netizens uploading gruesome photographs and defiant ideas onto Korea's burgeoning Internet and protesting against U.S. troops,[47] Hyochonli's tragedy would have hardly become a national issue. Moreover, once society got interested in ensuring a just and fair trial through trying Nino and Walker for negligent homicide under Korean laws, political deadlock became inevitable between Seoul and Washington, given their vastly dissimilar legal systems. The U.S. military insisted on holding a trial by jury with all panel members recruited from U.S. soldiers, as it was with all accidents involving GIs on public duties. The Korean society, by contrast, doubted whether U.S. soldiers sitting in as juries could try their fellow men in uniform in a just and fair way and it ended up calling for a trial by the Korean court. That was obviously not acceptable to Washington because it would have denied Nino and Walker their right to have a trial by jury as U.S. citizens.[48]

Even then, however, Hyochonli's tragedy would not have brought a severe breakdown in the MND's tight control over national agenda formation had there been no presidential election in December 2002. Seoul confronted not only a crisis in its security alliance with Washington but also a paralysis in its mechanism for crisis management. To explain this policy paralysis, it is necessary to bring in Korea's 2002 election as an intervening variable, which escalated the Hyochonli tragedy into an increasingly nonnegotiable issue involving political principles and legal justice. The election dramatically shook up Korea's bureaucratic policymaking processes because it was a critical election where Korea's allegedly rebellious "386 Generation"[49] rose en masse to mid-rank positions in the political parties, media, and NGOs responsible for political organization and campaigning, and its presumably nonconformist "X" and "N" generations, newly registered as voters and pressuring for an ideological realignment away from regionalism, decisively tilted politics toward moralistic reformism.[50] The septuagenarian "Three Kims" who personified Korea's old way of doing politics — regionalism and money politics — for thirty years were, moreover, readying for retirement from public life, too old and too discredited by their failures as president and prime minister. In addition, Korea's younger generations could challenge its established political system even more forcefully with new ideas, new organizations, and new faces.

Those myriad NGOs that kept alive the Hyochonli tragedy as a political issue were a product of this profound generational change. The 386 Generation became their organizational backbone after 1992, struggling for "postmaterialist" issues as rank-and-file members, once its frequently violent "class war" against what it called Korea's "neocolonial state monopoly capitalism" alienated society and boomeranged into the conservative regionalist political parties' triumph in presidential, national assembly, and local elections alike.[51] The political outsider Roh Moo-hyun likewise became the NMDP's presidential candidate in April 2002 only because his political party — hopelessly delegitimized by corruption, but also sensing a window of opportunity in the young people's hope to weed out regionalist politics and money politics by building a participatory democracy — decided to choose its candidate through newly instituted national primaries. Roh Moo-hyun soon demonstrated that the NMDP was right. Initially brushed aside as an easily roused moralistic rebel and even an unreliable populist by NMDP bosses and party cadres, Roh Moo-hyun surprised society by getting Korea's younger people to register as NMDP party members and support his bid for party nomination. These young activists worked from outside the NMDP even after Roh Moo-hyun's primary victory, maintaining a NGO-like fan club, *Nosamo*, as a campaign vehicle for Roh Moo-hyun in order to protect their image from getting dirtied by political association with one or another NMDP faction and to launch a moral critique against any NMDP politician who tried sabotaging Roh Moo-hyun's presidential bid from within the NMDP.[52]

This explosive "young power" explained why Lee Hoi-chang, a traditionalist with pro-American security views, took a very critical position on SOFA as frequently, consistently, and unambiguously as Roh Moo-hyun between June and December. Lee Hoi-chang was running for cover, if not trying to court young voters. Forty days after USFK rejected Korea's request to try Nino and Walker for negligent homicide under its laws,[53] Lee Hoi-chang called for enacting a new SOFA to recognize Korea's primary jurisdiction over legal disputes involving GIs while on public duty, lest he appear to have been bullied by U.S. policymakers into surrendering his people's basic rights for fair and just trial under Korean laws. Like most Koreans, moreover, he believed Korea could demand a SOFA revision without undermining U.S. military commitment because SOFA was a basic rights issue, disconnected from military security issues.[54] Consequently, while reiterating support for continued U.S. military presence in Korea, Lee Hoi-chang urged his Hannara party members to join in on a nationwide signature drive calling for SOFA revision on December 3 in order to catch up with Roh Moo-hyun in public support.[55] With Lee Hoi-chang trying to appear more reformist and nationalist on SOFA than Roh Moo-hyun to woo younger voters,[56] Korea no longer had a political force who contained anti-American sentiments from spreading throughout society by linking rights issues with military security issues, as its political right did before 2002. The two issues unlinked by Korea's conservative as well as progressive political forces, society continued to escalate its demand for SOFA revision, believing it could protect campside townspeople's basic rights without endangering Washington's willingness to station its troops in Korea.

Then there was George W. Bush's war on terror, which made many question even U.S. military troops' security role in Korea. Unfortunately for Lee Hoi-chang, Bush included Kim Jong Il's Pyongyang in an "axis of evil,"[57] a group of rogue states marked down for reprisal in his war on terror, only twenty months after Kim Dae-jung visited Pyongyang for a historic summit meeting. The hope for peace was then very high, with only 8.6 percent in one public opinion survey judging a military invasion from Pyongyang "highly possible."[58] The axis-of-evil speech in such a context made many view Washington not as a stabilizer deterring Pyongyang from launching a military attack, but as an irresponsible superpower ready to risk another Korean war while in pursuit of its larger global security goal. This looked even more likely because Pyongyang seemed too weak to attack, disintegrating economically as well as socially since its East European Soviet allies collapsed. To make Koreans even more apprehensive, Bush set goals and strategies unilaterally without closely consulting his allies. Given Korea's unequal alliance command structure with Washington in control of when to issue a DEFCON to put troops on alert, many argued that Korea was dangerously too trusting of U.S. intentions and could be dragged into war against its wishes. That Washington split into hawks and doves over how to respond to Pyongyang's decision to reactivate its Yongbyon nuclear facilities on December 12, 2002, did not help either. Pyongyang's hawkish words instantly made headlines in Korea, making many very anxious.[59]

This anxiety was visible even before tensions rapidly climbed up with Pyongyang's disclosure of its continuing nuclear development program in October 2002.[60] Figure 9.1 shows a public opinion map, with its vertical axis showing net support levels for Bush's war against terror and its horizontal axis displaying net policy receptivity ratios, which were calculated by subtracting negative appraisals from positive answers on one's perception of Washington's receptivity toward other countries' interests when formulating foreign policy, as discovered by a Pew Global Attitudes survey in June and July. Korea showed a strong antiwar consensus, with its people opposing the war on terror by a ratio of 72:24 and criticizing U.S. foreign policy as unilateralist by a ratio of 73:23. This placed Korea in Figure 9.1's most "anti-American" quadrant, Q3, with mostly unlikely Islamic countries as like-minded countries. Among nine others located in Q3, there existed only one other non-Islamic nation, Argentina, which saw itself as abandoned and betrayed by Washington during a deep socioeconomic crisis. That of ten surveyed nations with U.S. military troops only Turkey joined Korea in Q3 also shows how strong Korea's antiwar sentiments were.

Turkey was, after all, an Islamic country, partly identifying with Iraq and others who slandered Bush as waging a war against Muslim peoples. To say Korea was like Turkey in net support ratios for antiterrorist war as well as net policy receptivity ratios was only to acknowledge Korea's potential to become a trouble spot for U.S. policymakers. The "favorability ratio," measured by the Pew Global Attitudes survey by adding up those with positive views on Washington, stood at 52 percent in Turkey before it plunged by 22 percentage points amidst U.S. preparation for the war

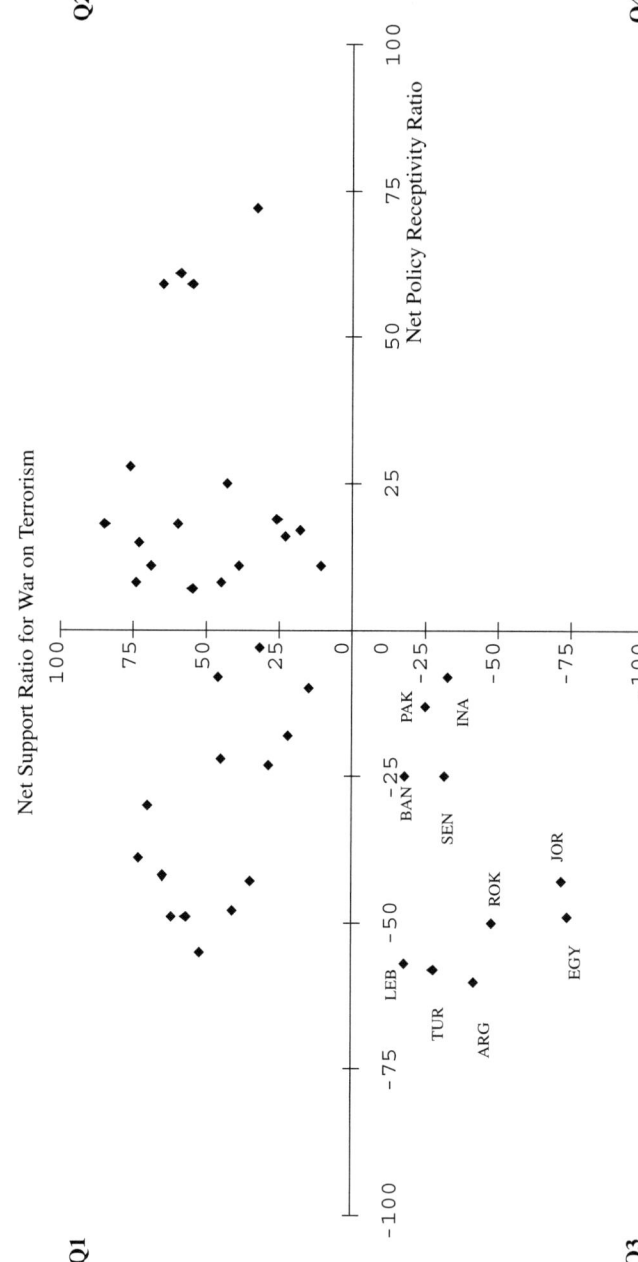

Figure 9.1 Public sentiments toward U.S. foreign policy goal and style. The net support ratio for war on terrorism was calculated by subtracting the percentage of respondents opposed from those in favor, when asked about U.S. efforts to fight terrorism. The net policy receptivity ratio was calculated by subtracting the percentage of respondents who answered "not too much" and "not at all" from those who answered "a great deal" and "a fair amount," when asked "to what extent the United States takes into account the interests of countries like [yours]?" The countries in Q3 are noted as follows: Argentina (ARG), Bangladesh (BAN), Egypt (EGY), Indonesia (INA), Jordan (JOR), Korea (ROK), Lebanon (LEB), Pakistan (PAK), Senegal (SEN), and Turkey (TUR). Source: Compiled from Q62 and Q72 in The Pew Research Center for the People and the Press, "The Pew Global Attitudes Project: What the World Thinks in 2002'" (Washington, DC, 2002), T-49 and T-59. In Korea, the survey was conducted between July 28 and August 10, 2002.

against terrorism.⁶¹ The potential for a similar slippage in favorable U.S. images obviously existed in Korea, too, if Bush unilaterally opted for a military solution to Pyongyang's nuclear facilities and missile development programs. This anxiety over war explained why Korea's public sentiments had greater similarities with underdeveloped Muslim societies, who all except one congregated in Q3,⁶² than with non-Islamic Asian nations with which it presumably shared common cultural and historical roots⁶³ or with industrialized nations resembling it in class stratification and industrial structure.⁶⁴ Nor did Korea's colonial past make it resemble Third World nations that mostly landed in either Q1 or Q2.⁶⁵

To sum up, Korea's military security community lost its tight control over policy discussions of SOFA issues partly because its political right, facing a profound partisan realignment, stopped acting as the brake on society's open dispute with U.S. policymakers, believing it could and should treat SOFA as a narrowly basic rights issue, unlinked from military security considerations. The control mechanism also broke down because with Bush's unilaterally driven war on terror and the massive entry into electoral politics by nonconformist young voters, Korea's progressive camp had a sizable constituency with which to experiment with new political ideas on the U.S. role in Korea. To increase the policy drift even more, Korea's progressives had a far better strategy than its right. The progressives successfully projected the struggle for SOFA revision as a protest against human rights violations rather than an anti-American agitation for U.S. military pullout in 2002. When Bush requested that Korea dispatch noncombat troops to Iraq in 2003, the progressives dexterously recast themselves as an antiwar — not anti-American — political force. The right, by contrast, backed SOFA revision in 2002, however intensely it feared a civil protest's turning into an anti-American rally by "leftist instigation," lest young voters looked at it as a political dinosaur still living in Korea's bygone Cold War era and accused it of depriving campside townspeople of their basic rights. However, by doing so, the right fueled anti-American sentiments even more and inadvertently strengthened its progressive rival's political base.

Rumsfeld Strikes Back

It looked like 2003 would usher in a new era in domestic politics and international relations, with a seemingly irreversible power shift toward Korea's newly legitimized progressive camp. The year, however, began with as much surprises as 2002. Writing for *New York Times*, former National Security Advisor Richard V. Allen depicted Korea as having walked into a politically neutral zone, with Roh Moo-hyun volunteering to act as a "mediator" between Pyongyang and Washington on nuclear issues. As Allen bluntly diagnosed, Korea had only two options: either stand with its U.S. ally on war against terrorism or "take another path."[66] Then, in early February, Rumsfeld expressed his high hope for talks to put the U.S.–Korea alliance on an equal partnership basis and showed interest in relocating the U.S. Second Division from Dongduchon and Uijongbu,[67] which rekindled ideological struggles in Korea. Many saw Rumsfeld as having a hidden agenda to tame Roh Moo-hyun even before his presidential inauguration on February 25 by threatening a staged U.S. military reduction. Some interpreted his words as sincere, mirroring his interest in protecting U.S. soldiers' lives through relocating the U.S. Second Division as far as possible from Pyongyang, whose nuclearization looked increasingly inevitable, given Roh Moo-hyun's very strong pacifist inclination. Still others believed Rumsfeld had only the good will to speed up LPP in order to avoid another tragedy like that at Hyochonli, which could wreck popular support for continued U.S. military presence in Korea.[68]

The truth was likely to be all three and more. As noted in "Military Security Constraints," above, U.S. troop reduction and relocation had been on the DoD's agenda since 1989, part of which was implemented before intelligence reports on Pyongyang's nuclear project interrupted EASI. Moreover, as analyzed in this section, in 1997 Armitage's NDP criticized the Cold War strategy of concentrating U.S. troops in a few fixed military bases in order to simultaneously engage in two regional theaters of war as a wrong strategy that only wasted resources for a very unlikely event. That Korea tied down one U.S. army division when fiscal austerity forced the DoD to downsize its ground forces from eighteen army divisions in 1987 to a mere ten by 1997 surely frustrated its military strategists. The military deterrence against Kim Jong Il, many U.S. policymakers argued, could be done much more cheaply with a slimmer USFK without hurting any deterrence capability if it restructured its forces into a genuinely interoperable joint force equipped with high-tech weapons. By proposing U.S. troop relocation in early 2003, then, Secretary Rumsfeld was simply doing what the DoD had wanted to do since 1989. The Korean defense ministry panicked when a DoD delegation formally proposed in March 2003 to draw up a "reorganization" plan for U.S. military troops by September and to implement it beginning in December, thus nullifying its earlier LPP pledge to spread out troop reduction and relocation over nine years. The DoD group, moreover, went into talks with the MND with a concrete road map for building an "equal" alliance. The delegation proposed withdrawing one brigade from Korea and relocating the U.S. Second Division's other remaining brigade to Pyongtaek and Osan, far away from the armistice line and Pyongyang's artilleries lined up along it, and safely below the Han River. The DoD road map, in other words, envisioned ending the U.S. Second Division's human tripwire role.[69]

The timing could not have been worse politically for Roh Moo-hyun. The security crisis precipitated by Pyongyang's admission of covertly developing a nuclear program with heavily enriched uranium in October 2002 only worsened, fracturing Korea from within into conservative hawks and progressive doves and burdening its economy with an added security risk. After threatening to rescind its nuclear freeze promised under an "agreed framework" with Washington in 1994, Pyongyang removed International Atomic Energy Agency (IAEA) seals and yanked monitoring cameras from its Yongbyon nuclear facilities on December 14. Twelve days later, it began moving a thousand or so fresh fuel rods into a five-megawatt reactor. The next day, Pyongyang resumed building two new reactors,[70] while expulsing IAEA inspectors from Yongbyon. Then, on January 10, 2003, it formally withdrew its Nuclear Nonproliferation Treaty membership.[71] Tension hit a new high on January 31 when Pyongyang moved some 8,000 spent fuel rods into an underground reprocessing facility.[72] The northern regime reactivated its hitherto mothballed five-megawatt reactor by February 27, too.[73] The next two months saw Seoul and Washington on a roller-coaster ride, continuously swinging between despair and relief, as Pyongyang talked very ambiguously and acted very deceptively regarding its true intention in order to maximize its bargaining leverage over Seoul and Washington.[74] Depending on how one interpreted its negotiator's words, actions, and even body language in a Three-Party Talk with Seoul, Washington, and Beijing in April, Pyongyang could be seen as having already begun reprocessing its 8,000 spent fuel rods, thus being only a few steps away from possessing nuclear weapons, or as finalizing its preparation for reprocessing.[75]

Rumsfeld was, then, proposing U.S. troop relocation when Korea needed more than ever unswerving U.S. military support to deter Pyongyang from escalating military tension. That he did so in spite of the dangers of Pyongyang's miscalculation of U.S. intentions was enough to alarm Seoul about the American military security commitment. Moreover, initiated as a remedy for or a retaliation against Korea's anti-American protests in 2002, Rumsfeld's proposal for U.S. troop relocation was inevitably received in Korea as a signal for a precipitous decline in American trust of Korea. Roh Moo-hyun, too, did not help when he openly criticized Bush for a hawkish view on how to handle Pyongyang and pledged to play a "lead role" in peacefully resolving the nuclear crisis. During his presidential campaign, he saw that role to be a "neutral mediator." The allies' rising discord amidst a nuclear crisis made many doubt Korea's ability to sustain peace and prosperity. Moody's Investor Service downgraded Korea's country credit ratings by two notches from A3 plus to A3 minus in February 2003, while Fitch Ratings warned it too would lower Korea's creditworthiness if the security crisis worsened. For every notch downgraded, society had to shoulder an additional five hundred million dollars in interest payments, investment decline, and export reduction every year.[76]

To be sure, society did not require a warning from international credit rating agencies to understand its economic vulnerability. The market was already very weak, paralyzed by numerous business frauds and policy failures, when Pyongyang escalated its nuclear blackmail beginning December 2002. The Financial Supervisory Commission charged many listed companies with account fraud on December 24,[77] making foreign investors seriously question its claim of success in upgrading prudential regulations since Korea's 1997 economic crisis. Then, on February 17, one month after an NGO filed a complaint against SK Global for massive illegal insider trading, public prosecutors issued a seizure and search warrant against top SK corporate executives. Five days later, SK Group Chairman Choi Tae-hyun was jailed for causing his stockholders damage totaling 207 billion won in his attempt to consolidate his corporate control.[78] While Korea's press anxiously reported rumors on public prosecutors' investigations spreading over into Hanhwa, Samsung, and LG chaebols for account fraud as well as irregular inheritance practices,[79] Kim Dae-jung's policy to exit from a recession in 1999 by stimulating consumption through encouraging household loans boomeranged, resulting in 2.96 million people with overdue credit cards, mortgages, and other personal loan payments by May 2003. Already, on January 22, Fitch Ratings identified household debts as a new threat obstructing banks from maintaining a healthy profit level.[80] The alliance discord, then, erupted when Seoul needed a robust alliance with Washington for not only military security but also economic reasons.

Moreover, as Korea's stock price index slid from 736.57 on December 3, 2002, to 515.24 by March 17, 2003,[81] conservative societal forces, which hitherto maintained a low profile in NGO activities and protest movements, given a seemingly impregnable hegemony forged by like-minded conservative newspapers and regionalist political parties in the political society, began organizing into a counter bloc in order to put military security on par with — if not higher than — SOFA and basic rights issues in Korea's national agenda. The talks on U.S. troop relocation provided a catalyst for the conservative societal forces' rush into action. The day celebrating Korea's holy March First Uprising against Japanese colonialism in 1919 saw 110 conservative religious groups assemble over a hundred thousand protesters in downtown Seoul to reiterate unswerving support for their *hyolmaeng*, or blood-shared alliance, with Washington. They also gave their protest a Cold War character by calling it an "anti-nuclear and anti-Kim Jong Il rally." The same day, Korea's progressive camp held an antiwar rally with much fewer than two thousand protesters against Bush's coming Iraqi war, which it saw as a precursor to a war against Pyongyang. The progressives called for independence from U.S. hegemony.[82]

Even before Roh Moo-hyun formally assumed presidential authority on February 25, 2003, then, he was being pressed very hard on three fronts simultaneously to tone down — if not drop — his progressive rhetoric on the U.S. role in Korea. First, Pyongyang escalated its nuclear threats, making it even more urgent for Seoul to secure unswerving U.S. support for its military defense. Second, Korea's already vulnerable economy stricken with account frauds and bad household loans saw its country's credit ratings downgraded further, as its political discord with Washington made many foreign investors increasingly skeptical of its ability to persuade Pyongyang not to proceed with its nuclear development program. Third, anti-American protests polarized society by compelling conservative groups into political organization, thereby emboldening the Hannara Party to use its legislative majority to keep Roh Moo-hyun in line. To preempt Pyongyang from amassing a nuclear arsenal, to thwart a further decline in Korea's credit ratings, and to prevent its political right from ideologically smearing his presidency, Roh Moo-hyun needed a friendly — if not loyal — Washington.

The top U.S. decision makers including Rumsfeld, however, made Roh Moo-hyun's situation even worse by unilaterally initiating talks on U.S. troop relocation that many interpreted as a signal for rising U.S. distrust of his presidency. When Roh Moo-hyun publicly requested the DoD to postpone talks on U.S. troop relocation and reduction until after Pyongyang gave up its nuclear ambition, its top policymakers argued that they could only opt for troop relocation, lest GIs walk into another tragic accident during a military drill in one or another urbanized training sites. That had to be avoided because it not only spread anti-American sentiments in Korea, but also jeopardized GIs' right to personal safety.[83] By setting an early deadline for a bilateral understanding on U.S. troop relocation and reduction, Rumsfeld linked SOFA back to military security issues and implicitly asked Roh Moo-hyun whether he was ready to push for SOFA revision even if it risked endangering military security. Roh Moo-hyun could not have a cake and eat it too, as he and many Koreans thought they could in 2002. He had to choose between SOFA revision and military security.

As late as in a nationally televised "Talk with People" in January and February 2003, president-elect Roh Moo-hyun talked very bravely, promising a sweeping change in Korea's SOFA provisos, wartime operational command structure, and even the Mutual Security Treaty.[84] After Rumsfeld elaborated his general proposal for an alliance reorganization into a specific plan for U.S. troop relocation and reduction in February and March, Roh Moo-hyun retreated, saying he would not seek a SOFA revision until after Pyongyang gave up on its nuclear development project.[85] To end public anxiety over a possibly irreversible political drift between Seoul and Washington, Roh Moo-hyun also moved very quickly to dispatch army engineers and medics to Iraq in spite of strong antiwar protests by NGOs — his primary electoral allies and supporters in 2002 — once Bush formally requested war support in early March.[86] As if to urge Washington to recompense his acts of bravery in Korea's domestic political arenas, he called for postponing all talks on U.S. troop relocation until a peaceful solution was found for Pyongyang's nuclear project when he addressed Korea's very unruly National Assembly to legislate his troop dispatch bill on April 2. A month later, at a summit meeting in Washington, Roh Moo-hyun personally asked Bush to delay U.S. troop relocation.[87]

To his conservative foes' surprise, moreover, Roh Moo-hyun even looked ready to accept in principle the DoD's new global strategic doctrine and its implications on USFK's role. Before a group of newly promoted brigadier generals and commodores, Roh Moo-hyun called for transforming USFK from a mere deterrent against Pyongyang into a regional balancer for Northeast Asia, ready to fly in and out of Korea to reinforce American power in another war zone.[88] That was precisely what his predecessors avoided — if not actively opposed — for many years, lest Beijing would see Seoul as following Washington's lead to encircle and contain Chinese military power. Moreover, again endorsing what was long advocated by Washington, Roh Moo-hyun pledged to make Korea's armed forces a "high-tech" war machine armed with modern information technology through increasing defense expenditure in order to prepare for eventual U.S. troop relocation and downsizing. Roh Moo-hyun, in other words, accepted the DoD's new global military strategy and its implications for Korea, but he asked for a delay in its implementation until after he resolved the crisis over Pyongyang's nuclear development. When Hannara criticized him for agreeing to end the U.S. Second Division's human tripwire role, Roh Moo-hyun lashed back, deploring its defeatist mentality as well as criticizing its misconception of U.S. security intentions. The U.S., he said, stationed its armed forces for "a goal larger than the military defense of Korea," and Rumsfeld's plan for U.S. troop relocation and reduction emerged and would proceed as part of changes in this larger global U.S. military strategy. Korea could ask for an adjustment in its schedule for reorganization but not a renunciation of its goal to restructure USFK. Moreover, Roh Moo-hyun declared, "it was wrong to view its troops as a substitute for Korea's own defense capability in any fundamental way."[89] The Korean military should take over the U.S. Second Division's role — albeit incrementally, in step with its transformation into a slim but powerful war machine, through purchasing high-tech U.S. weapons as well as encouraging Pyongyang's agreement to military disarmament. Roh Moo-hyun called his plan for gradual U.S. troop relocation paralleled with a concerted effort toward modernizing Korean military capability the position of a "pro-American independentist policy."[90]

Conclusion

Fifteen days before the summit meeting with Bush in Washington, Roh Moo-hyun held another televised "Talk with People," where he defined his ideology as "pro-American independentist."[91] That was a huge change from his presidential campaign days when he even looked to be siding with anti-American NGOs by brushing aside their conservative foes' alarm as based on an anachronistic "Cold War mentality." In his typical rebellious moment in 2002, Roh Moo-hyun even asked, "Why so much fuss over anti-American sentiments?"[92] The shift to the "pro-American independentist" position in 2003 occurred because Roh Moo-hyun realized he could not have a cake and eat it too. Demanding a SOFA revision as well as a transfer of wartime operational command could and did precipitate talks on an early U.S. troop relocation and reduction. If there was anyone who succeeded in having a cake and eating it too, it was ironically Rumsfeld's DoD, which seized Korea's protest for SOFA revision as an opportunity to initiate talks on U.S. troop redeployment and downsizing along its post–Cold War and post–9/11 global strategic doctrine, whose implementation Korea had resisted doggedly since 1992, given Pyongyang's rising nuclear threat.

That many Koreans, including Roh Moo-hyun, changed their minds about SOFA and U.S. military bases by March 2003 hardly persuaded Rumsfeld to drop his proposal for U.S. troop relocation and reduction. The DoD's demand for relocating U.S. troops early occurred because, with its Iraqi military campaign wrapped up in a mere three weeks, it believed even more strongly in its new military security doctrine's viability and speeded up its military redeployment plan worldwide;[93] the DoD also thought having the Second Division remain in thoroughly urbanized and heavily populated Dongduchon and Uijongbu jeopardized campside townspeople, GIs, and consequently Korean public support for U.S. military presence. The U.S., moreover, thought it could not and should not leave GIs vulnerable to an armed invasion from a possibly nuclearized Pyongyang just to satisfy Korea's demand for a human tripwire, which its military strategists criticized as not only an outdated but also a repulsive military concept, taking for granted heavy U.S. casualties in the event of war on the Korean peninsula.[94]

There was a political calculation, too. To end Korea's demand for SOFA revision and wartime operational command, as well as to raise its leverage in negotiations with the MND over where to relocate U.S. military troops and how to distribute the financial costs of troop relocation, the DoD had to look determined to relocate and downsize its troops. The strategy bore fruits soon. Landing in New York on May 12 on his way to Washington, Roh Moo-hyun said he would ask Bush to help "Korea in difficult time" by postponing troop relocation from Dongduchon and Uijongbu.[95]

That Roh Moo-hyun's nationalist project to create a more equal military alliance lasted only a year even when political power markedly shifted toward the rebellious 386 Generation and nonconformist X and N Generations in domestic politics visibly showed the power of international structural constraints noted in "A Crisis of Success" and "Rumsfeld Strikes Back," above. Korea depended on U.S. power for security and prosperity. Its newly emerging national identity as a major trade power deserving a more equal security alliance notwithstanding, Korea, surrounded by major world powers and facing a nuclear threat from its northern other half, was still a "small country" that could not stray afar from U.S. global, regional, and bilateral policy. Washington was its security underwriter, deterring Pyongyang from launching another armed attack with its 36,000 soldiers still poised as a human tripwire in Dongduchon and Uijongbu. The U.S. also constituted a strategic trade and investment partner without whom Korea could not prosper economically.[96] Then there was Korea's establishment, who looked to Washington as a model for liberal democracy and market capitalism, and its younger generations, who saw America as a pace setter in popular culture. The critical election in 2002 could abruptly break down the thoroughly bureaucratized security policymaking processes by throwing new ideas and new actors onto Korea's national political body, but only for a very brief time, because Korea's structural dependence on American power for security and prosperity was all too obvious and because its establishment exercised a veto power over Roh Moo-hyun's policy, once elections with the highly egalitarian rule of "one-person one-vote" ended. Without active U.S. support, Roh Moo-hyun could neither counter Pyongyang's nuclear threat, nor prevent a further deterioration in its financial instability, nor preempt conservative ideological backlashes.

The U.S. hegemony Korea rediscovered in 2003 was, however, dissimilar from the one it imagined during its Cold War days. The young 386, X, and N Generations, who made up an absolute majority in its electorate, did not share their parents' and grandparents' generations' *jaksarang*, or unrequited love, for America originating from before 1953, when Korea was rescued from communism by U.S. military troops. The young acquiesced in following U.S. leadership not because of its idealization of U.S. intentions, but because of Korea's harsh international political reality. Moreover, many older people subtly changed too, relieved by Roh Moo-hyun's distancing from anti-American NGOs, but also deeply troubled by Rumsfeld and his DoD aides' linking SOFA with military security in order to implement its global military strategy locally in Korea and regionally in Northeast Asia. That linkage strategy was a brilliant move in Rumsfeld's realpolitik chess board, but it was a shock to many older Koreans who hitherto saw America as a *hyolmaeng*, or military ally joined with Korea by blood. That rhetoric sounded too naïve even for Korea's older generations. The U.S. hegemony Korea rediscovered in 2003 was, then, one based on "hard power," with "soft power" seriously in decline.[97] And with it ended Korea's Cold War era, when people gave U.S. policymakers diffuse trust and loyalty, and was ushered in a new two-level political game in which Korean foreign policymakers had to take into account domestic political pressures to a degree unknown before.

Notes

This research is supported by a Korea University grant.

1. *Myongbun* means moral duty and obligation. The word is also frequently translated as justice or cause in English.
2. *Joongang Ilbo*, April 3, 2003.
3. *Joongang Ilbo*, April 5 and 7, 2003.
4. The Korean public overwhelmingly opposed Bush's Iraqi war by a ratio of 75.1 to 24.7 percent but split more or less evenly into 55.4 nays against 43.8 yeas on the dispatching of Korean noncombat troops in a national survey held on April 1. When asked whether support for U.S. war efforts would help Korean national interests, by contrast, 66.3 percent agreed and 32.4 percent disagreed. *Joongang Ilbo*, April 2, 2003.
5. The public support levels for Roh Moo-hyun and Lee Hoi-chang underwent two reversals in 2002. Roh Moo-hyun was initially favored by 55.0 to 33.6 percent on March 19 and 60.5 to 32.6 percent on April 15 when he won Korea's historically unprecedented presidential primary held by the NMDP. Then he saw his lead precipitously fall to 47.5 to 42.6 percent on May 25 and reversed to 36.3 to 48.9 percent on June 15 after he mistakenly adopted a regionalist election strategy and sided with Kim Dae-jung in spite of corruption scandals involving Kim Dae-jung's sons. The support rating for Roh Moo-hyun stayed in the low thirties against Lee Hoi-chang's low forties in a two-way race until Chung Mong-joon withdrew his candidacy in support of Roh Moo-hyun to forge a united front on November 24. The merger immediately raised Roh Moo-hyun's rating to 42.7 percent against Lee Hoi-chang's 35.2 percent by November 26 and eventually led to his victory on December 19. See *Joongang Ilbo*, December 20, 2002.

6. *Joongang Ilbo*, April 3, 2003.
7. See National Assembly debates as reported in *Joongang Ilbo*, April 9, 2003.
8. See Minister of Unification Lim Dong-won's statement at a national assembly hearing as reported by *Donga Ilbo*, April 19, 2001.
9. The left, pressuring for an immediate military pullout, hit only 6.3 percent, even in a public survey held on December 15, 2002, a day after a large anti-American political rally was organized in front of Seoul's city hall. Compiled from The East Asia Institute's survey results.
10. U.S. Department of Defense, *A Strategic Framework for the Asia-Pacific Rim: Looking toward the 21st Century* (Washington, DC: U.S. Government Printing Office, April 1990); and U.S. Department of Defense, *A Strategic Framework for the Asia-Pacific Rim: Report to Congress 1992* (Washington, DC: U.S. Department of Defense, May 1992).
11. The Office of International Security Affairs, Department of Defense, *United States Security Strategy for the East Asia-Pacific Region* (Washington, DC: U.S. Government Printing Office, February 1995).
12. Consult Yi Jeong-hun, "Haetbyot jeongchaekkwa 'jakgye 5027' gyejeong — jae yi hanbando jeonjaeng: guenal yihu (The sunshine policy and revised 'strategy plan 5027' in preparation for a second Korean war: after that day)," *Sindonga* (May 1999), 261, for U.S. strategy in the event of war with Pyongyang.
13. Hwang Dong-jun, Han Nam-seong, and Yi Sang-wuk, *Migukui daehan anbo jiwonkwa hanmi bangwi hyopryuk bangan jeonmang* (An evaluation of U.S. security support for Korea and a forecast on Korea-U.S. security cooperation measures) (Seoul: Minyoungsa, 1990), 69, 89–90.
14. Kim Il-young and Cho Seong-ryol, *Juhan migun: yeoksa, jaengjeom, jeonmang* (The United States Forces in Korea: history, issues and forecast) (Seoul: Hanul, 2003), 207.
15. Consult Yu Jae-gap, "Juhan migunae daehan han'gukui ipjang (The Korean position on the United States Forces in Korea)," in Kang Sung-hak et al., *Juhan migunkwa hanmi anbo hyopryuk* (The United States Forces in Korea and Korea-United States security cooperation) (Seoul: The Sejong Institute, 1996), 110–112.
16. Consult Yi Chun-keun, "Migukui sindongasia jeonryakkwa juhan migun (The United States' new East Asia strategy and the United States Forces in Korea), Kang Sung-hak et al., *Juhan migunkwa hanmi anbo hyopryuk* (The United States Forces in Korea and Korea-United States security cooperation) (Seoul: The Sejong Institute, 1996), 65.
17. See Yi Sam-song, *Miraeui yoksa'aeseo migukeun huimangin'ga* (Is America a hope in the future?) (Seoul: Dangdae, 1995), 206–209.
18. Roh Moo-hyun's "fireside chat" with a conservative Seoul International Forum, January 9, 2003. See *Joongang Ilbo*, January 10, 2003, for a report on some parts of his speech. Also see *Chosun Ilbo*, January 20, 2003, for his nationally televised talks on wartime operational command.
19. *Chosun Ilbo*, February 7, 8, and 9, 2003.
20. *Joongang Ilbo*, April 9 and 11, 2003.
21. SOFA defines the legal rights and responsibilities of the USFK and its "civilian component" over a wide range of issues from facility and land grant to taxation, custom duties, immigration, and criminal jurisdiction. See http://www.korea.army.mil/sofa/sofa1966_ui1991.pdf and http://www.korea.army. mil/sofa/2001sofa_english%20text.pdf for "Basic Agreement," "Agreed Minutes," and other related documents.
22. See Kyoung-Ryung Seong, "Civil Society and Democratic Consolidation in South Korea: Great Achievements and Remaining Problems," in *Consolidating Democracy in South Korea*, ed. Larry Diamond and Byung-Kook. Kim (Boulder, CO: Lynne Rienner Publishers, 2000), 87–109.
23. Including such a statement in a joint communiqué became virtually a ritual for an annually held bilateral Security Consultative Meeting. Consult Ministry of National Defense, Korea, *Gukbang baekseo* (white paper), various issues.
24. See *Chosun Ilbo*, January 14, 2003, for Roh Moo-hyun's conversation with U.S. Assistant Secretary of State for East Asian and Pacific Affairs James A. Kelly.
25. The U.S. Second Division, with 13,800 soldiers and civilian components, was headquartered in Dongduchon, where 73,502 people lived as residents in 2000. The Second Division

also maintained three camps in Uijongbu, another prospering satellite city near Seoul, with 355,380 inhabitants, as reported by Korea's 2000 national census. The situation was equally problematic in Camp Walker, where 7,800 GIs provided logistic support for USFK. With the residents growing from 919,953 people in 1970 to 2,480,578 by 2000, Daegu literally grew over Camp Walker, establishing the Dalsong District in 1981 and the Dalso District in 1987, both south of Camp Walker. What had been the outskirts of Daegu became a central district of the city in a mere seventeen years.

Then there were three U.S. military training grounds and shooting ranges in Paju, Maehyangli, and Pochon — respectively 28.0, 7.6, and 5.1 million *pyong* (3.3 m^2) in size, taking up much available land in each city, town, or county. Moreover, Paju and Pochon had a sizable population of 178,434 and 138,654 people in 2000, respectively. See *Joongang Ilbo*, July 19, 2001, for information on the location and size of U.S. military bases in Korea. The populations of the cities surrounding U.S. military bases and training grounds is compiled from the Korea National Statistics Office, *National Census*, 1970, 1980, and 2000.

26. The environment became a hot issue when a U.S. civilian component leaked a poisonous liquid from a U.S. military base into the Han River and subsequently tried to cover it up in 2000. As reported by Korea's environment ministry in a National Assembly Inspection and Audit session, U.S. troops were found responsible for environmental damage on twenty-six occasions between 1990 and 2000. They made no compensation in any of the twenty-six cases. See *Chosun Ilbo*, September 25 and November 3, 2000.
27. The Nogeunli tragedy occurred in July 1950, when the U.S. Seventh Cavalry Regiment's infantrymen massacred civilian refugees for three consecutive days until they joined their retreating regiment. The shooting was ordered because it was thought that Pyongyang's spies and soldiers had mingled in with refugees in order to hit U.S. military forces in their rear. The Nogeunli villagers continuously petitioned for a truth-finding since early 1961, but to no avail until two Associated Press reporters backed up their case with newly unclassified U.S. Air Force documents as well as interviews with a few surviving Seventh Cavalry Regiment soldiers. See *Chosun Ilbo*, September 29, 1999.
28. See http://mehyang.kfem.or.kr.
29. See http://www.usacrime.or.kr.
30. See http://antiusarmy.sungnam.net for information on the Seongnam branch of the campside town committee.
31. The Lawyers for a Democratic Society, established in 1988 by Korea's legal activists who defended political prisoners and labor activists during its authoritarian era, was one such mainstream NGO. The Citizens' Coalition for Economic Justice, also formed in 1988 and represented in every province, joined in frequently. The more progressive People's Solidarity for Participatory Democracy became an even more powerful lender of legitimacy to campside towns since its foundation in 1994.
32. *Chosun Ilbo*, January 19 and 20 and February 8, 2002.
33. Compare "Understanding Implementation of the Agreement under Article IV of the Mutual Defense Treaty between the United States of America and the Republic of Korea Regarding Facilities and Areas and the Status of United States Armed Forces in the Republic of Korea and Related Agreed Minutes" signed on July 9, 1966, with one signed on February 1, 1991. http://www.korea.army.mil/sofa/sofa1966_ui1991.pdf.
34. *Chosun Ilbo*, February 20, May 14, September 25, and November 3, 2000.
35. *Chosun Ilbo*, June 16, 2000.
36. See U.S. Joint Chiefs of Staff, "Joint Vision 2020," May 30, 2000. http://www.dtic.mil/jointvision/jvpub2.htm.
37. Consult U.S. Commission on National Security/21st Century, "New World Coming: American Security in the 21st Century," September 15, 1999, 6. http://www.nssg.gov/Reports/NWC.pdf.
38. See National Defense Panel, "Transforming Defense: National Security in the 21st Century," December 1997, iii. http://www.dtic.mil/ndp/FullDoc2.pdf.
39. See National Defense Panel, pp. 2, 23–24, 34.
40. See "Agreement between the United States of America and the Republic of Korea Amending the Agreement under Article IV of the Mutual Defense Treaty between the United States of America and the Republic of Korea, Regarding Facilities and Areas and the Status of United

States Armed Forces in the Republic of Korea of July 9, 1966," http://www.korea.army.mil/sofa/2001sofa_english%20text.pdf. For public criticism of Korea's 2001 SOFA, see *Chosun Ilbo*, December 28, 2000.

41. "Executive Summary: Land Partnership Plan under the United States and Republic of Korea Status of Forces Agreement," signed and approved by the SOFA Joint Committee on March 29, 2002, pp. 2–3. http://www.korea.army.mil/LPP/LPPExSum.pdf. See also Chosun libo, January 19, Feburary 8, and March 29, 2002.
42. The most challenging unanswered question was where and how to secure the 1.5 million pyong of land that Korea pledged to buy up for constructing new U.S. military bases in eight areas. The nearby towns and cities surely would protest if the LPP were implemented. To come up with $1.1 billion through land sales would be difficult, too, because many cities planned to construct public facilities and parks on their lands recovered from U.S. military troops. See *Chosun Ilbo*, May 25, 1999, and March 29, 2002.
43. See *Joongang Ilbo*, June 26; July 5, 24, and 30; August 5; October 1; and December 13, 2002.
44. *Joongang Ilbo*, September 16 and December 3, 7, and 14, 2002.
45. See *Joongang Ilbo*, June 29; July 4, 8, 10, 25, and 29; August 7; and November 24, 2002.
46. Especially see *Chosun Ilbo*, November 30 and December 4 and 15, 2002, for major candlelight vigils.
47. *Joongang Ilbo*, June 27 and 29 and July 3, 4, and 8, 2002. See also *Chosun Ilbo*, November 30 and December 4 and 15, 2002.
48. See *The Korea Times*, November 26, 2002, for a newspaper report on legal disputes between Seoul and Washington.
49. The name "386 Generation" came from their age (30 to 39 years old), their decade of college entrance (1980s), and their decade of birth (1960s).
50. The 386, X, and N Generations together make up a 2030 Generation, those in their twenties and thirties. They made up 49.7 percent of Korea's total electorate in 2002. For an analysis of generation gap in political values, consult Byung-Kook Kim, "The U.S.-South Korean Alliance in Crisis: Anti-American Challenges," *Journal of East Asian Studies* 3, no.2 (June-July 2003): 225–258.
51. For a detailed review of ideological struggles before 1992, see Pak Hyon-chae and Cho Hui-yeon, eds., *Palsip nyondae han'guk sahoi byondongkwa sahoi guseongchae nonjaengui jeon'gae* (The Korean society's transformation during the 1980s and the unfolding of the debate over its essential societal character) (Seoul: Juksan, 1989).
52. When the NMDP's *sinbijuryu*, or "new antimainstream" majority, threatened to reconvene a national primary in order to elect a new candidate after Hannara won a local election in June, this support group rescued Roh Moo-hyun by mobilizing young people for campaigning and fund-raising, as well as attacking the NMDP's *sinbijuryu* as a morally compromised and unprincipled political opportunist. Consult *Chosun Ilbo*, December 19 and 20, 2002.
53. *Chosun Ilbo*, August 7, 2002.
54. That society saw SOFA revision as a strictly basic rights issue independent from military security issues was fully shown in a nationwide public survey conducted by The East Asia Institute and *Joongang Ilbo* on December 15 and 16, 2002. Those who called for strengthening the military security alliance with Washington backed comprehensive or partial SOFA revision by a 97.1 to 2.9 ratio. Even President George W. Bush's politically most reliable and loyal Korean audience who "generally" or "actively" supported his "stern" policy against Pyongyang — 44.1 percent in The East Asia Institute's total sample —sided with partial or comprehensive SOFA revision by the ratio of 96.9 to 3.1. Consult http://www.eai.or.kr.
55. After Chung Mong-joon withdrew his candidacy in support for Roh Moo-hyun on November 24, 2002, Roh Moo-hyun's public support level jumped to exceed Lee Hoi-chang's by as many as 9.1 percentage points in opinion surveys. See *Joongang Ilbo*, December 3 and 20, 2002.
56. Roh Moo-hyun, by contrast, publicly declined from endorsing NGOs' petition for revising SOFA because it was "inappropriate for a presidential candidate to act like a NGO activist, however strongly one sympathized with NGO's cause." That ironically did not cost him much because he had already forged an image as a politician who could say "no" to Washington through his nonconformist political career since Korea democratized in 1987. See

Joongang Ilbo, December 9, 2002, for Roh Moo-hyun's position on NGOs' signature drive for SOFA revision.
57. See http://www.whitehouse.gov/news/releases/2002/01/20020129-11.html.
58. This sharply contrasted with 1995, when 36.8 percent saw a military invasion from Pyongyang as very likely. The same share hit 42.4 percent in 1997. Consult Sook-Jong Lee, "Sources of Anti-Americanism in Korean Society: Implications for Korea-U.S. Relations," 10, a paper presented at an international conference titled "Korea–U.S. Relations in Transition: Korea–U.S. Alliance in Retrospect and Prospects for a New Strategic Partnership," organized by the Sejong Institute, September 6, 2002.
59. Consult *Chosun Ilbo*, November 7, 9, 15, and 28 and December 12 and 15, 2002.
60. See *Chosun Ilbo*, October 17, 2002, for U.S. Assistant Secretary of State for East Asian and Pacific Affairs James A. Kelly's visit to Pyongyang between October 3 and 5, when Pyongyang disclosed its continuing nuclear development program.
61. The Pew Research Center for the People and the Press, "The Pew Global Attitudes Project: What the World Thinks in 2002" (Washington, DC: The Pew Research Center for the People and the Press, 2002), 4.
62. Of nine Muslim societies surveyed, only Uzbekistan showed up in Figure 9.1's Q2 quadrant. Those who fell into Q3 were Bangladesh, Egypt, Indonesia, Jordan, Lebanon, Pakistan, Senegal, and Turkey.
63. Of eight Asian nations surveyed by The Pew Research Center, only Bangladesh, Indonesia, and Pakistan — all Muslim nations — showed up with Korea in Q3 in Figure 9.1. The four other Asian societies —Confucian, Catholic, and Hindu societies — by contrast, all reside in Q1 (Japan) and Q2 (India, Philippines, and Vietnam).
64. The 2002 Pew Global Attitudes survey included six industrialized Western societies. Canada, France, Great Britain, Italy, and Japan were located in Figure 9.1's Q1, whereas Germany showed up in its Q2 quadrant.
65. Figure 9.1 shows only Senegal, a mostly Muslim society, in Q3. The nine other African countries were, by contrast, all located in its most "pro-American" Q2: Angola, Ghana, Ivory Coast, Kenya, Mali, Nigeria, South Africa, Tanzania, and Uganda. Eastern Europe was an even more homogeneous region in its public sentiment, albeit in a different direction: all six nations surveyed — Bulgaria, Czech Republic, Poland, Russia, Slovak Republic, and Ukraine — coalesced in Q1, where net support levels for war on terror were positive and net policy receptivity ratios were negative. Latin America, by contrast, was far more heterogeneous, with countries disbursed across Q1 (Bolivia, Brazil, and Mexico), Q2 (Guatemala, Honduras, Peru, and Venezuela), and Q3 (Argentina) by the ratio of 3:4:1.
66. See *New York Times*, January 16, 2003. Former Secretary of State James A. Baker III had even more disturbing words for NMDP Chairman Han Hwa-gap when he visited Washington. "When Corazon Aquino asked U.S. troops to leave," Baker reputedly said, "we left without any second thought.... When China seized some Filipino islands by force, she telephoned to ask whether we will let China get away with this. I said there were no U.S. soldiers in her country to prevent any such Chinese aggression.... The same applies to Korea" if she goes for U.S. military pullout. *Chosun Ilbo*, January 26, 2003.
67. Rumsfeld said, "U.S. military troops will leave Korea if its people desired so." The press reported similar statements from other "top" U.S. policymakers. See *Chosun Ilbo*, February 7, 8, and 9, 2003.
68. See *Chosun Ilbo*, February 7, 8, and 9, 2003.
69. *Chosun Ilbo*, March 4 and 20 and April 4 and 9, 2003.
70. The two new reactors under construction, respectively 50 and 200 megawatts in size, were expected to be completed in two or three years. If completed as scheduled, they could turn into a huge nuclear weapons factory by 2006 or 2007, together producing 55 bombs every year. Interview, April 20, 2003.
71. *Chosun Ilbo*, October 17 and December 12, 14, and 26, 2002, and January 10, 2003.
72. As jointly analyzed by Korean and American intelligence, Pyongyang could extract up to 35 kilograms of weapon-grade plutonium from its 8,000 spent fuel rods within six months after it began reprocessing. That amount could turn into between four and six nuclear bombs. See *Chosun Ilbo*, April 20, 2003.

73. With its five-megawatt nuclear reactor reactivated in February 2003, Pyongyang could have enough weapon-grade plutonium to produce one nuclear bomb every year, beginning September 2004. Interview, March 31, 2003.
74. See *Chosun Ilbo*, March 13; April 18, 21, and 25; and May 8, 2003, for contradictory intelligence reports on Pyongyang's reprocessing stage.
75. *Chosun Ilbo*, April 25–27, 2003.
76. Moody's Investor Service warned against another credit downgrading on March 15, 2003, if Korea failed to improve its nuclear crisis. See *Chosun Ilbo*, February 11 and March 15, 2003.
77. *Chosun Ilbo*, December 24, 2002.
78. *Chosun Ilbo*, January 9 and February 17 and 22, 2003.
79. *Chosun Ilbo*, February 24 and 26 and March 23, 2003.
80. See *The Korea Times*, May 7, 2003, and *Chosun Ilbo*, January 23, 2003.
81. See http://www.kse.or.kr/webkor/tong/tong_index.jsp.
82. *Chosun Ilbo*, March 2, 2003.
83. Interview with U.S. Embassy personnel in Seoul on January 22, February 11, and May 12, 2003.
84. *Chosun Ilbo*, January 19 and February 20, 2003.
85. *Chosun Ilbo*, April 4, 2003.
86. National Security Advisor La Jong-il publicly acknowledged Bush's request for war support on March 10. The president, on his part, convened a newly strengthened National Security Council ten days later to draw up Korea's response, then got cabinet approval for noncombat troop dispatch on March 21, and finally spoke before National Assembly Members on April 2 in order to pass his troop dispatch bill on a bipartisan basis. See *Chosun Ilbo*, March 11 and 21 and April 4, 2003.
87. *Chosun Ilbo*, May 5 and 15, 2003.
88. *Chosun Ilbo*, April 19 and 21, 2003.
89. *Chosun Ilbo*, April 19, 2003.
90. Consult http://www.president.go.kr/warp/app/broad/movie/list?meta_id=president. See also *Joongang Ilbo*, May 2, 2003.
91. *Joongang Ilbo*, May 2, 2003.
92. *Chosun Ilbo*, September 12, 2002.
93. The U.S. Department of Defense was reportedly accelerating troop relocation from Germany, Japan, Korea, Kuwait, Saudi Arabia, and Turkey into more friendly countries including Australia, Bulgaria, Qatar, and Rumania. See *Chosun Ilbo*, May 7, 2003.
94. *Chosun Ilbo*, March 19, 2003.
95. *Chosun Ilbo*, May 13, 2003.
96. The United States shared 20.7 percent in Korea's total exports and 15.9 percent in its imports in 2001. The United States also supplied 31.0 percent of its cumulative direct foreign investment and absorbed 27.4 percent of its overseas investment by 2002. Compiled from Korea National Statistical Office, http://kosis.nso.go.kr/cgi-bin/SWS_1020.cgi?KorEng=1&A_UNFOLD=1&TableID=MT_ATITLE&TitleID=R1&FPub=3&UserID=.
97. Consult Joseph S. Nye, Jr., *The Paradox of American Power: Why the World's Only Superpower Can't Go It Alone* (New York: Oxford University Press, 2002), for hard power and soft power.

Index

A

Afghanistan, 10, 33, 127, 140, 143–145, 155, 156, 159, 198, 200, 208
Africa, 9, 11, 12, 16, 18, 19, 33, 34, 36, 111, 168, 176, 181, 191, 193, 195, 201, 206, 249
African wars, 195
Airborne Warning and Control Systems, equipped warships, deployment of, Japan, 144
Air piracy, 205
Allen, Richard, 132, 133, 164, 237–238
Alliance for Progress, 49
Allies, 4, 7, 8, 11, 12, 14, 15–17, 19, 22–24, 82, 103, 104, 126, 138, 141, 144, 155, 193, 194, 198, 200, 202, 214, 227–230, 235, 242
al-Qaeda network, 33, 41, 45, 47
Alzugaray, Carlos, 212
Amazon
    countries, greater integration of, 182
    Protection System, 182
    region, 181–182
    Surveillance System, 182
American
    democratic paradigm, construction of, 186
    unilateralism, increase in negative sentiment about, 160–165
Andean
    Community, 79, 94–95, 100–101, 182
    countries, 79, 81, 94, 100
    Region, 81
Anglophone Caribbean, 202
Angola, 176, 179, 193, 196, 249

Anti-Americanism, 12, 220, 222
Antiterrorism, 159, 225
Anti-United States motivation, claims of, 61
APEC. *See* Asia Pacific Economic; Asia Pacific Economic Community
Argentina, 7, 10, 14, 17, 21, 23, 27, 28, 29, 30, 34, 36, 38, 49, 86, 88, 98, 99, 103, 107, 169, 172, 176, 180–183, 190, 191, 204, 235, 236, 249
Argentine-Brazilian Agency for Accounting and Control of Nuclear Materials, 181
Armistice agreement, 224
Armitage, Richard, 137, 162, 230
Army of National Liberation, 210, 211
Asian Monetary Fund, 15, 22, 24, 25, 31, 32, 51, 54, 61, 66, 74, 142
Asia Pacific
    Economic Community, 8, 15, 20, 24, 27, 31, 67, 68, 73, 147–148
    Economic Cooperation, 67, 145–146
Association
    of Caribbean States, 200
    of Southeast Asian Nations, 17, 22, 24–27, 29, 31, 32, 34, 46, 50, 55, 56, 63, 65–69, 71–73, 75, 76, 116, 118, 130, 131, 143, 146, 147, 158
    Free Trade Area, 18
    of Southeast Asian Nations Free Trade Area, 25
    of Southeast Asian Nations Plus Three, 15, 22, 31, 32, 56, 61–63, 65, 66, 69, 71, 72, 76, 155, 158
Asymmetric strategic requirements, 230
Australia, 18, 19, 20, 24, 25, 26, 31, 68, 72, 138, 144, 145, 155, 250

252 • Index

Authoritarian regimes, 2, 6, 7, 9, 13, 14, 16, 86, 194
    decline in tolerance for, 6
Authority structure, system of decentralized consensus formation, 150
AWACS. *See* Airborne Warning and Control Systems
Axis
    of evil, 47, 48, 140, 141, 205
    of populism, 40

B

Bahamas, 207
Balance United States power, 194
Bali, bombing of, 47
Bandwagon, 23, 24, 31
Banks, 9, 16, 41, 208, 240
Basic rights issues, 221, 226, 240
Bay of Pigs, 29, 36
Berlin Wall, 197, 198
Bilateral
    cooperation, 187, 195, 207
    free trade agreements, 64, 66, 67, 69, 70, 74
    swap arrangements, 66
Bin Laden, Osama, 16, 155
Bipolar, 20, 30, 51–53, 58, 60, 112
Bolivia, 39, 100, 102, 172, 182, 187, 249
Bolton, John, 210
Borders, United States ability to police, 96
Bosnia, 3, 4, 10, 11, 33
Brady Plan, 90
Brazil, 2, 3, 5, 7, 9–12, 14, 17–19, 21, 23, 25–30, 32–37, 39–41, 49, 79, 81, 88, 97–107, 165–192, 201, 249
    Argentina, reconciliation between, 21
    constitution of, nuclear activity, 172
    environmental issues, 170
    foreign policy of, 165–192
    human rights, 171
    international norms, rules, drive toward conformity with, 166–167
    international regimes, acceptance of, 170–173
    liberal institutionalists, 166
    regional hegemon, relations with, 184–188
    threats, 180–184
    United Nations, international security, 173–180

Bretton Woods, 82, 106
British model of normal statehood, 137–139
Brunei, 113
Budget in, 197
Bureaucracy, 22, 29, 77, 152
Burma, 121, 123
Bush, George W., 3, 29, 33, 36, 39, 41, 45, 47, 48, 103, 104, 143, 148, 185, 201, 206, 209, 212, 213, 220, 234–237, 235, 237, 239, 242–244
Business firms, 9, 16

C

Cambodia, 5, 7, 12, 14, 45, 71, 118, 121, 122, 125, 130, 144, 154, 156, 159, 177
    Vietnamese occupation of, 121–122
    Vietnam withdrawal, 122
Campside towns, 227, 247
Canada, 4, 5, 7, 11, 12, 14, 15, 18, 19, 22, 24, 25, 26, 31, 61, 67, 68, 75, 105–106, 106, 190, 204, 214, 216, 249
    Free Trade Agreement with United States, 105–106
Capital markets, liberalization of, 10, 17
Caribbean, 27, 34–36, 49, 54, 79, 81, 94–95, 94–97, 95, 97, 100, 101, 197, 199–202, 214, 216
    Basin, 81, 95, 96, 100, 101
    Basin Initiative, 95
    Community, 202, 216
    Tourism Organization, 202
Carter, Jimmy, 7, 14, 199, 205, 210
Castaneda, Jorge, 38, 41
Castro
    Fidel, 4, 11, 30, 37, 179, 190–192, 195, 196, 198, 201, 208, 214, 215
    Raul, 198
CDI. *See* Center for Defense Information
Center for Defense Information, frequency of military actions, 36–38
Central America, 5, 6, 12, 13, 27, 79, 90, 94–95, 95–97, 96, 97, 176
Centripetal authority structure, 152
Chaebol business conglomerates, 10, 240
Chavez, Hugo, 40–41, 41, 100, 205
Chemical weapons, 4, 11, 172, 173
Cheney, Richard, 16, 23, 223–226
Chen Shu bian, high risk behavior of, 129

Chiang Mai Initiative, 66
Chile, 7, 14, 18, 19, 24, 25, 26, 27, 31, 34, 39, 49, 75, 79, 80, 85, 97, 106, 107, 172
Chilean Manuel Rodriguez Patriotic Front, 210
China, 2, 4–6, 8–10, 11–13, 15–17, 18, 19, 20, 22–37, 43, 45, 48, 50, 51, 53–55, 59, 61–63, 65, 66, 68–76, 96, 111–133, 141, 143, 145–147, 149, 150, 154–161, 164, 180, 193, 194, 202, 203, 249
    economic influence in Eastern Asia, 50–51
    as emerging superpower, 5–6
    hegemony along borders, demand for, 119
    leadership, political legitimacy, survival of, 128
    naval strategy, similar to Soviet Union, 114–115
    replacing United States, Japan's trading, economic partner, 160–161
    Russian weaponry, reliance on, 114
    South Korea, diplomatic relations between, normalization, 123–124
Choice between variables in, 20
Christian Democratic Party, 6
Civilian
    advisers, 193
    aircraft, shooting down over international waters, 207
    power, 145, 154, 162, 163
    supremacy, 197
Civil wars, 13, 20, 29, 36, 212
Clark Airbase, transfer to Philippine government, 44
Clear mandates, definition of, 179–180
Client states, 13, 14, 17, 21, 24, 44, 50
Clinton, William, 38, 39, 40, 49, 53, 73, 91, 185, 206, 213
Coast Guard, 194, 206, 207
Coexistence between major powers, 13–14
Cold War, 1–6, 8–14, 16, 19–21, 23, 26, 28, 30, 33–38, 40, 42, 43, 48, 49, 51–53, 59, 60, 80, 85–90, 92, 93, 102, 103, 112–115, 119, 120, 122, 123, 125, 127, 129, 136, 137, 149, 153, 154, 157, 170, 171, 174, 176, 177, 184, 187, 188
    United States, policy shift in strategy, 153
Collapse of Soviet Union, worldwide effects of, 3–6

Collective security, 14, 20, 21, 23–25, 27, 30–32, 62, 175, 176, 178
    functional demand for, 62
    institutionalized forms of, 14
Colombia, 4, 10, 11, 17, 27, 29, 34, 38, 40–42, 100, 103, 182, 183, 187, 210
Communist
    governments, 193, 194, 202
    parties, 1
    regimes, 2, 9, 11–15, 193
    market-oriented economic changes adopted by, 8
Comprehensive Test Ban Treaty, 173
Confidence-building measures, 206
Congress, 91, 99, 104, 105, 199, 201
Conservative, 25, 27, 32, 34, 40, 118, 155, 210, 220, 233, 234, 239–244, 246
Consolidated democracies, consensus of, 7
Conspiracy theories, 62
Constructivism, 59
Conventional war, removal of, 3
Convention
    for Prohibition of Biological Weapons, 173
    for Prohibition of Chemical Weapons, 173
Cooperation with the United States, 46, 117, 126, 187, 205
Costa Rica, 38, 86, 176
Costs of United States military presence, 223
Cotonou Convention, 201, 202
CRS. *See* United States Congressional Research Service
Cuba, 3–8, 10–15, 19, 26, 29, 30, 33, 34, 36, 38–40, 49, 79, 96, 97, 190, 193–216
    Air Force, 207
    Communist Party, 196
    Constitution of 1976, 196
    diplomatic corps, 200
    Eastern Army, 206
    global military deployments, 196
    international economic, 203–205
    internationally induced adjustments in, 195–198
    lobbying, 199
    Pax Americana and, 29
    remittances from Cuban Americans, 197
    security agreement, 205
    security cooperation, United States, 208
    security issues, 208–212

United States, cooperation with, 205–208
United States policies toward, 11, 198
visa rules, 213
Cuban
　Air Force, 207
　Democracy Act, 199, 200
　Democracy and Solidarity Act, 200
　Guardafronteras, 207
　migration, 206
Currency, 24, 56, 66, 96, 100, 135, 139, 181

D

Dae-jung, Kim, 229, 234, 240
da Silva, President Luiz Inacia Lula, 3, 11, 18, 168, 174
DEA. *See* Drug Enforcement Administration
Debt crisis, 9, 15, 16, 21, 22, 28, 39, 49, 85, 90, 184
Declaration of Mendoza, 172
Defense Intelligence Agency, 206, 210, 216
Democracy, 14, 15, 18, 19, 45, 49, 52–54, 80, 87, 89, 95, 107, 127, 129, 139, 145, 153, 155, 167, 172, 178, 186, 192, 199–201, 233, 244, 246, 247
　enlargement of, 45
　clause, 7
Democratic
　consolidation, international
　　response to, 11
　peace, 51
　People's Republic of Korea, 3, 4, 5, 6, 12, 27, 28, 29, 30, 47–48, 123, 219–249
　negotiations with United States, People's Republic of China's role as host for, 124–125
　nuclear power, 159–160
　　response to, 156
　nuclear weapons program, diplomacy over, 124
　process, insulation of Ministry from, 188
　regimes, 1, 6, 13, 38, 39, 89
　wave, use of hard power to support, 39
Democratization, 6–8, 7, 13–15, 21, 28, 45, 54, 63, 64, 80, 87–90, 102, 167, 182, 188, 200, 201, 222–224
　of access to information, 102
　worldwide processes of, 6–9

Department of Defense, 38, 46, 131, 132, 221, 246, 250
Desert Storm, 16, 23
Detente, 208
Deterred United States military, 5
Developmental state, waning of, 151
Development credits, 195
Diaspora, 197
Diminished United States power use, pattern of, 34
Diplomatic corps, 28, 35, 200
Dissident group suppression, Japan, 155
Domestic economy, production for, production for export, change to, 87
Dominant size of United States economy, 82
Dominican Republic, 39, 96, 107, 176, 202
Drug Enforcement Administration, 187
Drugs
　premiums, 42
　trafficking in, 5, 12, 29, 36, 41–42, 168, 187, 208, 212
Dynamic power game, 22
Dynastic transition, 4, 11

E

EAEG. *See* East Asian Economic Grouping
EAFTA. *See* East Asian Free Trade Area
EAS. *See* East Asian Summit
EASG. *See* East Asian Study Group
East Africa, 193
East Asia, 1–76, 98, 111–120, 125, 126, 129–132, 140, 141, 143, 154, 163, 215, 223, 224, 246, 248. *See also* specific area of
　bipolar stability, 52–53
　community proposal, 63
　financial crisis, 18, 45
　financial crisis of 1997, 9, 45
　regionalism, 23–30, 30–33, 55–57, 56, 60–66, 69–76
　future of, 64
　United States hostility toward, 24–25
　United States hegemony, confrontation between, 72
East Asian
　Economic Grouping, 15, 22, 61, 62, 64, 65, 74
　Free Trade Area, 63–66, 65, 69, 70
　Study Group, 65, 75
　Summit, 64, 65, 66, 70

tigers, 83
Visionary Group, 65, 75
Strategic Initiative, 23, 223
Eastern Europe, 6, 13, 20, 38, 39, 96, 143, 193, 249
East Timor separatist movement, 118–119
Economic
    crisis, 56, 62–64, 62–66, 74, 75, 81, 84, 86, 90, 93, 102, 103, 107, 204, 240
    depression, 9, 16, 39
    globalization, 90, 92–93, 151
    appraisal of, 15
    forces of, 146
    leadership, 152–153
    opportunities offered by, 101
    technological advances associated with, 88
    United States power and, 81–83
    hard power, 49–51
    integration, process of, 57
    power, compliment to, 120–121
    reform, 18, 54, 85–87, 86, 100, 107, 116, 153
    political costs of, 87
    sanctions, 4, 11, 41, 47, 49, 124, 200
        Cuba, condemnation of, 200
    values, United States, triumph of, 39
Ecuador, 38, 40, 42, 100–102, 101, 102, 172, 182
Educational exchanges, 85–86
Electronic intelligence center at Lourdes, Cuba, 197
El Salvador, 5, 12, 38–40, 96, 107, 176, 212
Enterprise of the Americas Initiative, 78, 95
Environmental
    issues, Brazil, 170
    protection, development, incompatibility between, 170–171
Equal alliance, security vulnerability, conflict between, 29–30
Equal security alliance, 29, 244
Espionage, 156, 209–211, 210–211
Ethiopia, 196
Europe, 1–3, 5–14, 17, 18, 20, 22, 23, 24–30, 32–39, 51, 53, 58, 61, 75, 76, 85, 90, 93, 96, 98, 107, 111, 132, 139, 141, 143, 176, 193, 195, 196, 202, 229, 249. *See also* specific country
European
    Coal and Steel Community, 20, 27, 28
    Commission, 200
    Economic Community, 6, 13, 20, 27, 32

    Free Trade Association, 18, 19, 20, 25, 26
    Monetary System, 25, 32
    Parliament, 200
    Union, 7, 14, 17, 19, 20, 24, 26, 27, 31, 58, 67, 69, 71, 73, 90, 102, 135, 139, 158, 168, 186, 200–204, 214
Euskadi ta Askatasuna, 210, 211
Expansion in United States foreign policy ambitions, 33–34
Exporters, 9, 16
Extradition treaty, 211
Extraterritorial reach of United States law, 200

F

Federal
    Bureau of Investigation, 207
    Republic of Germany, 5
    Reserve Board, 14
Financial system, 11, 18, 86, 90
Fitch Ratings, 240
Florida, 10, 40, 97, 205, 211, 212, 216
Force structure, transformation of, 16–17
Ford, Gerald, 199
Foreign
    capital, 10, 17, 96, 106
    exchange earner, 197
    investment, 93, 94, 115, 121, 123, 131, 197, 216
    policy, design of, 188
Formal independence, commitment to, 126
Fourth Party Congress of 1991, 197
Fox, Vicente, 41
France, 4, 5, 11, 12, 20, 23, 27, 30, 90, 125, 132, 138, 141–142, 141–143, 163, 180, 190, 212, 213, 249
Franco, Francisco, 38
Free riding, 17, 24, 227
Free trade, 77–106
    political costs of, 105
    Agreement of the Americas, 7, 14, 17, 20, 24, 27, 30, 37, 50, 61, 67, 81, 92, 94, 95, 97–106, 98, 99, 100, 101, 102, 103, 104, 106
    agreements, 14, 21, 25–27, 27, 29–33, 32, 34, 35, 56, 60, 61, 64, 65, 67–74, 76, 79, 94, 95, 99, 101, 105, 117, 136, 140, 143, 145–148, 146, 147
    Area of the Americas, 17, 27, 50, 61, 67, 78, 81, 92, 94, 97–106, 186, 190

French leadership style, Japanese leadership style, difference between, 142
French model of normal statehood, 141–143
FTAA. *See* Free Trade Area of the Americas

G

GATT. *See* General Agreement on Tariffs and Trade
Gaulism, 142
General Agreement on Tariffs and Trade, 2, 9, 10, 17, 21, 28, 79, 83, 105
Generalized System of Preferences, trade access benefits, 46
Genocide, Khmer Rouge, 122–123
German model of normal statehood, 139–141
Germany, 4, 5, 11, 12, 20, 23, 25, 27, 30, 32, 58, 82, 138–141, 139, 143, 149, 153, 155, 162, 163, 184, 204, 249, 250
Globalization, 15, 18, 22, 25, 31, 38, 79–83, 81, 82, 88, 90, 92–93, 101, 105, 146, 148, 151, 152, 163, 167–169, 193, 198
 appraisal of, 15
 forces of, 146
 leadership, 152–153
 requirements of leaders, 152–153
 technological advances associated with, 88
 United States power and, 81–83
Globalophile, 15, 22
Globalophobe, 15, 22
Great Britain, 23
Great powers, local powers, power differential between, 112
Grenada, 29, 36, 202
Growth of military strength, among allied, client states, 44
GSP. *See* Generalized System of Preferences
Guantanamo, 3, 10, 29, 36, 40
Guatemala, 5, 12, 39, 96, 176, 212, 249

H

Haiti, 3, 4, 7, 10, 11, 14, 37, 39, 91, 96, 175, 178, 179, 198, 202
Hannara Party, 220, 231–232, 234
Hard power, soft power, distinguished, 35
"Hard shell" conception of sovereignty, 198–199
Health care, 193, 208, 214

Hegemon, 15, 22, 23, 29, 30, 51, 80, 184, 199
Hegemony, 28, 29, 32, 36, 40, 56, 60, 67, 72–74, 77–79, 82, 90, 92, 96, 98, 102, 111, 114, 118–123, 125, 126, 130, 131, 148, 180, 184, 199, 214, 240, 241, 245
Helms-Burton Act, 201, 207
Hoi-Chang, Lee, 234
Hostages, mutual, strategy of, 23
Humanitarian assistance, 201, 209
Human
 rights norms, 7
 tripwire, 223, 226, 231, 239, 244
Hurricane Michelle, 209
Hurtado, Miguel de la Madrid, 21, 28
Hussein, Saddam, 13
Hyochonli, 232–233

I

Iberoamerican summits, 200, 201
Ibrahim, Anwar, 8
Ideology, 12–14, 19–21, 27, 28, 53, 78, 79, 81, 83, 91–93, 130, 185, 194–197, 199, 202, 210, 212, 214, 220, 222, 226, 233, 238, 243, 244, 248
Illegal Cuban migration, 206
Illicit drugs. *See* Drugs, trafficking in
IMF. *See* International Monetary Fund
Imperialism, 40, 163, 196
Import substitution, 21, 78, 79, 83–85, 84, 92, 106
Imports, 22, 50, 93, 98, 100, 116, 121, 195, 203–205, 209, 250
India, 2, 9, 28, 35, 123, 180, 249
Indian Ocean, Japanese naval operations in, 143–145
Indochina, history of, 119–120
Indonesia, 15, 47, 113, 116, 117–118, 118
Industrial policies, 22
Information, democratization of access to, 102
Initiative for Development in East Asia, 72–74
Institutionalization, 14, 27, 62, 65, 74–76, 78, 79, 103
Institutionalized declination, management of free trade, 82
Insurgencies, 5, 38
Interamerican Court of Human Rights, 171
Inter-American Development Bank, 198
Interdependence, 14, 21, 23, 30, 31, 38, 55, 57, 63, 68, 75, 82, 96, 97, 99, 106, 138, 167

Interests Sections, 205
Intergovernmentalism, liberal, 58
International
    academic and cultural exchanges, 209
    Atomic Energy Agency, 21, 172, 211, 239
    credit rating agencies, 240
    debt, 16, 203
    donations, 203, 204
    Monetary Fund, 2, 9, 11, 12, 14, 15, 18, 19, 21, 22, 24, 31, 49–51, 56, 61, 62, 66, 74, 83, 92, 107, 185
    order, nature of, debate on, 189
    organizations, 14, 130, 169, 183, 202, 209
        institutionalization of, 92
    regime-abiding, 28
    strategy, 194, 212
    terrorism, 4, 11, 16, 23, 41, 45–46, 103–104, 140, 183, 194, 210
    tourism, Cuba's development of, 213
Internet, 80, 88, 152, 222, 232
Interoperable joint force, 230, 238
Iraq, 3, 4, 6, 10, 11, 13, 20, 23, 33, 47, 89, 103, 119, 127, 138, 140, 141, 159, 160, 161, 174, 175, 198, 199, 208, 219, 220, 235, 237, 241, 242, 243, 245
Irish Republican Army, 210, 211
Islamist terror network, 45–46
Italy, 23, 30, 190, 204, 216, 249

J

Jamaica, 96, 207
Japan, 3, 6, 9, 10, 12, 13, 15, 16, 18, 19, 20, 22–30, 43, 44, 48, 50, 54, 56, 59, 62–76, 82, 90, 93, 102, 107, 112–117, 120, 123, 135–164, 174, 204, 222, 223, 249, 250
    constitution of, 28, 35, 145, 159
        Article Nine, 145, 153
    France, commonalities between, 141–142
    Germany, commonalities between, 139
    normal statehood, 135–164
    People's Republic of China
        economic conflict between, 72–77
        rivalry over control of region, 63
    United Kingdom, commonalities between, 137–138
    United States, Security Treaty, 136

Japanese
    –Chinese joint communique, 157
    –Korean joint communique, 157
    leadership style, French leadership style, difference between, 142
    nationalism, 140
    networks, 72
    polity, Sectoral protectionism within, 147
    –Singapore Economic Partnership Agreement, 67, 68
    –United States Security Treaty, 153–154
        abrogation of, 160
Jemaah Islamiyah, 47
Joint Chiefs of Staff, 16, 38, 229, 247
Joint Declaration of Security and on Revised Guidelines for Defense Cooperation, 44
Jong Il, Kim, 229
JSEPA. *See* Japan-Singapore Economic Partnership Agreement

K

Kennedy, John F., 14, 78, 209
Keohane, Robert, 14, 21, 31, 38
Khmer Rouge, leadership for genocide, prosecution of, 122–123
Khrushchev, Nikita, 13, 20, 209
Komei Party, 155
Kooni Fire Range, 228
Korea, 2–12, 20, 24, 25, 27–30, 47–48, 80, 85, 112, 119, 123–124, 219–250.
    See also North Korea; South Korea
    domestic politics, 226–231
    election in, 231–243
    military security constraints, 222–226
    negotiations with United States, People's Republic of China's role as host for, 124–125
    nuclear power, 159–160
        response to, 156
    nuclear weapons program, diplomacy over, 124
    People's Republic of China, diplomatic relations between, 123–124
    reduced United States military presence in, 124–125
    security goals, United States, 226–231
    stock price index, 240
    success of, 221–231

United States, Combined Forces
Command, 223
United States forces in, 221, 224–225,
242
Kosovo, 3, 10, 33, 119, 132, 154
Kumpulan Mujahideen Malaysia, 47
Kuwait, 13, 20, 250

L

Land armies, 21, 27, 120
Land Partnership Plan, 230, 248
Laos, 71, 130, 193, 194
Latin America, 1–54, 75, 77–107, 111, 169,
182, 184, 187, 212, 214, 215, 249. *See also*
specific countries of
    Canada, comparison between,
        105–106
    free trade, 77–106
    zone of democratic peace, 52
Leadership, 10, 11, 21, 24, 65–66, 245
Leninist party-state, 27
Liberal
    Democratic Party, 152, 155
    global trade regime, 23
    intergovernmentalism, 58
Liberalism, 58, 167
Liberal Party, 155
Limited wars, 14, 21
Local powers, great powers, power differential
between, 112
Lome Convention, 201
Lourdes, Cuba, 197, 204–205
Lusophone countries, 29, 36

M

Maehyangli, 228, 247
Mahathir, Mohammed, 3, 8, 10, 15, 56, 64
Malaysia, 3, 8, 45–47, 51, 53, 61, 67, 72, 113,
116, 118, 130, 132
    Philippines, territorial dispute between,
        118
Manila, United States, bilateral exchange of
favors between, 46
Marcos, Ferdinand, 7, 14
Maritime superiority, 35
Market-based success stories, examples of, 85
Market-model of development, sustainability
of, impact of Latin American domestic
politics on, 102–103

Market-oriented economic practices, spread
of, 2
Market-oriented reforms, 9, 11–12
    worldwide processes of, 9–13
Market reforms, pressure for, 90
Marxist-Leninist party, 202
Mayazawa Plan, 66
McCaffrey, General Barry, 207, 216
Medical
    collaboration, 209
    diplomacy, 214
Meiji system, 150
MERCOSUR, 7, 14, 17–21, 23–28, 30, 31, 34,
37, 38, 67, 97–100, 107, 190
    creation of, 170
Mexico, 2, 5–7, 9–20, 22, 25–27, 30, 31, 34, 37,
38, 42, 49, 67, 68, 75, 79, 81, 86, 88, 89,
95–98, 100–103, 107, 190, 191, 200, 204,
215, 249
    Caribbean Basin, 95–97
    United Kingdom and, 5
    United States relations, 7
Middle East, 9, 13, 18, 33, 34, 36, 100, 111,
130, 132, 230. *See also under* specific
country
Migration, 3, 5, 10, 12, 29, 36, 87, 96, 205,
206, 208, 212
    agreement, 206
Military Committee, 224
Ministry of National Defense, Korea,
221, 246
Missile
    crisis of 1962, 195, 197
    delivery systems, 4, 11
    Technology Control Regime, 173
Monetary
    cooperation in East Asia, 66
    support system, institutionalized
        declination of, 82
Monroe Doctrine, original old Pax
Americana, 35
Montes, Ana Belen, 211
Moody's Investor Service, 240
Moo-hyun, Roh, 3, 225–226, 226, 234,
237–245, 243–244
MTCR. *See* Missile Technology Control
Regime
Multilateral Evaluation Mechanism, 186
Multilateral institutions, 4, 14, 15, 18, 22, 29,
36, 83, 189, 198, 200, 202
Multilateralism, 22, 91, 103, 104, 167, 184,
198, 202, 203

Mutual hostages, strategy of, 23
Mutual Security Treaty, 242

N

NAC. *See* New Agenda Coalition
NAFTA. *See* North American Free Trade Agreement
Narcotics production, trafficking, war against, 41–42
National
    Campaign for Eradication of Crime by United States Troops, 228
    Defense Panel, 23, 38, 230, 247
    Human Rights Commission, 232
Nationalism, 16, 125, 133, 140, 198
National Security Strategy, Bush administration, 33–34
NATO. *See* North Atlantic Treaty Organization
Nature of international order, debate on, 189
Naval supremacy, geographical advantage of, 112–113
Neofunctionalism, 57, 59
Neoliberal consensus, in East Asia, 64
Neoliberalism, 86, 102
Neorealist, 75, 194, 199–203, 214
Neorealist multilateralism, 202, 203
Netizens, 222, 232–233
New Agenda Coalition, 172
New Conservative Party, 155
New Jewel Movement, 202
New kinds of leaders, search for, 152
Newly industrializing countries, 10, 17
New Millennium Democratic Party, 220
New Zealand, 18, 20, 25, 68, 72, 191
NGO, 222, 227, 228, 230, 232, 234, 240, 247, 248
Nicaragua, 5, 12, 38, 39, 49, 176, 196, 212
Nixon administration, 205
Nogeunli, 227, 247
Nonaligned Movement, 194
Nonintervention, principle of, Brazil, 190
Nonproliferation, 28, 36, 47, 160, 165, 169, 170, 172, 173, 179, 181, 184, 191, 192, 212, 225, 239
Noriega, Manuel Antonio, 7, 14
Normal statehood, 28, 35, 135, 145, 150–159, 153
    ambitions for, 161
    British model, 137–139
    defined, 135
    French model, 141–143
    German model, 139–141
    leadership, exercise of, 150–153
    models of, 137–143
North Africa, 36, 193
North American Free Trade Agreement, 5, 7, 8, 12, 14, 15, 17–21, 20, 22, 24–28, 30, 31, 37, 50, 61, 67, 69, 70, 94–95, 95, 105, 106, 107
North Atlantic Treaty Organization, 3, 10, 14, 21, 139, 141, 143, 145, 162, 175
    challenge need for, 3
Northeast Asia, 18, 20, 22–24, 25, 26, 29–31, 33, 45, 63, 113, 123, 125, 160, 242, 245
    regionalism, United States hostility toward, 24–25
North Korea, 3–6, 4, 5, 6, 10–13, 12, 27–29, 28, 29, 30, 34–36, 43, 45, 47–48, 48, 53, 70, 119, 123–125, 138–141, 150, 154, 155, 156, 157, 159–162, 160, 162, 171–174, 176–180, 186, 187, 190, 192, 193, 194, 196, 199, 202, 211, 213, 215, 221, 229, 230, 231, 234, 237, 238, 240, 241, 243, 245
    negotiations with United States, People's Republic of China's role as host for, 124–125
    nuclear power, 159–160
    response to, 156
    nuclear weapons program, diplomacy over, 124
North Vietnam, invasion of South Vietnam, 121
Nosamo, 234
Nuclear
    -armed communist states, conflicts with, 42–43
    development program, Korea, disclosure of, 235
    energy, 21, 28, 192
    nonproliferation, 21, 28, 47, 160, 170, 173, 181, 212, 225, 239
    Nonproliferation Treaty, 47, 212, 239
    Suppliers Group, 172
        membership in, 172
    war, 4, 11, 38, 43
    weapons, 3, 6, 10, 13, 43, 45, 47, 48, 123–125, 191, 192, 212, 229, 239, 249
Nye, Joseph, 14, 16, 21, 23, 31, 35, 38, 54, 137, 163, 212, 223, 250
Nye Report, 23, 223

O

OAS. *See* Organization of American States
Official aid, alternatives to, 49
Offshore capital market facilities, 10
Okinawa, 43
Olympics, 213
Open international markets, reestablishment of, 92
Open regionalism, 15
OPIC. *See* Overseas Private Investment Corporation
Organization for Economic Cooperation and Development, 11, 18, 221
Organization of American States, 89, 91, 94
    nonintervention resolution included in, 94
Osama bin Laden, 16, 155
Overseas Private Investment Corporation, credit line, 46

P

Pacific Ocean, 28, 35, 201
Panama, 3, 4, 7, 10, 11, 14, 39, 40, 91, 96, 100, 198
Paraguay, 7, 14, 21, 28, 39, 107, 168, 172, 180, 183
Paraguayan War, 180
Parana River system, 21
Paris Accords, 122
Pax
    Americana. *See under* specific country
    Britannica, 112
    Latin Americana, 53
    Sinica, 119–125
    violence of Cold War, contrast between, 125
    Sino-Americana, emergent, 53
Peace, 2, 5, 6, 9, 12, 13, 14, 20, 21, 22, 28, 29, 30, 35, 37, 45, 51–54, 69, 73, 81, 83, 111–115, 117, 119, 121–123, 125–127, 129–133, 141, 149, 153
Peacetime operational command, 224, 225
People Power Revolution, 45
People's Republic of China, 2, 4–6, 5, 6, 8–10, 9, 10, 12, 13, 18, 19, 20, 22–30, 23, 24, 25, 27, 28, 29, 30, 111–133
    economic influence in Eastern Asia, 50–51
    as emerging superpower, 5–6

hegemony along borders, demand for, 119
Japan
    economic conflict between, 72–77
    rivalry over control of region, 63
    naval strategy, similar to Soviet Union, 114–115
    replacing United States, Japan's trading, economic partner, 160–161
    rise of, 139
    Russian weaponry, reliance on, 114
    South Korea, diplomatic relations between, normalization, 123–124
    stable relationship with, 159
    uncontested land power, 120
Peron, Juan, 21
Persian Gulf War, abstention from, 178
Peru, 10, 17, 38, 39, 86, 100, 107, 168, 182, 187, 249
Petroleum, 195, 205
Philippines, 4, 7, 11, 14, 19, 26, 43–47, 46, 50, 54, 113, 115–118, 116, 117, 123, 132, 161, 249
    Malaysia, territorial dispute between, 118
    prohibition of foreign troops fighting on national soil, 46–47
Pinochet, Augusto, 7, 14
Plan Colombia, 40–41, 187
Plaza Accord, 63
Political, economic power, disparity, Latin America, United States, 78–79
Political
    Bureau, 197
    parties, 18, 19, 20, 25, 26, 233, 240
    regime's survival, fundamental goal, 198
    risk, 29, 36, 194
    stability, 2, 9, 96, 118, 121
    systems, opening of, 1–2
Portugal, 201
Post-Cold War era, 91
Powell, Colin, 210
Power, way of exercising, 60
Power concentration, multipolarity in, 52
Preference ordering, process of, 140–141
Primary enemy, 221
Prime Minister Mohammed Mahathir, 3
Prisoners of war, 208
Production for domestic economy, production for export, change to, 87
Protectionist measures, 83
Proxy wars, 13, 20

Putin, 205
Pyongyang, 148–150
    nuclear development program, 223

Q

Quebec Summit of Heads of State and Government, 7, 14

R

Reagan administration, 38, 205
Realism, 58, 60, 76, 219, 220
Reciprocal trade liberalization, challenge of, 50
Reduction of United States troops, 16
Regional integration, 29, 30, 33, 56–60, 57, 63–68, 74–76, 165, 181, 185, 189
    facilitators of, 59
    supply-side conditions, 57–58
Regionalism, 15, 17–20, 17–23, 22–27, 24–27, 29–34, 30, 31, 37, 38, 55–57, 59–67, 69–76, 78, 92, 146, 162, 192, 233
    perception of, 60–61
    three kinds of, 17–23
Regional
    military security, importance of, 21
    policy makers, ideology of, 78–79
    security, 20, 27, 29, 51–53, 189
Regulation, 9, 14, 16, 21, 168
Remittances from Cuban Americans, 197
Repatriation, 196, 206
Republic of Korea, 2
Revolutionary Armed Forces of Columbia, 41, 210, 211
    indictment of members of, 41
Revolution in Military Affairs, 44
RMA. *See* Revolution in Military Affairs
Rogue states, 14, 21, 23, 155, 210, 230, 234
Roh Moo-hyun, 219
Rumsfeld, Donald, 17, 24, 25, 225, 237–239, 237–243, 241–245, 249
Russia, 12, 19, 27, 34, 113, 120, 138, 141, 154, 155, 196, 197, 203–205, 249
Russo-Japanese War, 120

S

SAFTA. *See* South American Free Trade Area
Sayyaf, Abu, 46

SEATO. *See* Southeast Asian Treaty Organization
Second Declaration of Havana, 196
Second Division, United States, 223, 227, 232, 238, 246
Security commitment, American military, Korea, 239
Security community, 51–52
Security Council, 174
Self-Defense Force, 138
Self-image, as middle power, 97
Seoul
    political reorientation in, 48
    United States, political deadlock between, 232–233
September 11 attacks, 4, 11, 16, 23, 26, 33, 34, 45, 47, 103–104, 117, 138, 143, 144, 191, 195, 205, 208, 209, 212, 214, 216
Sheehan, General John, 206
Singapore, 18, 19, 25, 26, 28, 35, 44–47, 51, 67–70, 73–75, 113, 116–118, 117, 123, 130, 147
Single-party political system, 199
Sino-Japanese, 23
SIPAM. *See* Amazon Protection System
SIVAM. *See* Amazon Surveillance System
Social Democracy, 6
Soft power, 21, 35, 73, 96, 97, 130, 195, 212–214, 245
    exercise of, 195
    hard power, distinguished, 35
    sources of, 96
South America, 21, 22, 24, 29, 30, 34, 40, 67, 88, 96, 98, 99, 186
South American Free Trade Area, 98, 99
Southeast Asia, 5, 6, 12, 13, 17, 22, 24, 25, 28, 29, 31, 32, 35, 42, 44, 45, 68, 71–73, 113, 114, 118–121, 125, 139, 153, 163. *See also under* specific country
Southeast Asian Treaty Organization, dissolution of, 44
Southern Command, 207
Southern Cone, 79, 100, 165, 176
South Korea, 2, 3, 6–19, 20, 22–27, 29–34, 36, 37, 42–45, 48, 50, 54, 56, 63–65, 69, 70, 73–75, 80, 85, 123–125, 132, 146, 154, 158, 219–249
    diplomatic relations between, normalization of, People's Republic of China, 123–124
    reduced United States military presence in, 124–125

Soviet Union, 1–5, 8–12, 13, 15, 16, 20, 22, 26–28, 33–35, 38, 90, 96, 113–114, 118–120, 122, 123, 125, 130, 149, 154, 162, 193, 195–197
    collapse of, 1–2, 3–6, 34, 120
Spain, 38, 80, 85, 144, 190, 200, 201, 203, 204, 211, 216
Special relationship, idea of, 137–139
Stalin, Joseph, 13, 20, 53
State enterprises, 9, 16, 203
State ownership, 199
State sovereignty, 168, 169, 181, 189
Status of Forces Agreement, 222, 248
Stealth imperialism, 40
Stockholm Conference, 170–171
Strategy of insertion, 166–167
Stroessner, Alfredo, 7, 14
Structural adjustment, 196
Subic Bay, withdrawal of forces from, 44
Submarine capabilities, Chinese development of, 115
Sugar, 195, 197, 204
Sunshine policy, 125
Supply-side conditions, regional integration, 57–58
Supranational, 17, 18, 22, 23
Suriname, 202

T

TaeWoo, Roh, 226
TAFTA. *See* Trans Atlantic Free Trade Area
Taiwan, 6–8, 7, 8, 10, 13–15, 17, 19, 26, 28, 38, 43, 45, 48, 50, 53, 72, 73, 76, 84, 85, 112, 113, 115, 117, 125–129, 125–130, 132, 133, 146, 154, 158
    declaration of sovereign independence, 128–129
    Relations Act, 45
    Strait
        deterrence dynamics in, 126
        hegemony over, 126
Tariff rates, 10, 17, 98, 107
Technological advances, globalization and, 81
Territorial status quo, 27, 34
Terrorism, 4, 11, 12, 16, 19, 23, 26, 33, 41, 45–46, 46, 73, 103–104, 140, 183, 194, 195, 205, 207, 208, 210, 212, 214, 229
Terrorists. *See* Terrorism
Thailand, 7, 10, 11, 14, 17, 18, 19, 26, 43–45, 47, 50, 51, 53, 68, 75, 121, 125, 130, 147

Thermonuclear war, removal of, 3
Thirty years war, 38
Tokugawa system, 150
Torricelli, Robert, 199, 201
Tourism, 35, 69, 72, 107, 197, 202–204, 213
Trade, dependency on, 115–116
Trade
    blocs, 17–18
    embargo, 209
    liberalization, 2, 9, 10, 12, 17, 19, 39, 50, 69–71, 73, 98, 104, 116, 147, 148
    Promotion Authority, 91, 104–105
Traditional deterrence policy, failure of in Korea, 230
Trafficking in narcotics, war against, 41–42
Trans Atlantic Free Trade Area, 61
Transnational criminal organizations, 187
Transnationalism, 14, 15, 17, 21, 22, 24, 59, 63, 183, 184, 187
Transnational societies, institutions, 59
Trans-regional cooperation, 67
Treasury Department, 61
Treaty
    of Asuncion, 21
    of Montevideo, 180
    of Rome, 6, 13
    of Tlatelolco, 21, 172, 191, 212
Trollope's Ploy, 209
Truman, Harry, 13
Two-China policy, 28
Two-power standard *vs.* global standard, 112

U

Unilateralism, 22, 24, 25, 81, 91, 103, 104, 160
    bias for, 15
    renewed, tendencies toward, 103–104
Unipolar, 13, 15, 17, 20, 22, 24, 53, 102, 192
United Kingdom, 5, 12, 80, 81, 85, 137, 138, 141–145, 155
    Japan, commonalities between, 137–138
United Malays National Organization, 8, 15
United Nations, 4, 7, 13, 14, 20, 123, 138, 141, 154, 157, 159, 165, 173, 178, 179, 191, 192, 224
    General Assembly, 183, 200
    Register of Conventional Arms, 173
United States
    allies, 15, 19, 24, 194, 198, 200, 230
    economic values, 39
    government silence, 61

hegemony
  deepening of, 90
  East Asia, confrontation between, 72
image, rise, fall of, 15
leadership, 3, 4, 14, 17
maritime superiority, 28
market, access to, 93
military power, 2–3
  diminished exercise of, 35–48
  economic power reinforcement of, 115
  history of, 35
  policies of, alienation of United States allies, 198
  power of economic ideas, 85
  primacy, 194
  regionalism, 23–30
  Second Division, 223
  security policy, 23, 186
  Southern Command, 207
  unilateralism, 18, 20
United States Commission on National Security, 229, 247
United States Congressional Research Service, inventory of, 35–36
United States–Singapore Free Trade Agreement, 73, 76
  significance of, 73–74
Uribe, Alvaro, 211
Uruguay, 7, 10, 14, 17, 21, 28, 38, 86, 99, 107, 172, 176, 180
Uruguay Round of General Agreement of Tariffs and Trade, 10, 17
USSFTA. *See* United States-Singapore Free Trade Agreement

V

Vargas, Getulio, 21
Venezuela, 10, 17, 38, 40, 54, 88, 97, 100, 103, 107, 170, 182, 190, 204, 205, 249
Vietnam, 5, 8, 9, 12, 15, 16, 28, 35, 36, 43–45, 71, 112, 118, 119, 121, 122, 125, 130, 132, 148, 193, 194, 249
  diplomatic, economic relations, reestablishment, 5
  withdrawal from, 36, 118

Visa rules, 213
Voluntary globalization, 193–194
Vulnerability, 14, 21, 25, 29, 32, 36, 91, 128, 203, 240

W

Waltz, Kenneth, 60, 76, 135, 199, 215
Warsaw Pact, 3, 10
  dissolution of, 3
Wartime operational command, 223, 225, 243, 244
Washington consensus, 185
  challenge of, 40
  imposition of, 62
Weapons of mass destruction, 11, 23, 125, 140, 173, 209, 210
Western Europe, 3, 6, 10, 11, 13, 18, 20, 22, 23, 27, 29, 30, 37, 58, 75
West Germany, 23
  NATO's integration of, 23
Westphalian notion of sovereignty, 135
Woods, Bretton, 82
World Bank, 26, 41, 49, 54, 78, 198
World Trade Organization, 2, 50–51, 55, 101–102, 105, 140, 148, 152, 169, 201
World War II, 7, 9, 13, 14, 16, 20, 21, 27, 28, 35, 78, 79, 81, 82, 92, 113, 136, 141, 158, 162, 173
WTO. *See* World Trade Organization

X

X generation, Korea, 244–245

Y

Yen bloc, 23, 24, 31
Yew, Lee Kuan, 25, 32
Yokosuka, 43
Yongbyon nuclear facilities, 235, 239
Yongsan Army Base, 228
Young-sam, Kim, 225
Yugoslavia, 3